2

Story and Art by
Rumiko Takahashi

CONTENTS

Story thus far...

When Nanoka Kiba was seven years old, she was orphaned in a violent accident. Now she is a third-year student in middle school. One day she passes the spot where the accident occurred and is miraculously transported to the Taisho Era. There she meets an exorcist named Mao who informs her that she is not a human but an ayakashi, and it's possible that, like Mao, she has been cursed by Byoki, a cat demon. Before Nanako can process all of this, she and Mao encounter a cult whose members, like Byoki, seek to achieve immortality. Nanako agrees to help Mao infiltrate the cult in order to investigate their priestess, Shoko...

Chapter 1:
The Origins of the Ogre God

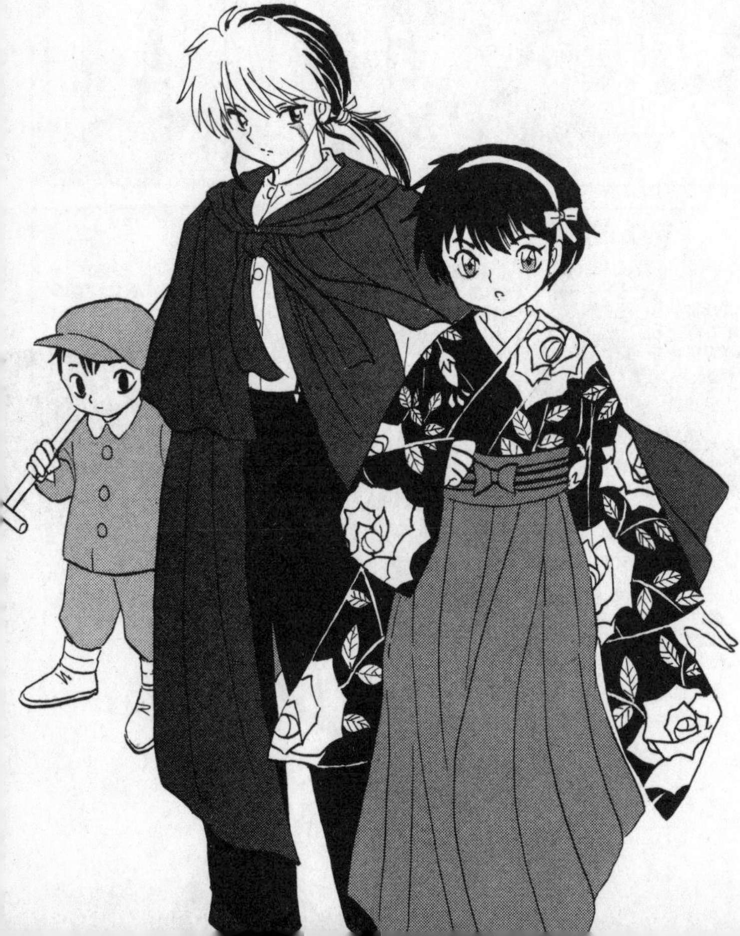

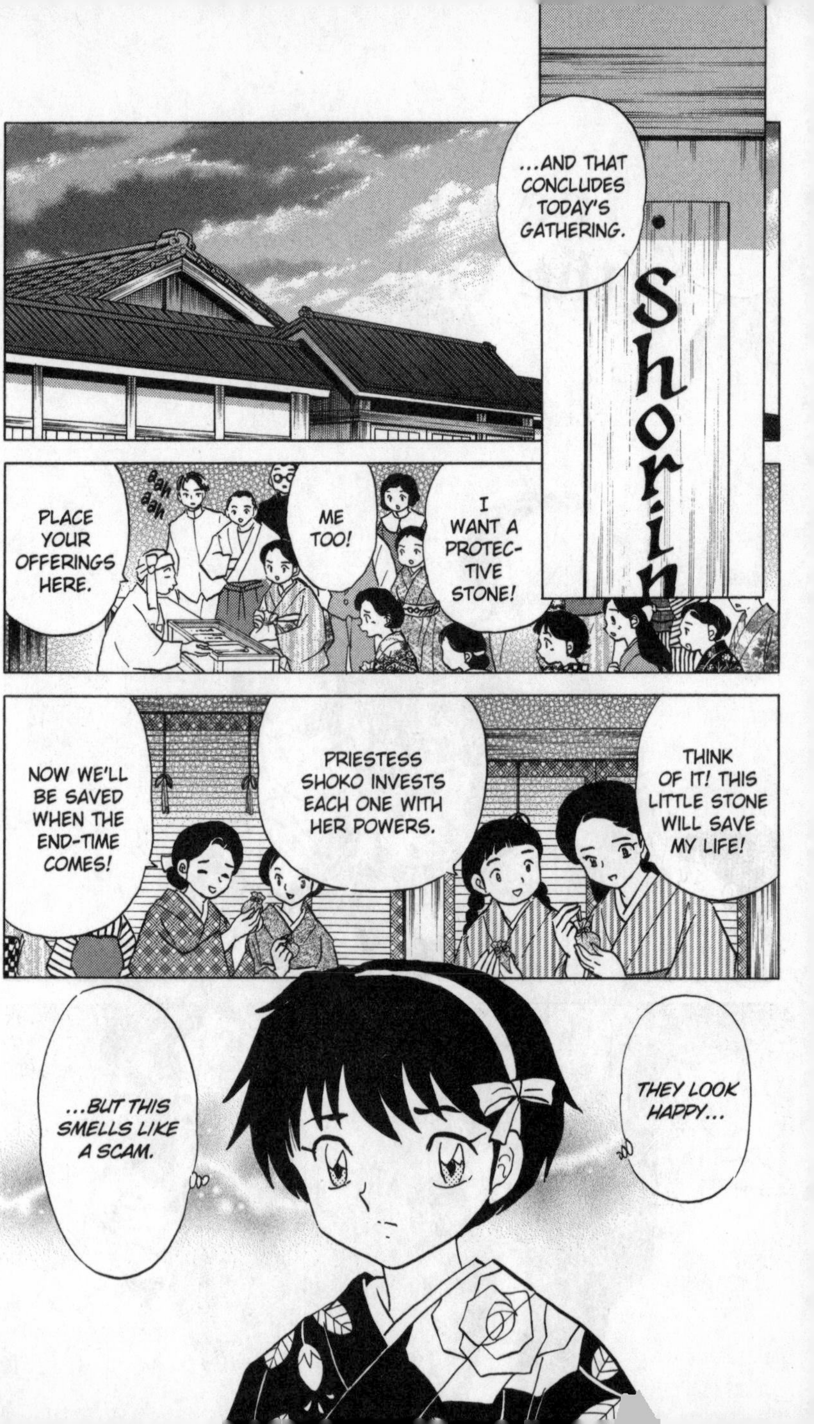
...AND THAT CONCLUDES TODAY'S GATHERING.
Shorin
I WANT A PROTEC-TIVE STONE!
ME TOO!
PLACE YOUR OFFERINGS HERE.
THINK OF IT! THIS LITTLE STONE WILL SAVE MY LIFE!
PRIESTESS SHOKO INVESTS EACH ONE WITH HER POWERS.
NOW WE'LL BE SAVED WHEN THE END-TIME COMES!
THEY LOOK HAPPY...
...BUT THIS SMELLS LIKE A SCAM.

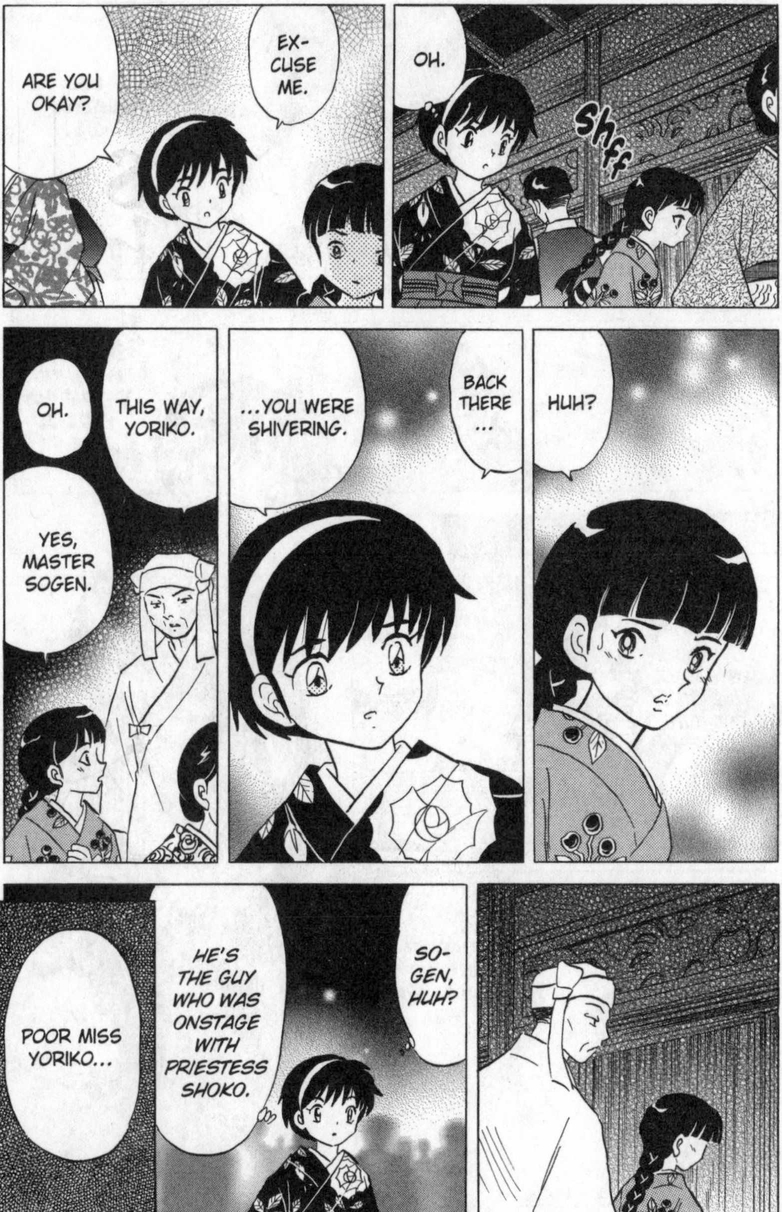
OH.
SHFF
EX-CUSE ME.
ARE YOU OKAY?
HUH?
BACK THERE...
...YOU WERE SHIVERING.
THIS WAY, YORIKO.
OH.
YES, MASTER SOGEN.
SO-GEN, HUH?
HE'S THE GUY WHO WAS ONSTAGE WITH PRIESTESS SHOKO.
POOR MISS YORIKO...

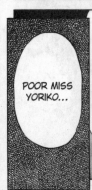

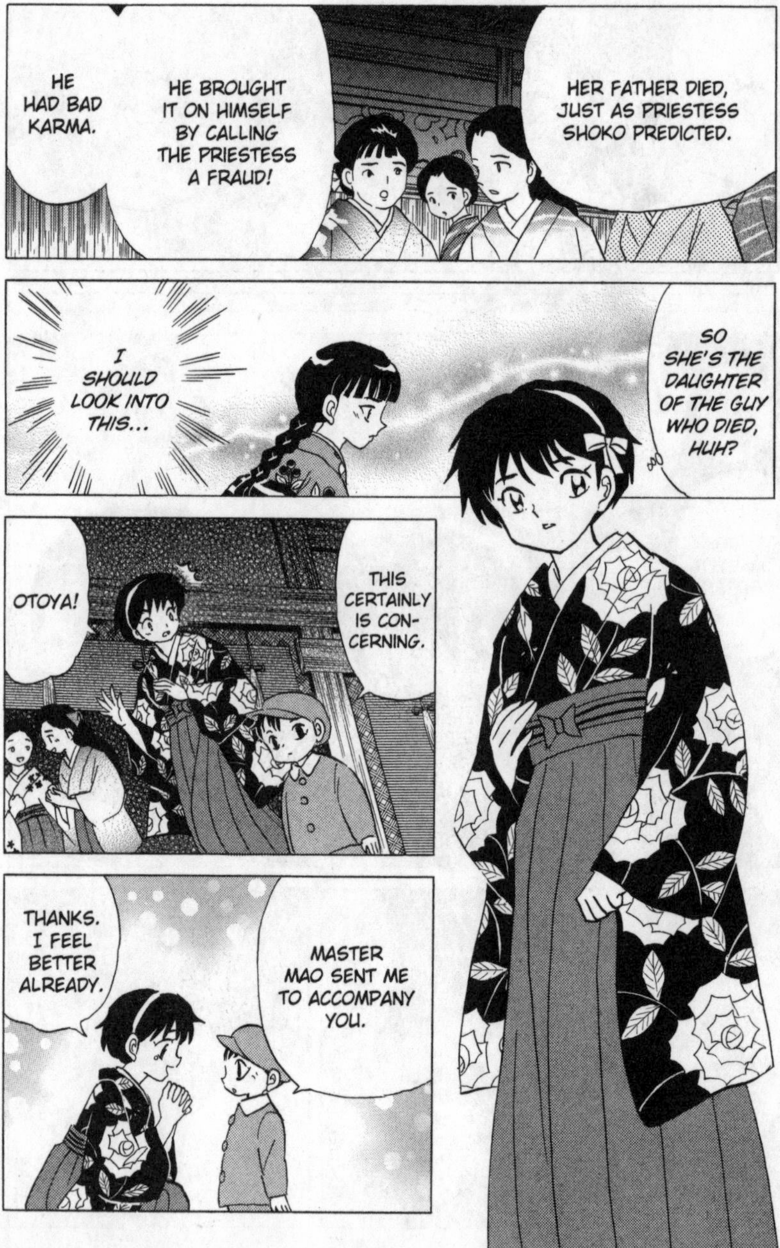
HER FATHER DIED, JUST AS PRIESTESS SHOKO PREDICTED.
HE BROUGHT IT ON HIMSELF BY CALLING THE PRIESTESS A FRAUD!
HE HAD BAD KARMA.
SO SHE'S THE DAUGHTER OF THE GUY WHO DIED, HUH?
I SHOULD LOOK INTO THIS...
THIS CERTAINLY IS CON- CERNING.
OTOYA!
MASTER MAO SENT ME TO ACCOMPANY YOU.
THANKS. I FEEL BETTER ALREADY.

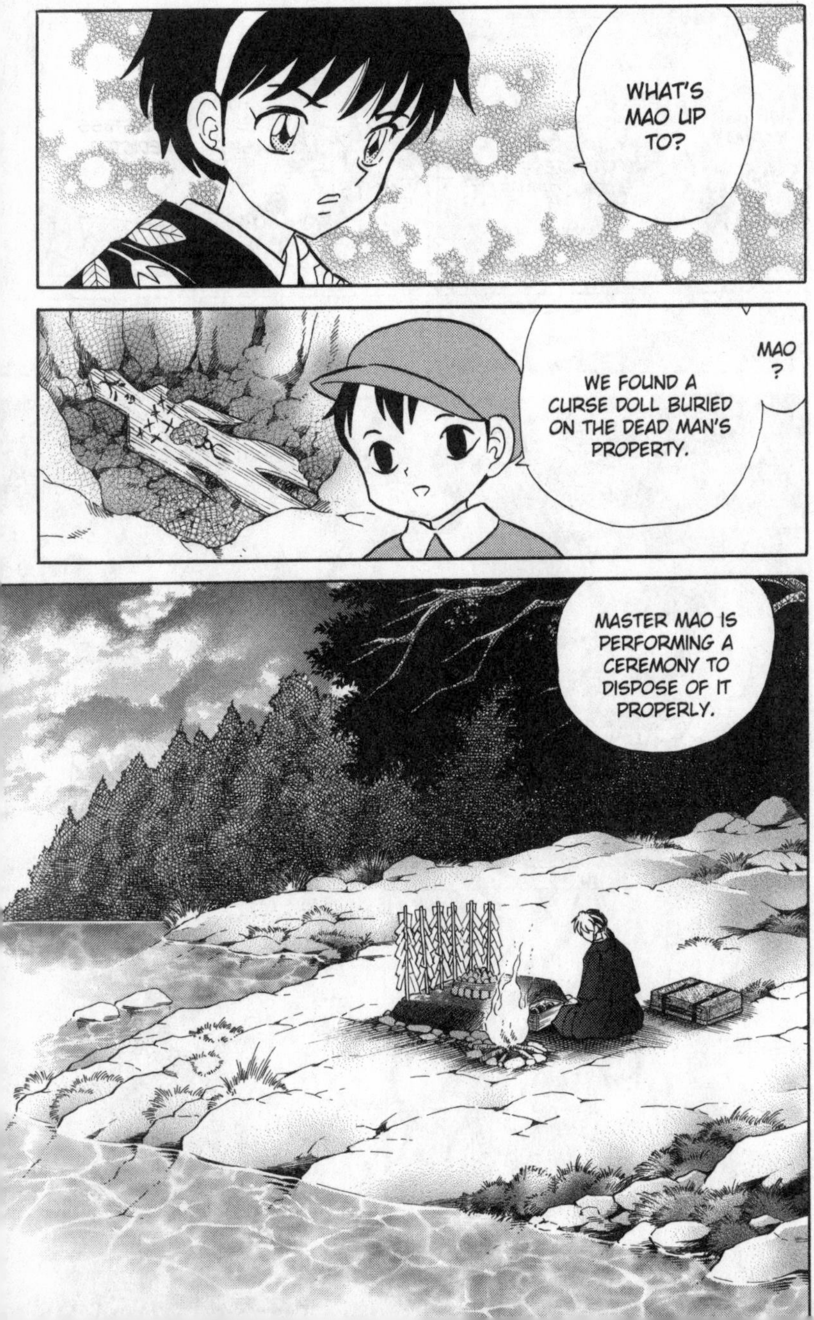
WHAT'S MAO UP TO?
MAO ?
WE FOUND A CURSE DOLL BURIED ON THE DEAD MAN'S PROPERTY.
MASTER MAO IS PERFORMING A CEREMONY TO DISPOSE OF IT PROPERLY.

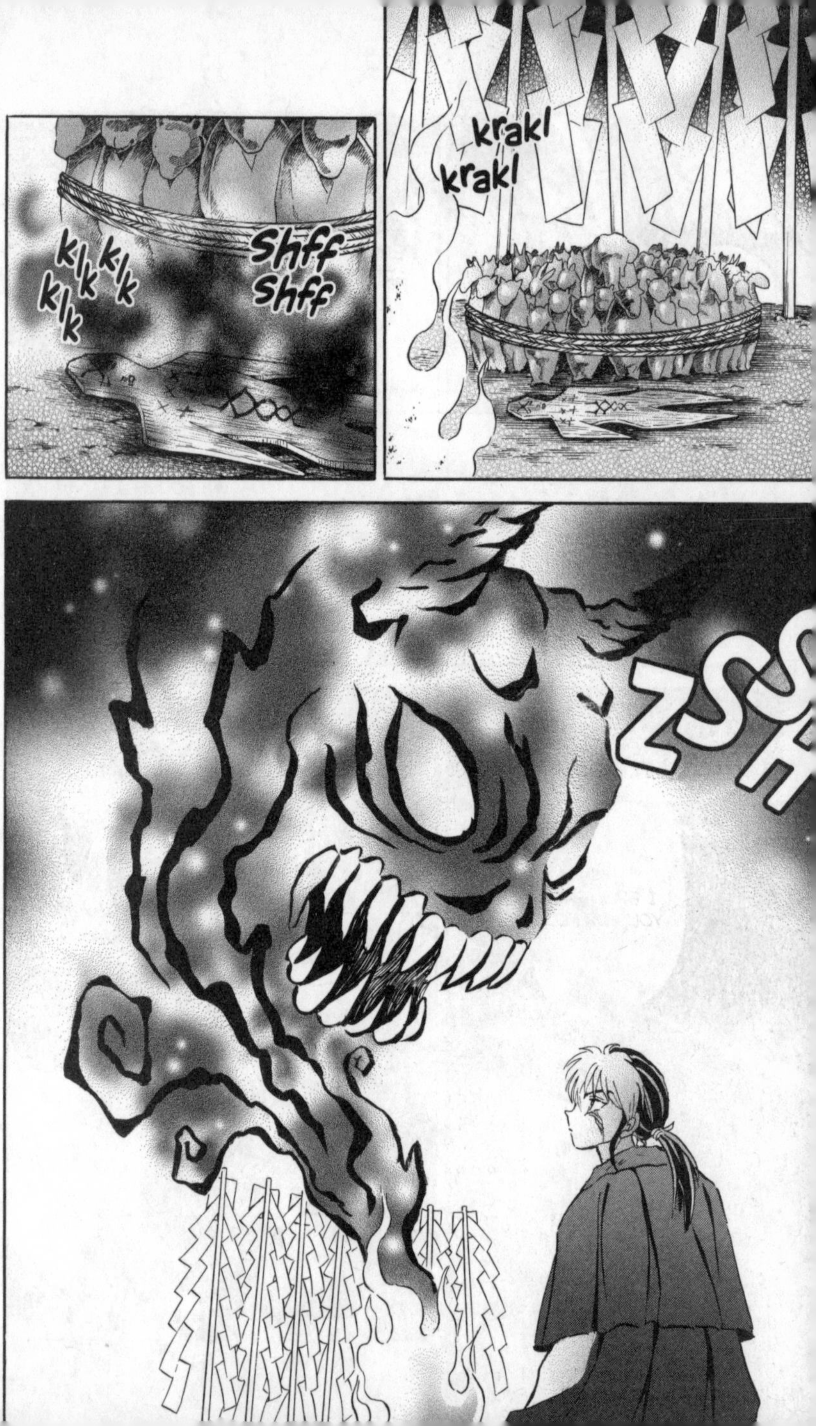
krakl
krakl
klk klk
klk
shff
shff
ZSSH

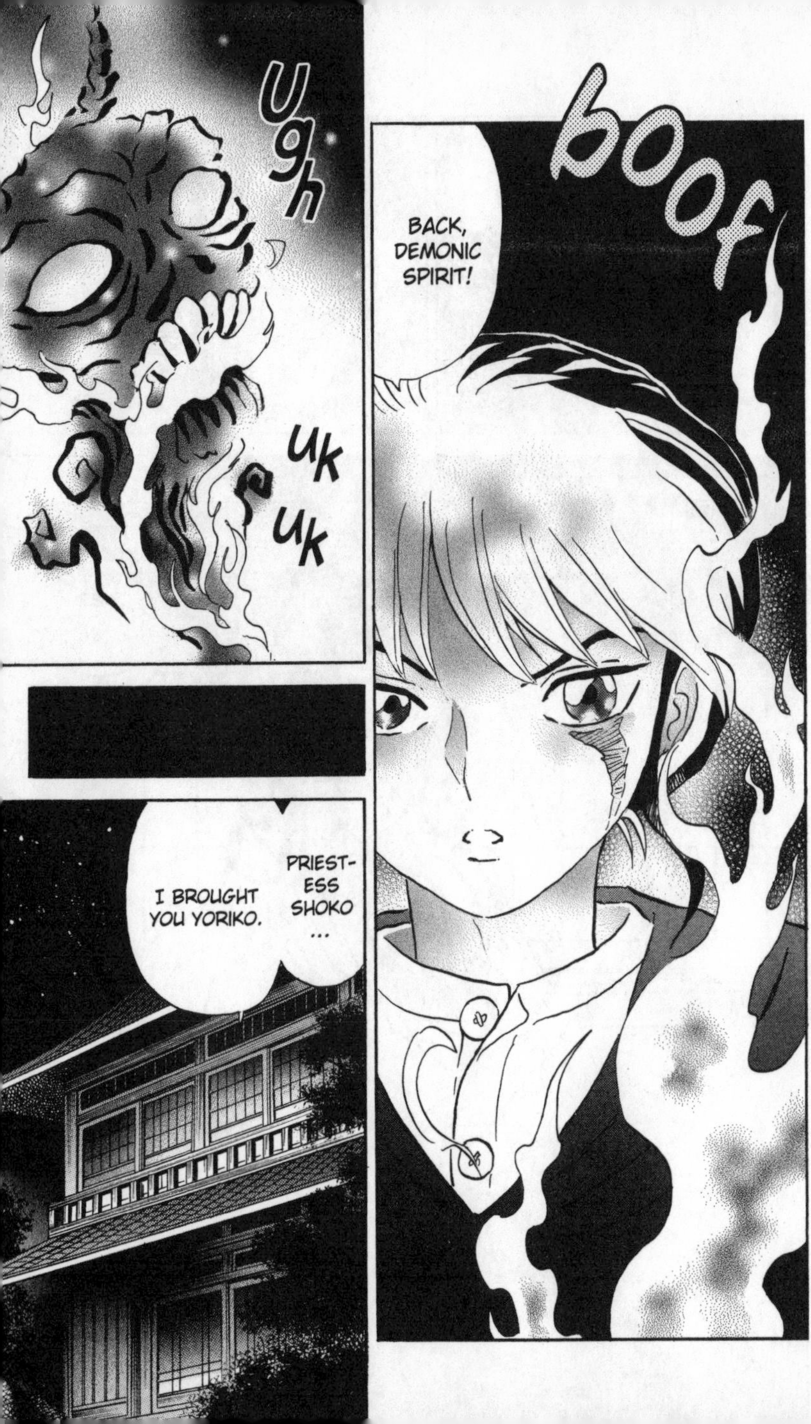
BOOF
BACK, DEMONIC SPIRIT!
Ugh
UK UK
PRIEST-ESS SHOKO ...
I BROUGHT YOU YORIKO.

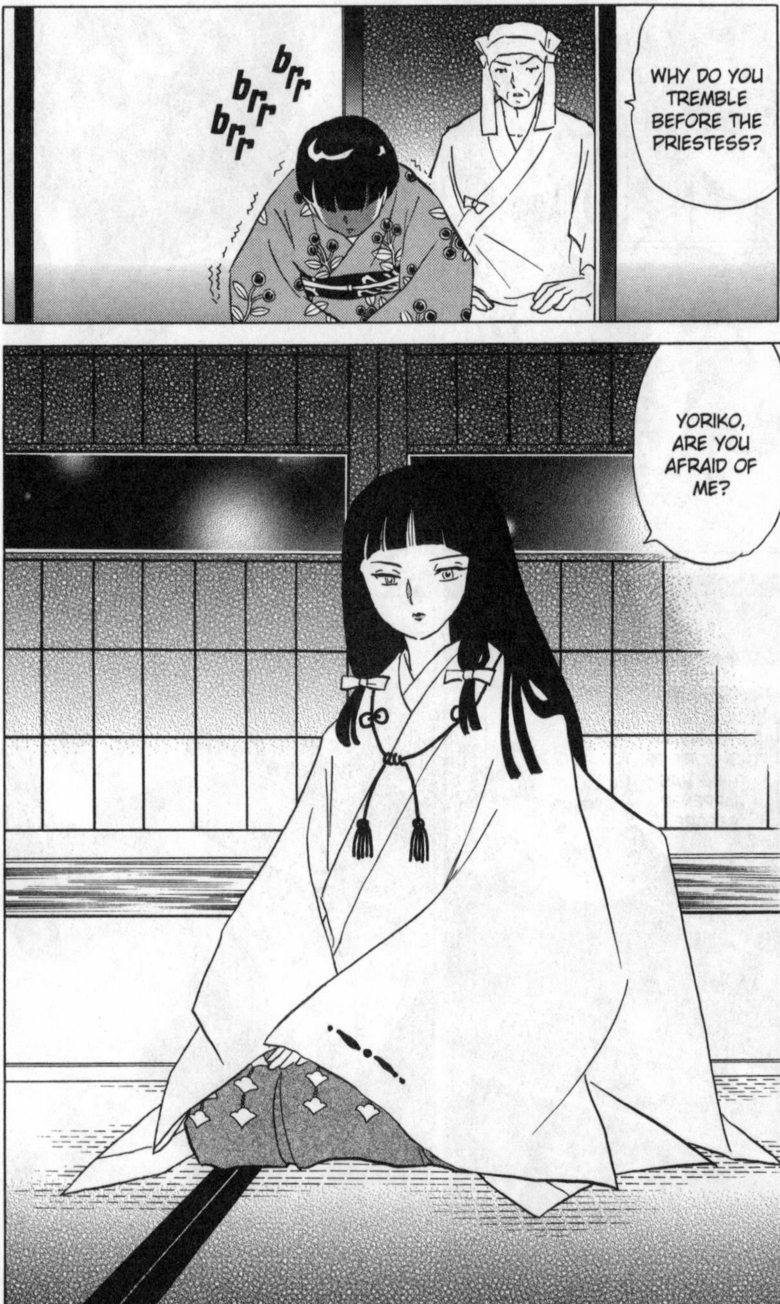
WHY DO YOU TREMBLE BEFORE THE PRIESTESS?
brr brr brr
YORIKO, ARE YOU AFRAID OF ME?

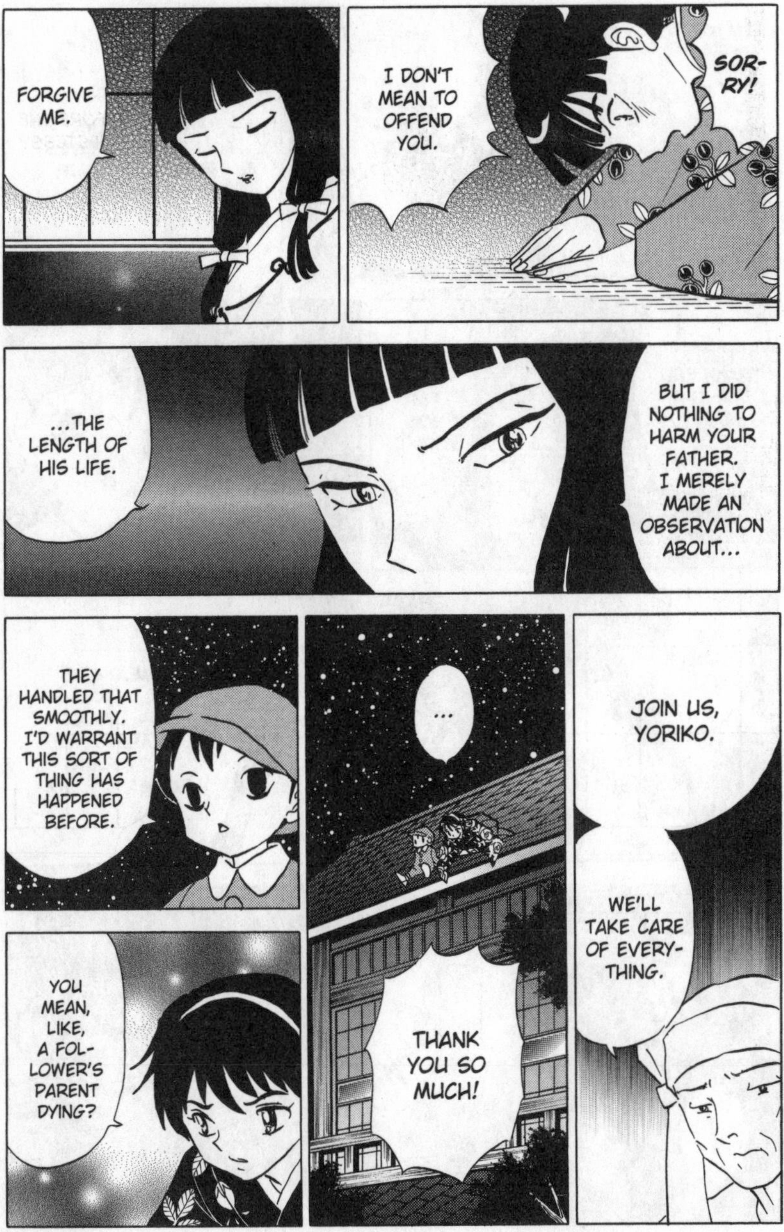
SOR-RY!
I DON'T MEAN TO OFFEND YOU.
FORGIVE ME.
BUT I DID NOTHING TO HARM YOUR FATHER. I MERELY MADE AN OBSERVATION ABOUT...
...THE LENGTH OF HIS LIFE.
JOIN US, YORIKO.
WE'LL TAKE CARE OF EVERY-THING.
...
THANK YOU SO MUCH!
THEY HANDLED THAT SMOOTHLY. I'D WARRANT THIS SORT OF THING HAS HAPPENED BEFORE.
YOU MEAN, LIKE, A FOL-LOWER'S PARENT DYING?

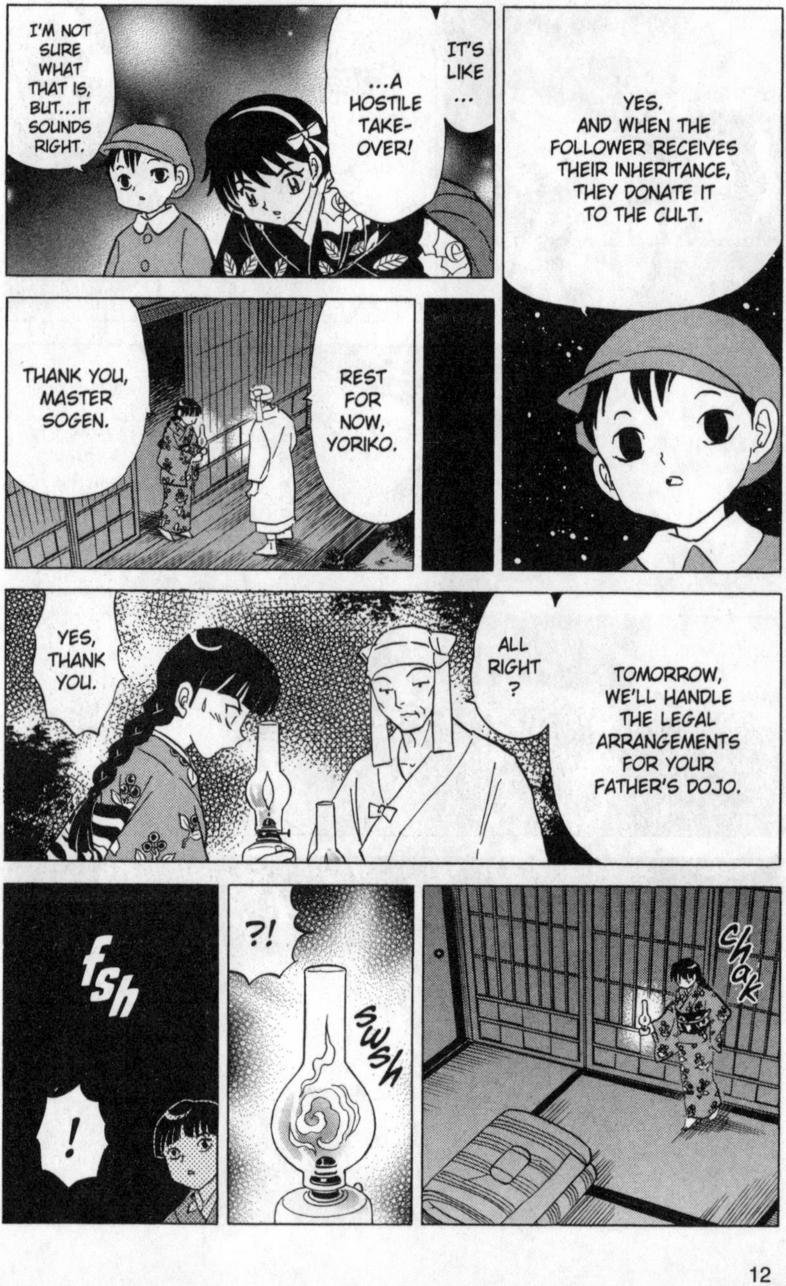
YES.
AND WHEN THE FOLLOWER RECEIVES THEIR INHERITANCE, THEY DONATE IT TO THE CULT.
IT'S LIKE ...
...A HOSTILE TAKE-OVER!
I'M NOT SURE WHAT THAT IS, BUT...IT SOUNDS RIGHT.
REST FOR NOW, YORIKO.
THANK YOU, MASTER SOGEN.
TOMORROW, WE'LL HANDLE THE LEGAL ARRANGEMENTS FOR YOUR FATHER'S DOJO.
ALL RIGHT?
YES, THANK YOU.
chak
?!
swsh
fsh
!

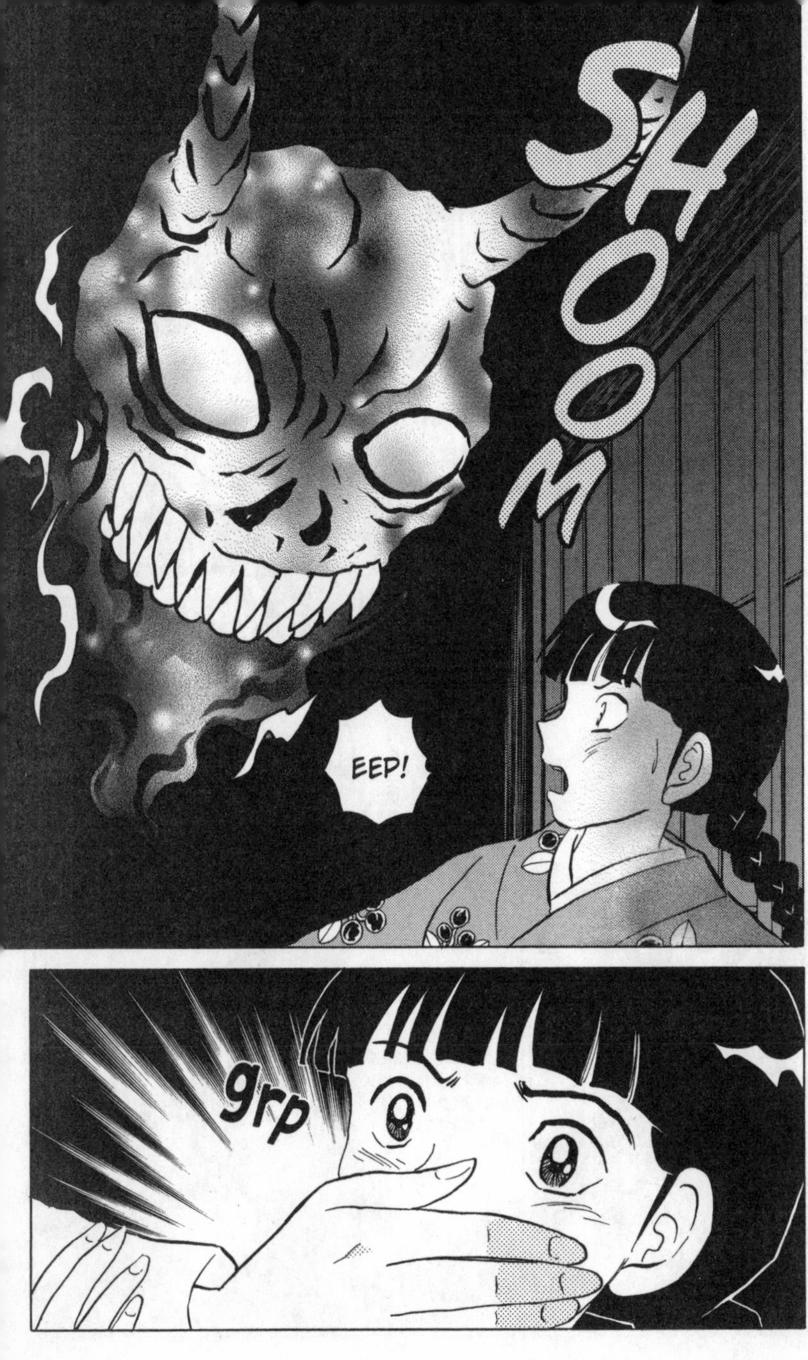
SHOOOM
EEP!
grp

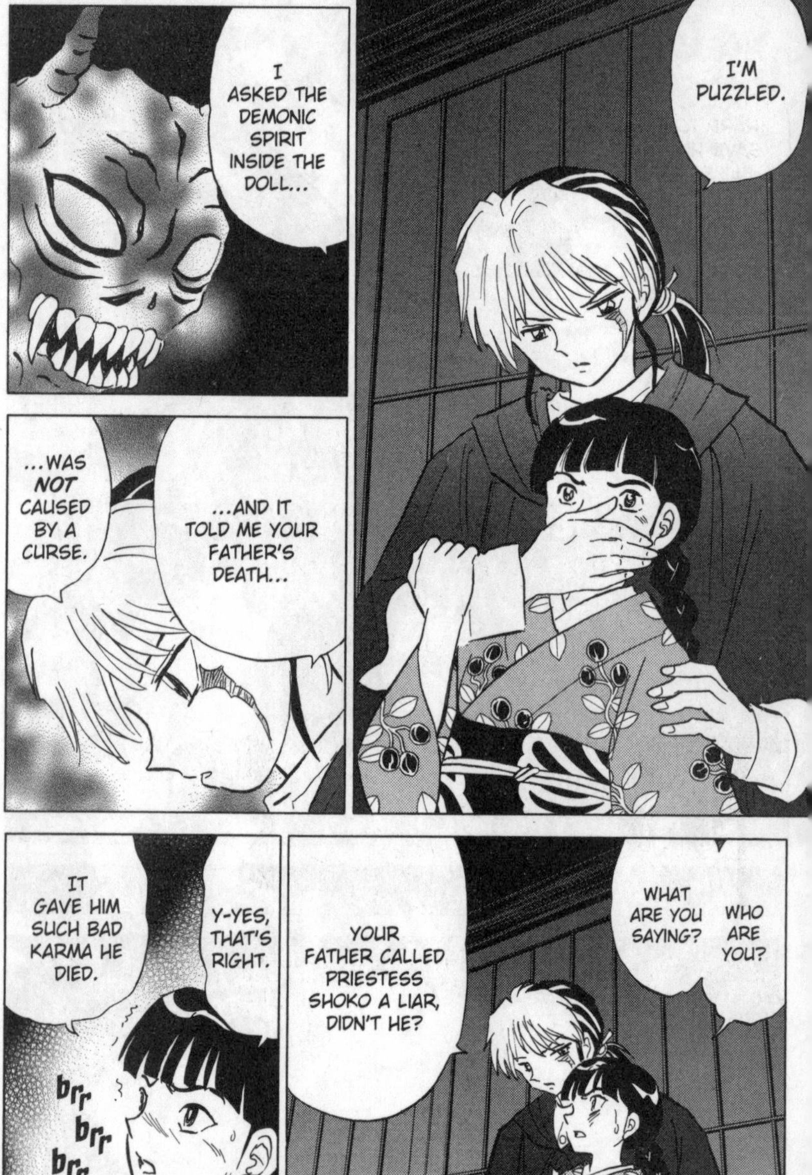
I'M PUZZLED.
I ASKED THE DEMONIC SPIRIT INSIDE THE DOLL...
...AND IT TOLD ME YOUR FATHER'S DEATH...
...WAS *NOT* CAUSED BY A CURSE.
WHO ARE YOU?
WHAT ARE YOU SAYING?
YOUR FATHER CALLED PRIESTESS SHOKO A LIAR, DIDN'T HE?
Y-YES, THAT'S RIGHT.
IT GAVE HIM SUCH BAD KARMA HE DIED.
brr brr brr

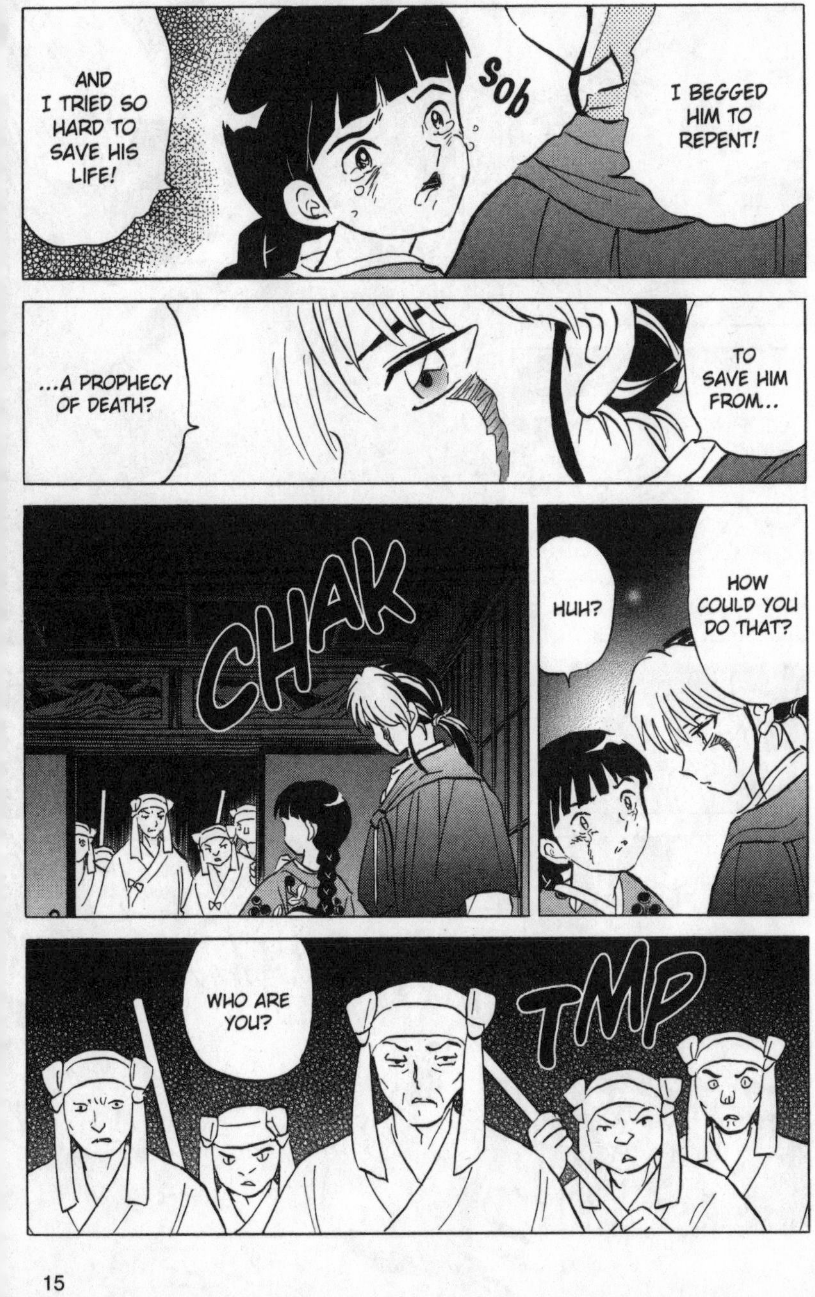
I BEGGED HIM TO REPENT!
Sob
AND I TRIED SO HARD TO SAVE HIS LIFE!
TO SAVE HIM FROM...
...A PROPHECY OF DEATH?
HOW COULD YOU DO THAT?
HUH?
CHAK
TMP
WHO ARE YOU?

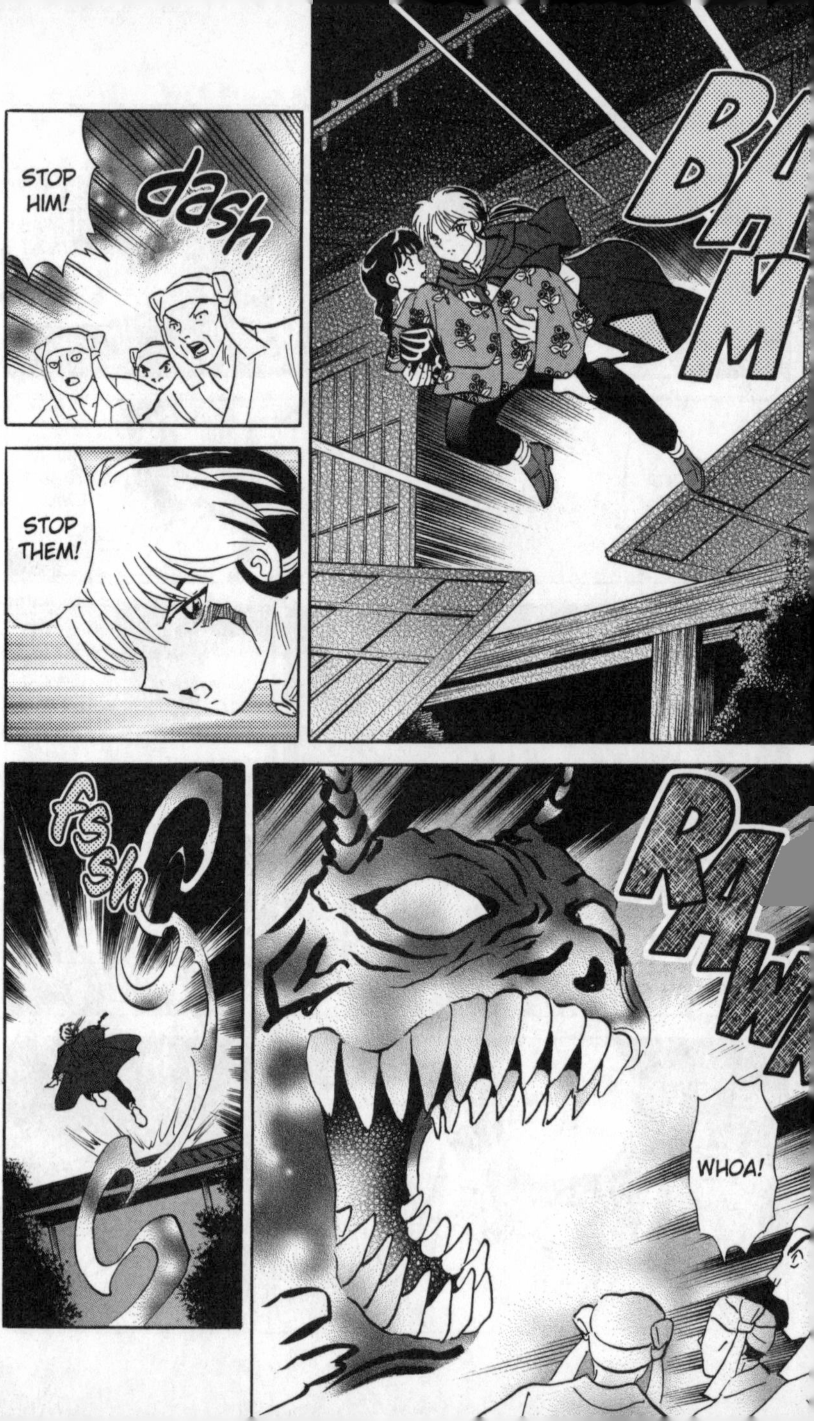
BAM
STOP HIM!
dash
STOP THEM!
RAW
WHOA!
fssh

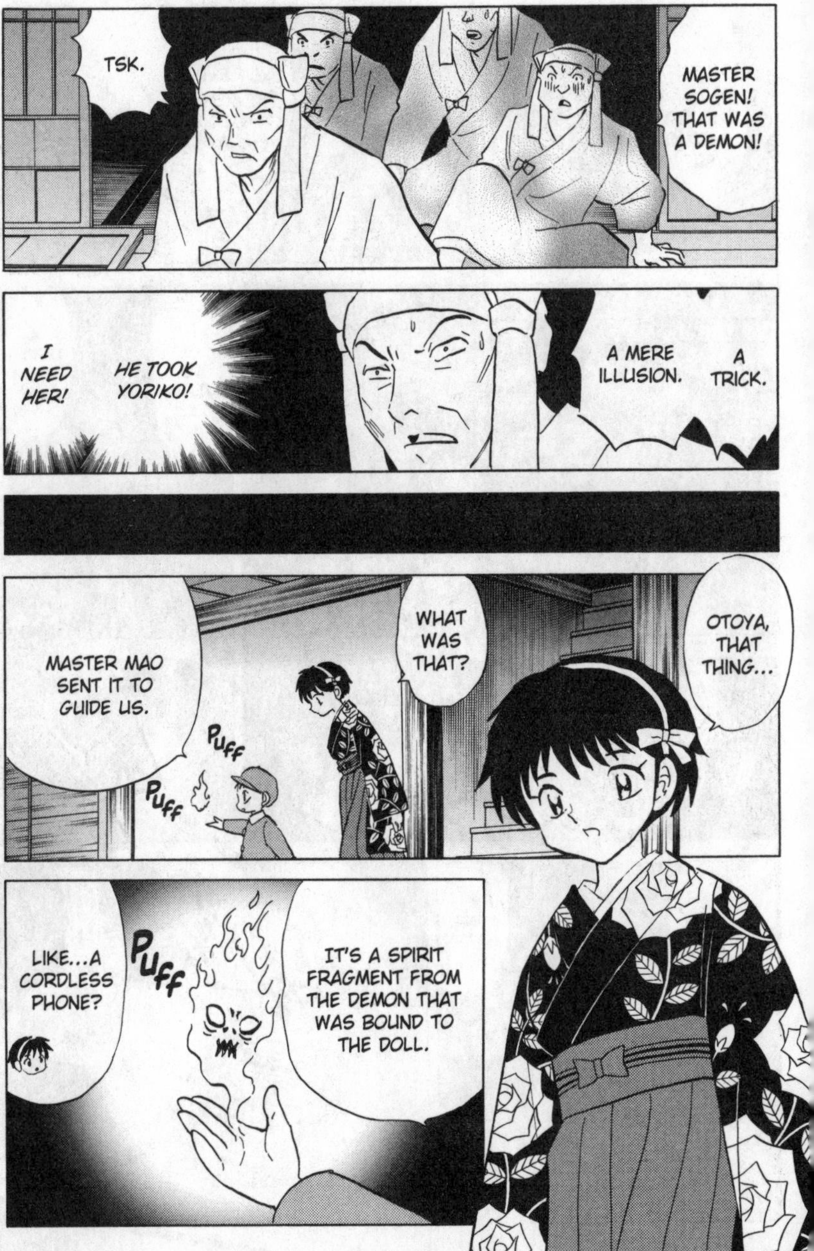
MASTER SOGEN! THAT WAS A DEMON!
TSK.
A TRICK.
A MERE ILLUSION.
HE TOOK YORIKO!
I NEED HER!
OTOYA, THAT THING...
WHAT WAS THAT?
MASTER MAO SENT IT TO GUIDE US.
PUFF
PUFF
IT'S A SPIRIT FRAGMENT FROM THE DEMON THAT WAS BOUND TO THE DOLL.
PUFF
LIKE...A CORDLESS PHONE?

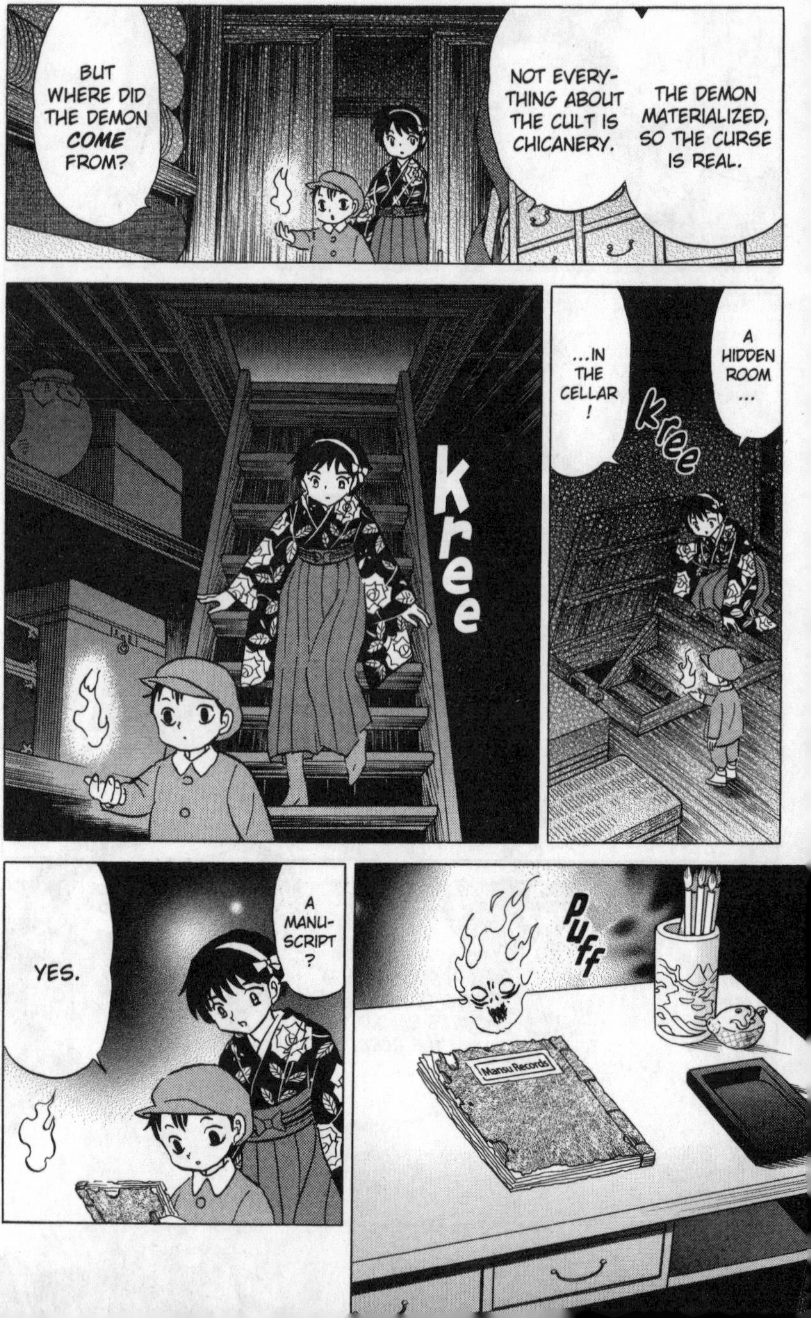
THE DEMON MATERIALIZED, SO THE CURSE IS REAL.
NOT EVERY-THING ABOUT THE CULT IS CHICANERY.
BUT WHERE DID THE DEMON **COME** FROM?
A HIDDEN ROOM ...
kree
...IN THE CELLAR!
kree
Puff
Mansu Records
A MANU-SCRIPT?
YES.

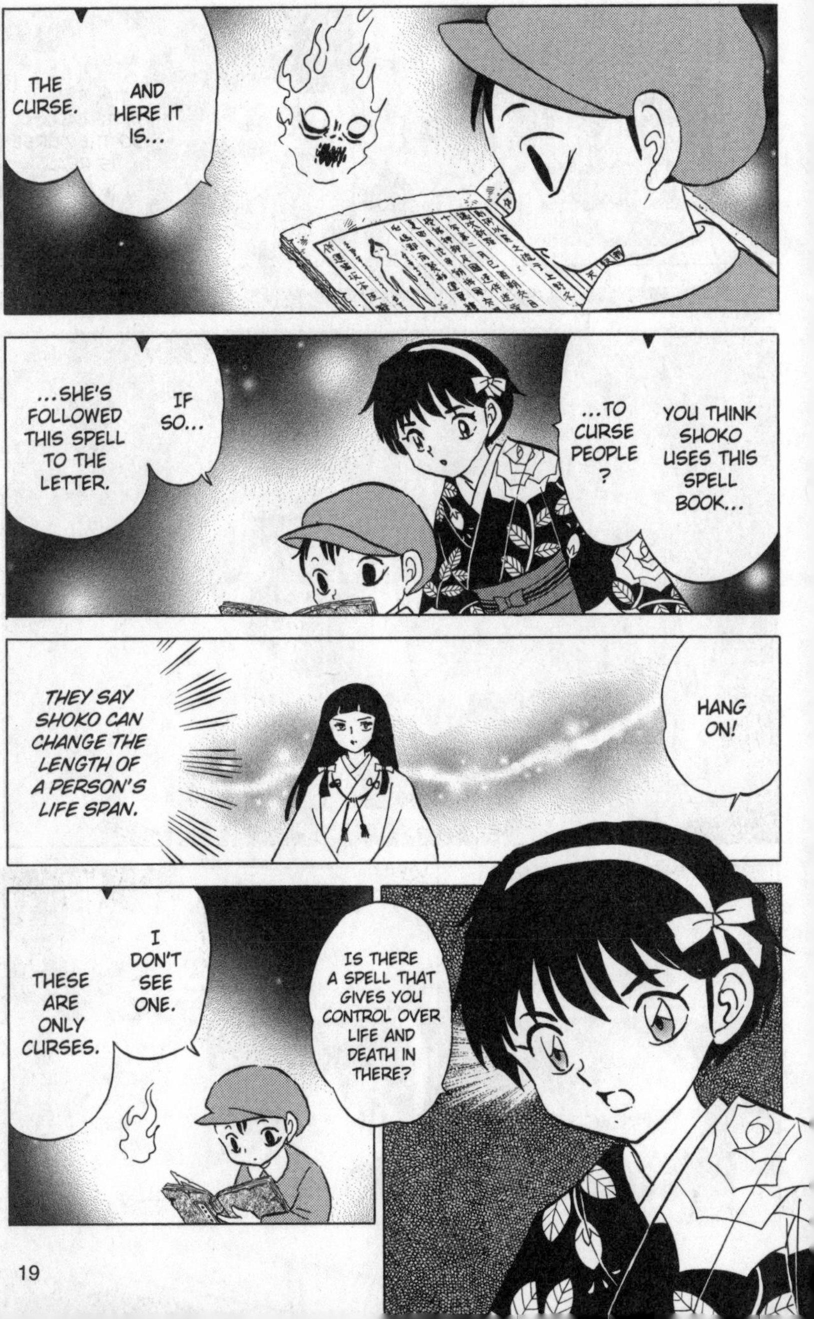
AND HERE IT IS...
THE CURSE.
YOU THINK SHOKO USES THIS SPELL BOOK...
...TO CURSE PEOPLE?
IF SO...
...SHE'S FOLLOWED THIS SPELL TO THE LETTER.
HANG ON!
THEY SAY SHOKO CAN CHANGE THE LENGTH OF A PERSON'S LIFE SPAN.
IS THERE A SPELL THAT GIVES YOU CONTROL OVER LIFE AND DEATH IN THERE?
I DON'T SEE ONE.
THESE ARE ONLY CURSES.

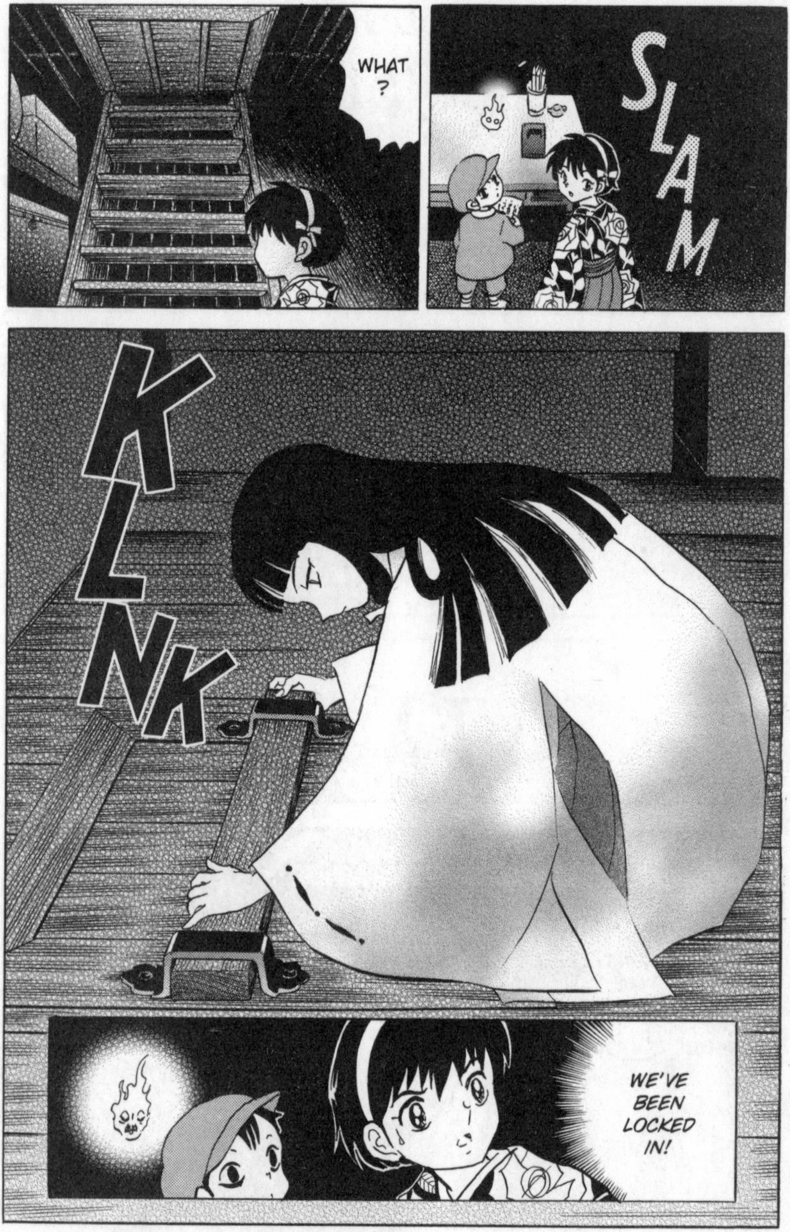
SLAM
WHAT ?
KLLNK
WE'VE BEEN LOCKED IN!

Chapter 2:
Other Face of the Cult

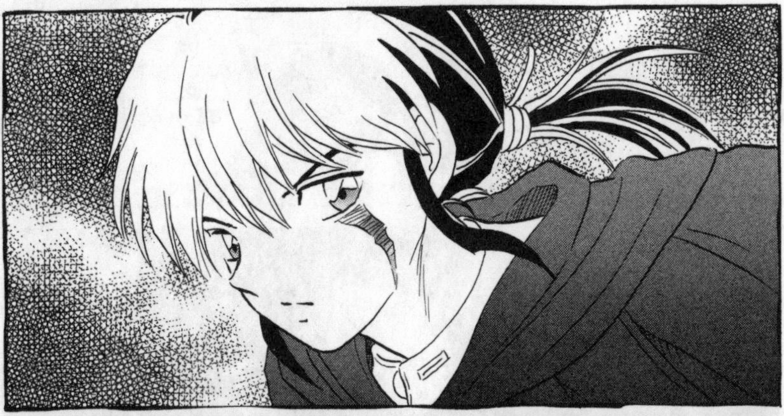

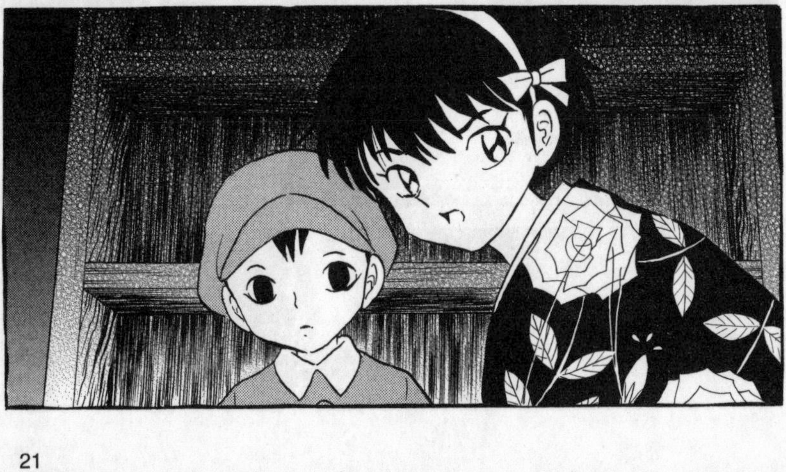

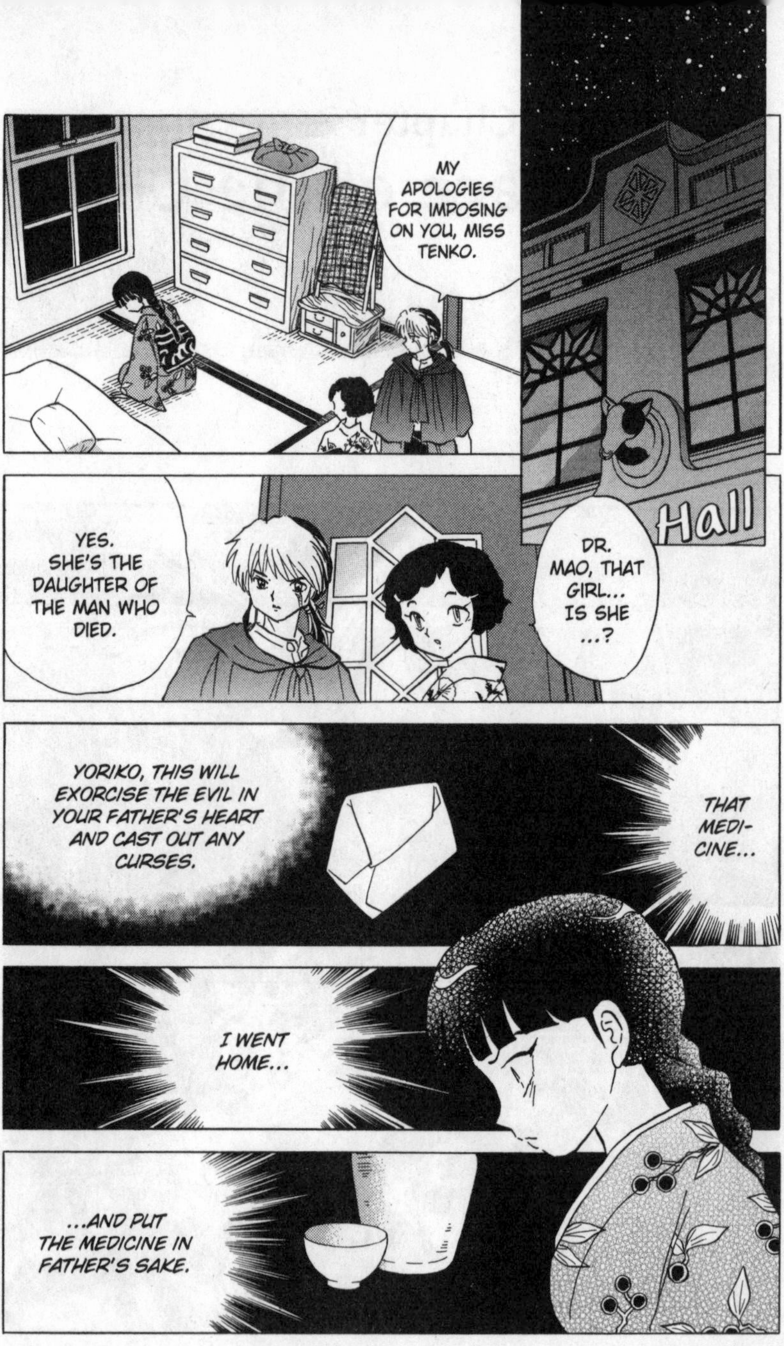
Hall
MY APOLOGIES FOR IMPOSING ON YOU, MISS TENKO.
DR. MAO, THAT GIRL... IS SHE ...?
YES. SHE'S THE DAUGHTER OF THE MAN WHO DIED.
THAT MEDICINE...
YORIKO, THIS WILL EXORCISE THE EVIL IN YOUR FATHER'S HEART AND CAST OUT ANY CURSES.
I WENT HOME...
...AND PUT THE MEDICINE IN FATHER'S SAKE.

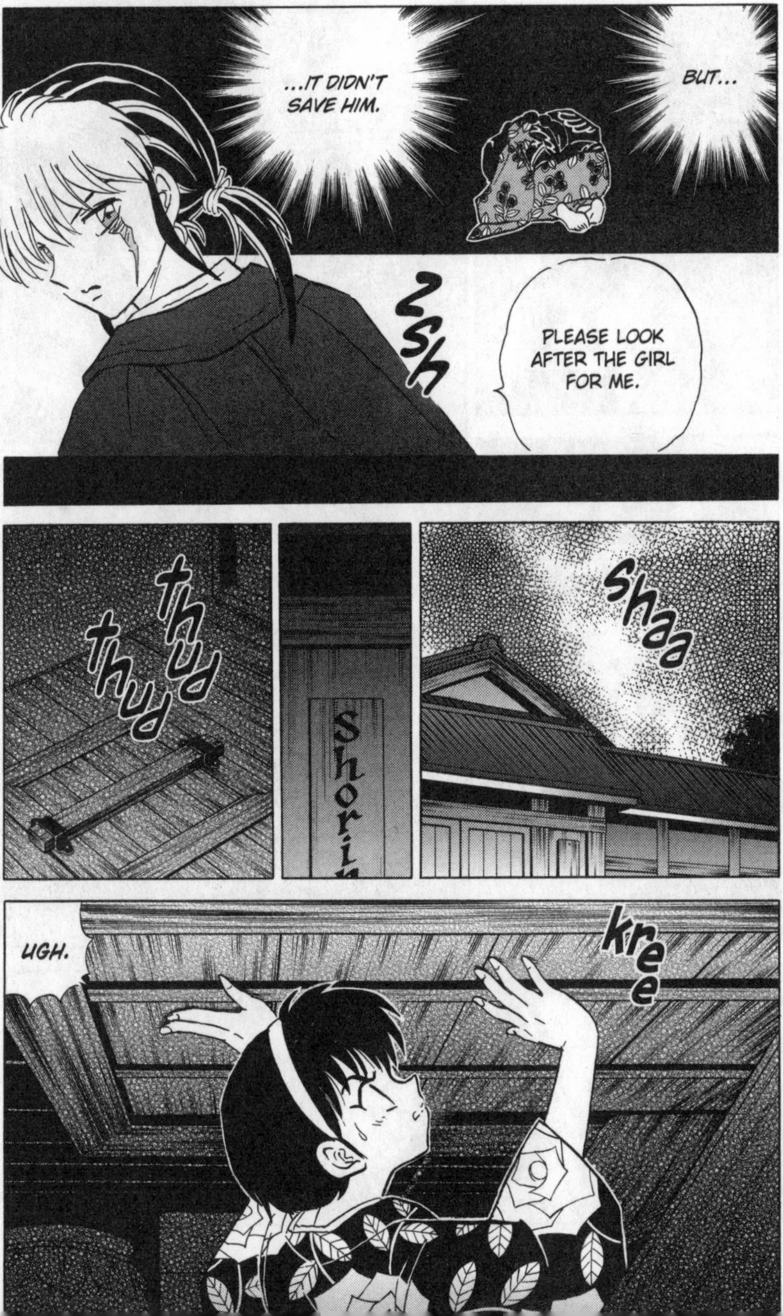
BUT...
...IT DIDN'T SAVE HIM.
zsh
PLEASE LOOK AFTER THE GIRL FOR ME.
shaa
thud thud
kree
UGH.

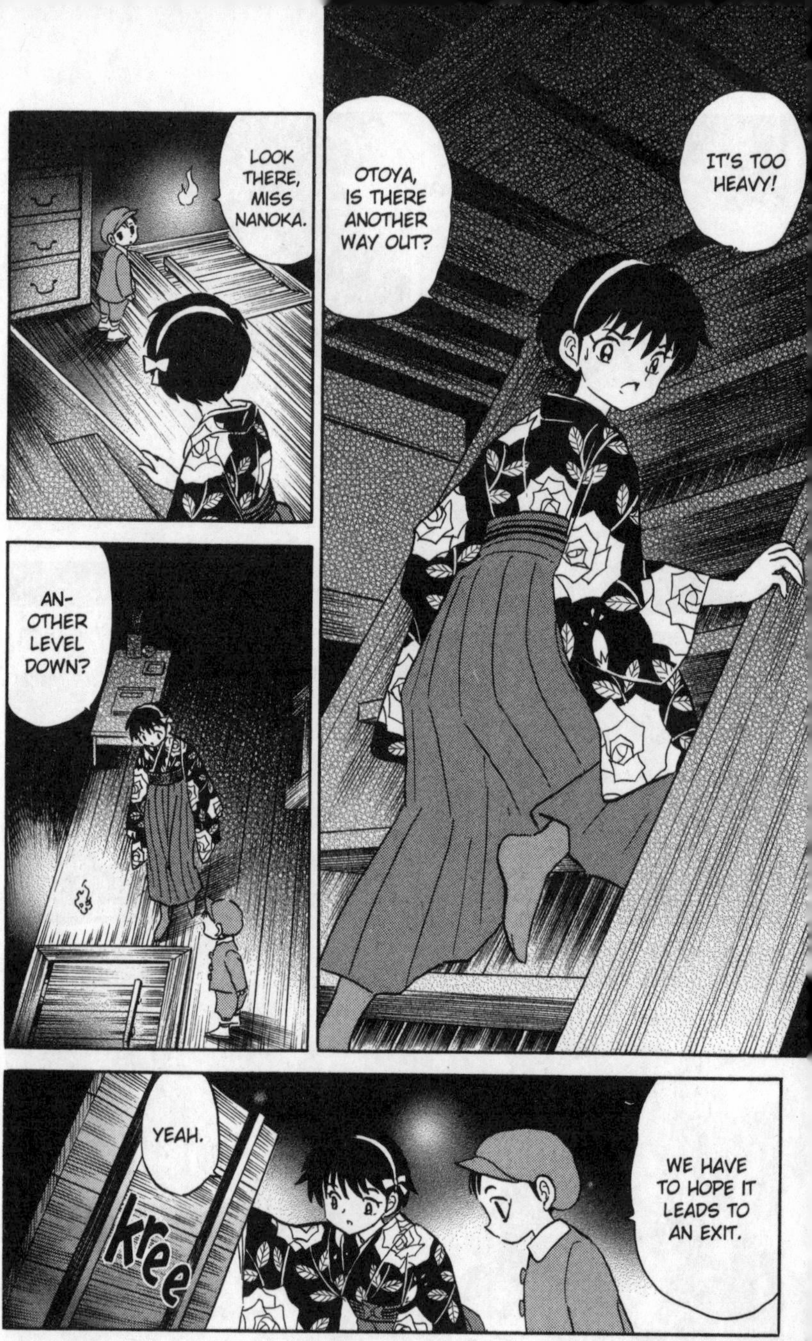
IT'S TOO HEAVY!
OTOYA, IS THERE ANOTHER WAY OUT?
LOOK THERE, MISS NANOKA.
AN-OTHER LEVEL DOWN?
WE HAVE TO HOPE IT LEADS TO AN EXIT.
YEAH.
kree

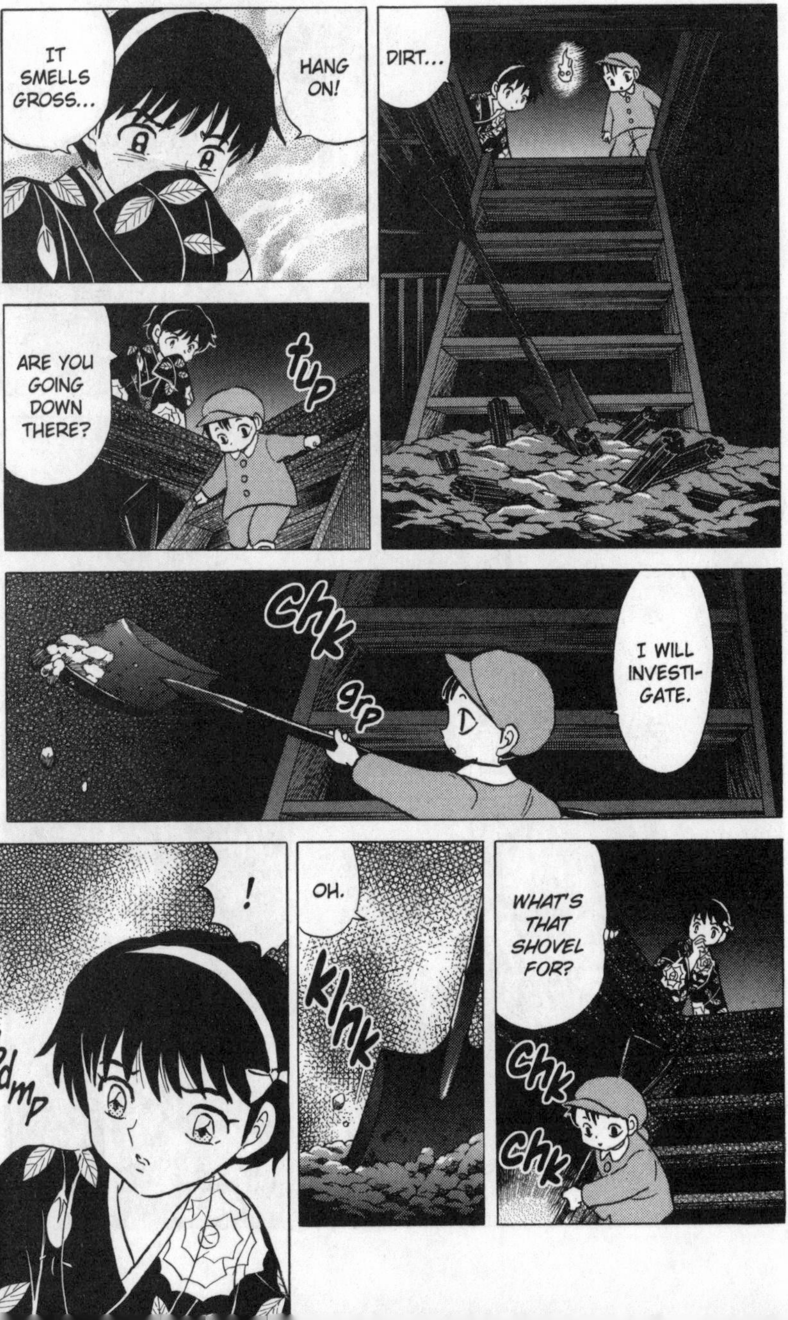
DIRT...
HANG ON!
IT SMELLS GROSS...
ARE YOU GOING DOWN THERE?
tup
I WILL INVESTI-GATE.
chk
grp
WHAT'S THAT SHOVEL FOR?
chk
chk
OH.
klink
!
bdmp

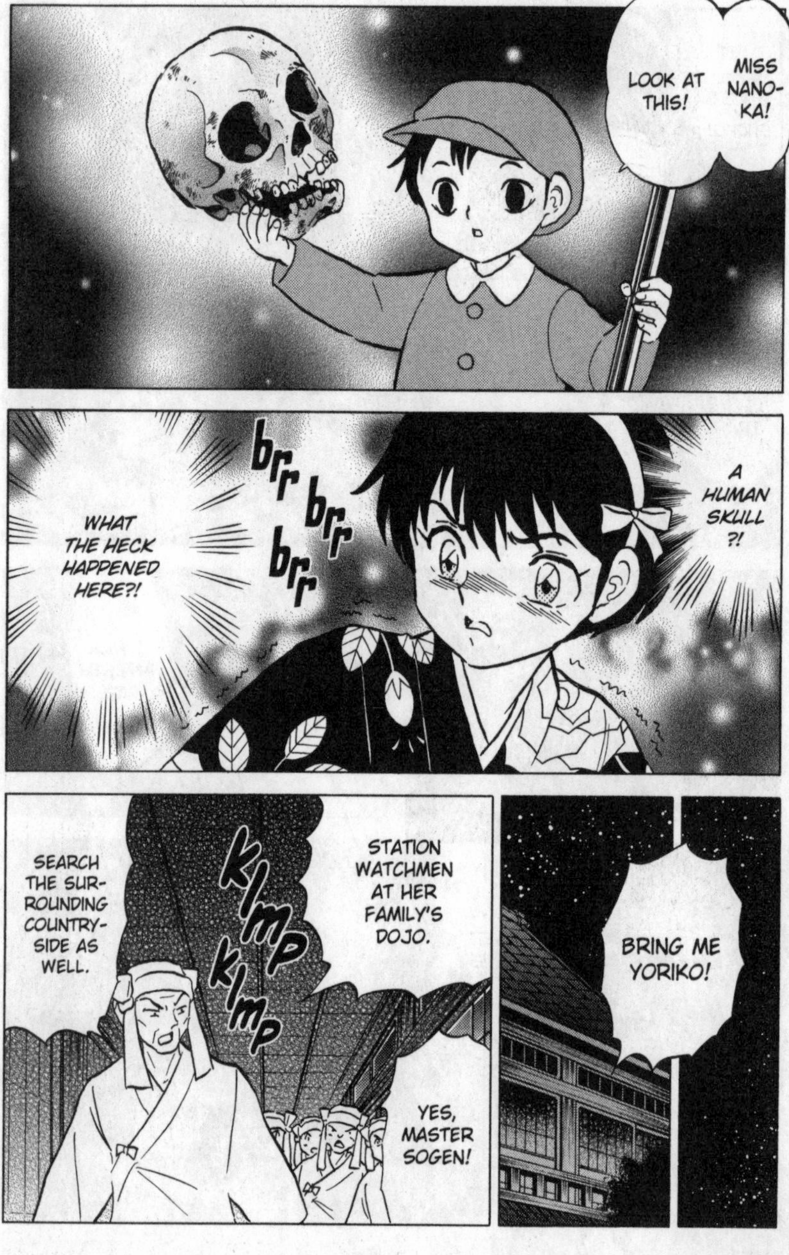
MISS NANO-KA!
LOOK AT THIS!
A HUMAN SKULL ?!
brr brr brr
WHAT THE HECK HAPPENED HERE?!
BRING ME YORIKO!
STATION WATCHMEN AT HER FAMILY'S DOJO.
SEARCH THE SUR-ROUNDING COUNTRY-SIDE AS WELL.
klmp klmp
YES, MASTER SOGEN!

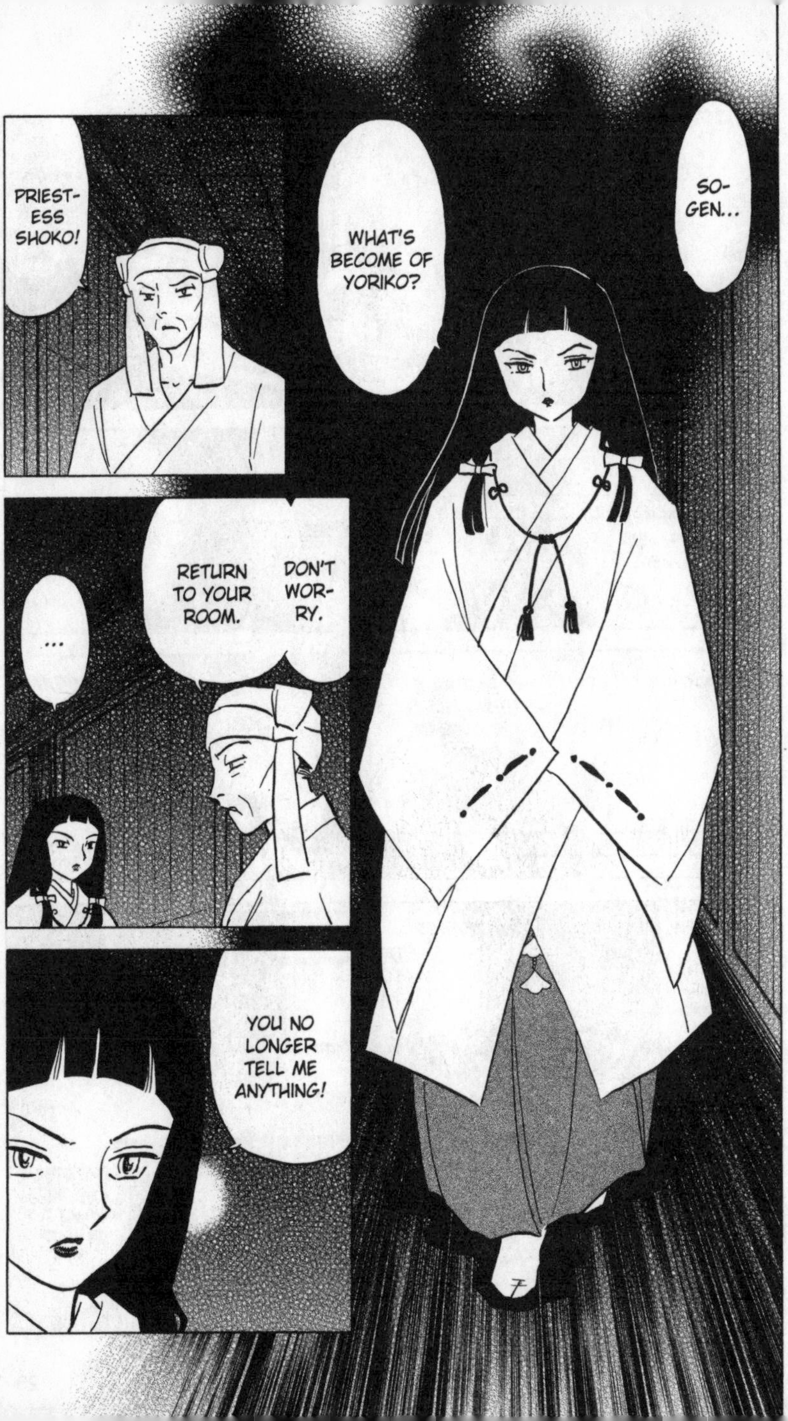
SO-GEN...
WHAT'S BECOME OF YORIKO?
PRIEST-ESS SHOKO!
DON'T WOR-RY.
RETURN TO YOUR ROOM.
...
YOU NO LONGER TELL ME ANYTHING!

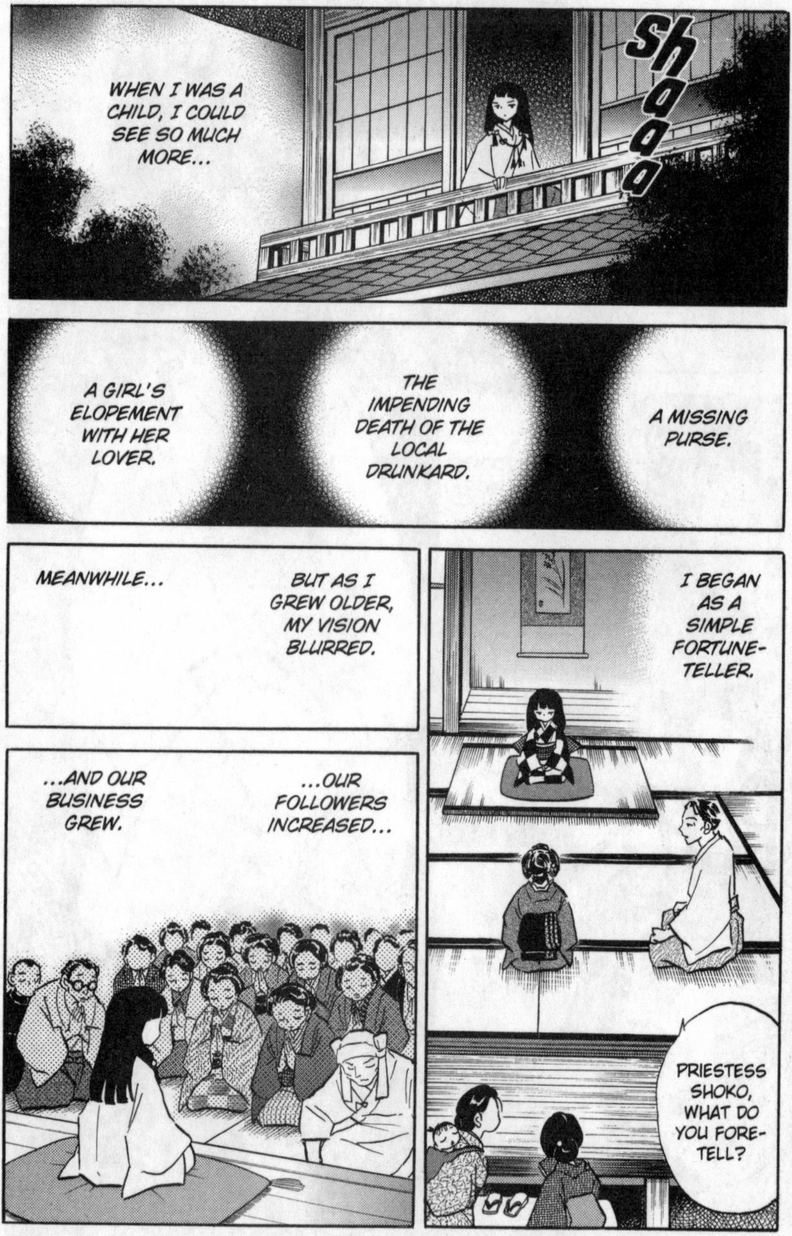
Shaaa
WHEN I WAS A CHILD, I COULD SEE SO MUCH MORE...
A MISSING PURSE.
THE IMPENDING DEATH OF THE LOCAL DRUNKARD.
A GIRL'S ELOPEMENT WITH HER LOVER.
I BEGAN AS A SIMPLE FORTUNE-TELLER.
BUT AS I GREW OLDER, MY VISION BLURRED.
MEANWHILE...
...OUR FOLLOWERS INCREASED...
...AND OUR BUSINESS GREW.
PRIESTESS SHOKO, WHAT DO YOU FORE-TELL?

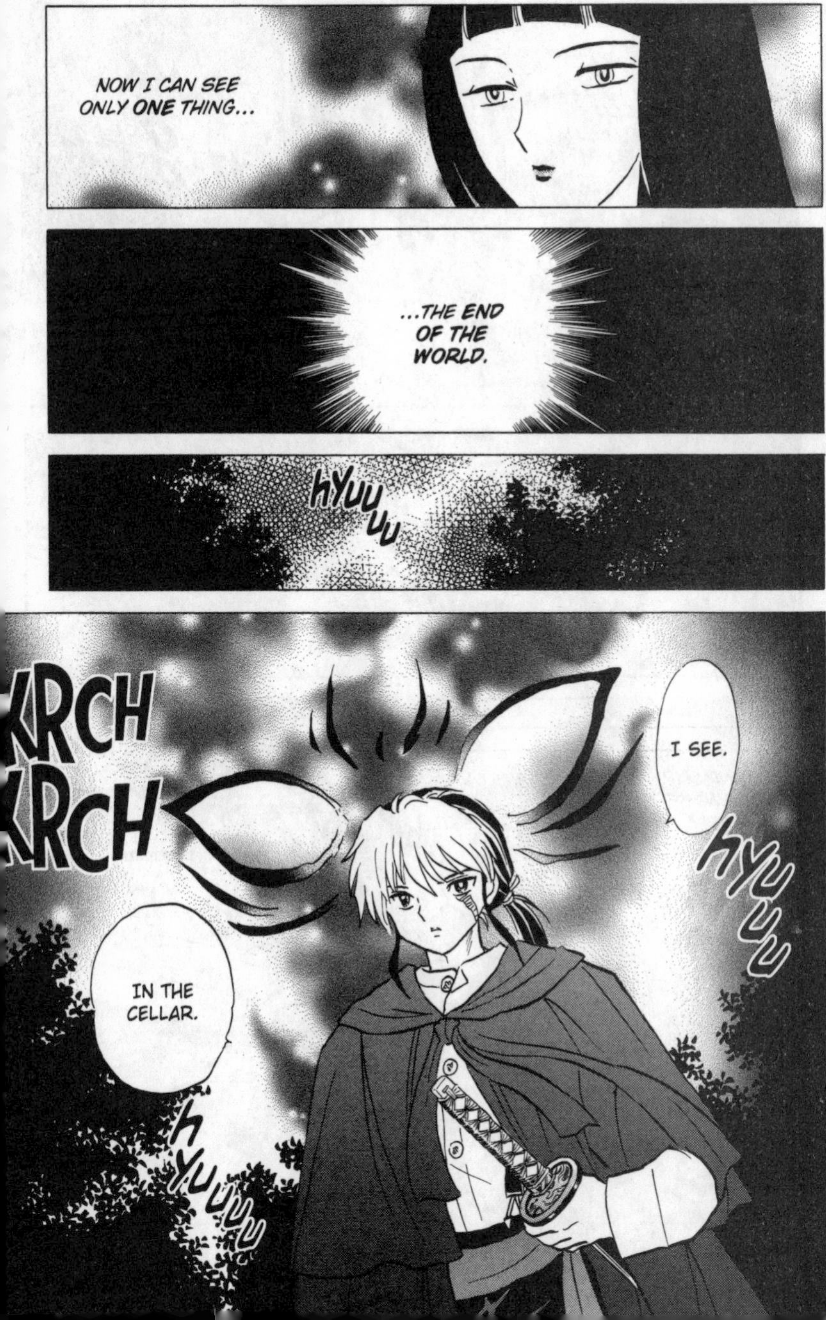
NOW I CAN SEE ONLY ONE THING...
...THE END OF THE WORLD.
hYUUUUU
I SEE.
hYUUU
KRCH
KRCH
IN THE CELLAR.
hYUUUU

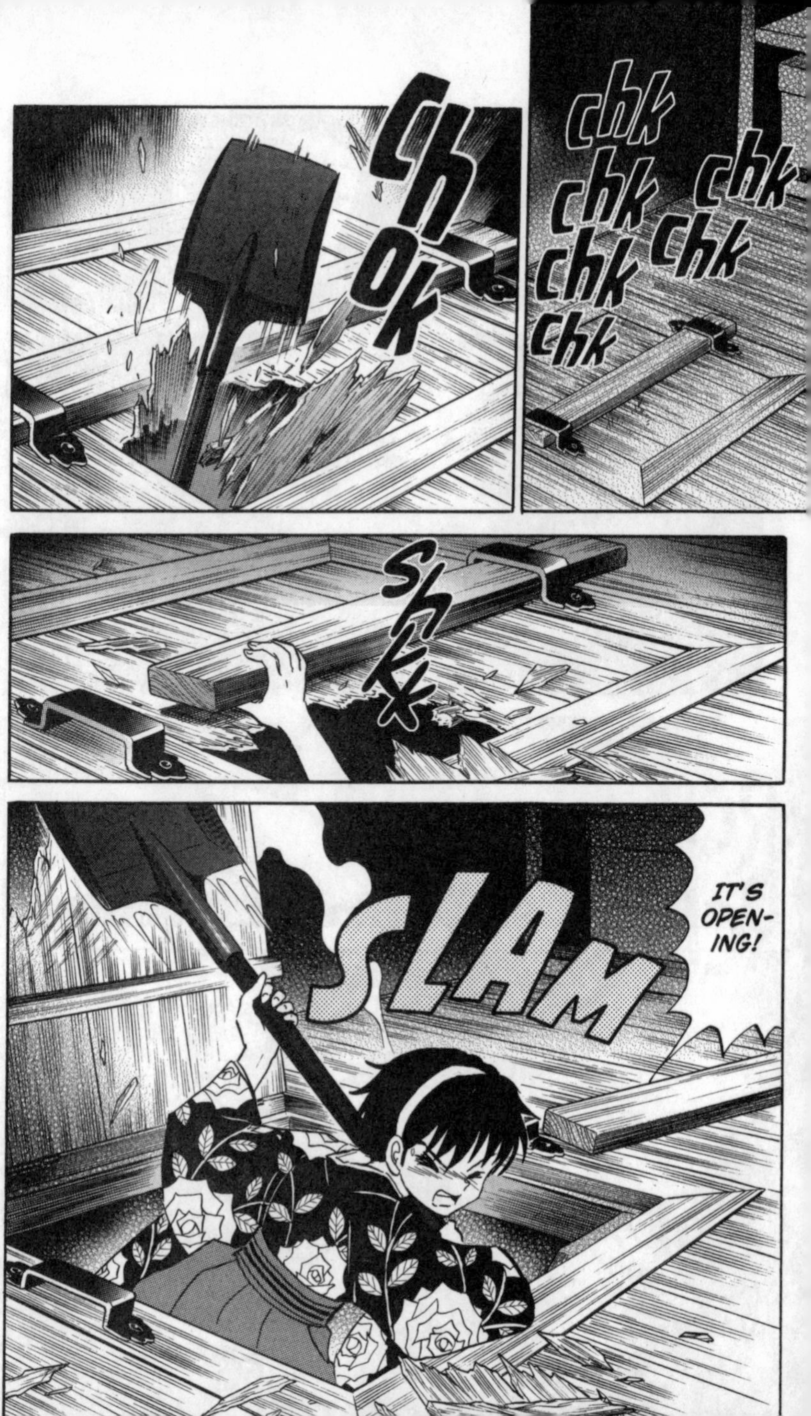
chk chk
chk chk chk chk
CHOK
SHKK
IT'S OPENING!
SLAM

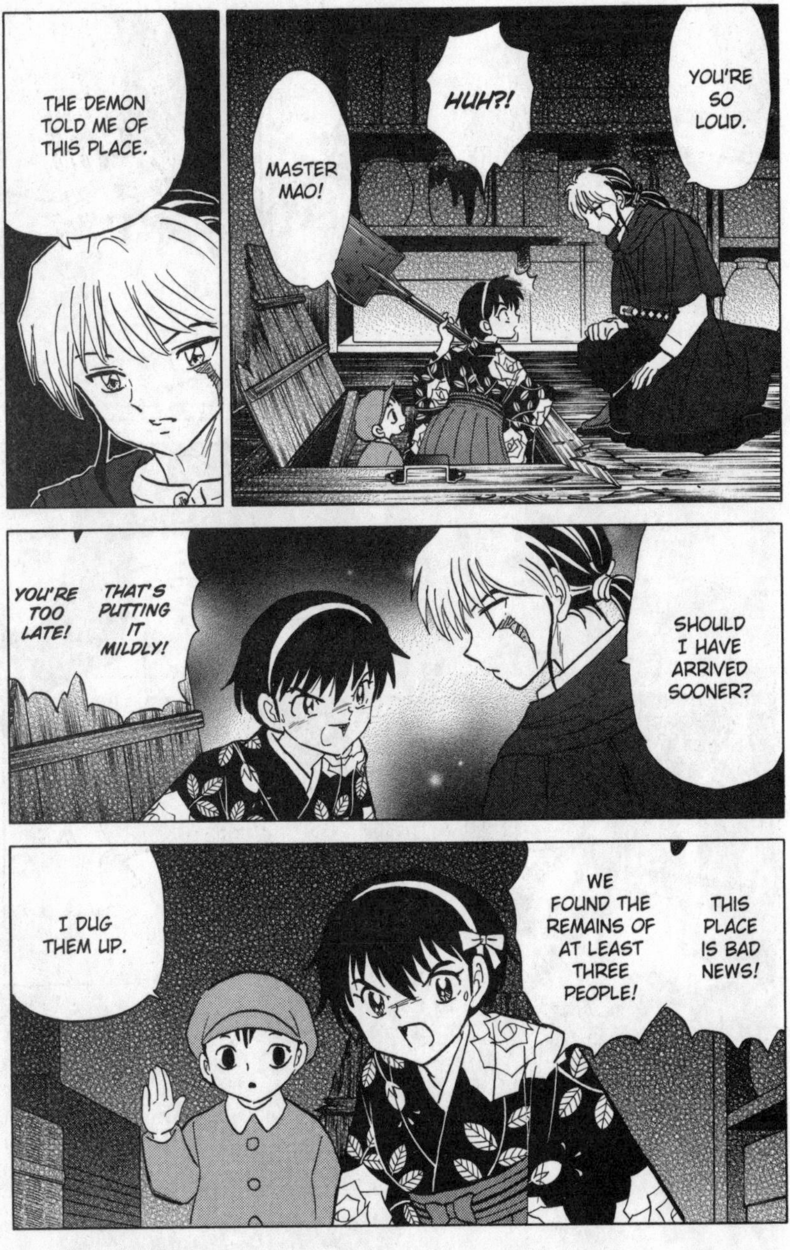
YOU'RE SO LOUD.
HUH?!
MASTER MAO!
THE DEMON TOLD ME OF THIS PLACE.
SHOULD I HAVE ARRIVED SOONER?
THAT'S PUTTING IT MILDLY!
YOU'RE TOO LATE!
THIS PLACE IS BAD NEWS!
WE FOUND THE REMAINS OF AT LEAST THREE PEOPLE!
I DUG THEM UP.

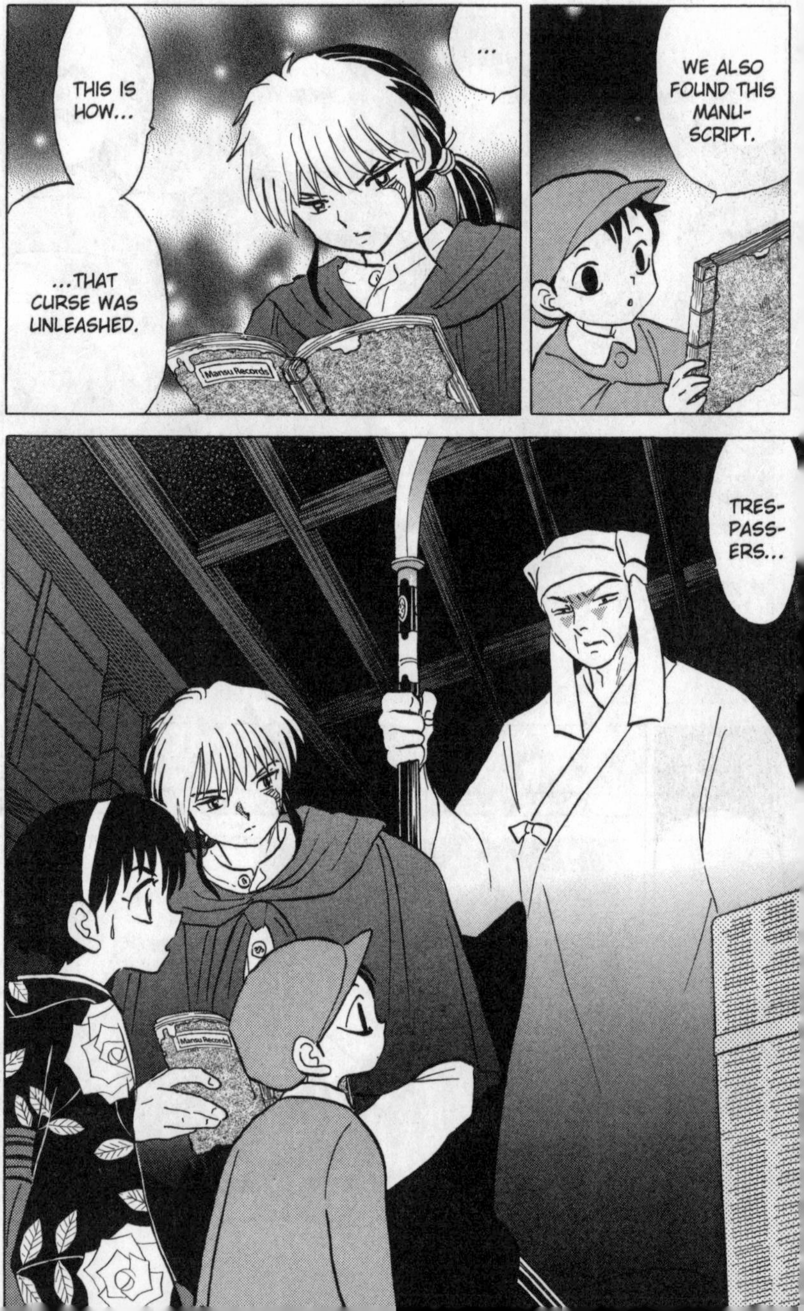
WE ALSO FOUND THIS MANU-SCRIPT.
...
THIS IS HOW...
Mansu Records
...THAT CURSE WAS UNLEASHED.
TRES-PASS-ERS...
Mansu Records

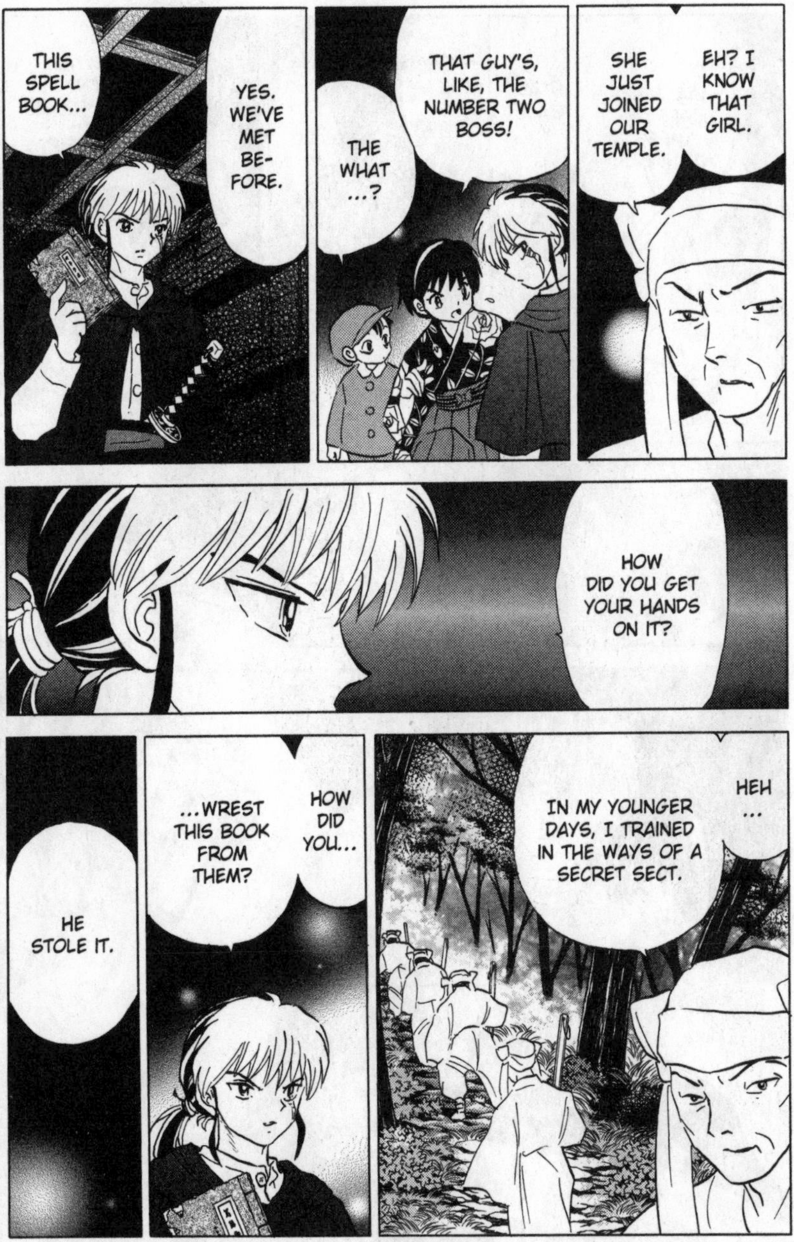
EH? I KNOW THAT GIRL.
SHE JUST JOINED OUR TEMPLE.
THAT GUY'S, LIKE, THE NUMBER TWO BOSS!
THE WHAT ...?
YES. WE'VE MET BE-FORE.
THIS SPELL BOOK...
HOW DID YOU GET YOUR HANDS ON IT?
HEH ...
IN MY YOUNGER DAYS, I TRAINED IN THE WAYS OF A SECRET SECT.
HOW DID YOU...
...WREST THIS BOOK FROM THEM?
HE STOLE IT.

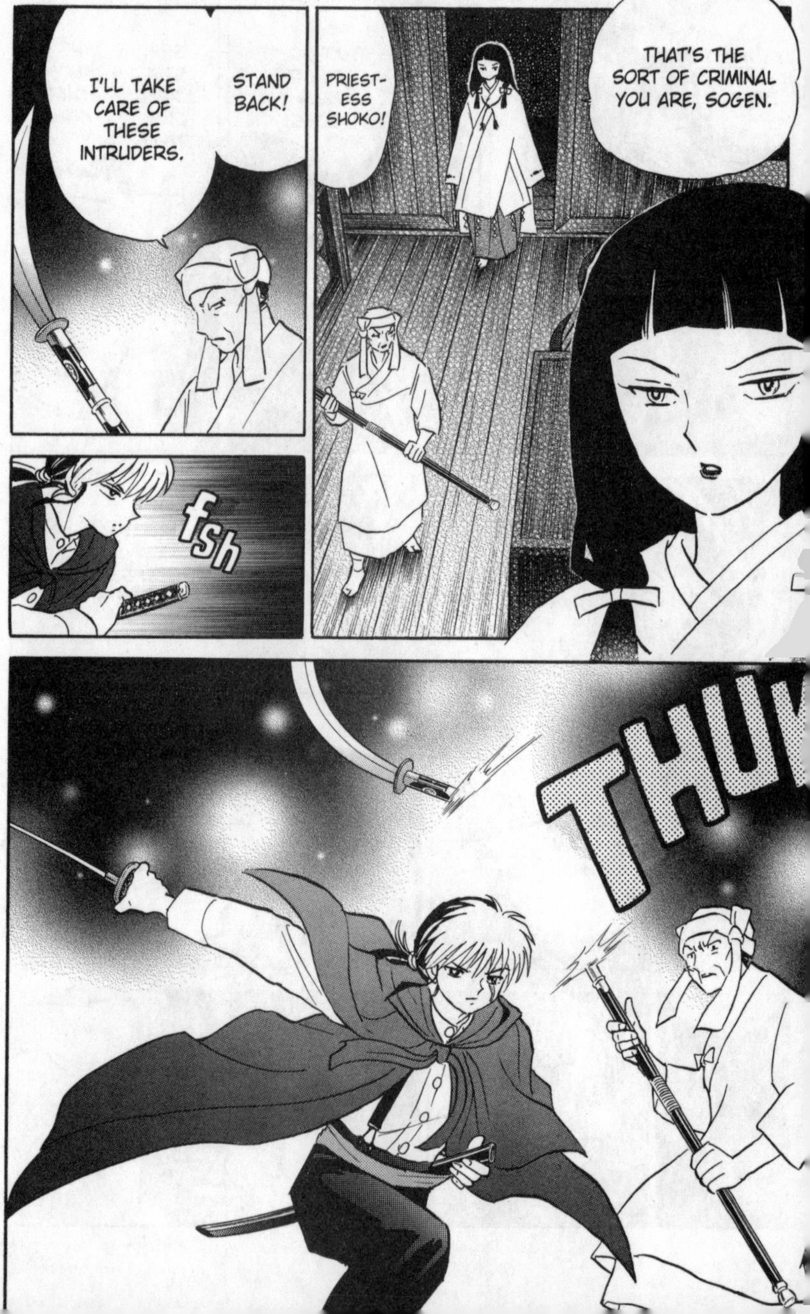
THAT'S THE SORT OF CRIMINAL YOU ARE, SOGEN.
PRIEST-ESS SHOKO!
STAND BACK!
I'LL TAKE CARE OF THESE INTRUDERS.
fsh
THUK

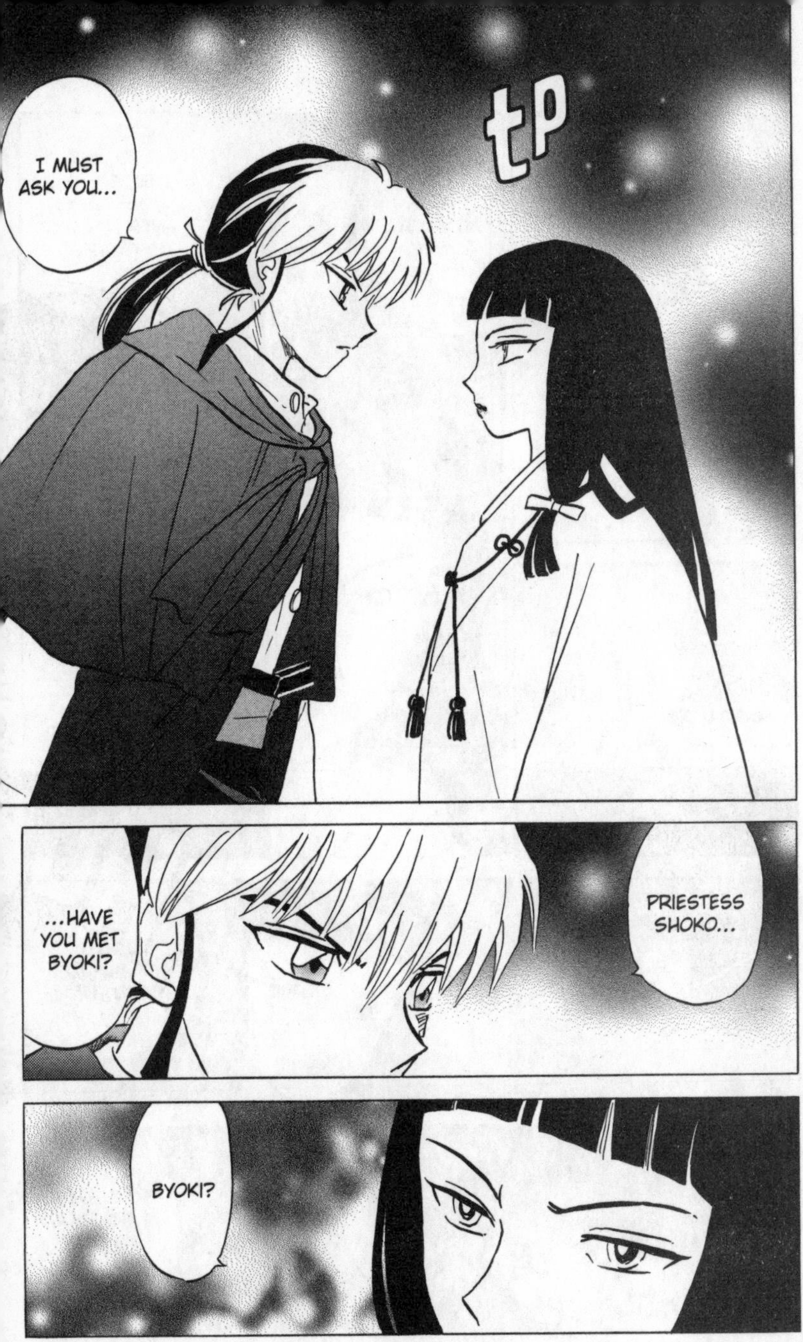
tp
I MUST ASK YOU...
PRIESTESS SHOKO...
...HAVE YOU MET BYOKI?
BYOKI?

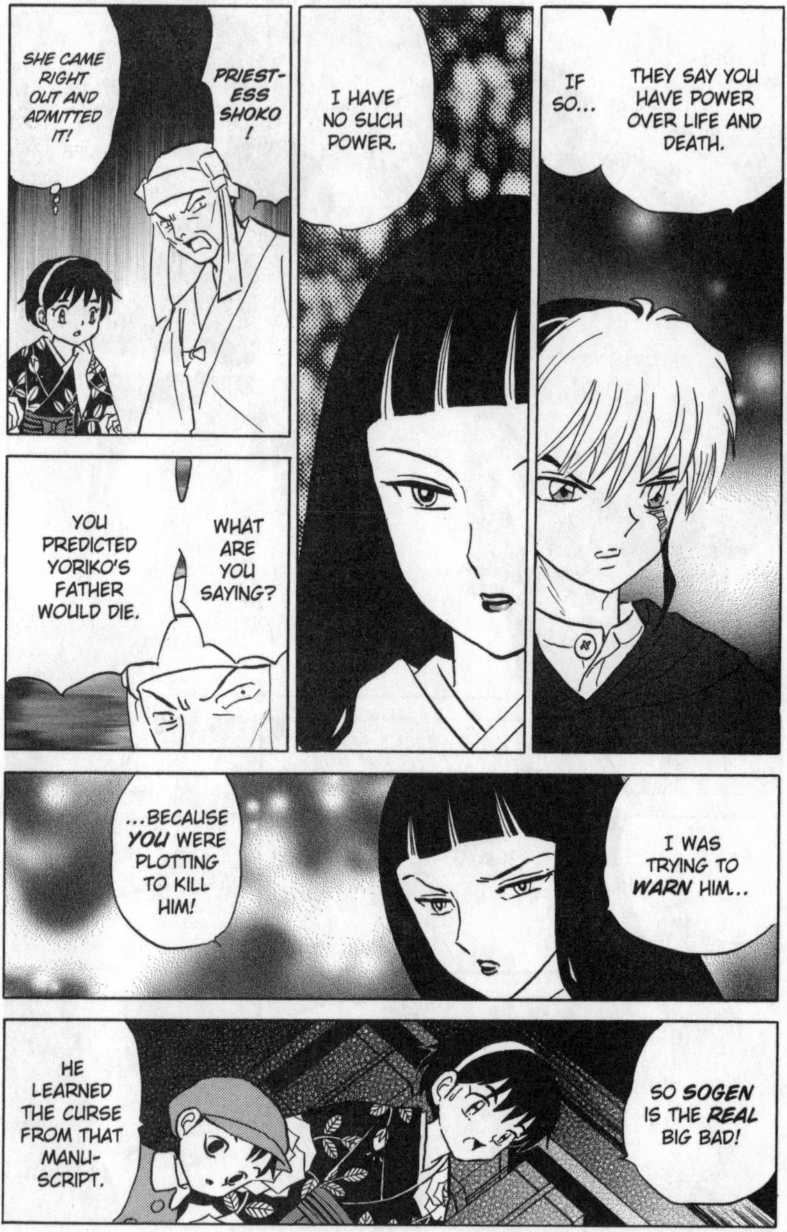
THEY SAY YOU HAVE POWER OVER LIFE AND DEATH.
IF SO...
I HAVE NO SUCH POWER.
PRIEST-ESS SHOKO!
SHE CAME RIGHT OUT AND ADMITTED IT!
WHAT ARE YOU SAYING?
YOU PREDICTED YORIKO'S FATHER WOULD DIE.
I WAS TRYING TO WARN HIM...
...BECAUSE YOU WERE PLOTTING TO KILL HIM!
SO SOGEN IS THE REAL BIG BAD!
HE LEARNED THE CURSE FROM THAT MANU-SCRIPT.

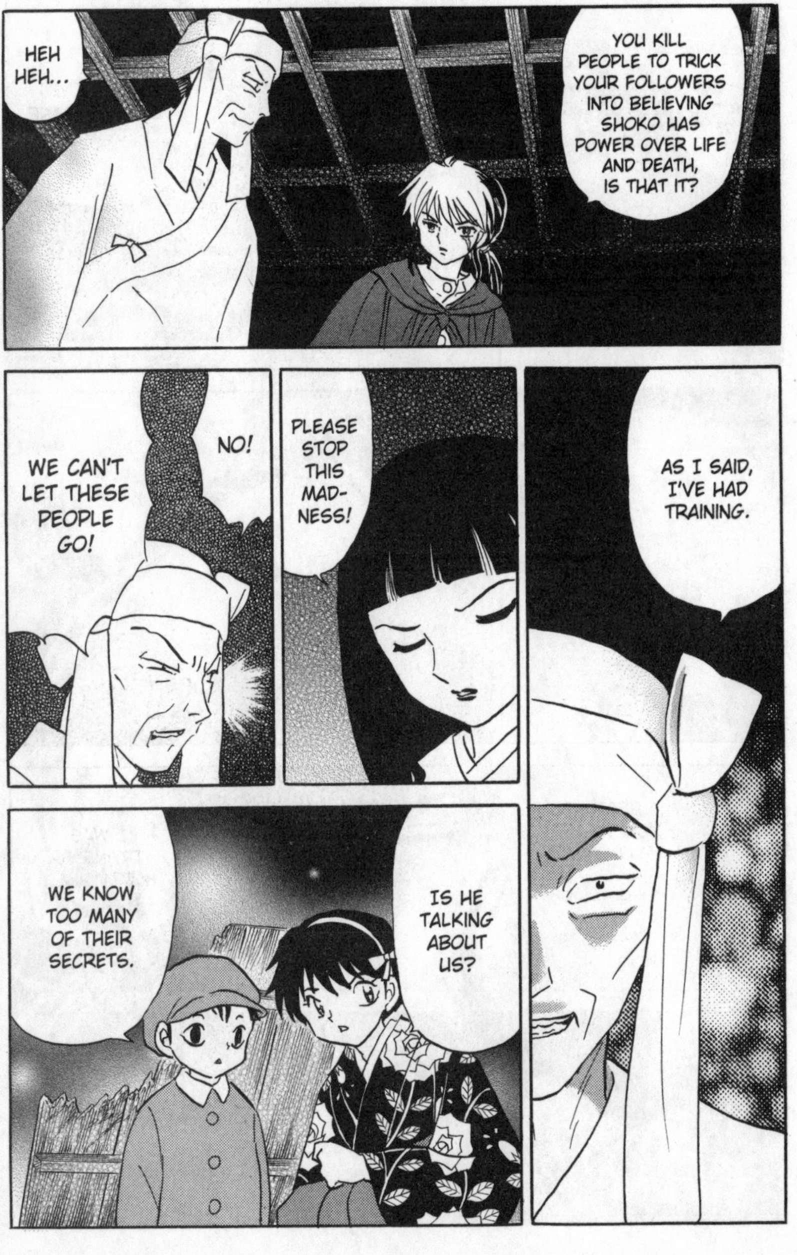
YOU KILL PEOPLE TO TRICK YOUR FOLLOWERS INTO BELIEVING SHOKO HAS POWER OVER LIFE AND DEATH, IS THAT IT?
HEH HEH...
AS I SAID, I'VE HAD TRAINING.
PLEASE STOP THIS MAD-NESS!
NO!
WE CAN'T LET THESE PEOPLE GO!
IS HE TALKING ABOUT US?
WE KNOW TOO MANY OF THEIR SECRETS.

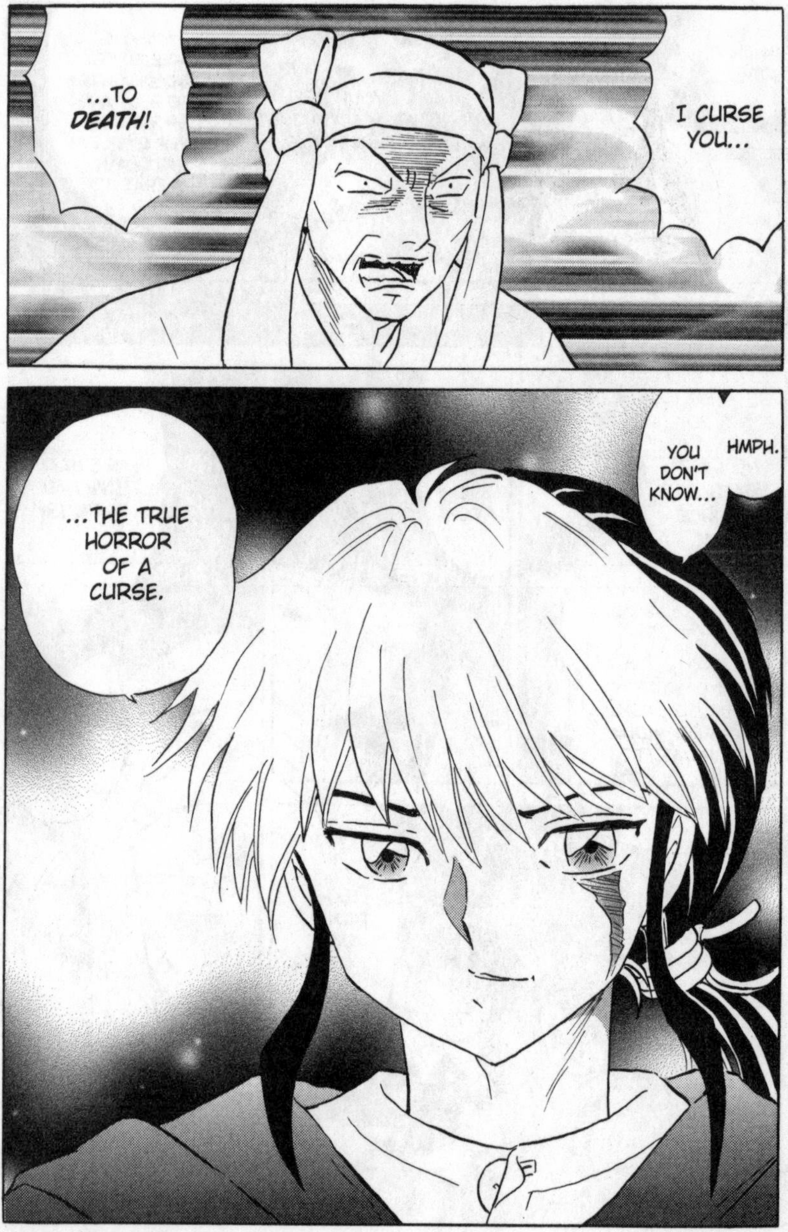
I CURSE YOU...
...TO *DEATH!*
HMPH.
YOU DON'T KNOW...
...THE TRUE HORROR OF A CURSE.

Chapter 3: The Curse Returns

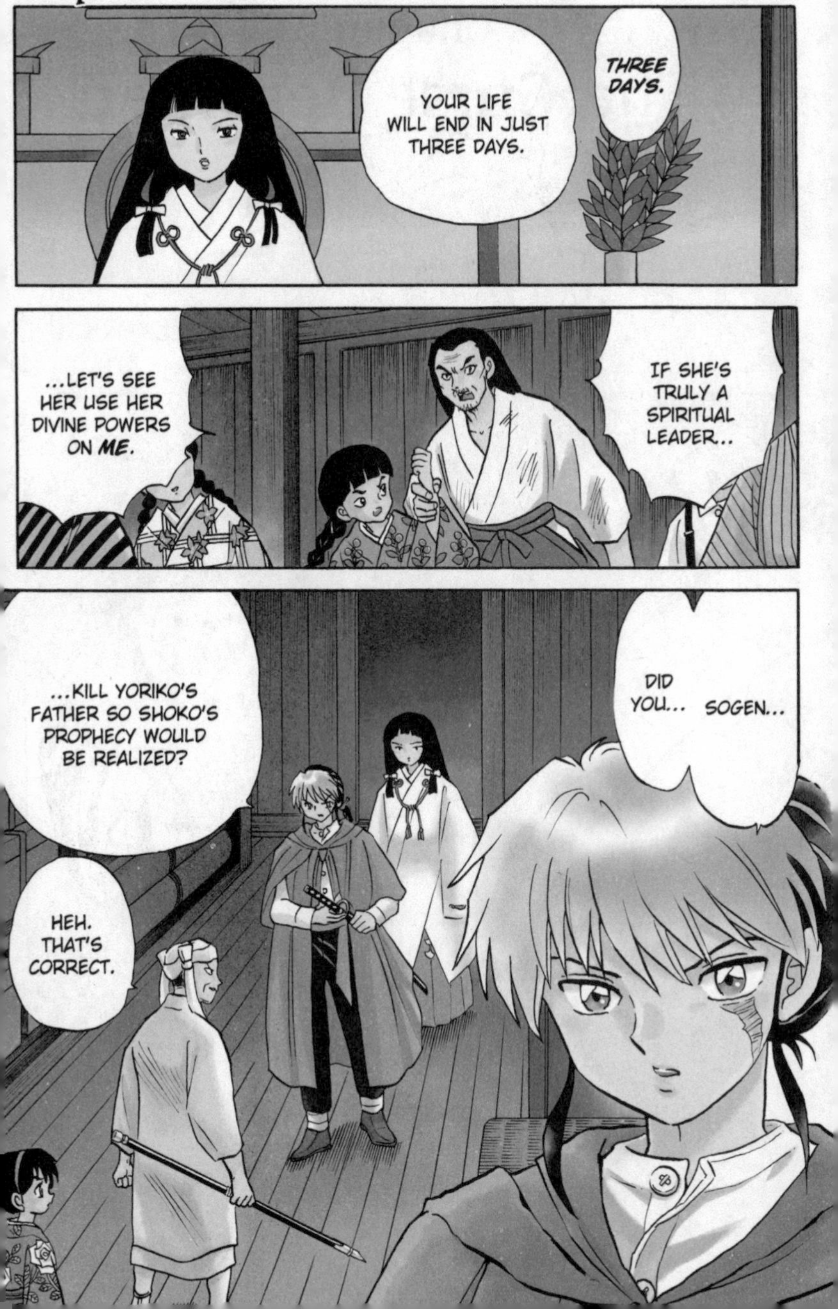
THREE DAYS.
YOUR LIFE WILL END IN JUST THREE DAYS.
IF SHE'S TRULY A SPIRITUAL LEADER...
...LET'S SEE HER USE HER DIVINE POWERS ON *ME*.
DID YOU...
SOGEN...
...KILL YORIKO'S FATHER SO SHOKO'S PROPHECY WOULD BE REALIZED?
HEH. THAT'S CORRECT.

Chapter 3:
The Curse Returned

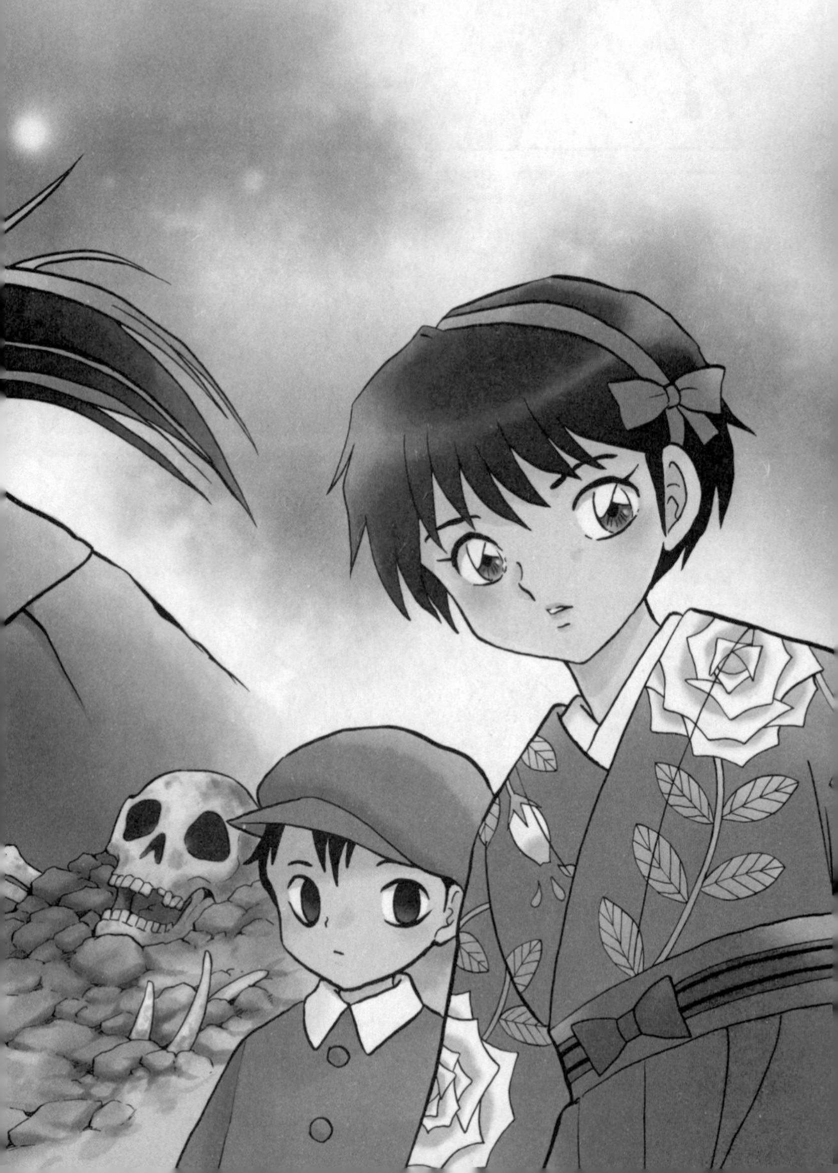

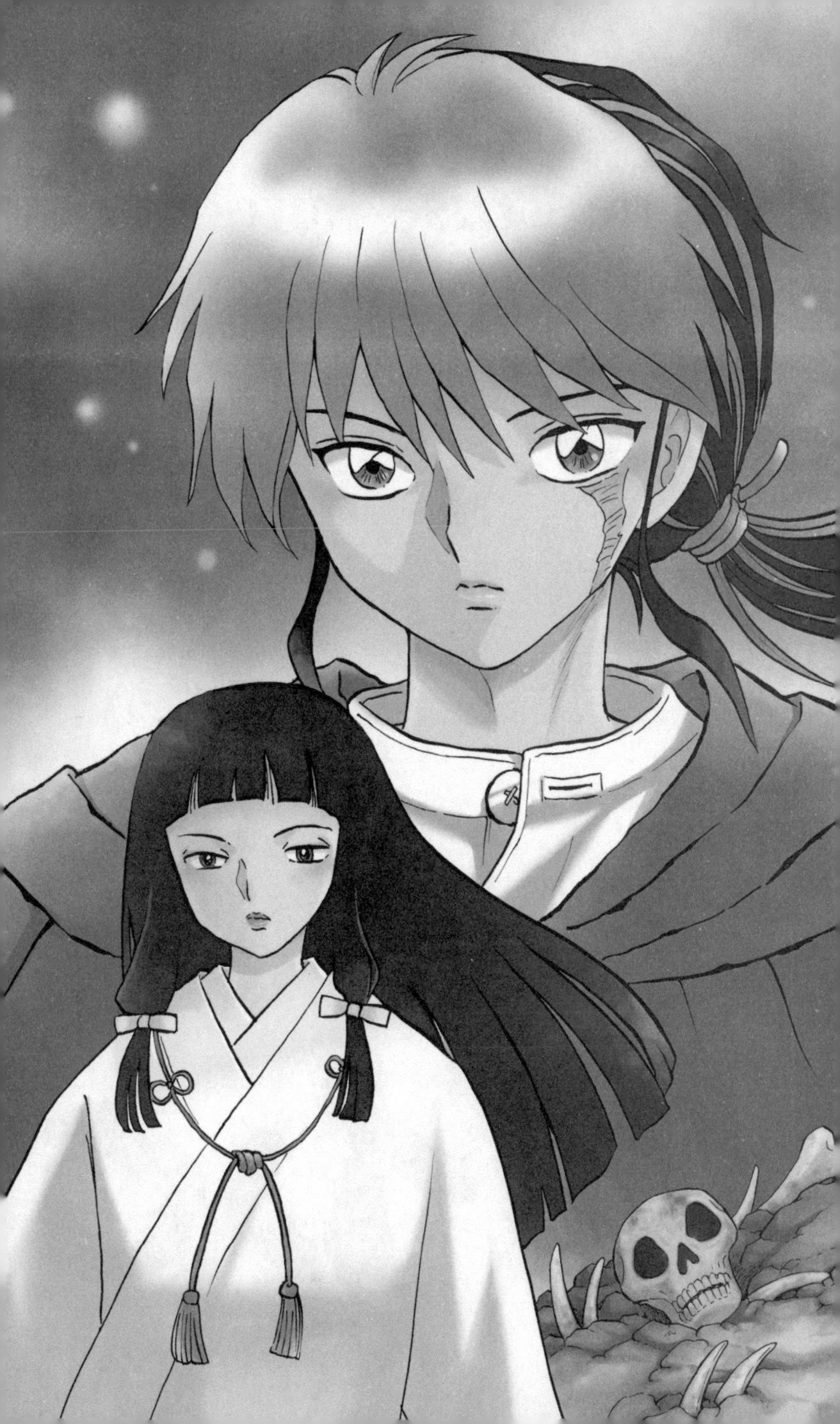

MAO

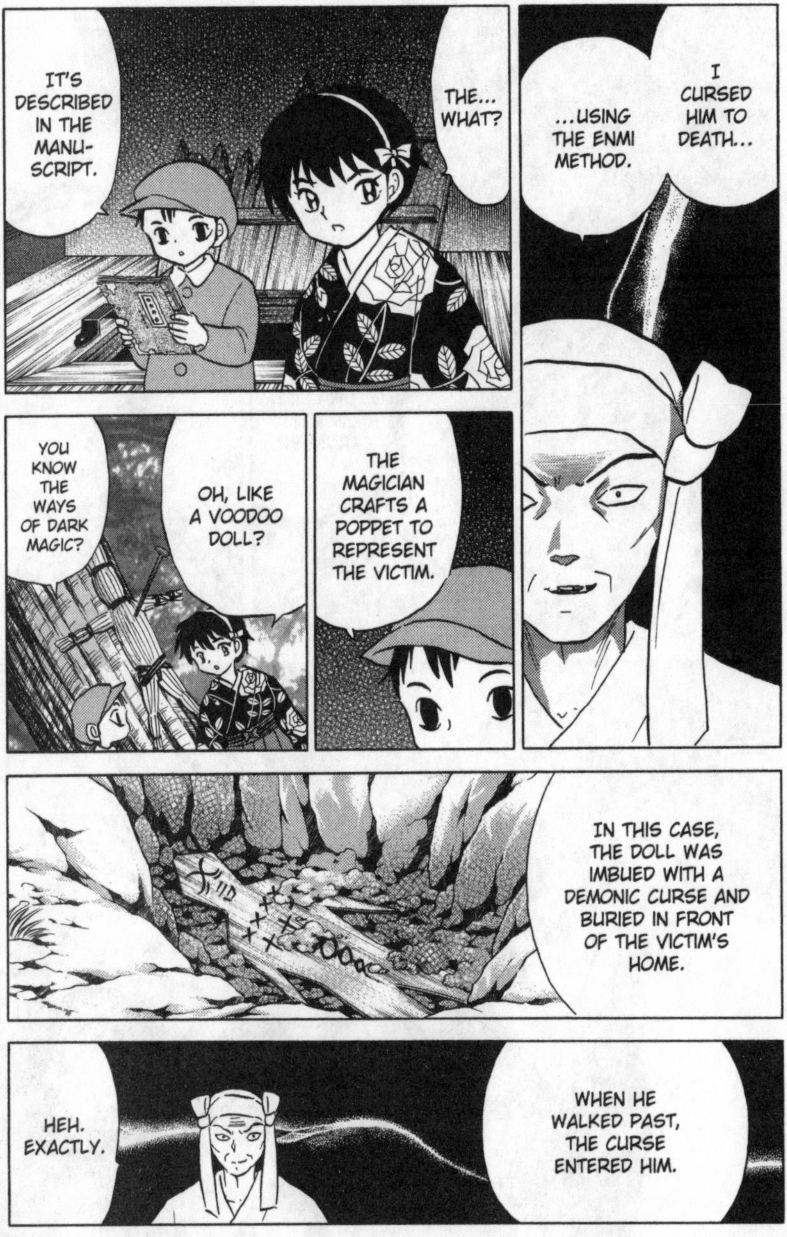
I CURSED HIM TO DEATH...
...USING THE ENMI METHOD.
THE... WHAT?
IT'S DESCRIBED IN THE MANU-SCRIPT.
THE MAGICIAN CRAFTS A POPPET TO REPRESENT THE VICTIM.
OH, LIKE A VOODOO DOLL?
YOU KNOW THE WAYS OF DARK MAGIC?
IN THIS CASE, THE DOLL WAS IMBUED WITH A DEMONIC CURSE AND BURIED IN FRONT OF THE VICTIM'S HOME.
WHEN HE WALKED PAST, THE CURSE ENTERED HIM.
HEH. EXACTLY.

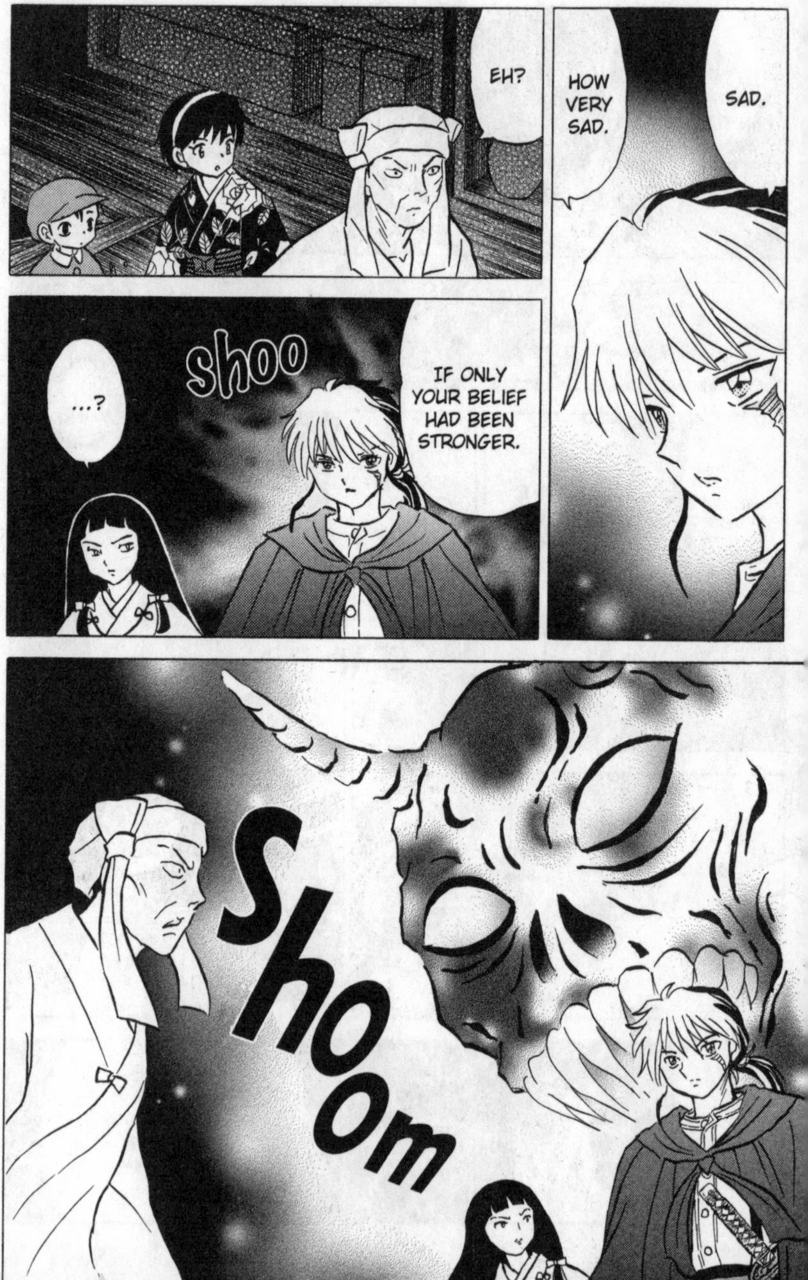
SAD.
HOW VERY SAD.
EH?
IF ONLY YOUR BELIEF HAD BEEN STRONGER.
shoo
...?
Shoom

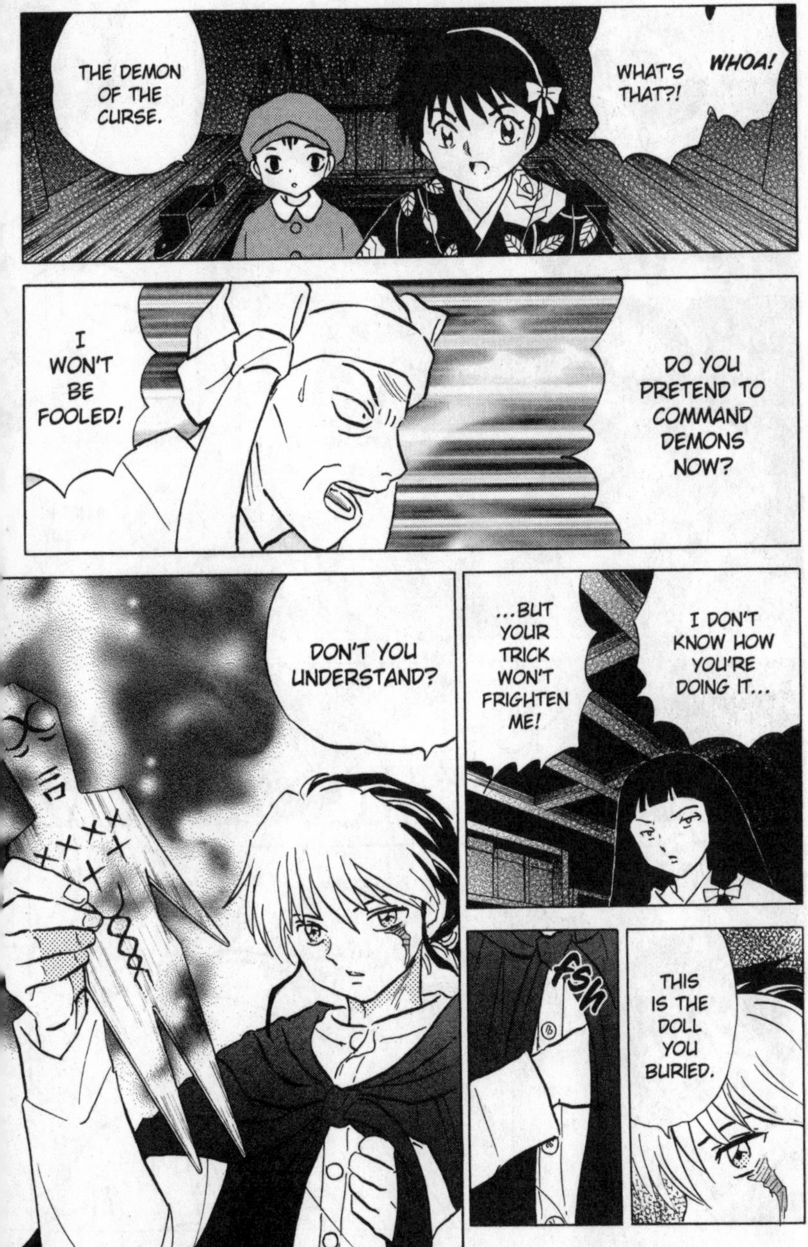
WHOA!
WHAT'S THAT?!
THE DEMON OF THE CURSE.
DO YOU PRETEND TO COMMAND DEMONS NOW?
I WON'T BE FOOLED!
I DON'T KNOW HOW YOU'RE DOING IT...
...BUT YOUR TRICK WON'T FRIGHTEN ME!
THIS IS THE DOLL YOU BURIED.
FSH
DON'T YOU UNDERSTAND?

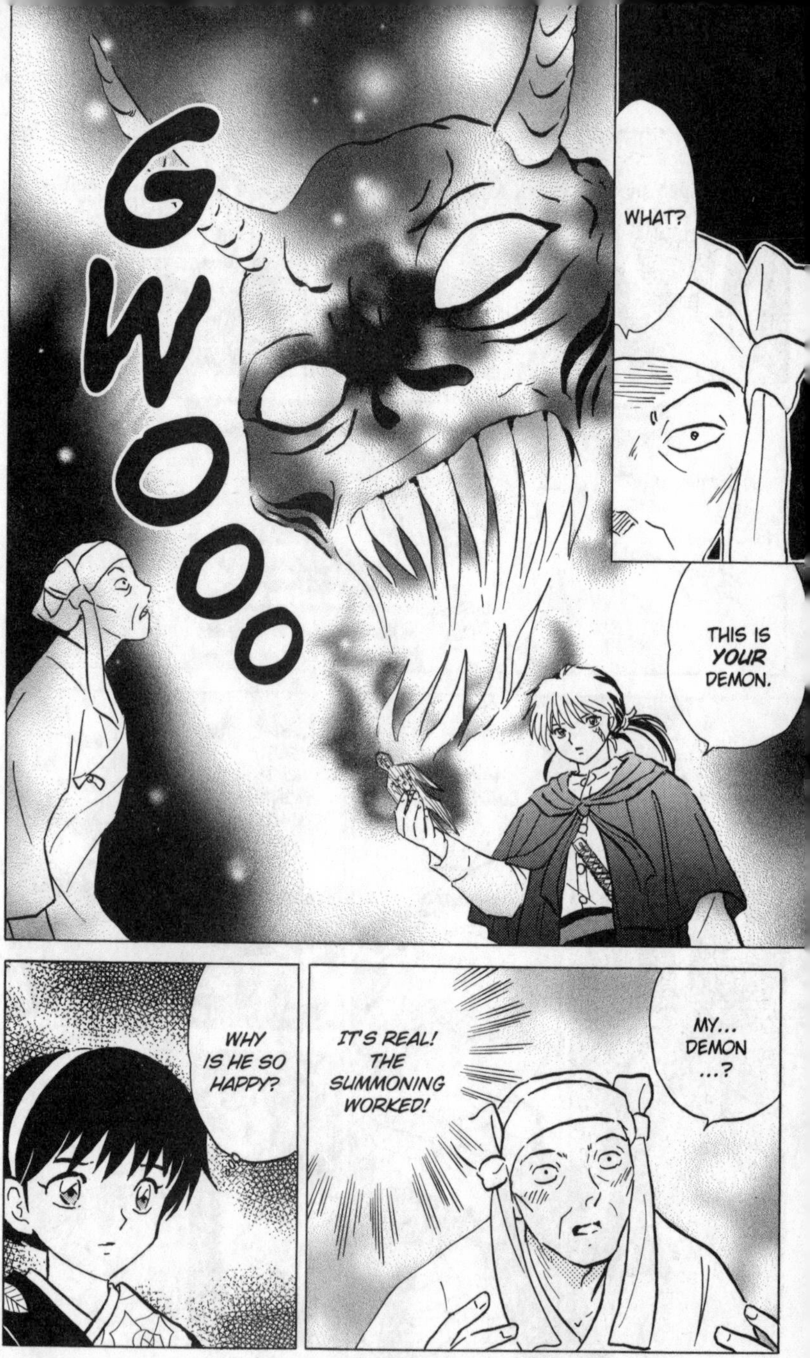
WHAT?
GWOOOO
THIS IS YOUR DEMON.
MY... DEMON ...?
IT'S REAL! THE SUMMONING WORKED!
WHY IS HE SO HAPPY?

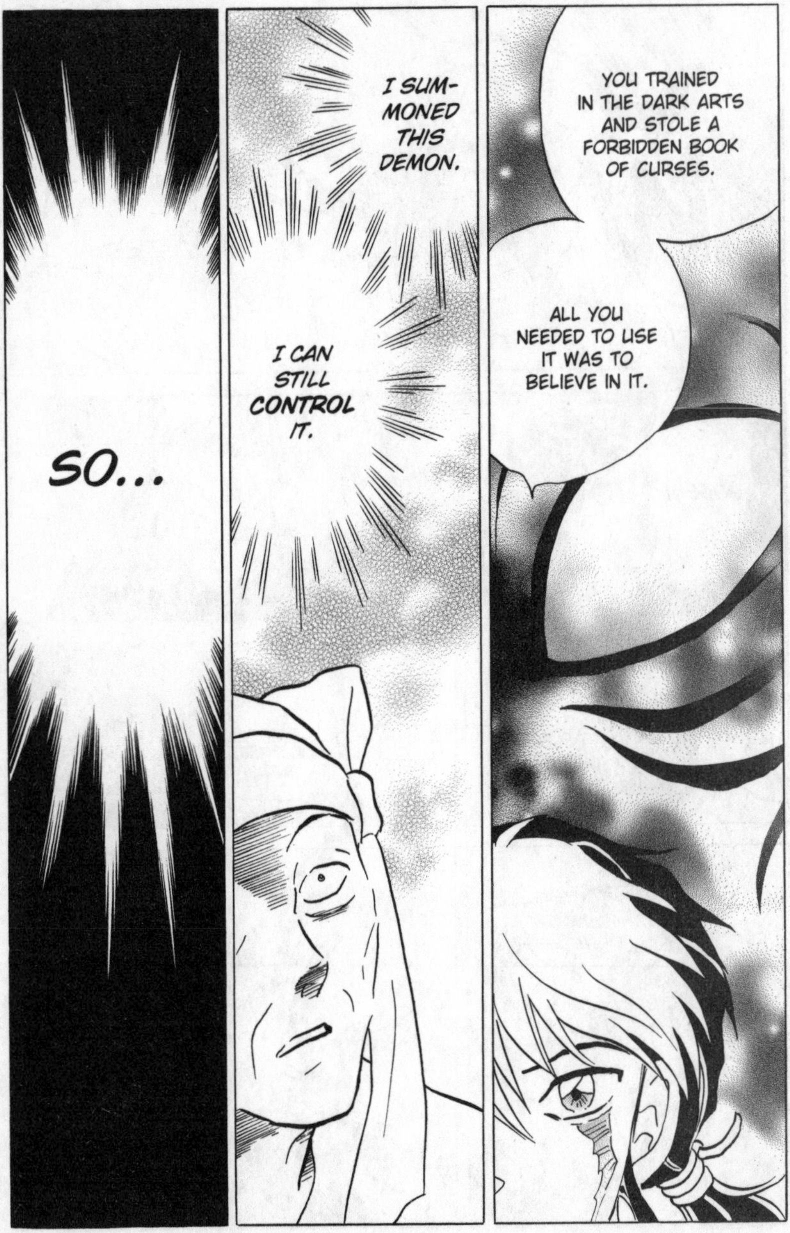
YOU TRAINED IN THE DARK ARTS AND STOLE A FORBIDDEN BOOK OF CURSES.
ALL YOU NEEDED TO USE IT WAS TO BELIEVE IN IT.
I SUMMONED THIS DEMON.
I CAN STILL CONTROL IT.
SO...

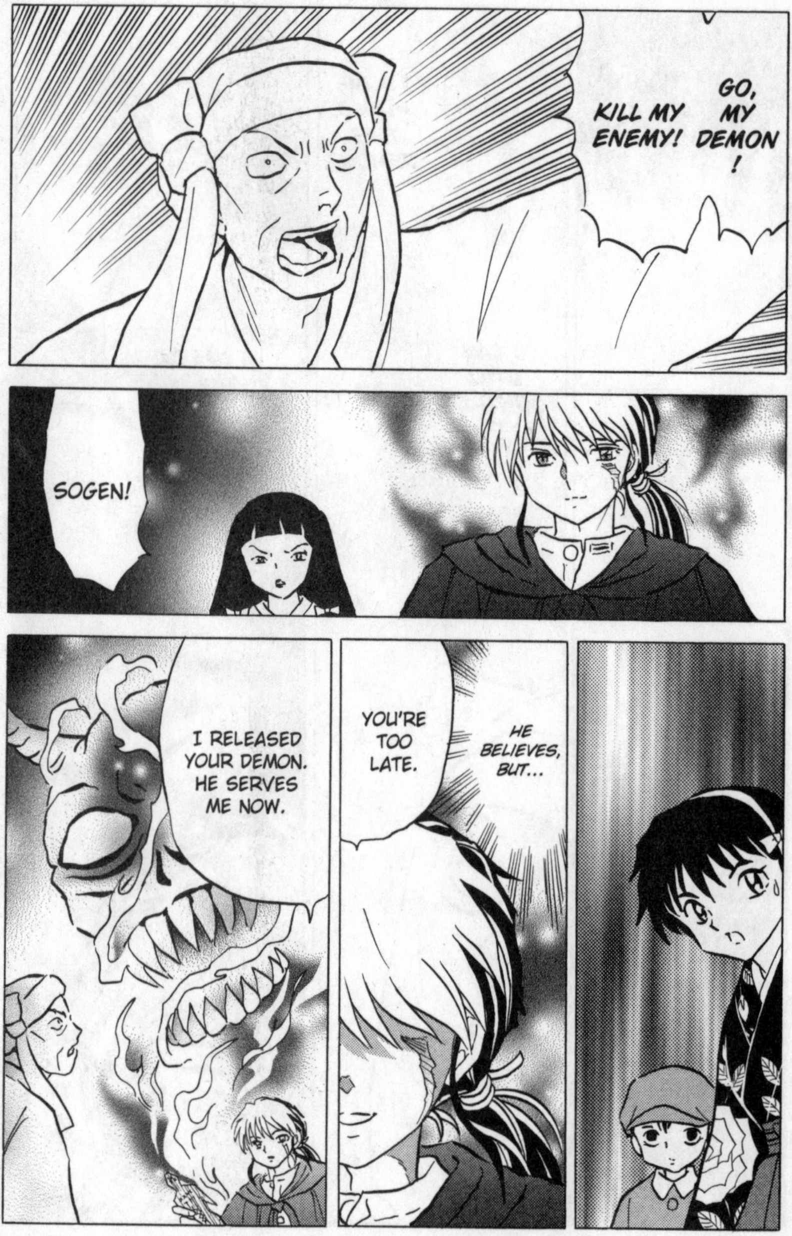
GO, MY DEMON!
KILL MY ENEMY!
SOGEN!
HE BELIEVES, BUT...
YOU'RE TOO LATE.
I RELEASED YOUR DEMON. HE SERVES ME NOW.

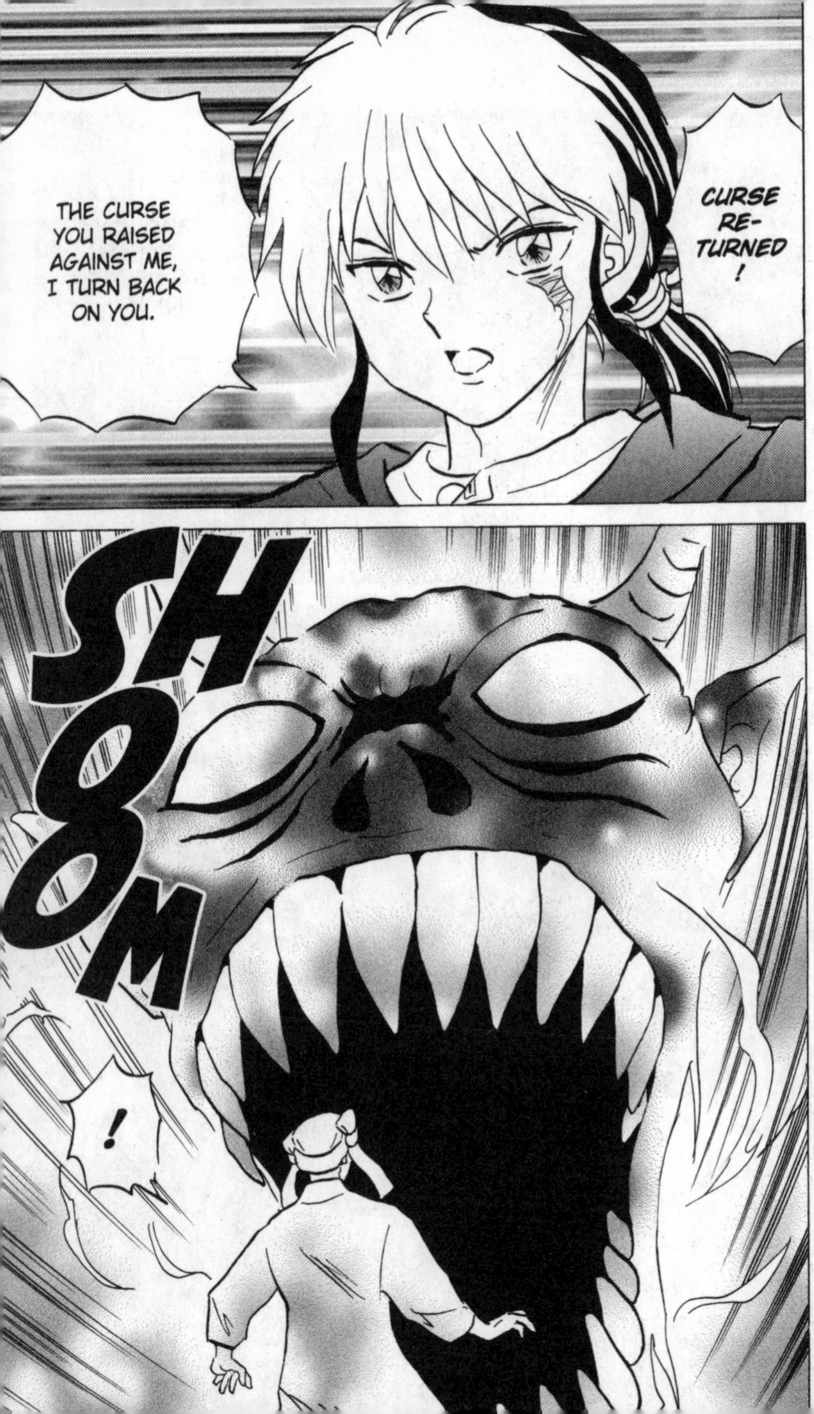
CURSE RE-TURNED!
THE CURSE YOU RAISED AGAINST ME, I TURN BACK ON YOU.
SHOOM
!

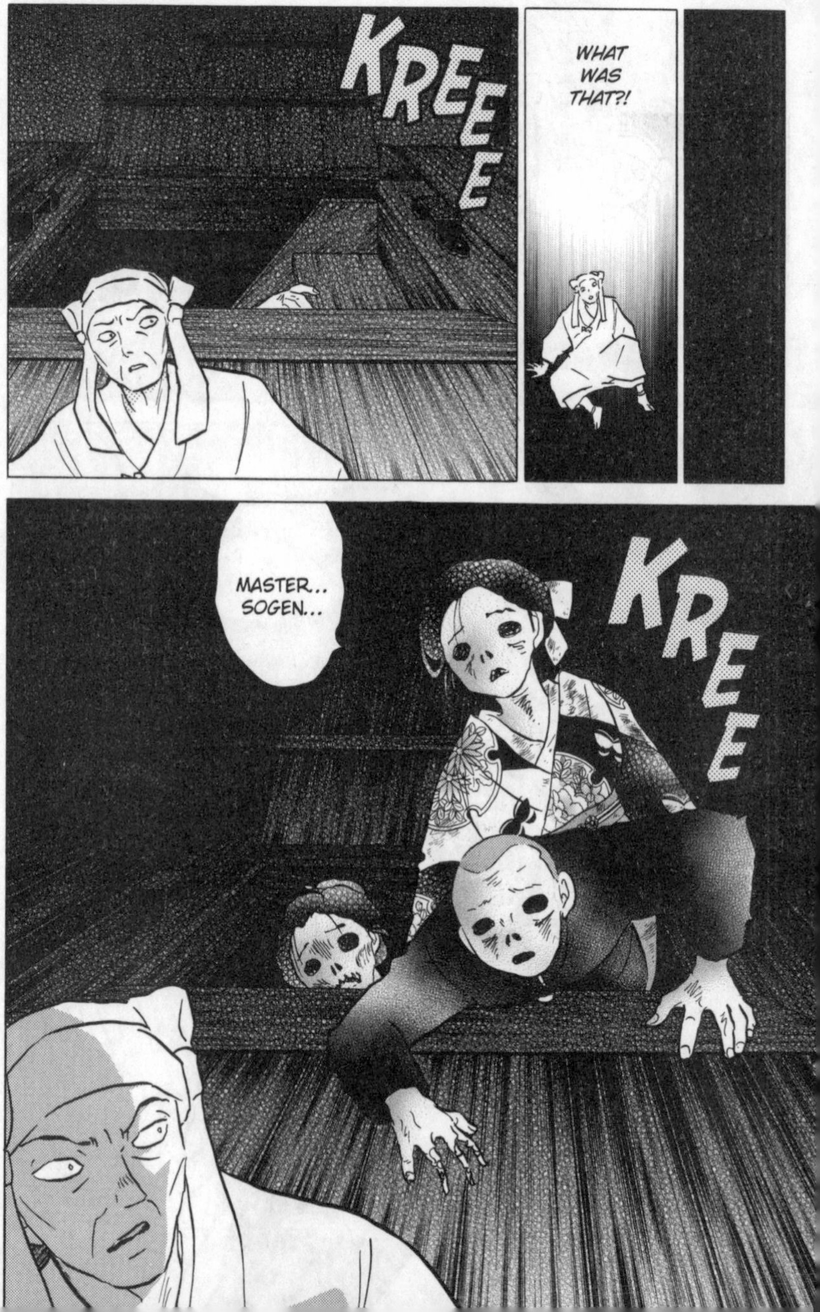
WHAT WAS THAT?!
KREEE
MASTER... SOGEN...
KREE

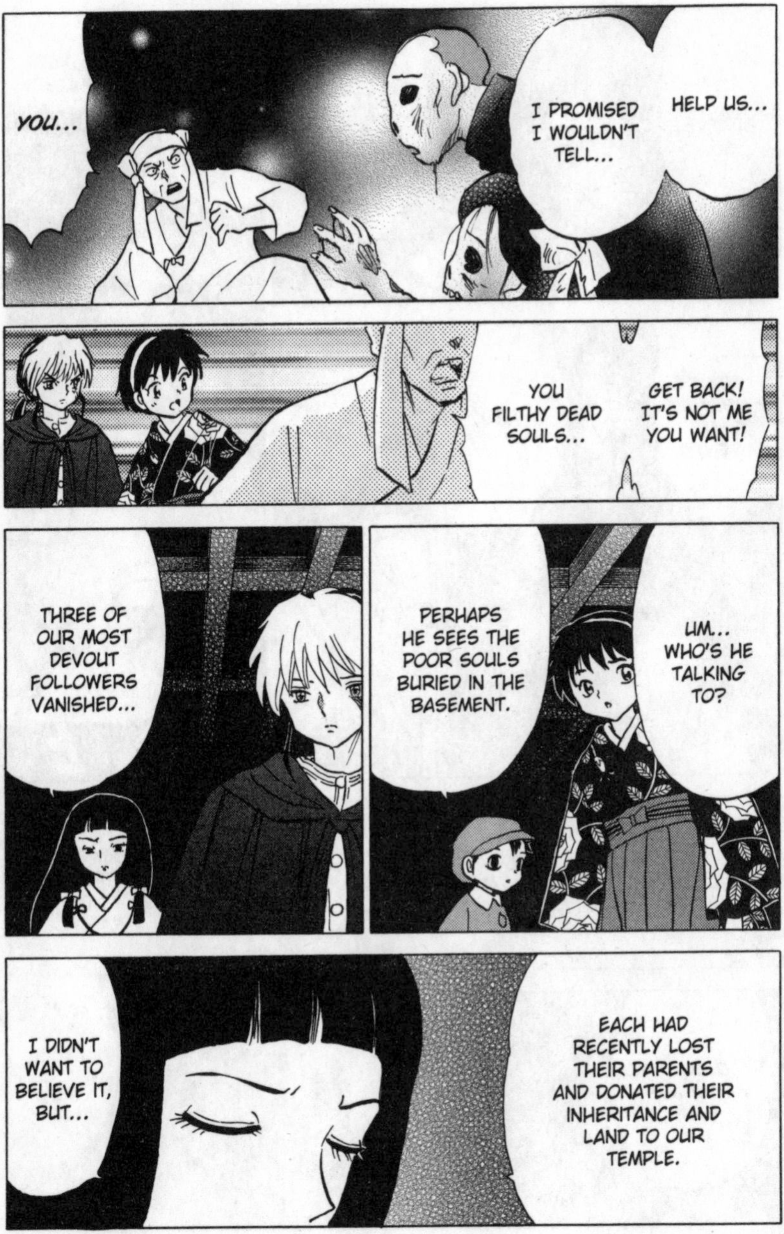
HELP US...
I PROMISED I WOULDN'T TELL...
YOU...
GET BACK! IT'S NOT ME YOU WANT!
YOU FILTHY DEAD SOULS...
UM... WHO'S HE TALKING TO?
PERHAPS HE SEES THE POOR SOULS BURIED IN THE BASEMENT.
THREE OF OUR MOST DEVOUT FOLLOWERS VANISHED...
EACH HAD RECENTLY LOST THEIR PARENTS AND DONATED THEIR INHERITANCE AND LAND TO OUR TEMPLE.
I DIDN'T WANT TO BELIEVE IT, BUT...

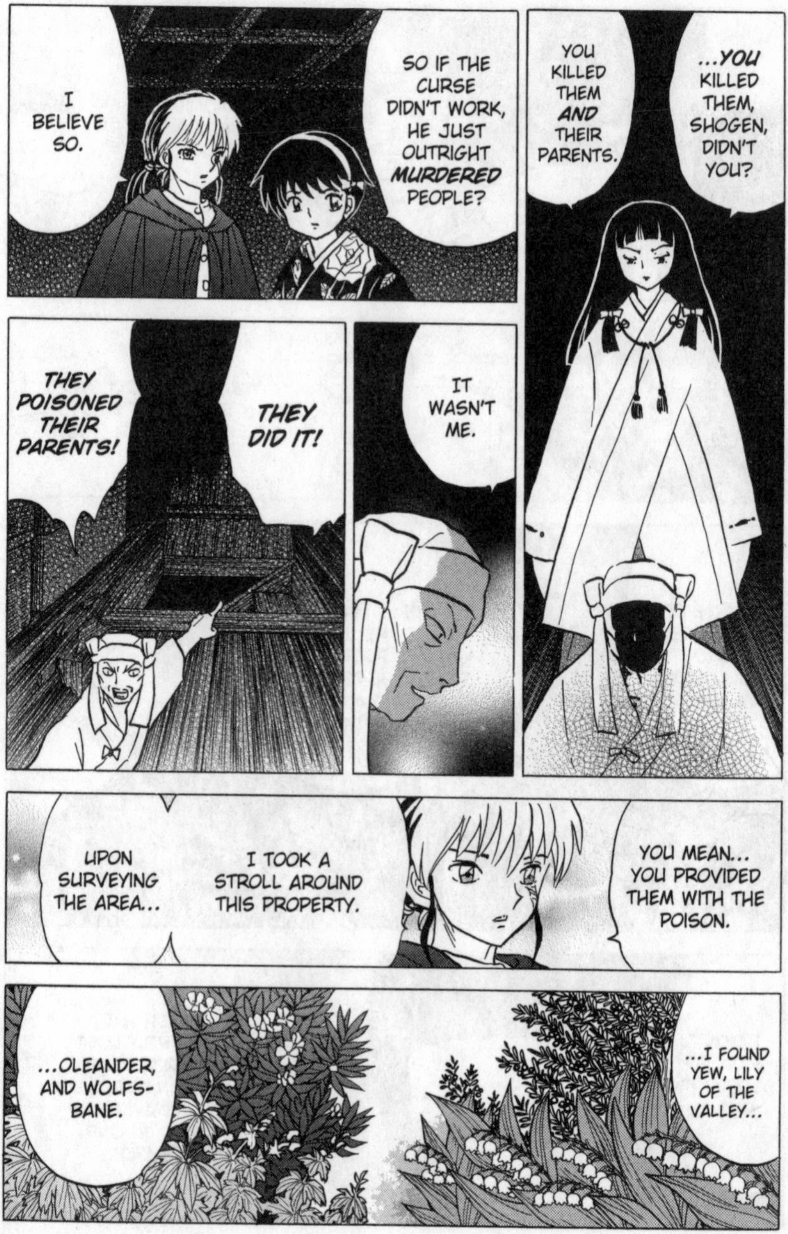
...YOU KILLED THEM, SHOGEN, DIDN'T YOU?
YOU KILLED THEM AND THEIR PARENTS.
SO IF THE CURSE DIDN'T WORK, HE JUST OUTRIGHT MURDERED PEOPLE?
I BELIEVE SO.
IT WASN'T ME.
THEY DID IT!
THEY POISONED THEIR PARENTS!
YOU MEAN... YOU PROVIDED THEM WITH THE POISON.
I TOOK A STROLL AROUND THIS PROPERTY.
UPON SURVEYING THE AREA...
...I FOUND YEW, LILY OF THE VALLEY...
...OLEANDER, AND WOLFS-BANE.

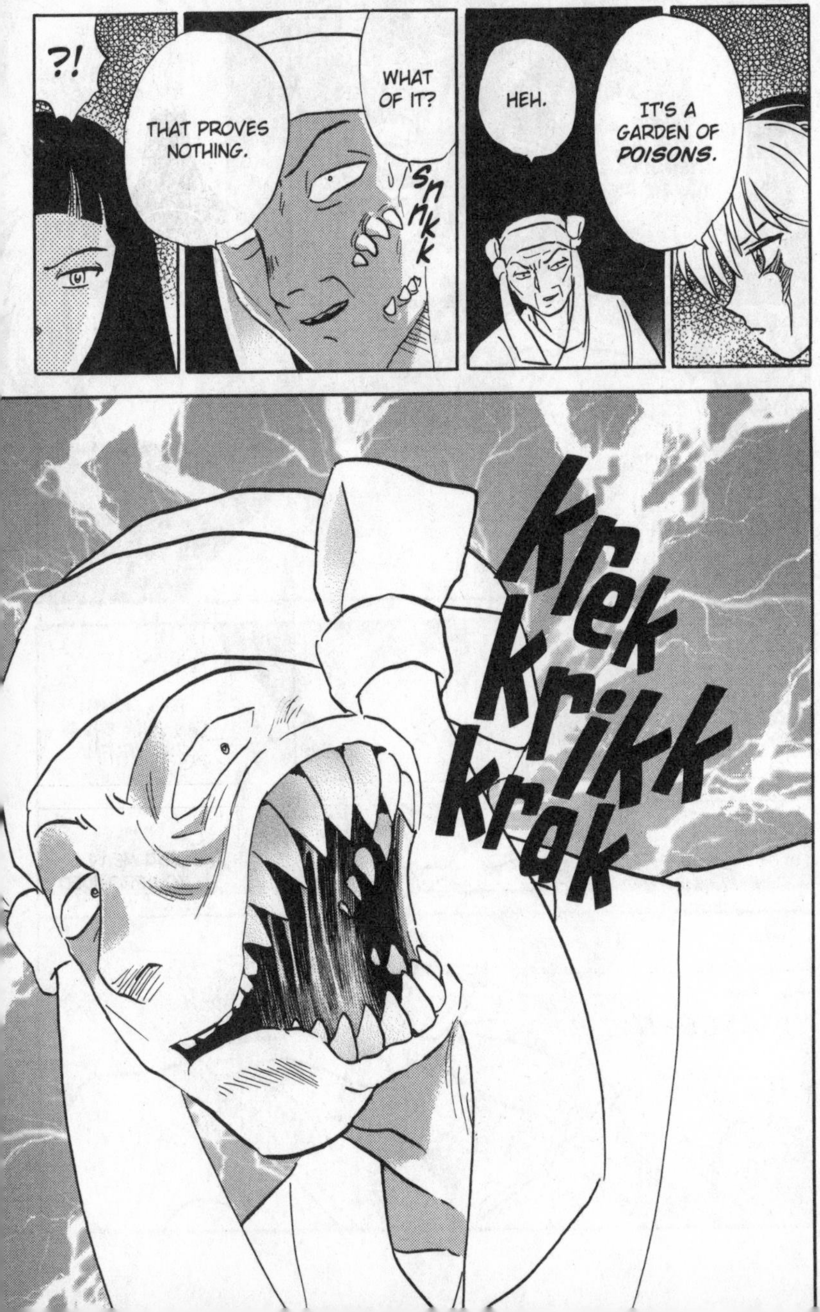

IT'S A GARDEN OF POISONS.
HEH.
WHAT OF IT?
snnkk
THAT PROVES NOTHING.
?!
krek krikk krak

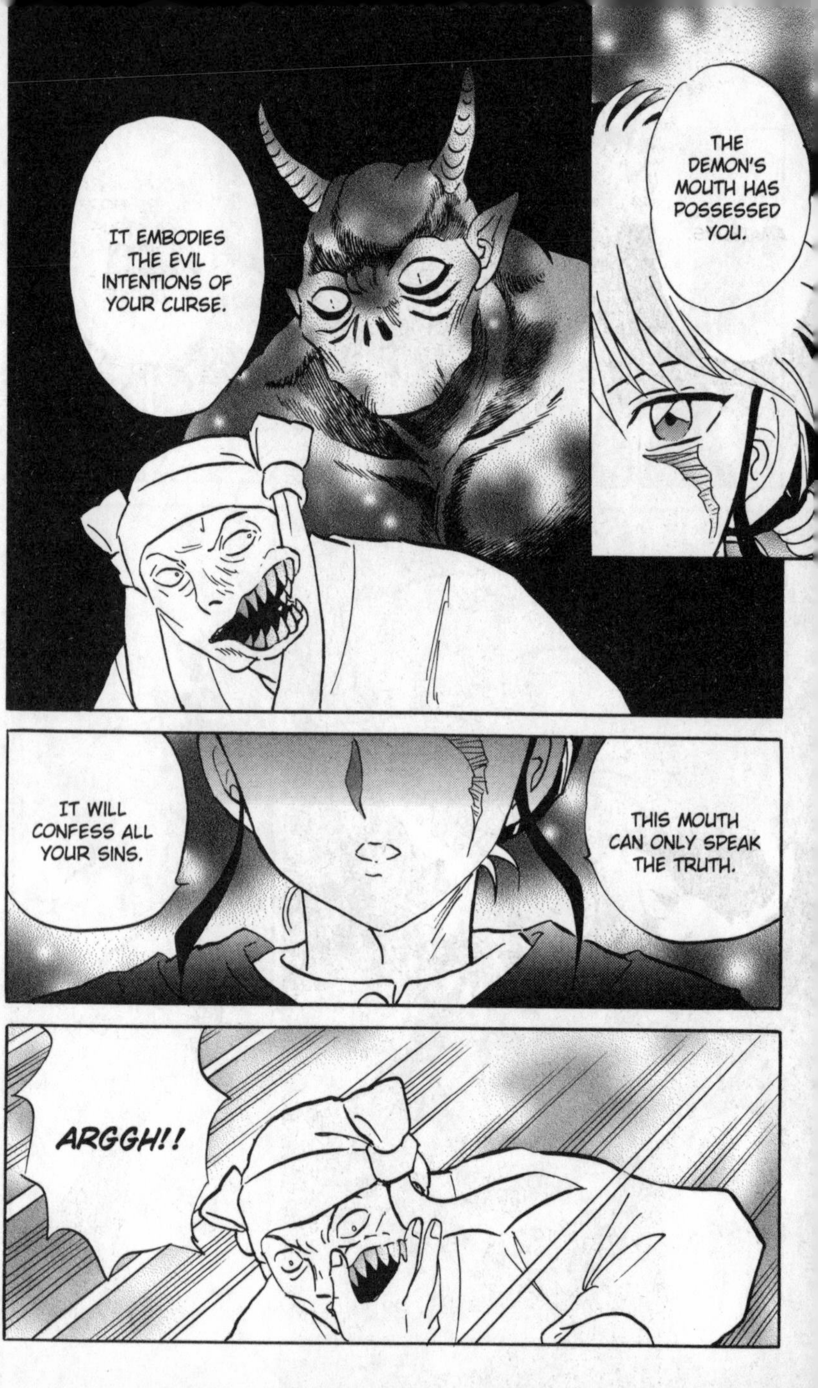
THE DEMON'S MOUTH HAS POSSESSED YOU.
IT EMBODIES THE EVIL INTENTIONS OF YOUR CURSE.
THIS MOUTH CAN ONLY SPEAK THE TRUTH.
IT WILL CONFESS ALL YOUR SINS.
ARGGH!!

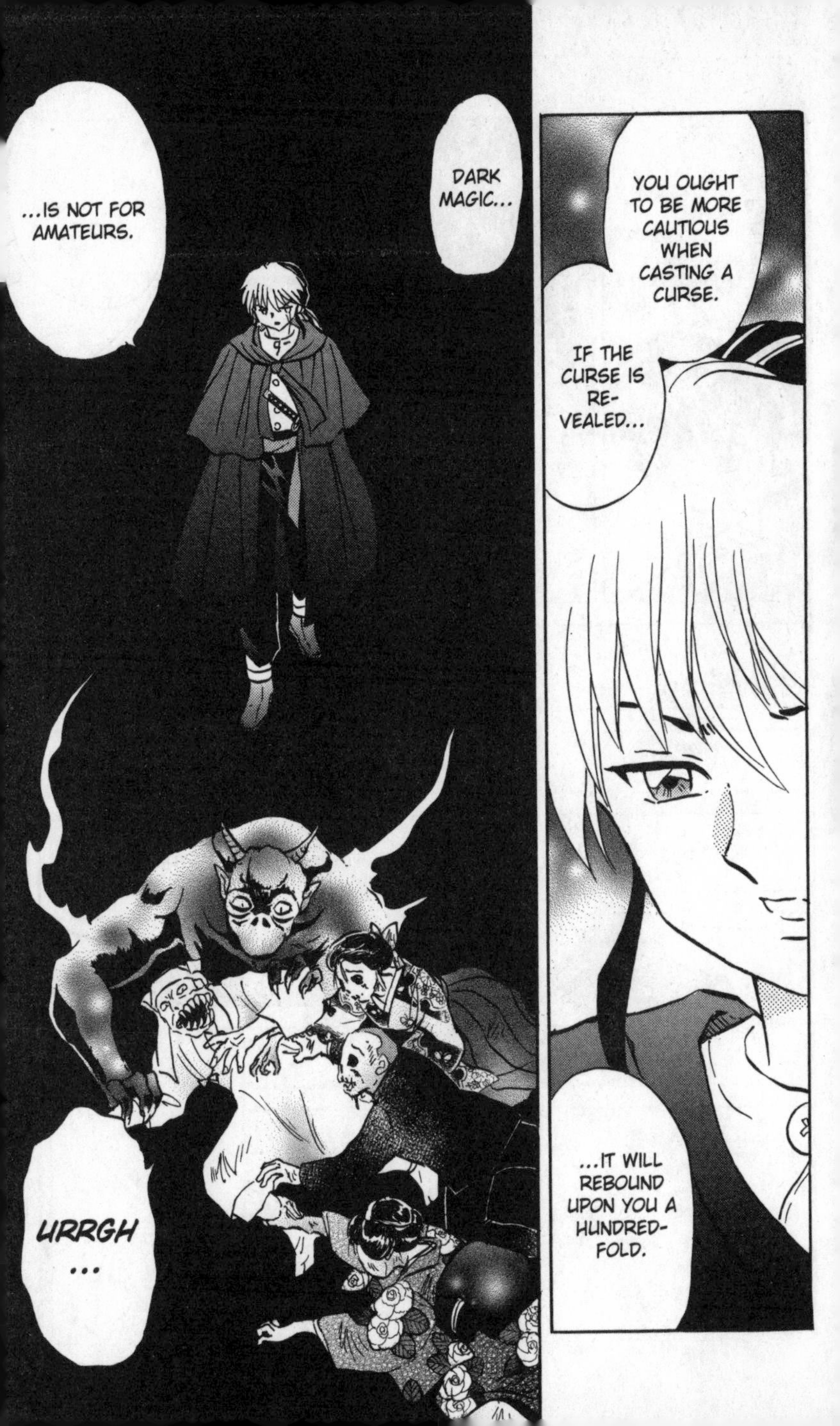
YOU OUGHT TO BE MORE CAUTIOUS WHEN CASTING A CURSE.
IF THE CURSE IS RE-VEALED...
...IT WILL REBOUND UPON YOU A HUNDRED-FOLD.
DARK MAGIC...
...IS NOT FOR AMATEURS.
URRGH ...

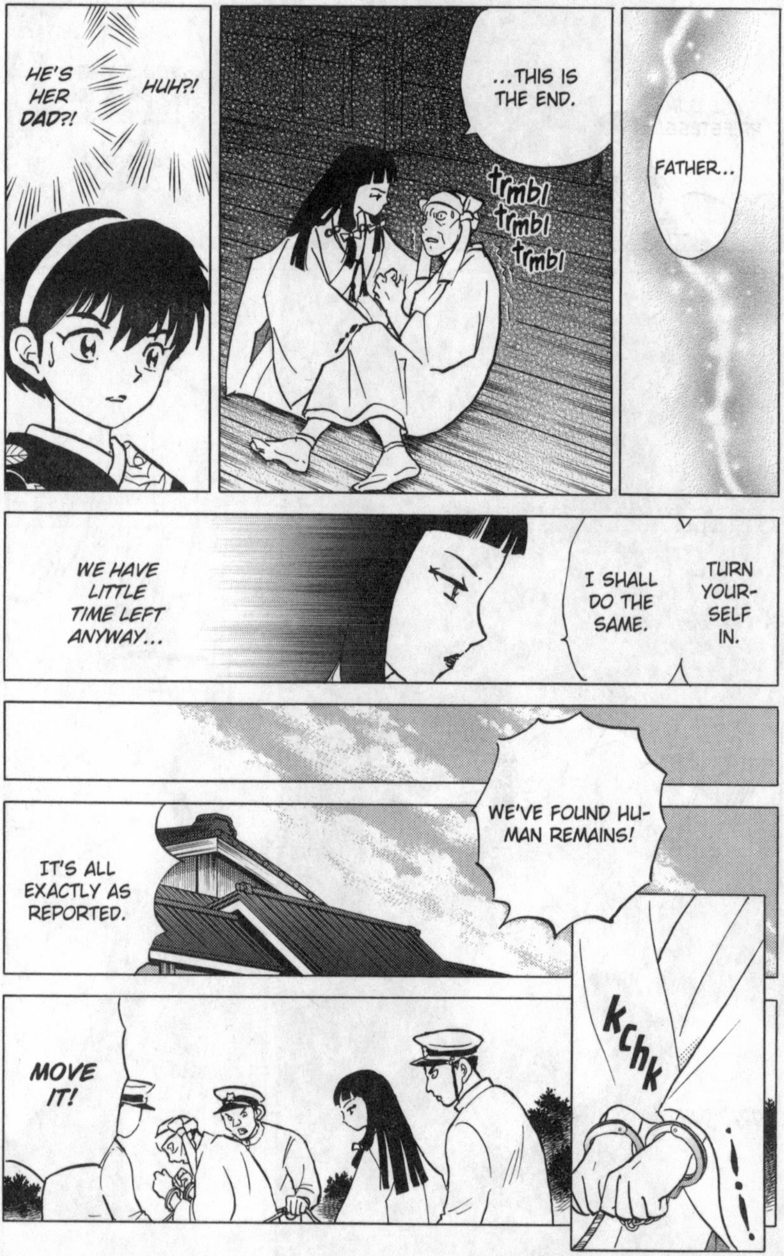
FATHER...
...THIS IS THE END.
trmbl trmbl trmbl
HUH?!
HE'S HER DAD?!
TURN YOURSELF IN.
I SHALL DO THE SAME.
WE HAVE LITTLE TIME LEFT ANYWAY...
WE'VE FOUND HUMAN REMAINS!
IT'S ALL EXACTLY AS REPORTED.
kchk
!
MOVE IT!

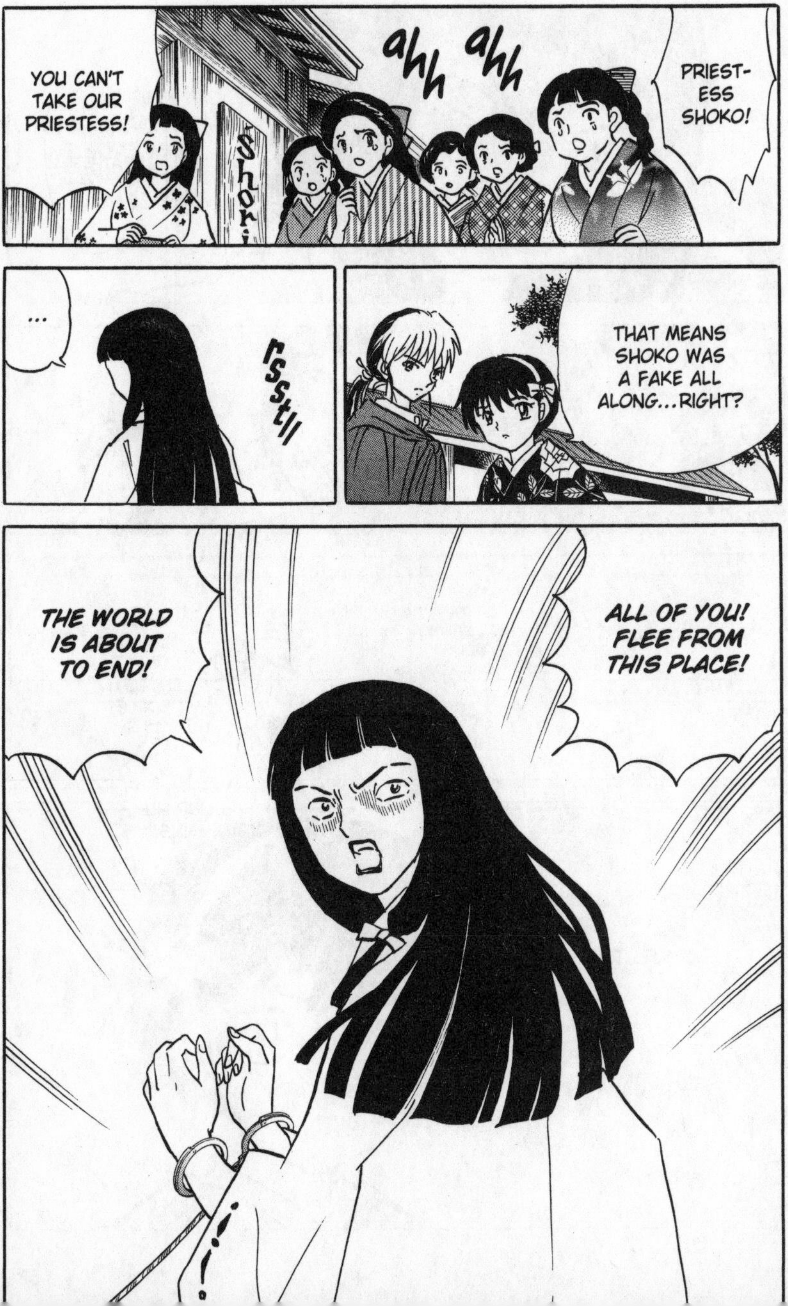
PRIEST-ESS SHOKO!
ahh ahh
Shori
YOU CAN'T TAKE OUR PRIESTESS!
THAT MEANS SHOKO WAS A FAKE ALL ALONG...RIGHT?
rsst
...
ALL OF YOU! FLEE FROM THIS PLACE!
THE WORLD IS ABOUT TO END!

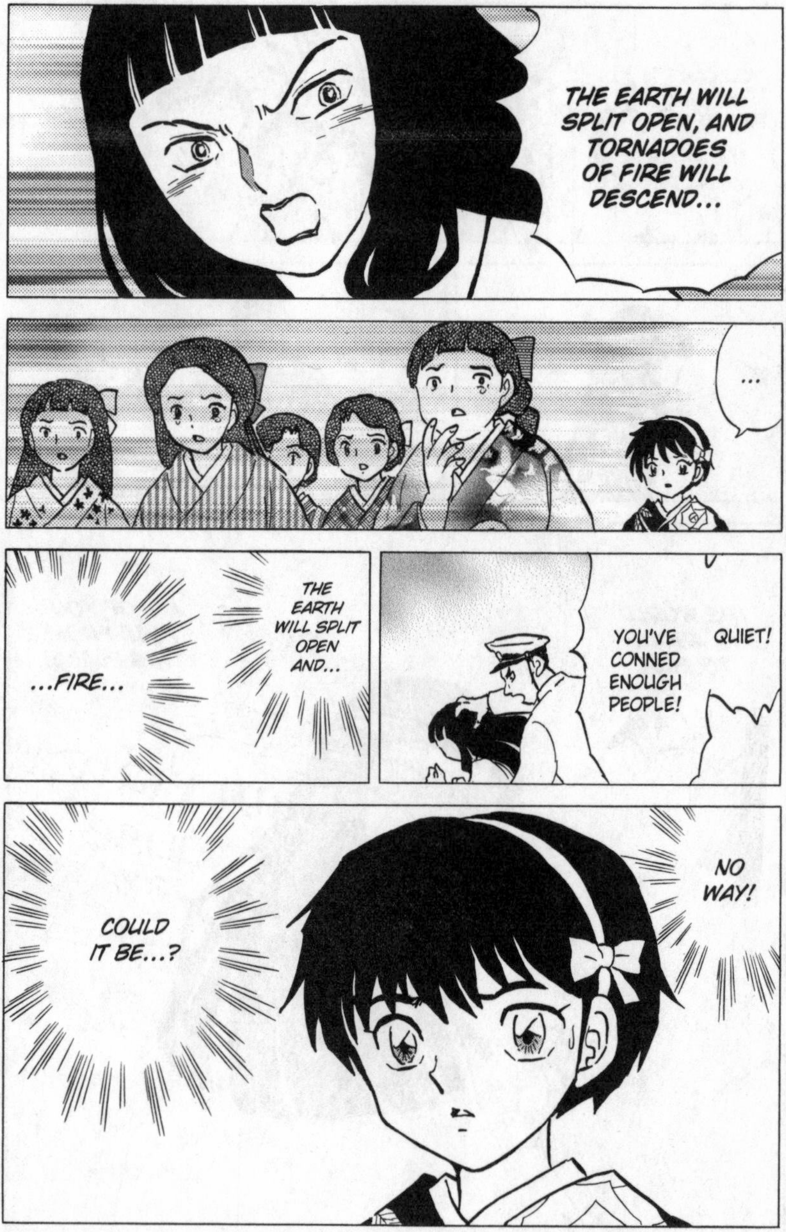
THE EARTH WILL SPLIT OPEN, AND TORNADOES OF FIRE WILL DESCEND...
...
QUIET!
YOU'VE CONNED ENOUGH PEOPLE!
THE EARTH WILL SPLIT OPEN AND...
...FIRE...
NO WAY!
COULD IT BE...?

Chapter 4: Priestess Shoko's Prophecy

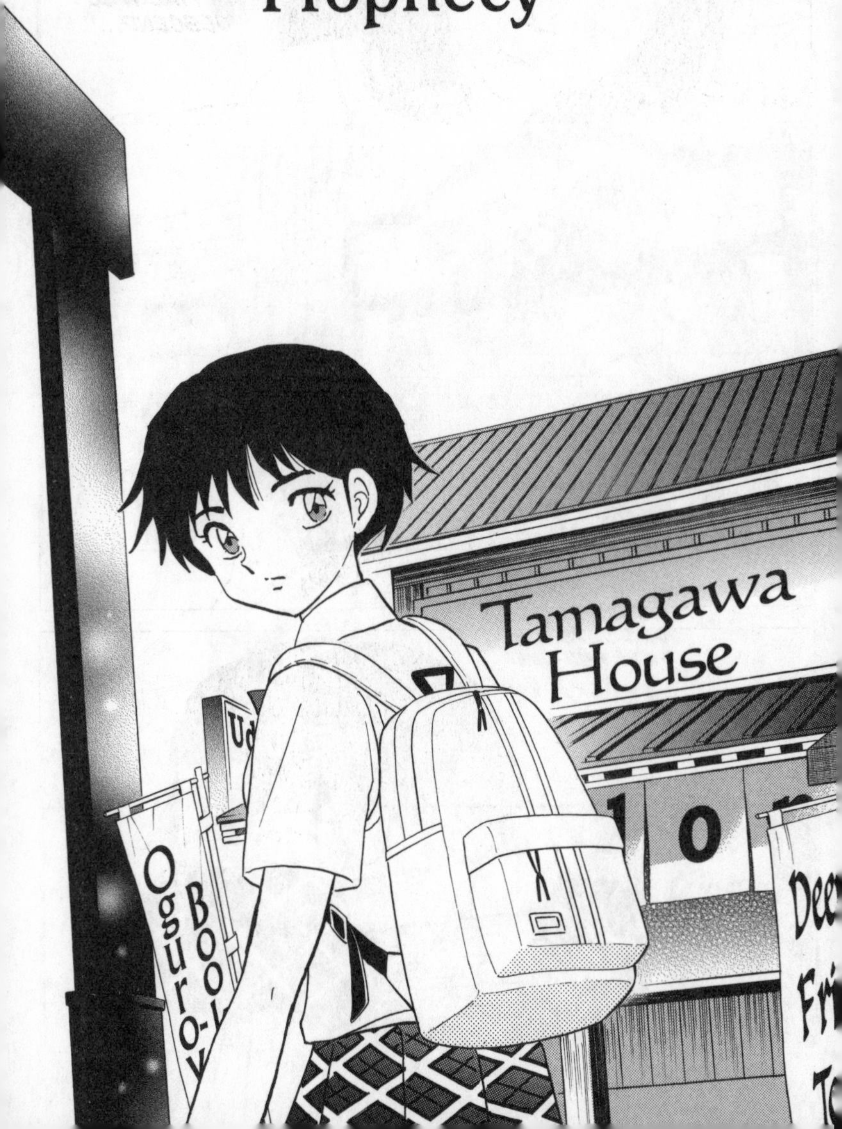
Tamagawa House

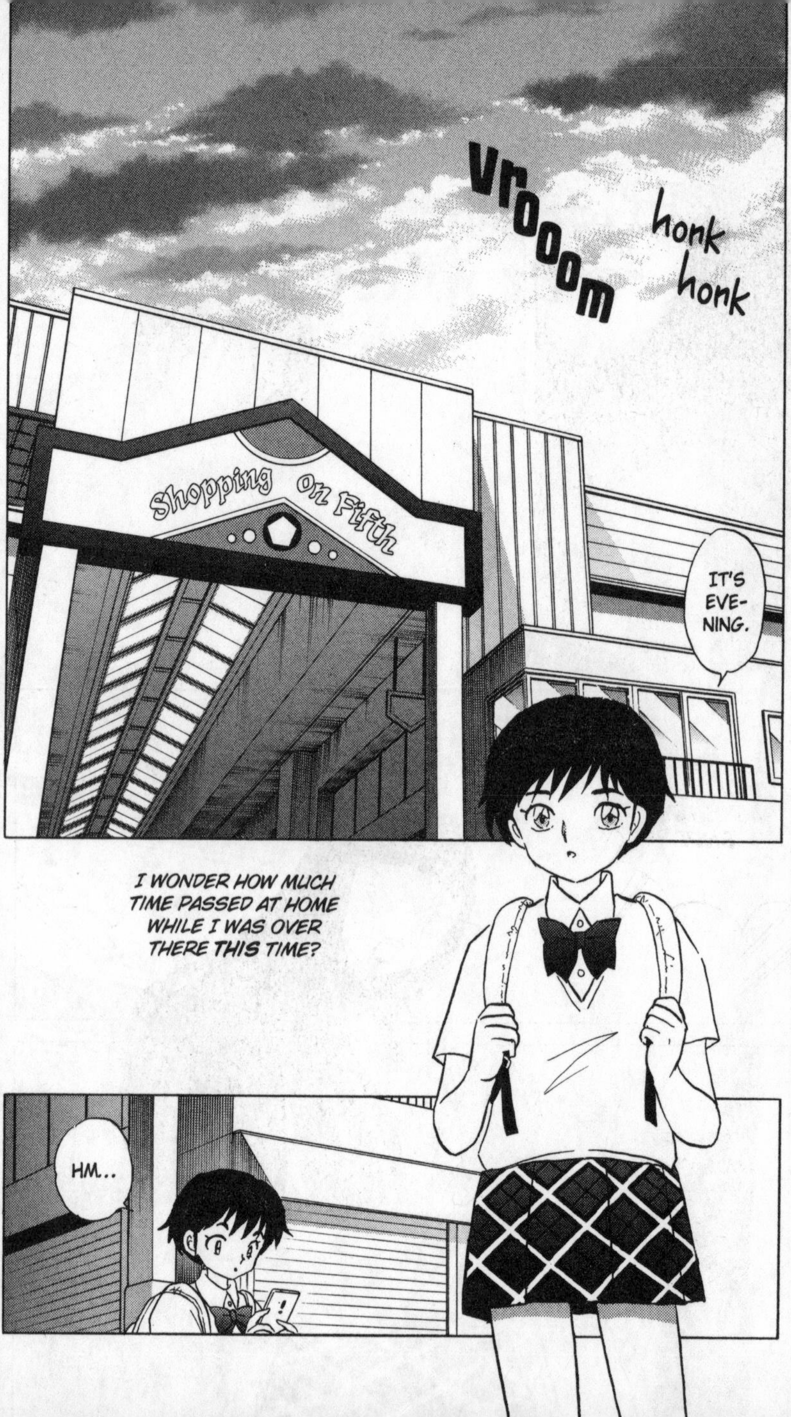
honk honk
vrooom
Shopping on Fifth
IT'S EVENING.
I WONDER HOW MUCH TIME PASSED AT HOME WHILE I WAS OVER THERE **THIS** TIME?
HM...

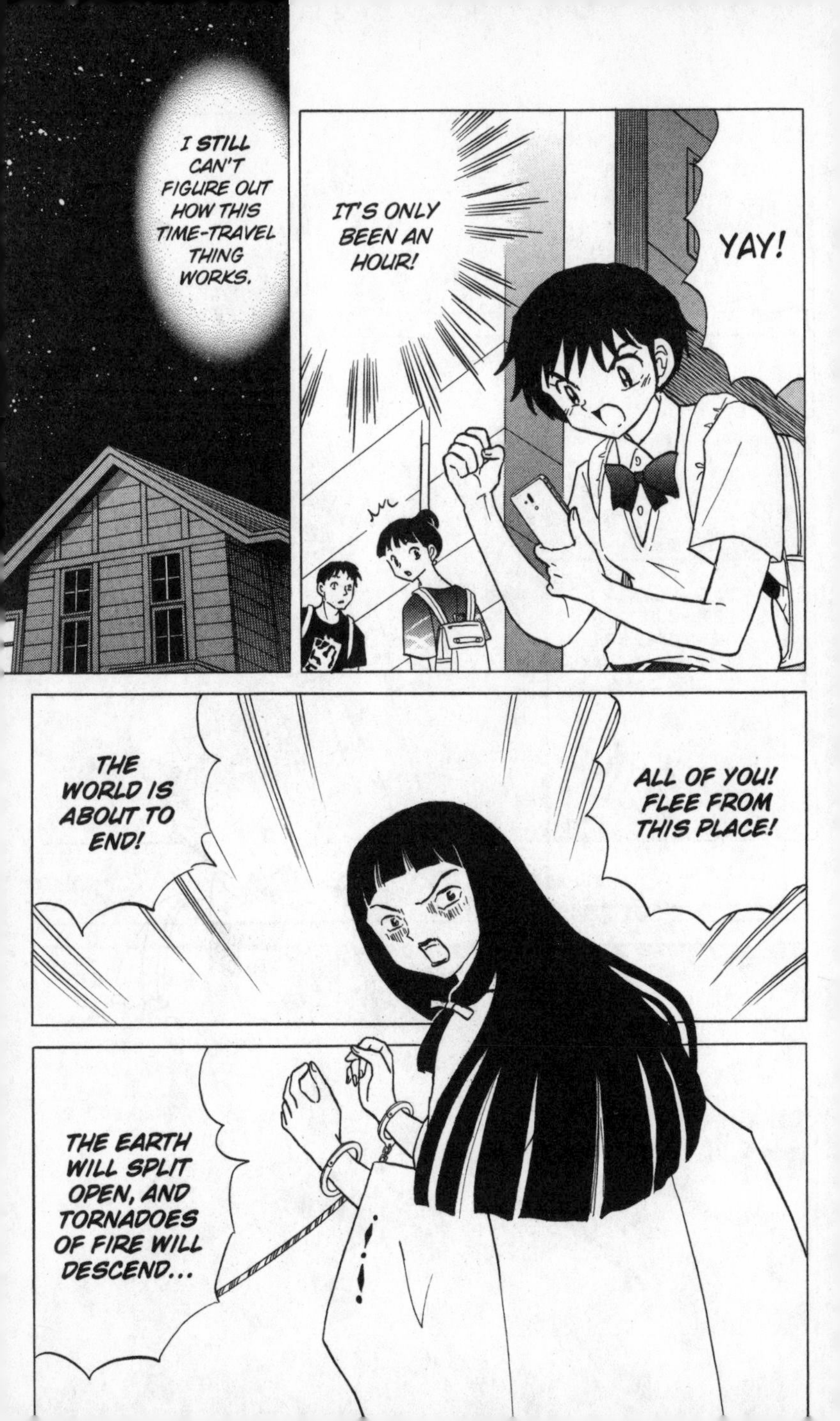
YAY!
IT'S ONLY BEEN AN HOUR!
I STILL CAN'T FIGURE OUT HOW THIS TIME-TRAVEL THING WORKS.
ALL OF YOU! FLEE FROM THIS PLACE!
THE WORLD IS ABOUT TO END!
THE EARTH WILL SPLIT OPEN, AND TORNADOES OF FIRE WILL DESCEND...

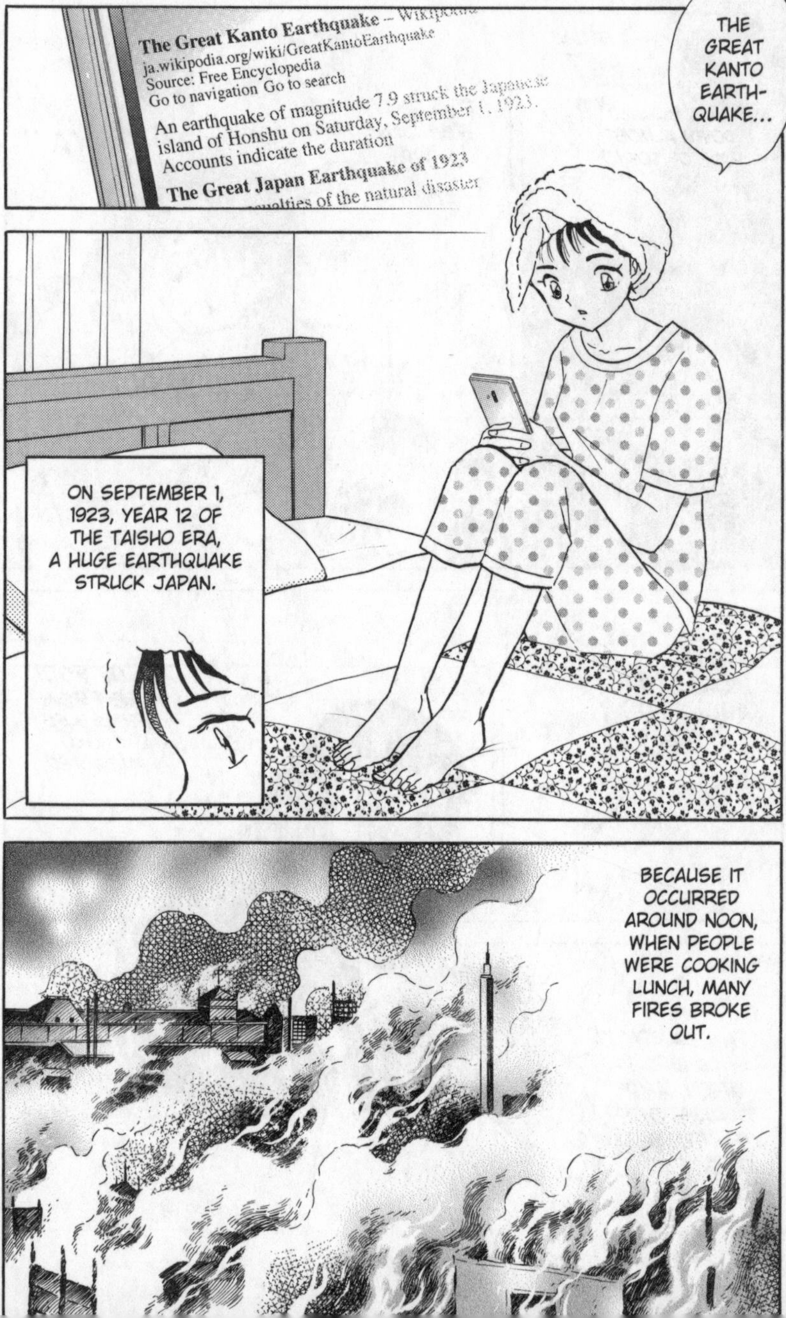
THE GREAT KANTO EARTHQUAKE...
The Great Kanto Earthquake – Wikipedia
ja.wikipodia.org/wiki/GreatKantoEarthquake
Source: Free Encyclopedia
Go to navigation Go to search
An earthquake of magnitude 7.9 struck the Japanese island of Honshu on Saturday, September 1, 1923.
Accounts indicate the duration
The Great Japan Earthquake of 1923
of the natural disaster
ON SEPTEMBER 1, 1923, YEAR 12 OF THE TAISHO ERA, A HUGE EARTHQUAKE STRUCK JAPAN.
BECAUSE IT OCCURRED AROUND NOON, WHEN PEOPLE WERE COOKING LUNCH, MANY FIRES BROKE OUT.

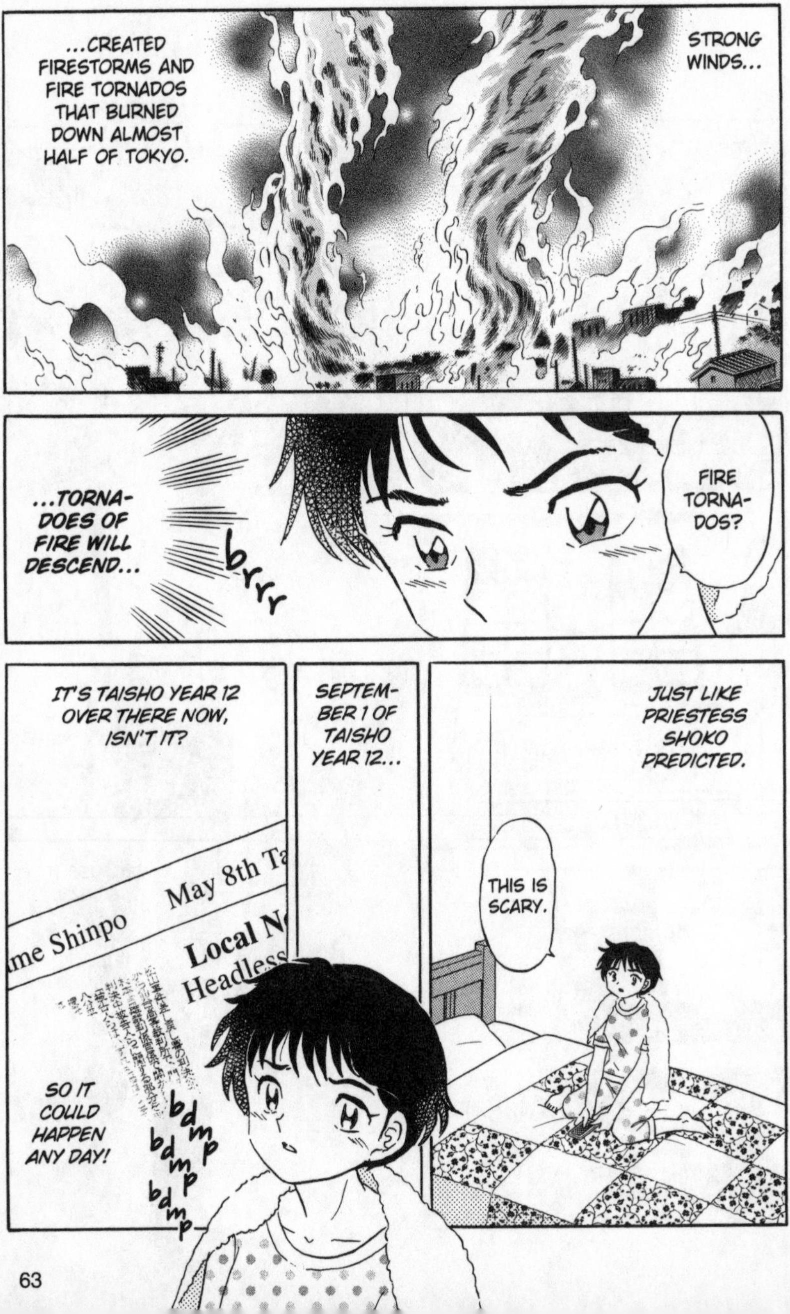
STRONG WINDS...
...CREATED FIRESTORMS AND FIRE TORNADOS THAT BURNED DOWN ALMOST HALF OF TOKYO.
FIRE TORNA-DOS?
...TORNA-DOES OF FIRE WILL DESCEND...
brrr
JUST LIKE PRIESTESS SHOKO PREDICTED.
THIS IS SCARY.
SEPTEM-BER 1 OF TAISHO YEAR 12...
IT'S TAISHO YEAR 12 OVER THERE NOW, ISN'T IT?
May 8th Ta
me Shinpo
Local N
Headless
SO IT COULD HAPPEN ANY DAY!
bdmp bdmp bdmp

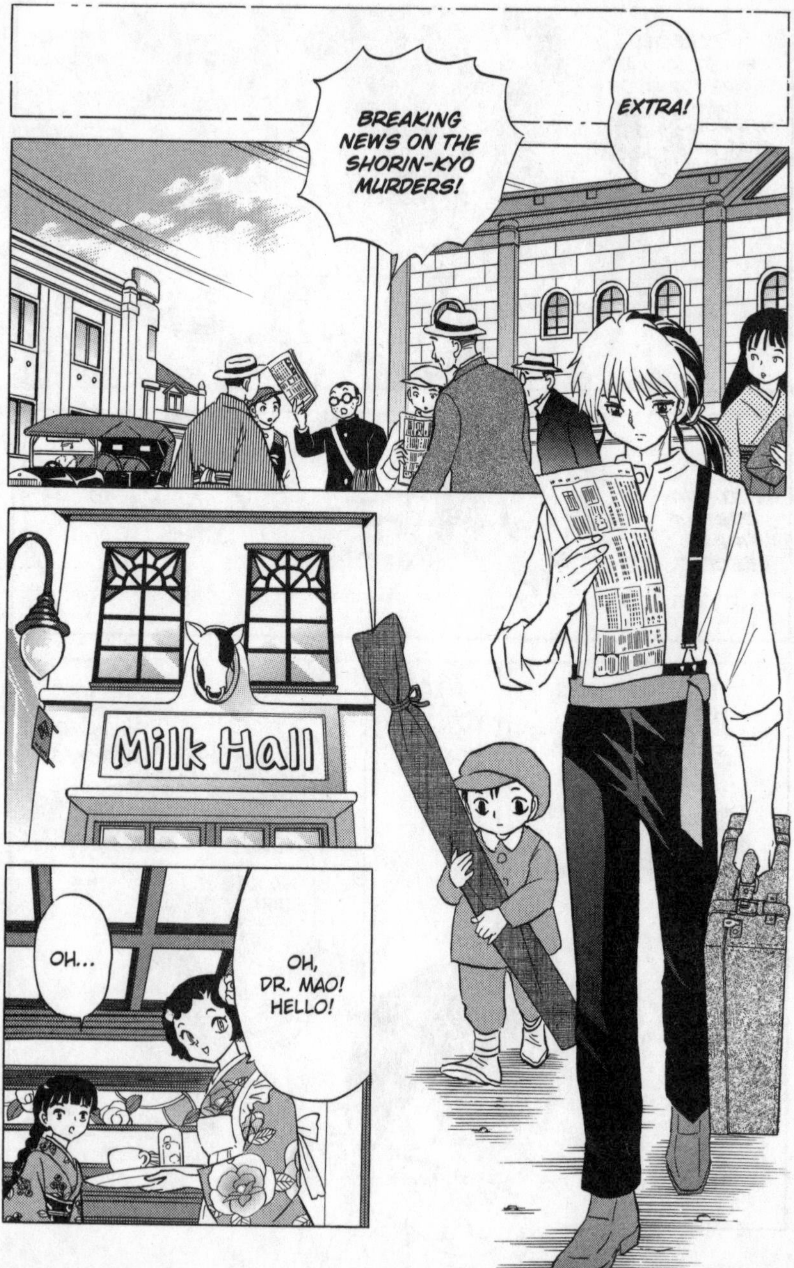
EXTRA!
BREAKING NEWS ON THE SHORIN-KYO MURDERS!
Milk Hall
OH, DR. MAO! HELLO!
OH...

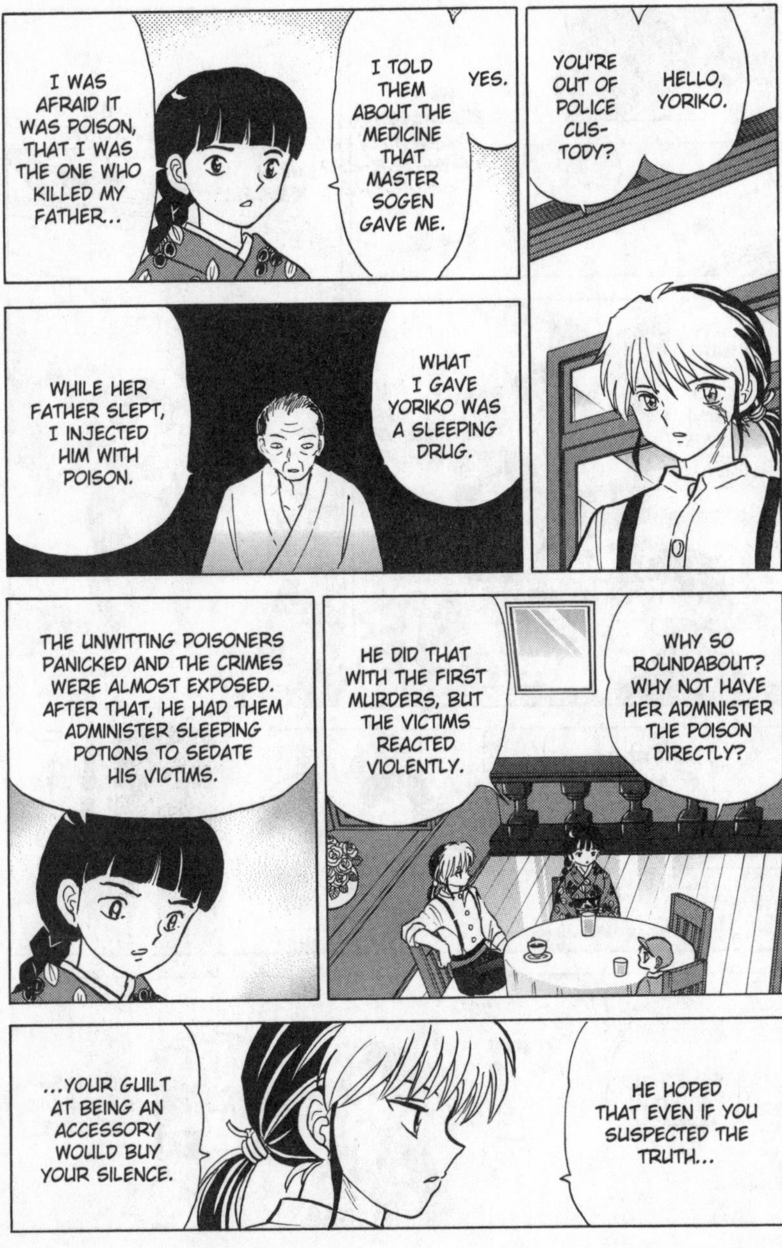
HELLO, YORIKO.
YOU'RE OUT OF POLICE CUS-TODY?
YES.
I TOLD THEM ABOUT THE MEDICINE THAT MASTER SOGEN GAVE ME.
I WAS AFRAID IT WAS POISON, THAT I WAS THE ONE WHO KILLED MY FATHER...
WHAT I GAVE YORIKO WAS A SLEEPING DRUG.
WHILE HER FATHER SLEPT, I INJECTED HIM WITH POISON.
WHY SO ROUNDABOUT? WHY NOT HAVE HER ADMINISTER THE POISON DIRECTLY?
HE DID THAT WITH THE FIRST MURDERS, BUT THE VICTIMS REACTED VIOLENTLY.
THE UNWITTING POISONERS PANICKED AND THE CRIMES WERE ALMOST EXPOSED. AFTER THAT, HE HAD THEM ADMINISTER SLEEPING POTIONS TO SEDATE HIS VICTIMS.
HE HOPED THAT EVEN IF YOU SUSPECTED THE TRUTH...
...YOUR GUILT AT BEING AN ACCESSORY WOULD BUY YOUR SILENCE.

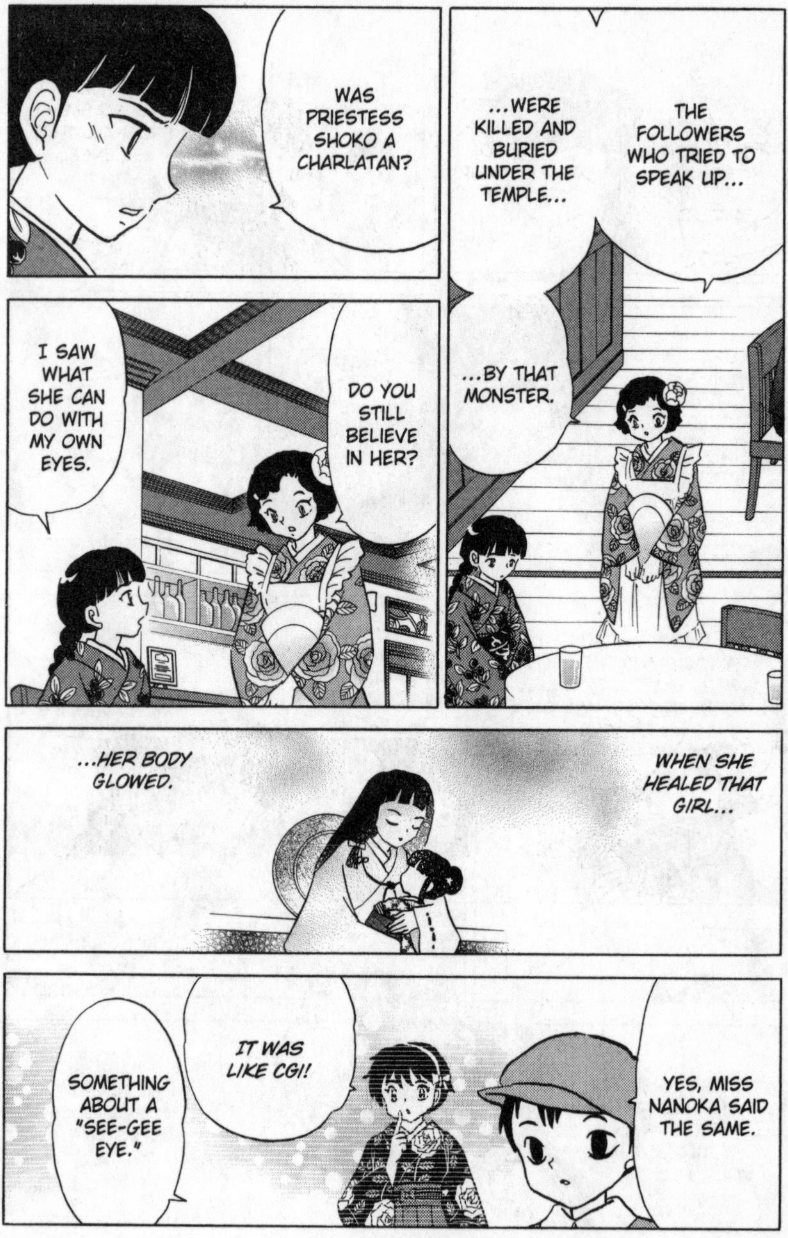
THE FOLLOWERS WHO TRIED TO SPEAK UP...
...WERE KILLED AND BURIED UNDER THE TEMPLE...
...BY THAT MONSTER.
WAS PRIESTESS SHOKO A CHARLATAN?
DO YOU STILL BELIEVE IN HER?
I SAW WHAT SHE CAN DO WITH MY OWN EYES.
WHEN SHE HEALED THAT GIRL...
...HER BODY GLOWED.
YES, MISS NANOKA SAID THE SAME.
IT WAS LIKE CGI!
SOMETHING ABOUT A "SEE-GEE EYE."

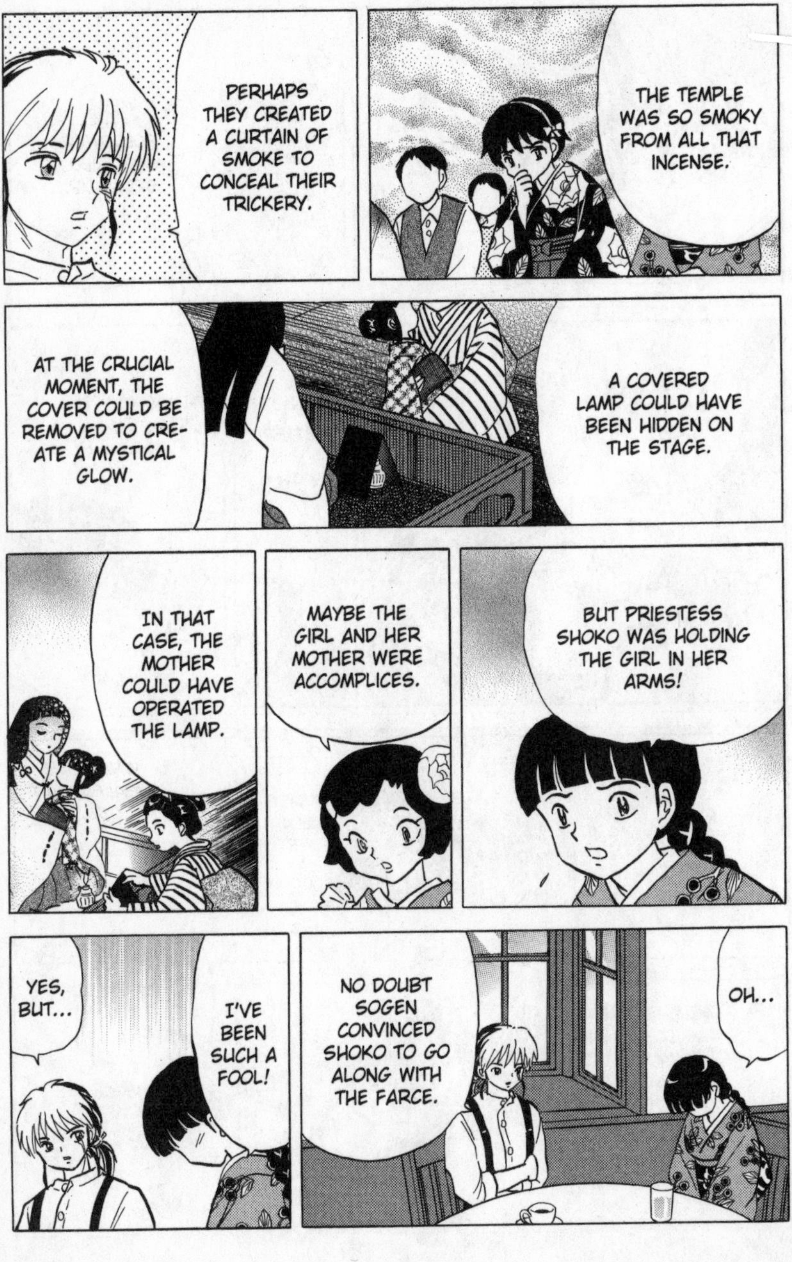
THE TEMPLE WAS SO SMOKY FROM ALL THAT INCENSE.
PERHAPS THEY CREATED A CURTAIN OF SMOKE TO CONCEAL THEIR TRICKERY.
A COVERED LAMP COULD HAVE BEEN HIDDEN ON THE STAGE.
AT THE CRUCIAL MOMENT, THE COVER COULD BE REMOVED TO CRE-ATE A MYSTICAL GLOW.
BUT PRIESTESS SHOKO WAS HOLDING THE GIRL IN HER ARMS!
MAYBE THE GIRL AND HER MOTHER WERE ACCOMPLICES.
IN THAT CASE, THE MOTHER COULD HAVE OPERATED THE LAMP.
OH...
NO DOUBT SOGEN CONVINCED SHOKO TO GO ALONG WITH THE FARCE.
I'VE BEEN SUCH A FOOL!
YES, BUT...

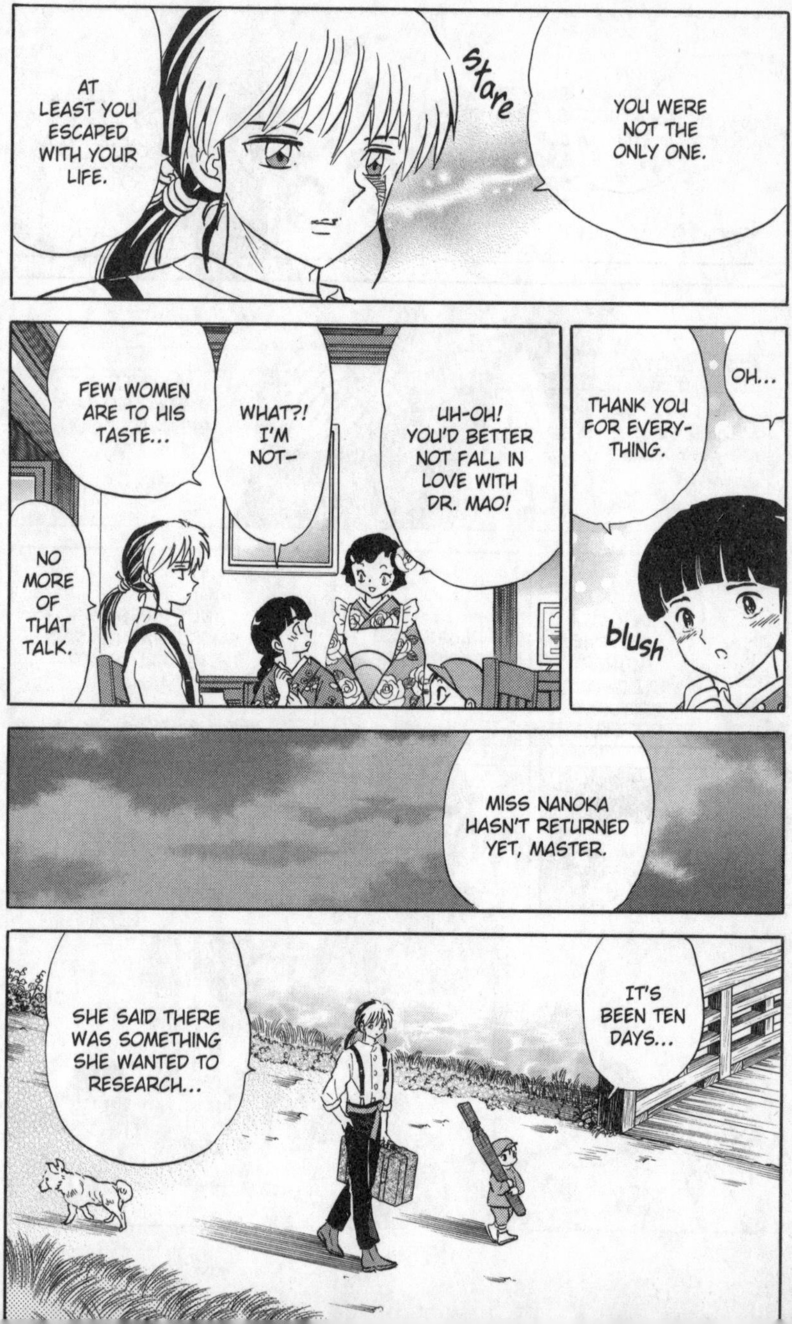
YOU WERE NOT THE ONLY ONE.
stare
AT LEAST YOU ESCAPED WITH YOUR LIFE.
OH...
THANK YOU FOR EVERY-THING.
blush
UH-OH! YOU'D BETTER NOT FALL IN LOVE WITH DR. MAO!
WHAT?! I'M NOT-
FEW WOMEN ARE TO HIS TASTE...
NO MORE OF THAT TALK.
MISS NANOKA HASN'T RETURNED YET, MASTER.
IT'S BEEN TEN DAYS...
SHE SAID THERE WAS SOMETHING SHE WANTED TO RESEARCH...

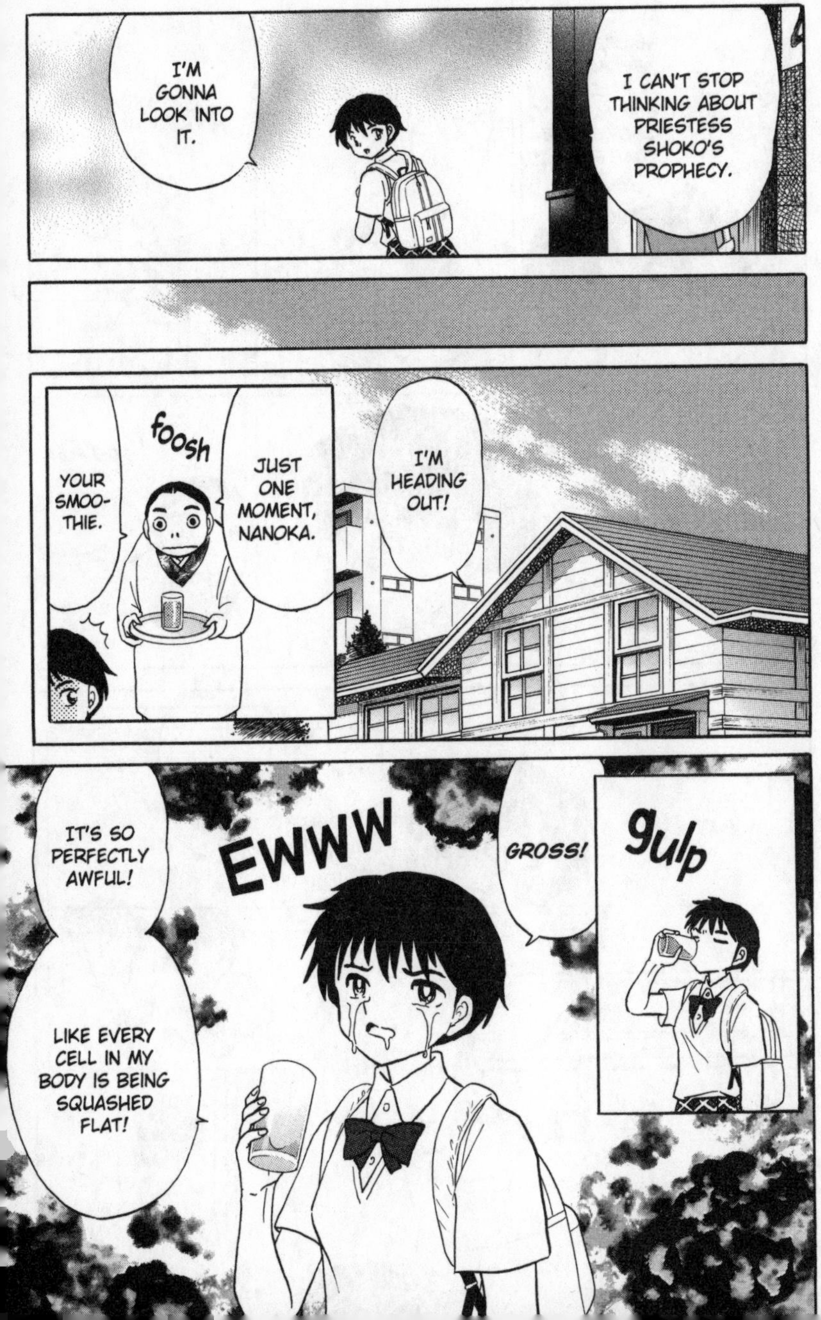
I CAN'T STOP THINKING ABOUT PRIESTESS SHOKO'S PROPHECY.
I'M GONNA LOOK INTO IT.
I'M HEADING OUT!
JUST ONE MOMENT, NANOKA.
foosh
YOUR SMOO-THIE.
gulp
GROSS!
EWWW
IT'S SO PERFECTLY AWFUL!
LIKE EVERY CELL IN MY BODY IS BEING SQUASHED FLAT!

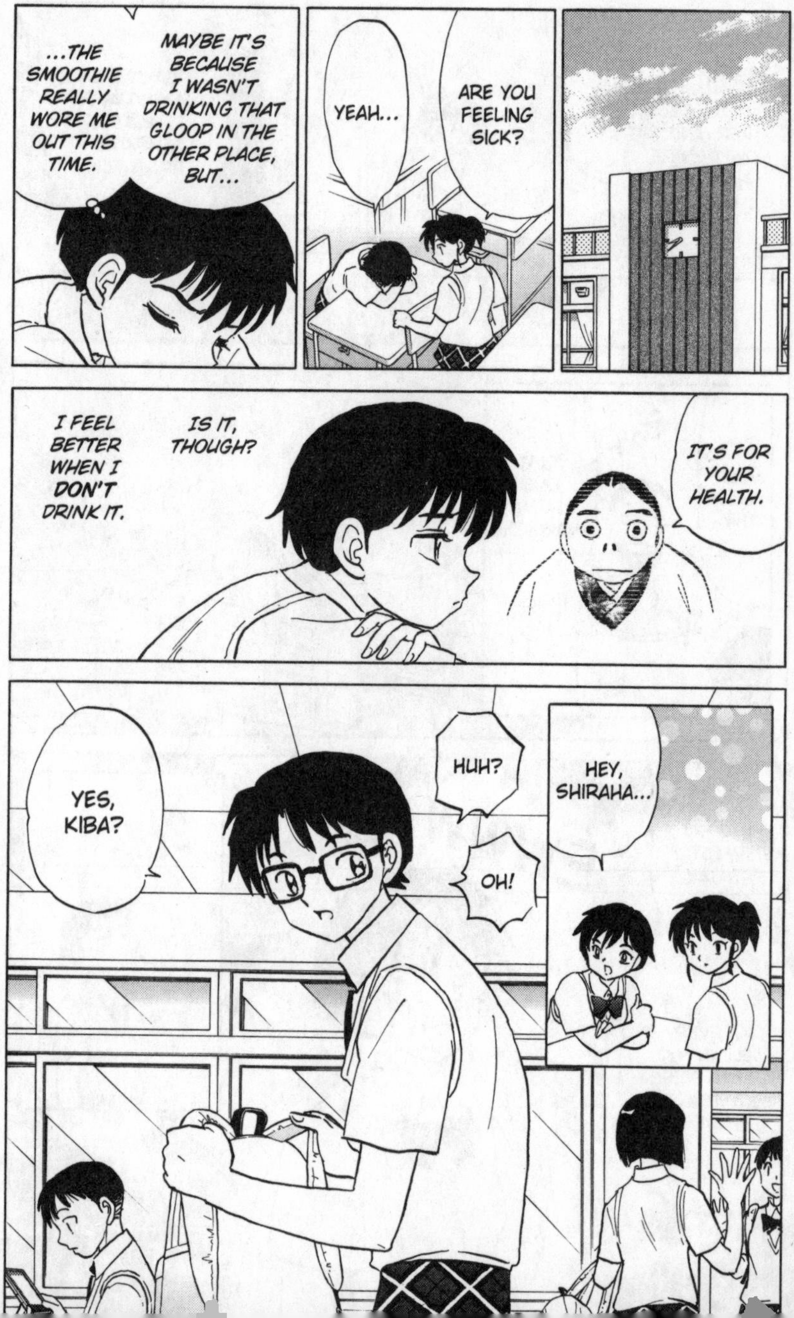
ARE YOU FEELING SICK?
YEAH...
MAYBE IT'S BECAUSE I WASN'T DRINKING THAT GLOOP IN THE OTHER PLACE, BUT...
...THE SMOOTHIE REALLY WORE ME OUT THIS TIME.
IT'S FOR YOUR HEALTH.
IS IT, THOUGH?
I FEEL BETTER WHEN I DON'T DRINK IT.
HEY, SHIRAHA...
HUH?
OH!
YES, KIBA?

WOULD YOU MIND HELPING ME OUT AGAIN?
SURE. WHAT'S UP?
OH MY GOSH, ARE THEY A *THING* NOW?
MAY-BE!
SHE KNOWS HE LIKES HER, AND NOW THEY'RE HANGING OUT...
I HAVE TO WARN MAO ABOUT THE QUAKE!
BUT HOW IS IT RELATED TO THAT OLD SHOPPING AREA?
THE GREAT KANTO EARTHQUAKE HAPPENED ON SEPTEMBER 1 AT 11:58 A.M.
THE SINKHOLE ACCIDENT THAT KILLED MY PARENTS...
...WAS ALSO ON SEPTEMBER 1, AROUND NOON.

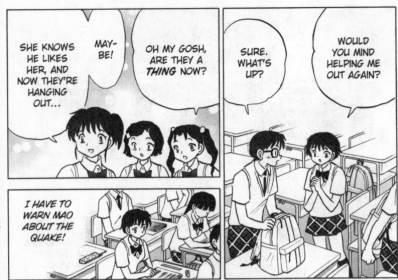

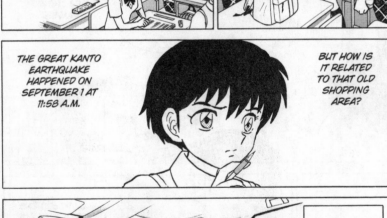

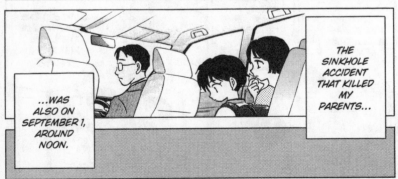

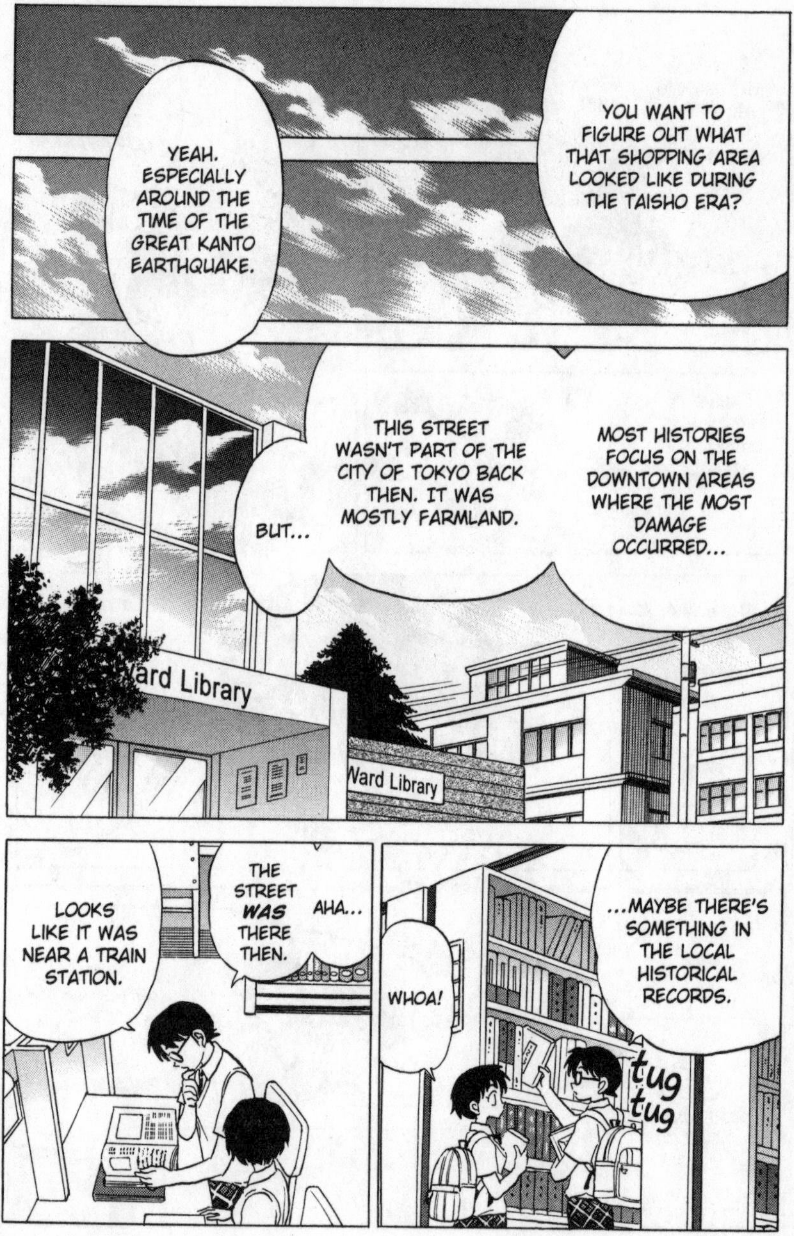
YOU WANT TO FIGURE OUT WHAT THAT SHOPPING AREA LOOKED LIKE DURING THE TAISHO ERA?
YEAH. ESPECIALLY AROUND THE TIME OF THE GREAT KANTO EARTHQUAKE.
MOST HISTORIES FOCUS ON THE DOWNTOWN AREAS WHERE THE MOST DAMAGE OCCURRED...
THIS STREET WASN'T PART OF THE CITY OF TOKYO BACK THEN. IT WAS MOSTLY FARMLAND.
BUT...
ard Library
ard Library
...MAYBE THERE'S SOMETHING IN THE LOCAL HISTORICAL RECORDS.
WHOA!
tug tug
AHA...
THE STREET *WAS* THERE THEN.
LOOKS LIKE IT WAS NEAR A TRAIN STATION.

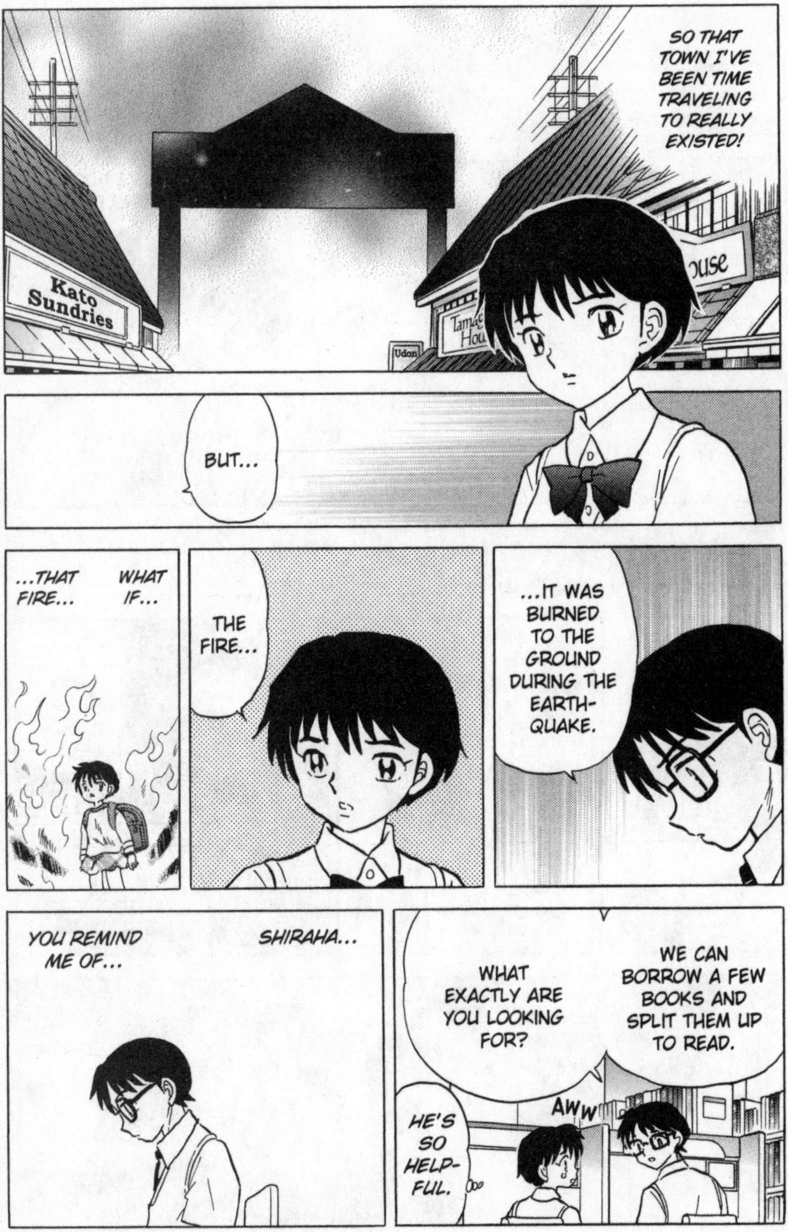
SO THAT TOWN I'VE BEEN TIME TRAVELING TO REALLY EXISTED!
Kato Sundries
Udon
BUT...
...IT WAS BURNED TO THE GROUND DURING THE EARTH-QUAKE.
THE FIRE...
WHAT IF...
...THAT FIRE...
WE CAN BORROW A FEW BOOKS AND SPLIT THEM UP TO READ.
WHAT EXACTLY ARE YOU LOOKING FOR?
AWW
HE'S SO HELP-FUL.
SHIRAHA...
YOU REMIND ME OF...

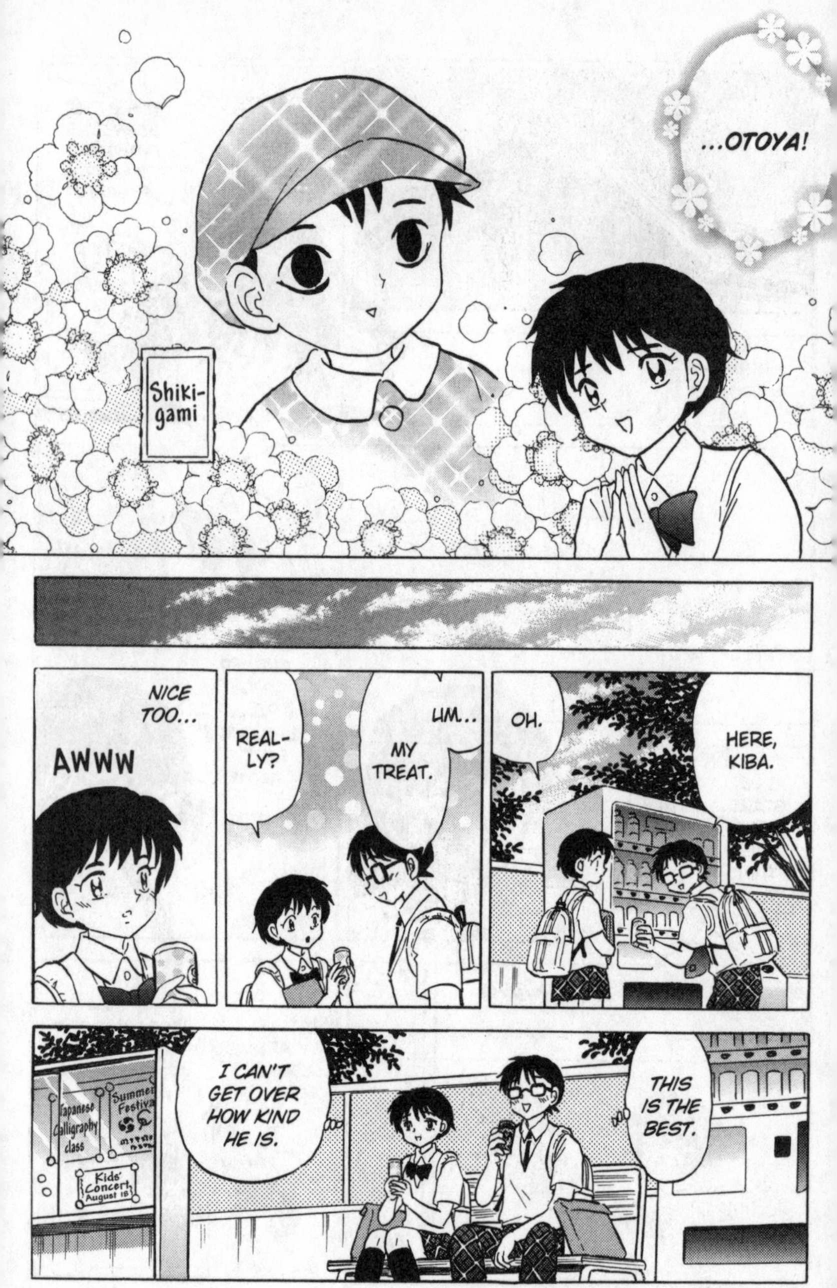
...OTOYA!
Shiki-gami
HERE, KIBA.
OH.
UM... MY TREAT.
REAL-LY?
NICE TOO...
AWWW
THIS IS THE BEST.
I CAN'T GET OVER HOW KIND HE IS.
Japanese Calligraphy class
Kids' Concert August 18

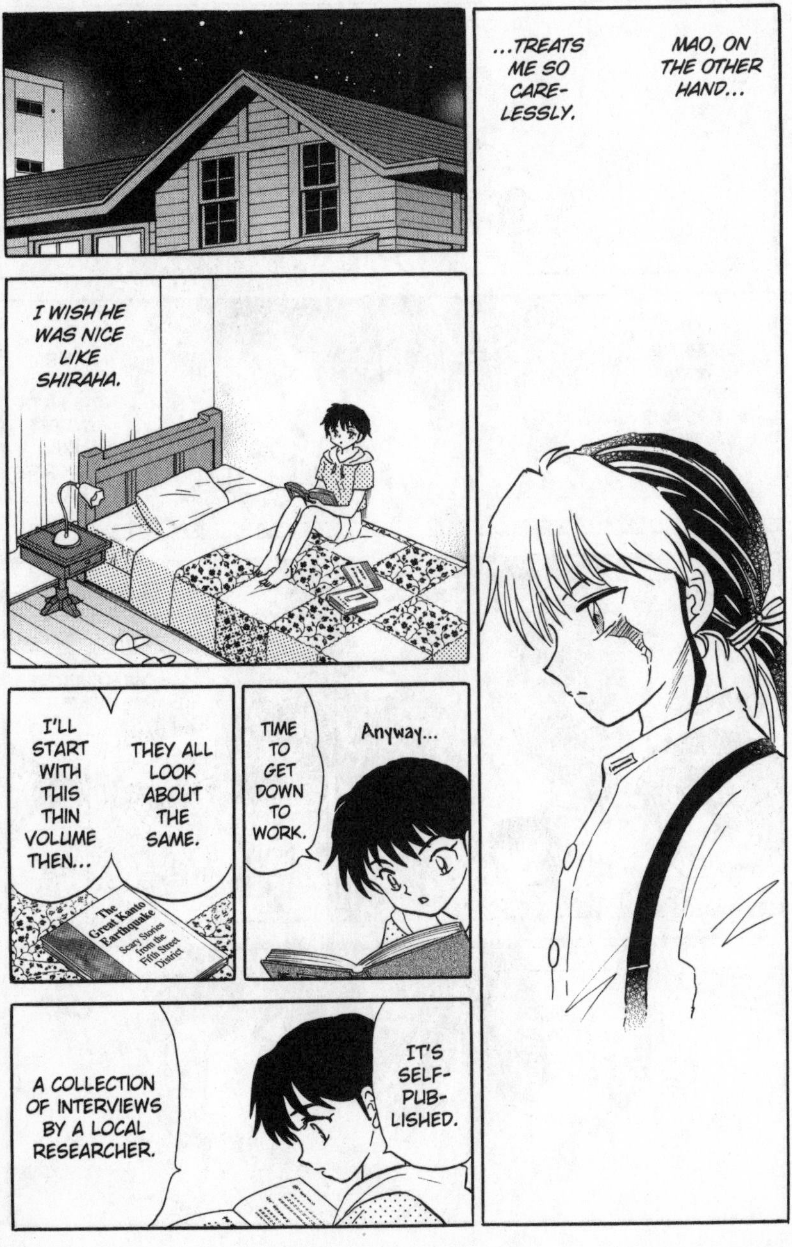
MAO, ON THE OTHER HAND...
...TREATS ME SO CARE-LESSLY.
I WISH HE WAS NICE LIKE SHIRAHA.
Anyway...
TIME TO GET DOWN TO WORK.
THEY ALL LOOK ABOUT THE SAME.
I'LL START WITH THIS THIN VOLUME THEN...
The Great Kanto Earthquake
Scary Stories from the Fifth Street District
IT'S SELF-PUB-LISHED.
A COLLECTION OF INTERVIEWS BY A LOCAL RESEARCHER.

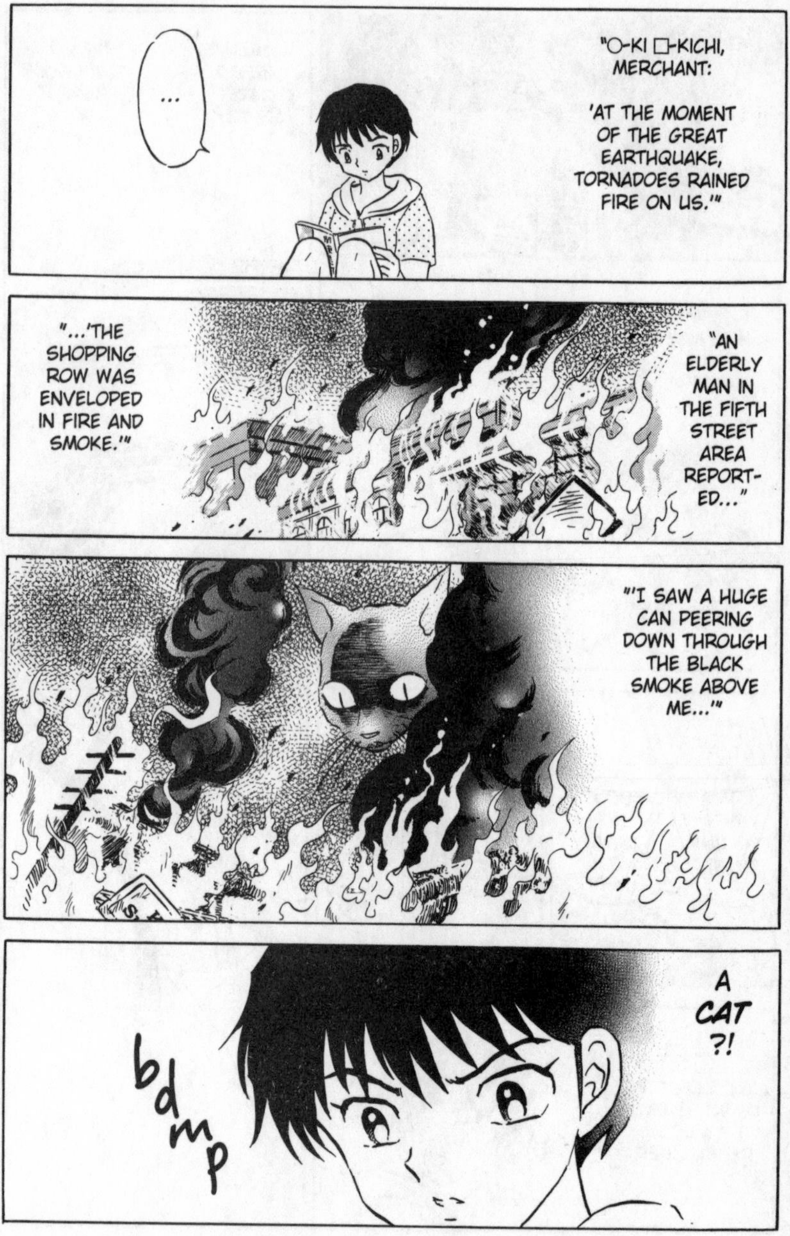
"○-KI □-KICHI, MERCHANT:
'AT THE MOMENT OF THE GREAT EARTHQUAKE, TORNADOES RAINED FIRE ON US.'"
...
"AN ELDERLY MAN IN THE FIFTH STREET AREA REPORTED..."
"...'THE SHOPPING ROW WAS ENVELOPED IN FIRE AND SMOKE.'"
"'I SAW A HUGE CAN PEERING DOWN THROUGH THE BLACK SMOKE ABOVE ME...'"
A CAT?!
bdmp

Chapter 5:
The Keystone

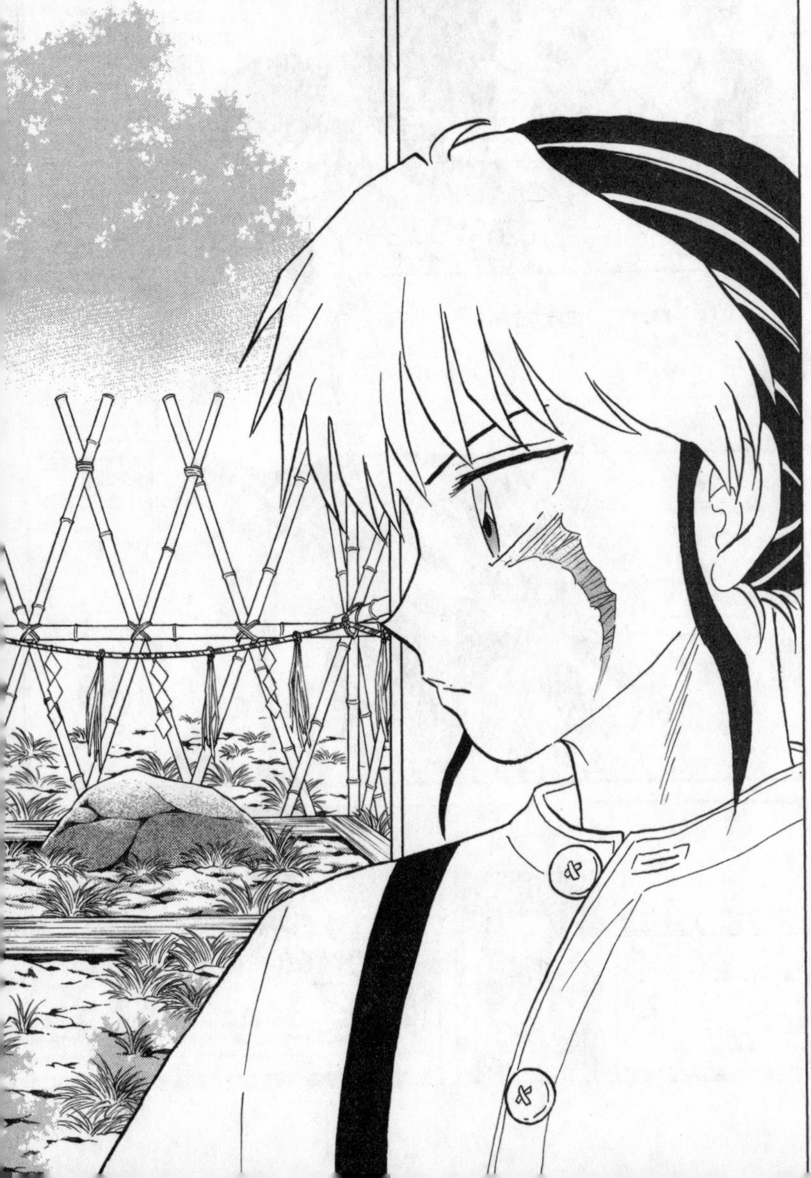

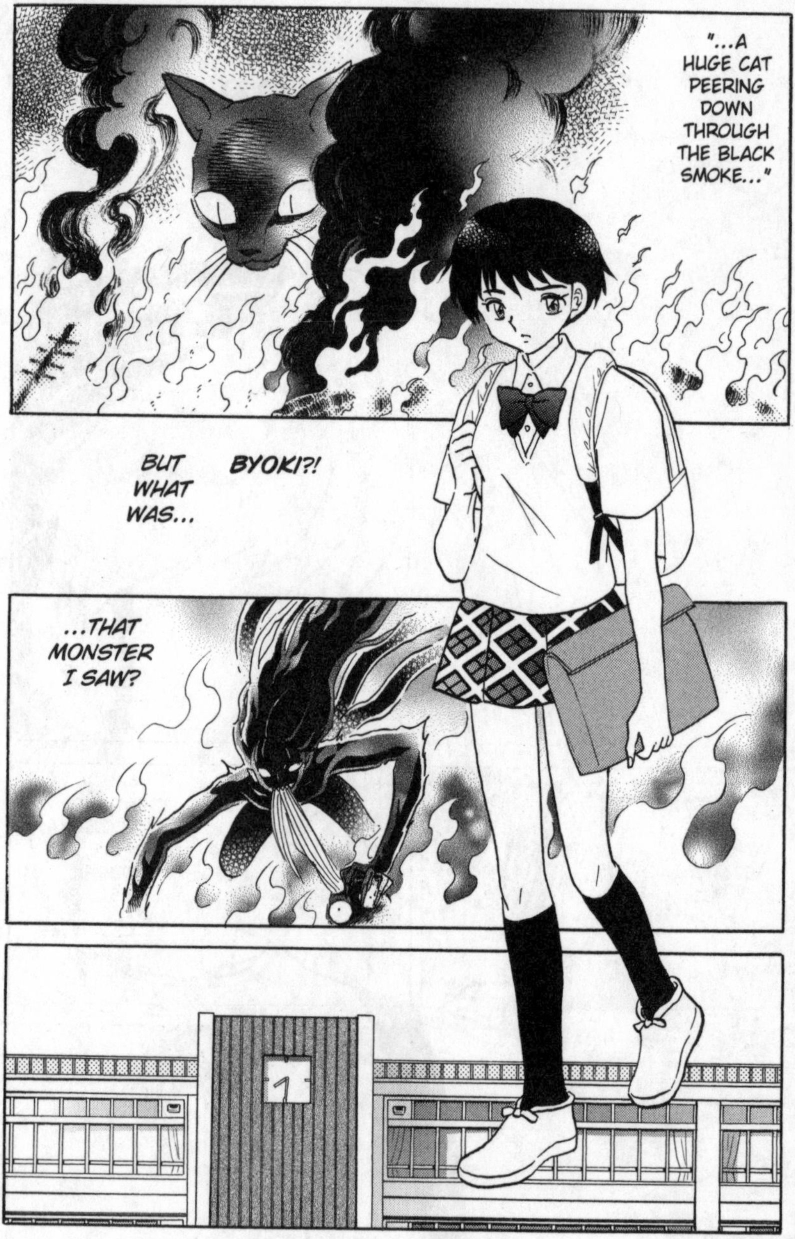
"...A HUGE CAT PEERING DOWN THROUGH THE BLACK SMOKE..."
BYOKI?!
BUT WHAT WAS...
...THAT MONSTER I SAW?

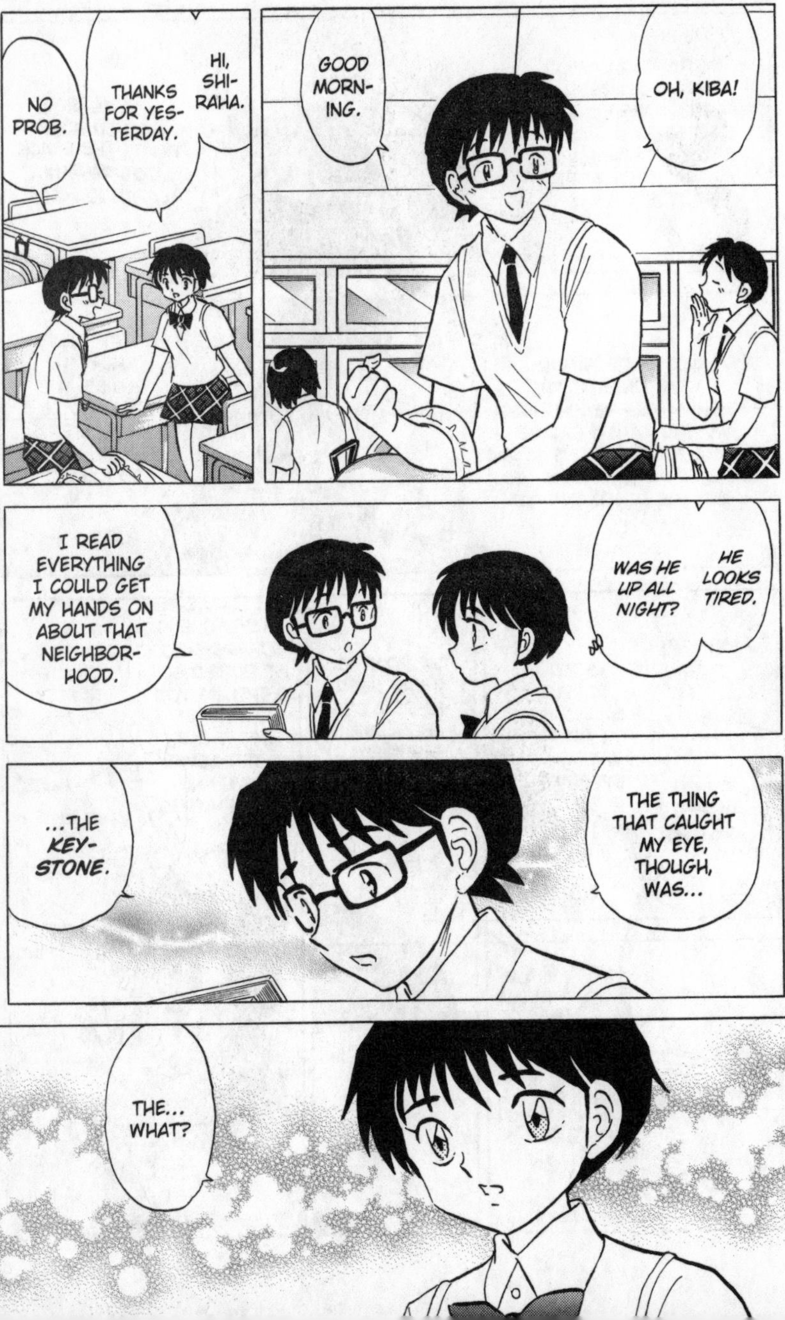
OH, KIBA!
GOOD MORN-ING.
HI, SHI-RAHA.
THANKS FOR YES-TERDAY.
NO PROB.
HE LOOKS TIRED.
WAS HE UP ALL NIGHT?
I READ EVERYTHING I COULD GET MY HANDS ON ABOUT THAT NEIGHBOR-HOOD.
THE THING THAT CAUGHT MY EYE, THOUGH, WAS...
...THE *KEY-STONE*.
THE... WHAT?

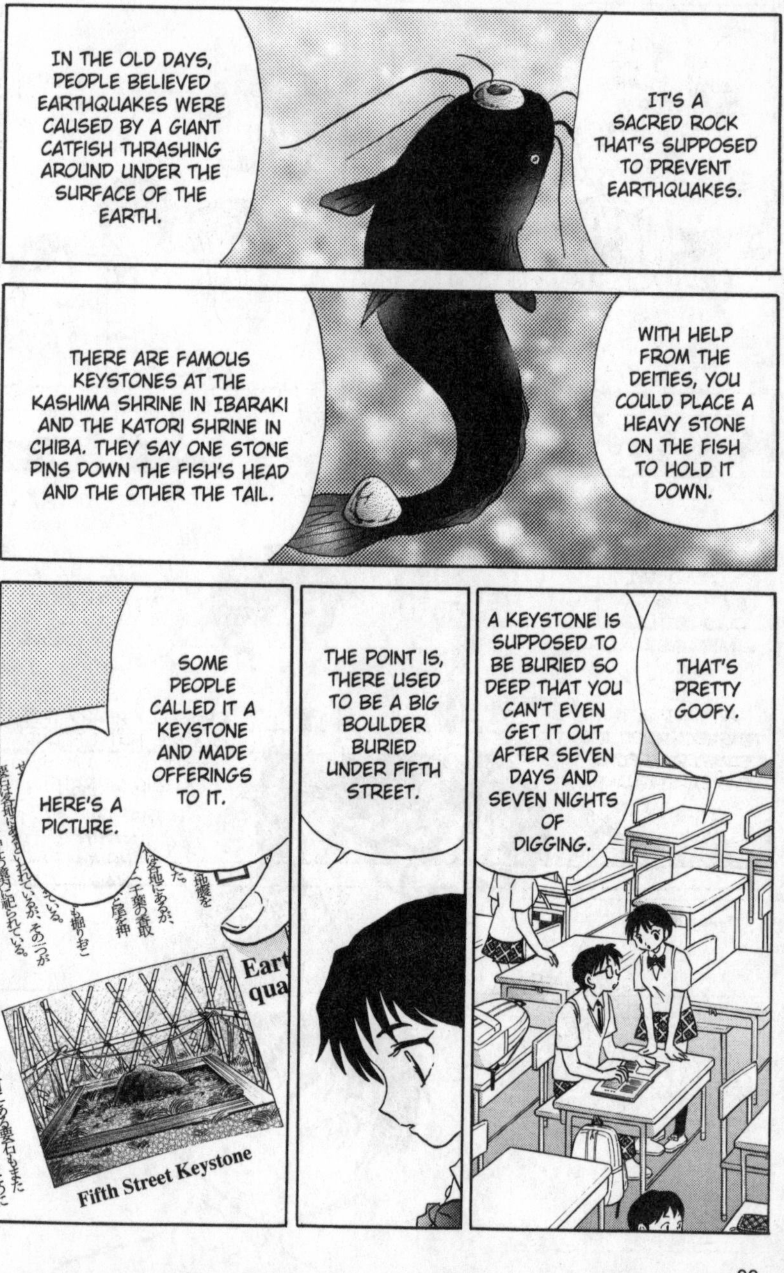
IT'S A SACRED ROCK THAT'S SUPPOSED TO PREVENT EARTHQUAKES.
IN THE OLD DAYS, PEOPLE BELIEVED EARTHQUAKES WERE CAUSED BY A GIANT CATFISH THRASHING AROUND UNDER THE SURFACE OF THE EARTH.
WITH HELP FROM THE DEITIES, YOU COULD PLACE A HEAVY STONE ON THE FISH TO HOLD IT DOWN.
THERE ARE FAMOUS KEYSTONES AT THE KASHIMA SHRINE IN IBARAKI AND THE KATORI SHRINE IN CHIBA. THEY SAY ONE STONE PINS DOWN THE FISH'S HEAD AND THE OTHER THE TAIL.
A KEYSTONE IS SUPPOSED TO BE BURIED SO DEEP THAT YOU CAN'T EVEN GET IT OUT AFTER SEVEN DAYS AND SEVEN NIGHTS OF DIGGING.
THAT'S PRETTY GOOFY.
THE POINT IS, THERE USED TO BE A BIG BOULDER BURIED UNDER FIFTH STREET.
SOME PEOPLE CALLED IT A KEYSTONE AND MADE OFFERINGS TO IT.
HERE'S A PICTURE.
Fifth Street Keystone

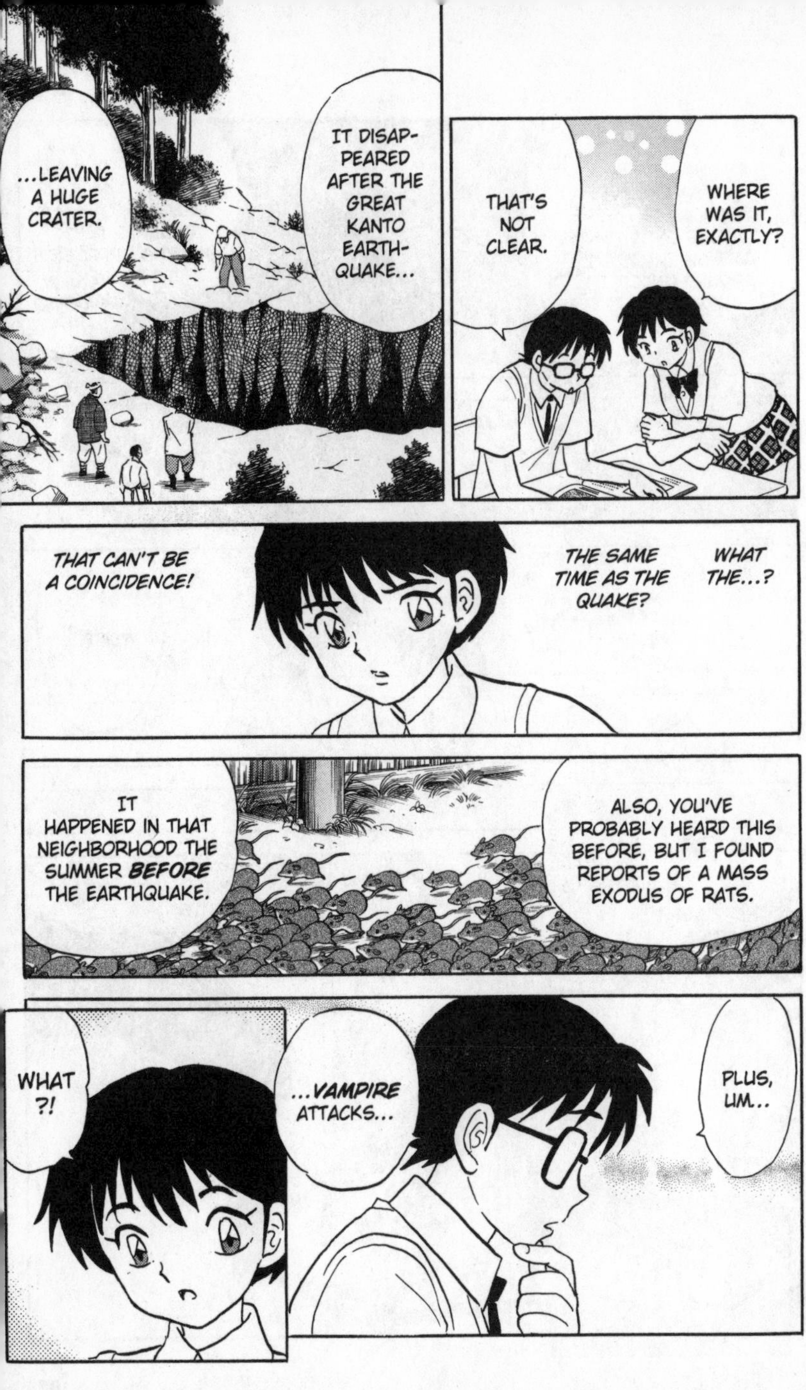
WHERE WAS IT, EXACTLY?
THAT'S NOT CLEAR.
IT DISAPPEARED AFTER THE GREAT KANTO EARTHQUAKE...
...LEAVING A HUGE CRATER.
WHAT THE...?
THE SAME TIME AS THE QUAKE?
THAT CAN'T BE A COINCIDENCE!
ALSO, YOU'VE PROBABLY HEARD THIS BEFORE, BUT I FOUND REPORTS OF A MASS EXODUS OF RATS.
IT HAPPENED IN THAT NEIGHBORHOOD THE SUMMER ***BEFORE*** THE EARTHQUAKE.
PLUS, UM...
...***VAMPIRE*** ATTACKS...
WHAT?!

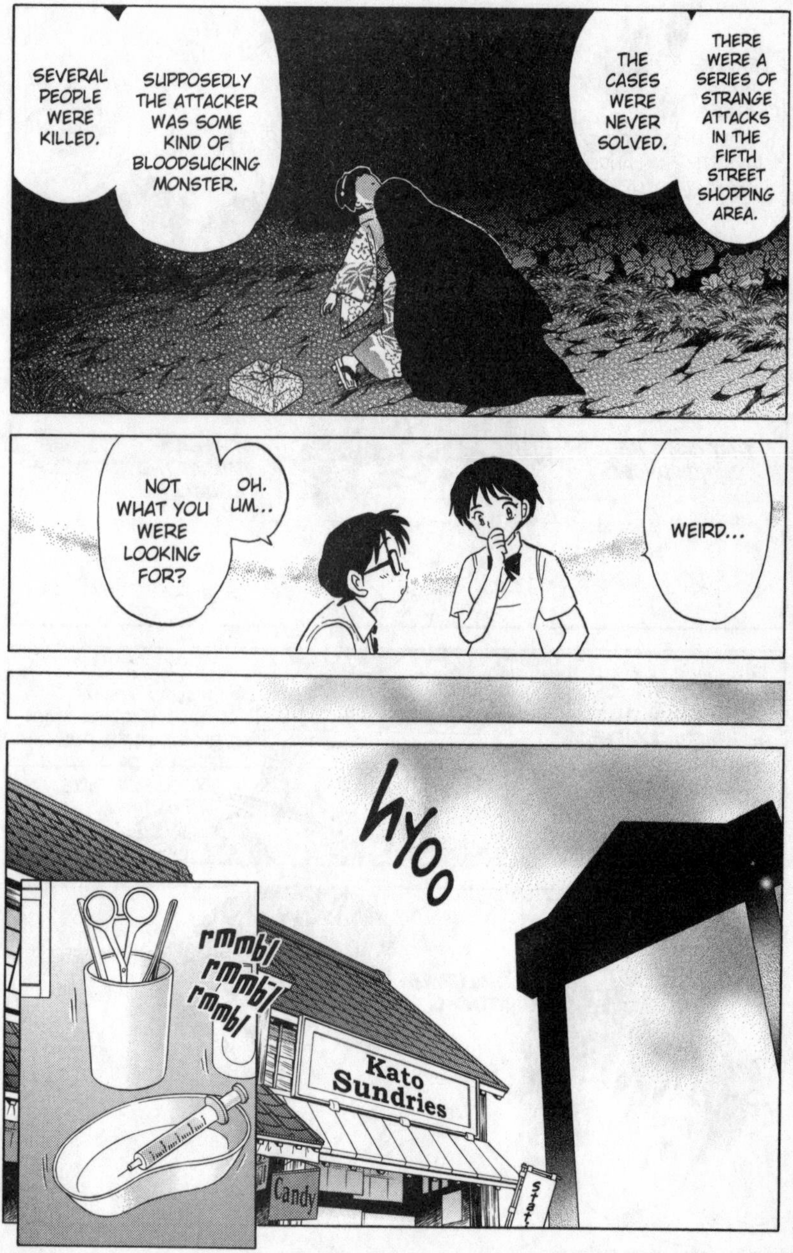
THERE WERE A SERIES OF STRANGE ATTACKS IN THE FIFTH STREET SHOPPING AREA.
THE CASES WERE NEVER SOLVED.
SUPPOSEDLY THE ATTACKER WAS SOME KIND OF BLOODSUCKING MONSTER.
SEVERAL PEOPLE WERE KILLED.
WEIRD...
OH. UM...
NOT WHAT YOU WERE LOOKING FOR?
hyoo
Kato Sundries
Candy
rmmbl rmmbl rmmbl

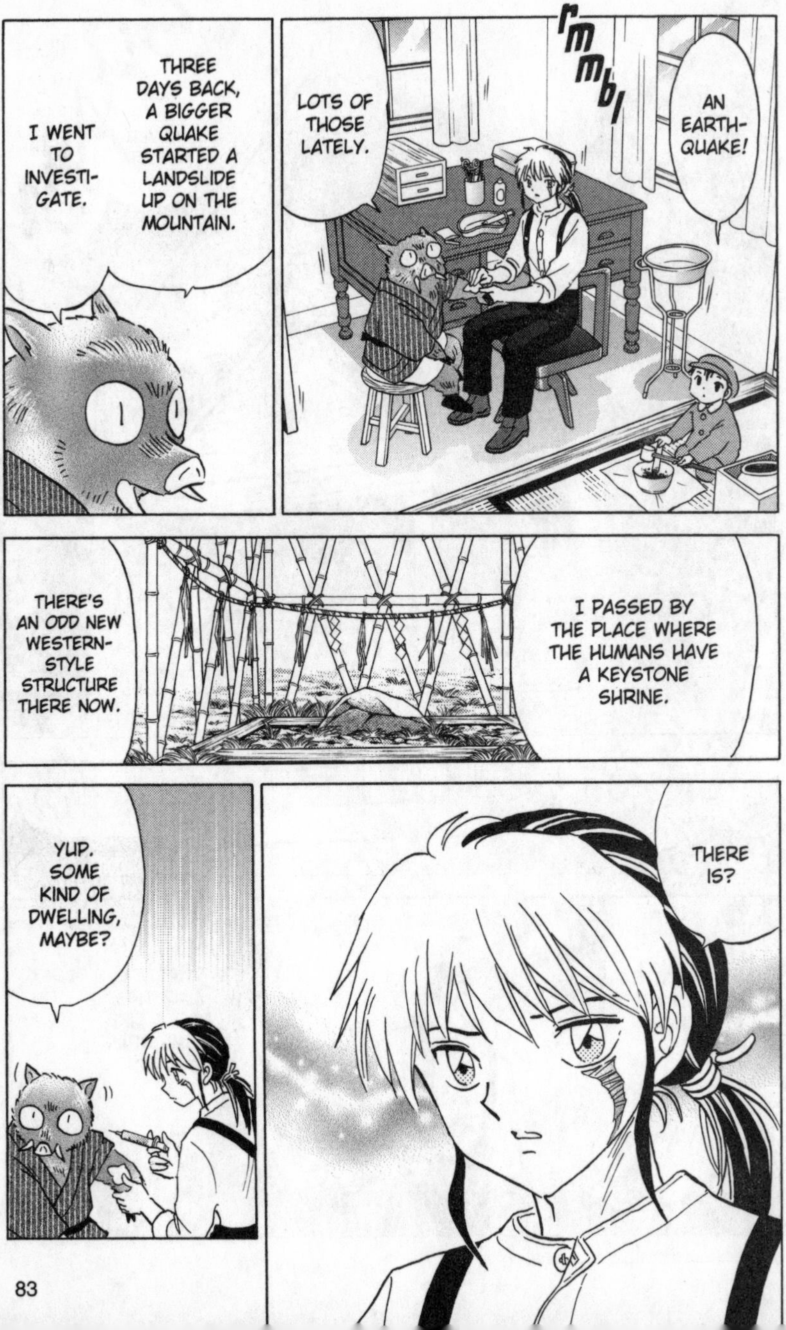
rmmbl
AN EARTH-QUAKE!
LOTS OF THOSE LATELY.
THREE DAYS BACK, A BIGGER QUAKE STARTED A LANDSLIDE UP ON THE MOUNTAIN.
I WENT TO INVESTI-GATE.
I PASSED BY THE PLACE WHERE THE HUMANS HAVE A KEYSTONE SHRINE.
THERE'S AN ODD NEW WESTERN-STYLE STRUCTURE THERE NOW.
THERE IS?
YUP. SOME KIND OF DWELLING, MAYBE?

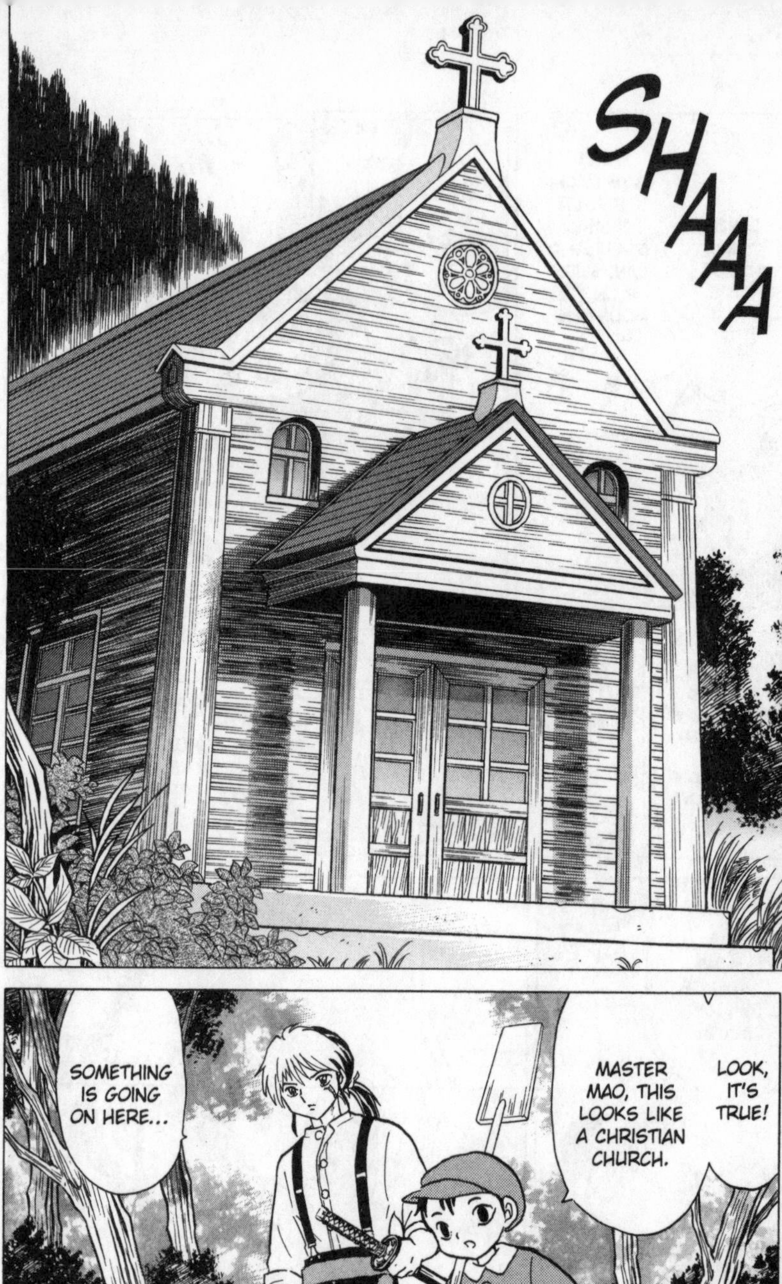
SHAAAA
LOOK, IT'S TRUE!
MASTER MAO, THIS LOOKS LIKE A CHRISTIAN CHURCH.
SOMETHING IS GOING ON HERE...

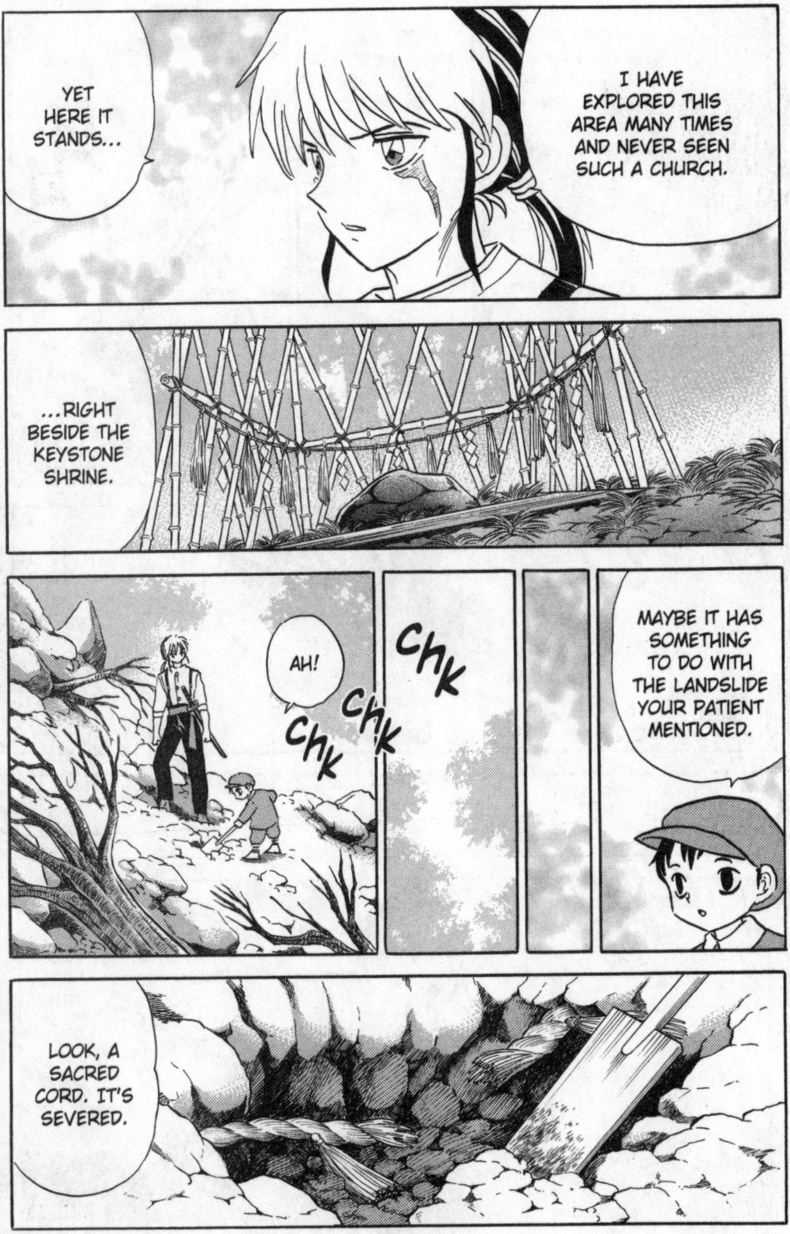
I HAVE EXPLORED THIS AREA MANY TIMES AND NEVER SEEN SUCH A CHURCH.
YET HERE IT STANDS...
...RIGHT BESIDE THE KEYSTONE SHRINE.
MAYBE IT HAS SOMETHING TO DO WITH THE LANDSLIDE YOUR PATIENT MENTIONED.
CHK
CHK
CHK
AH!
LOOK, A SACRED CORD. IT'S SEVERED.

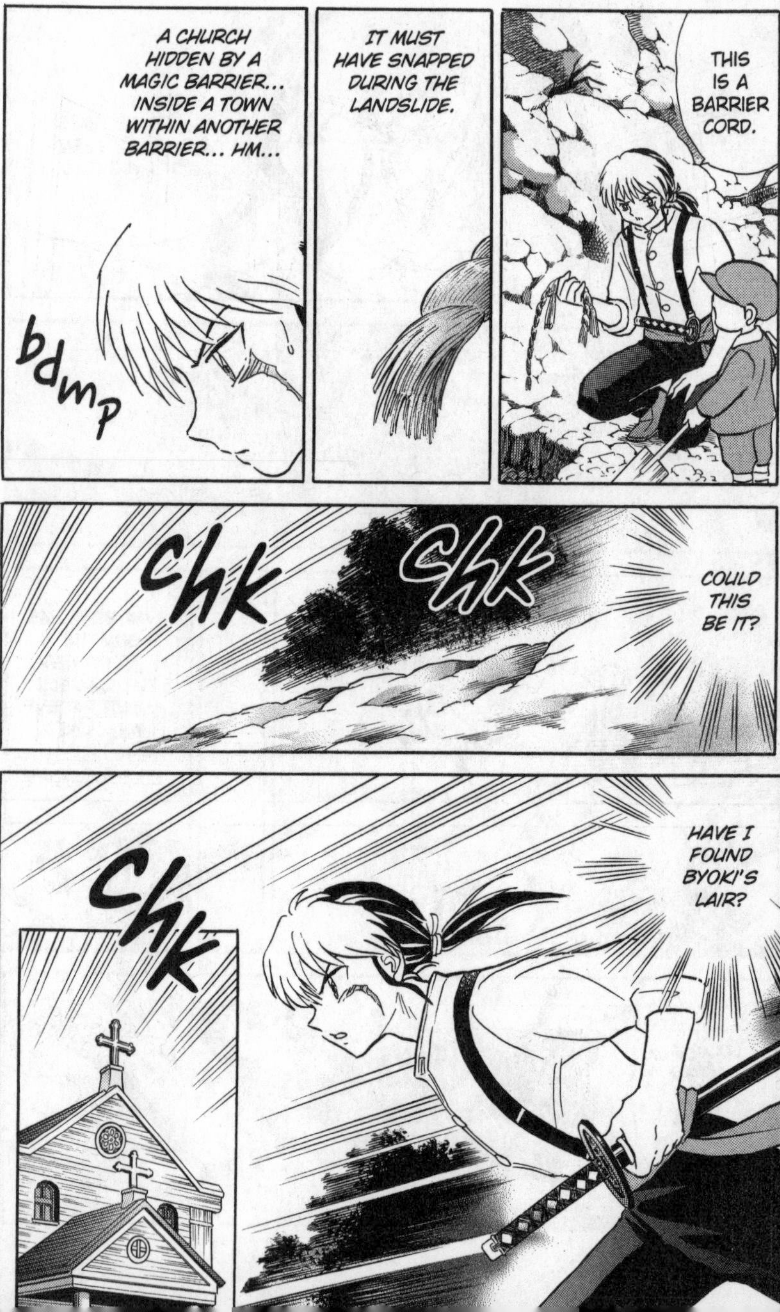
THIS IS A BARRIER CORD.
IT MUST HAVE SNAPPED DURING THE LANDSLIDE.
A CHURCH HIDDEN BY A MAGIC BARRIER... INSIDE A TOWN WITHIN ANOTHER BARRIER... HM...
bdmp
COULD THIS BE IT?
Chk
Chk
HAVE I FOUND BYOKI'S LAIR?
Chk

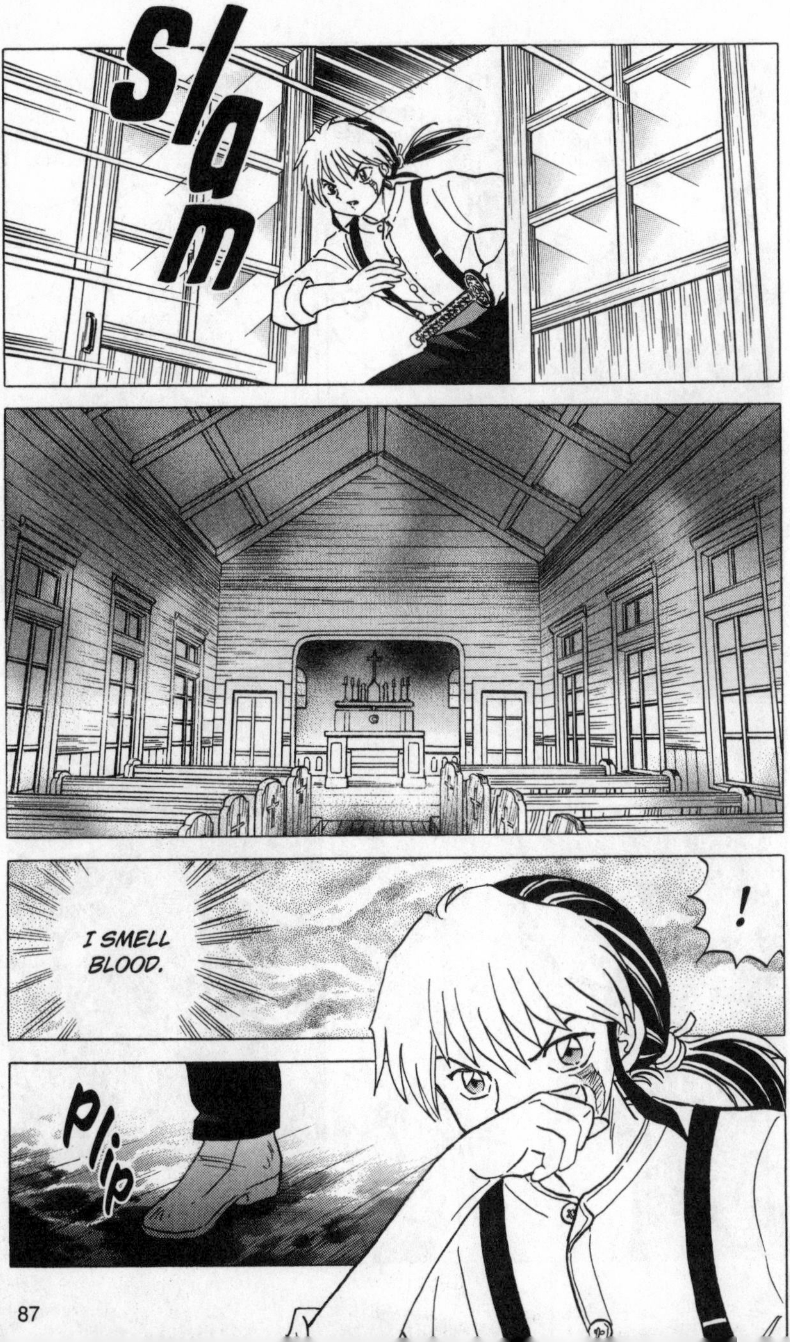
Slam
!
I SMELL BLOOD.
plip

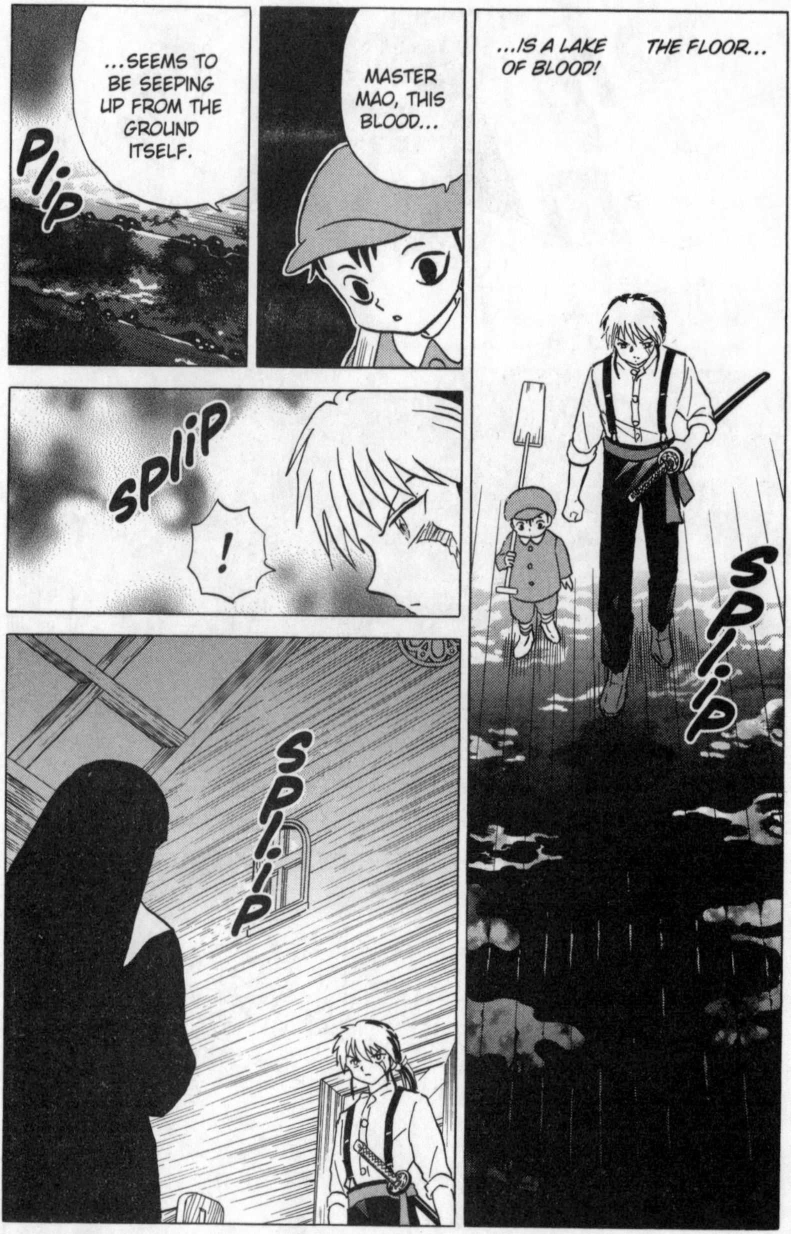
THE FLOOR...
...IS A LAKE OF BLOOD!
SPLIP
MASTER MAO, THIS BLOOD...
...SEEMS TO BE SEEPING UP FROM THE GROUND ITSELF.
Plip
SPLIP
!
SPLIP

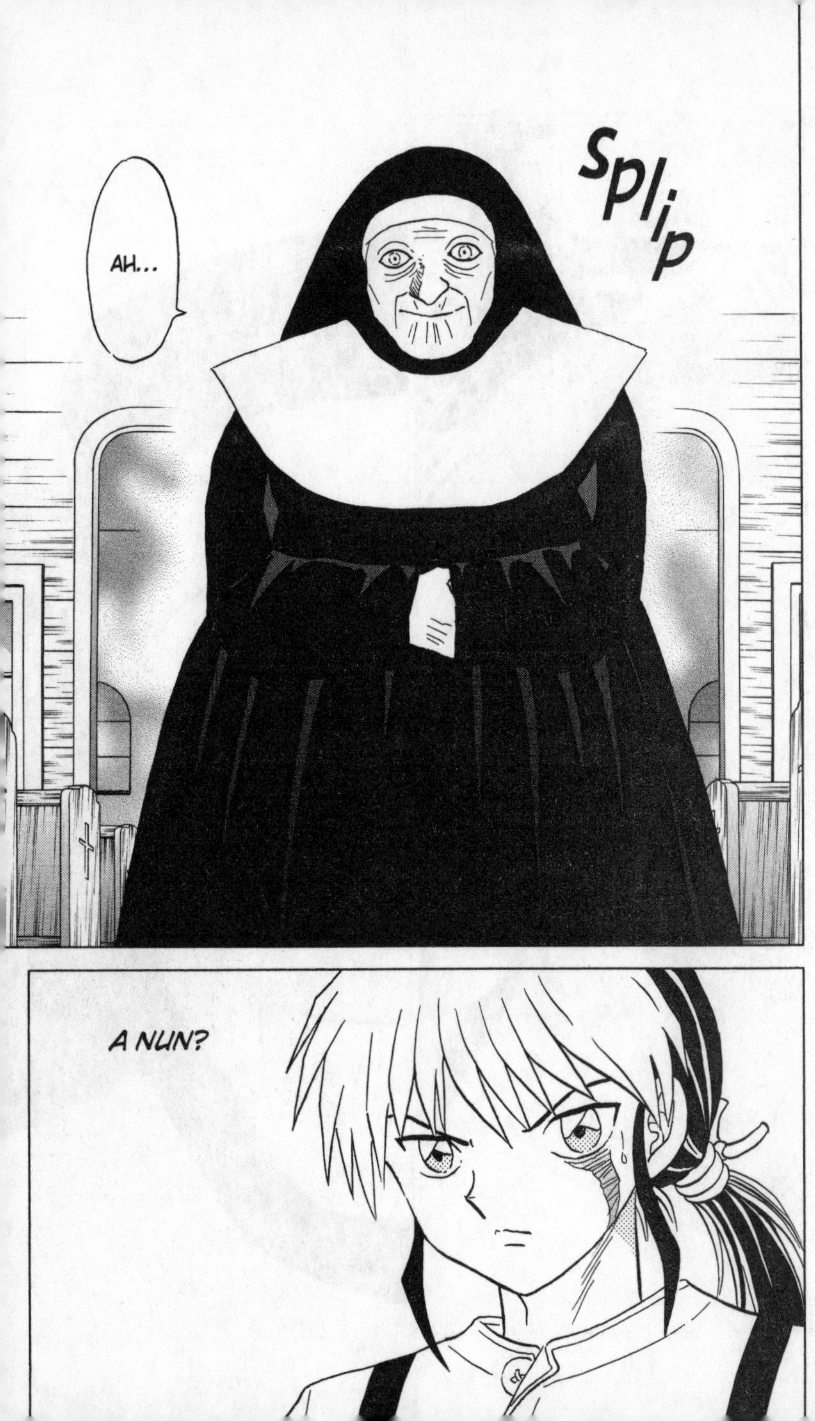
SPLIP
AH...
A NUN?

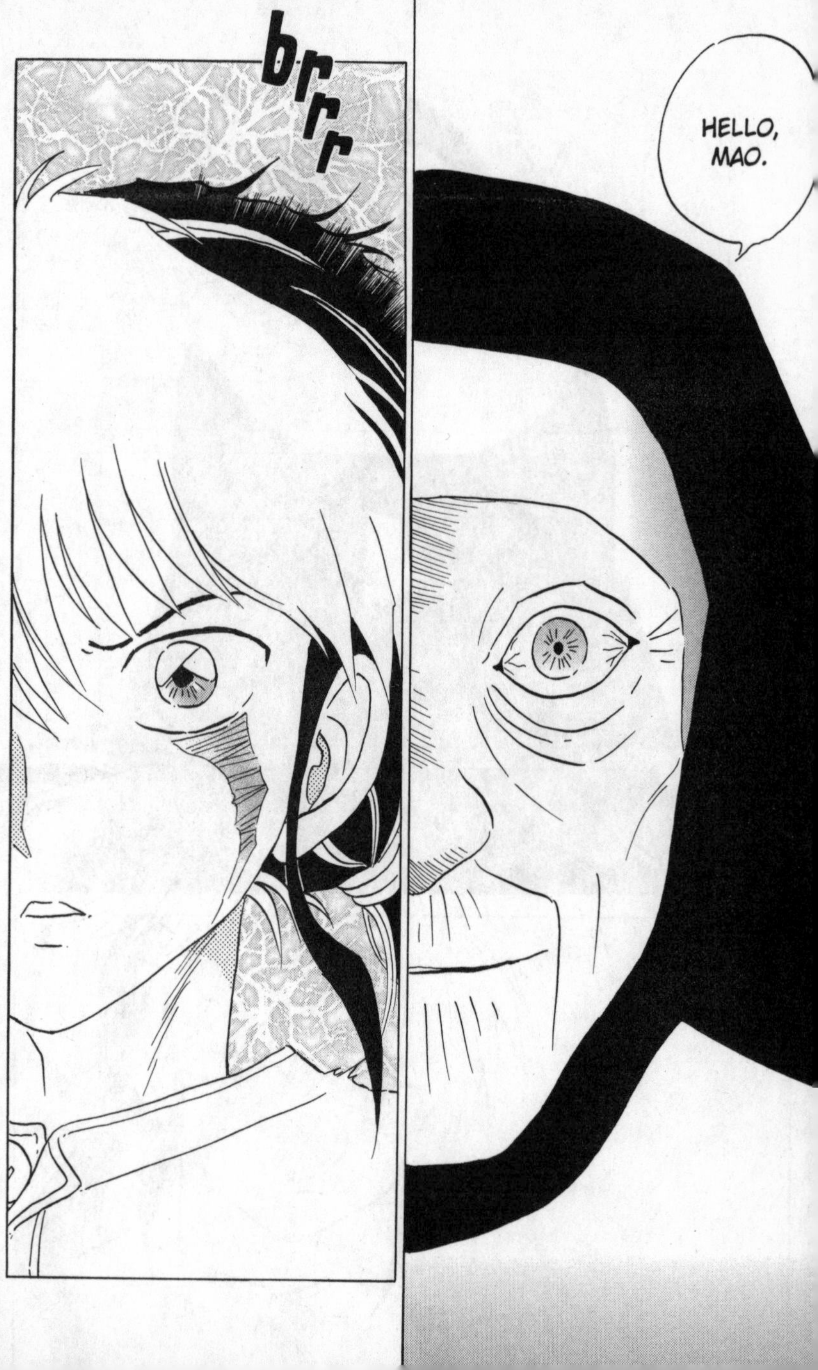
HELLO, MAO.
brrr

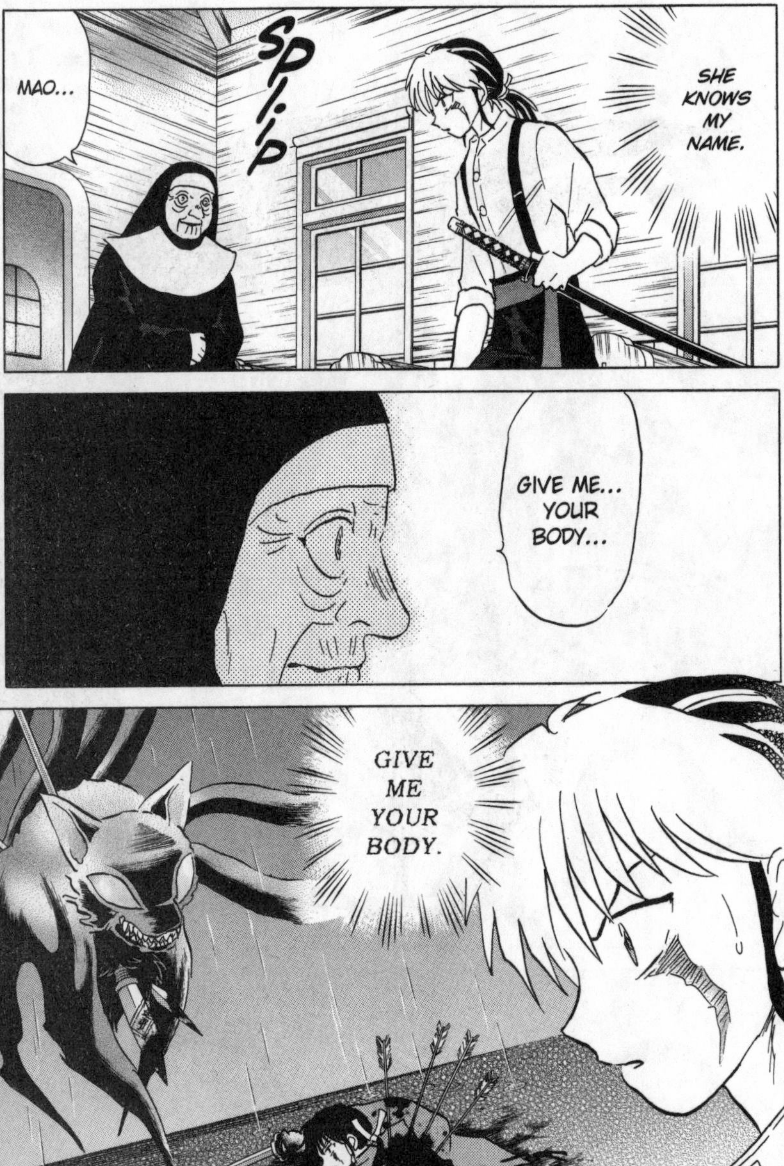
SHE KNOWS MY NAME.
SPLIP
MAO...
GIVE ME... YOUR BODY...
GIVE ME YOUR BODY.

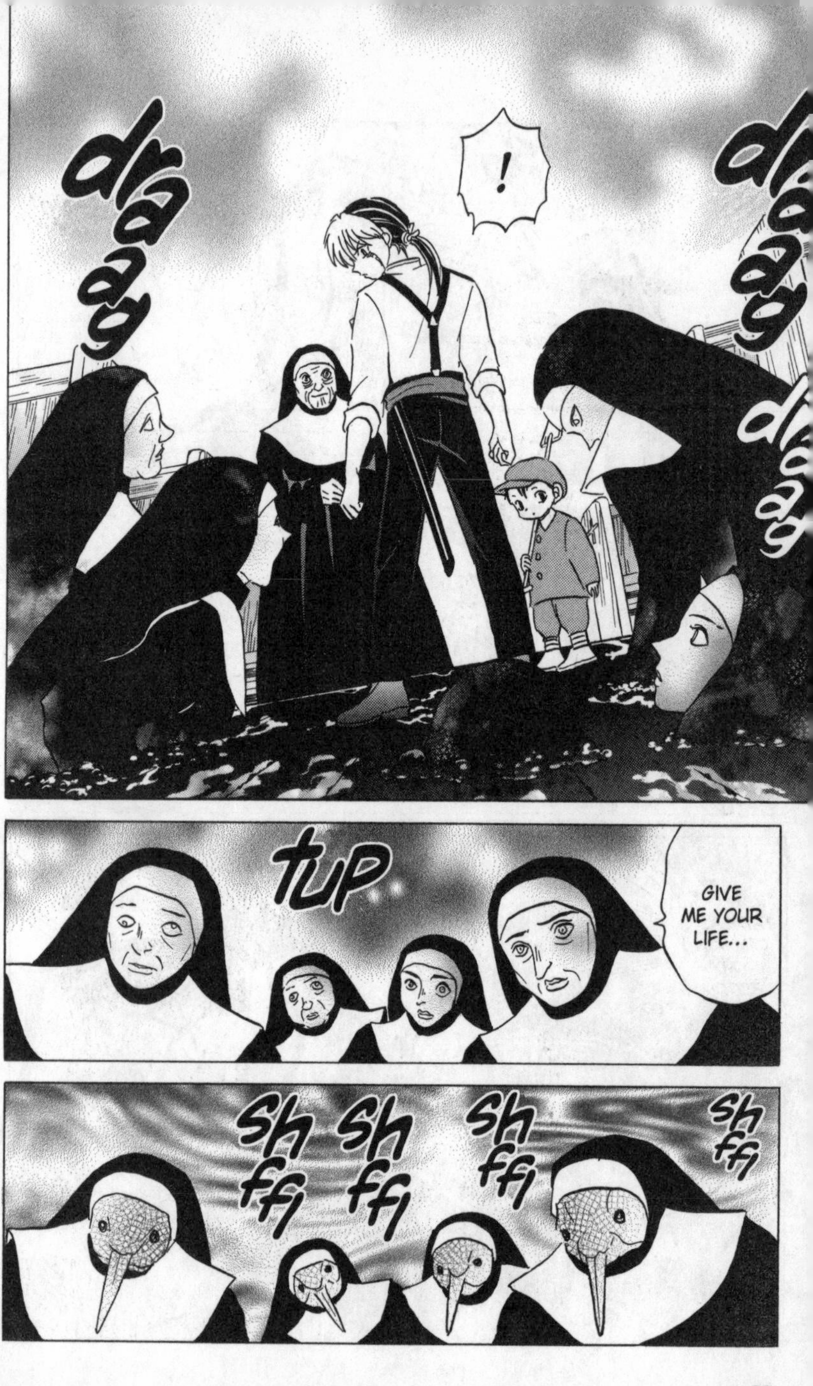
draag
draag
!
draag
GIVE ME YOUR LIFE...
tup
shffl
shffl
shffl
shffl

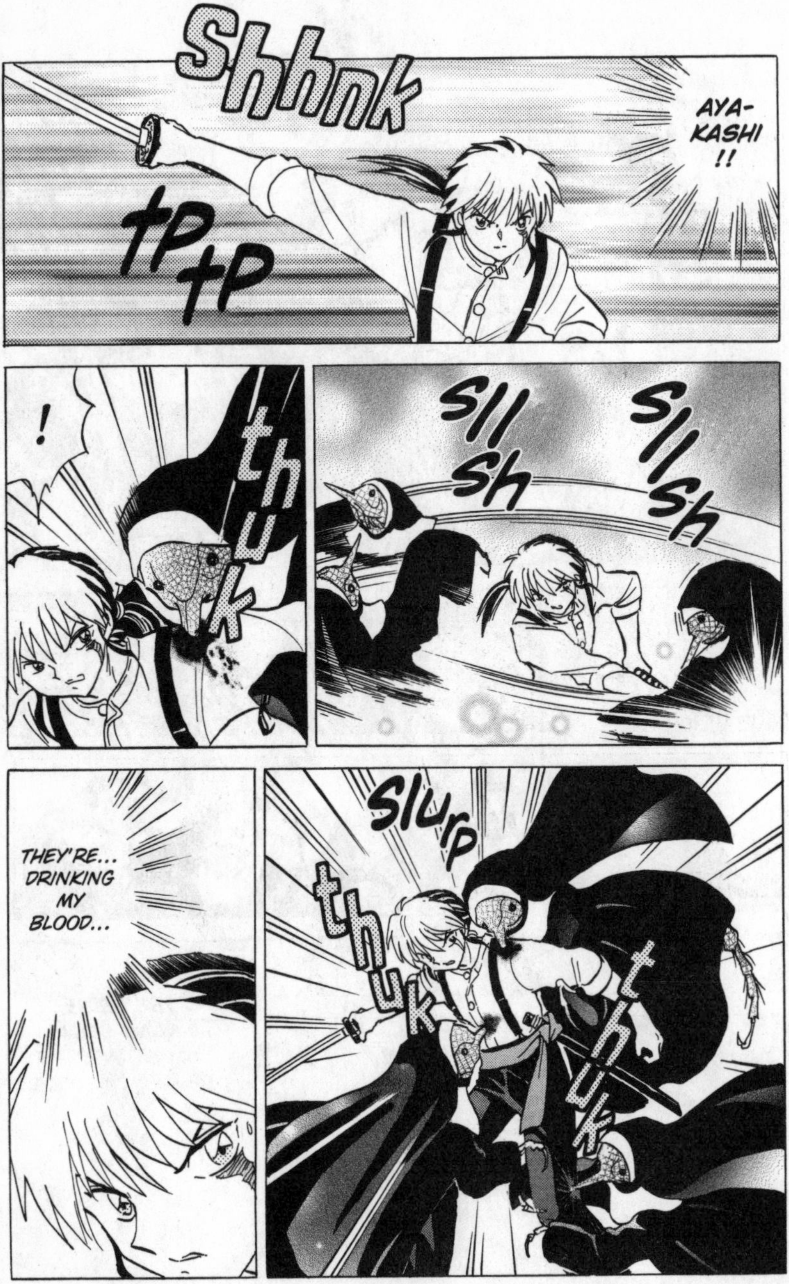
AYA-KASHI !!
Shhnk
tp tp
Sllsh
Sllsh
!
thuk
slurp
thuk
thuk
THEY'RE... DRINKING MY BLOOD...

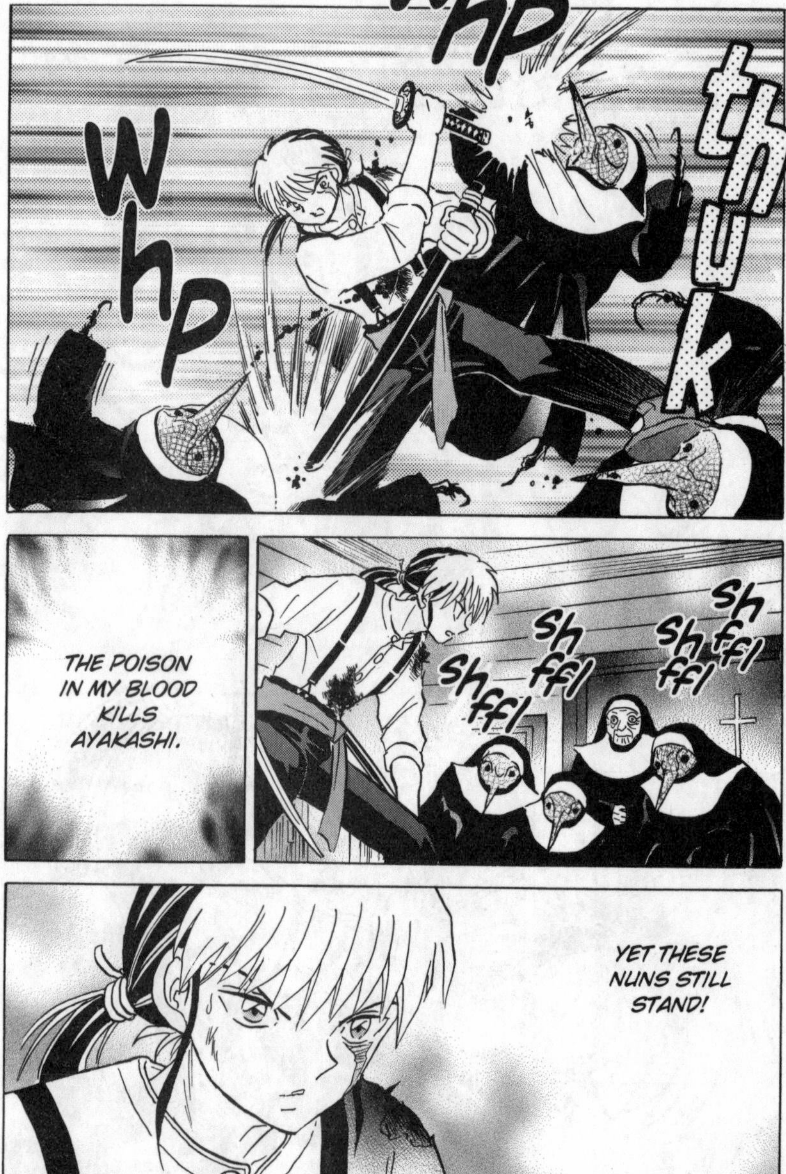
THUK
WHP
WHP
SHFFL
SHFFL
SHFFL
SHFFL
THE POISON IN MY BLOOD KILLS AYAKASHI.
YET THESE NUNS STILL STAND!

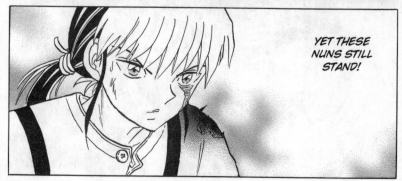

Chapter 6:
Guardian of the Barrier

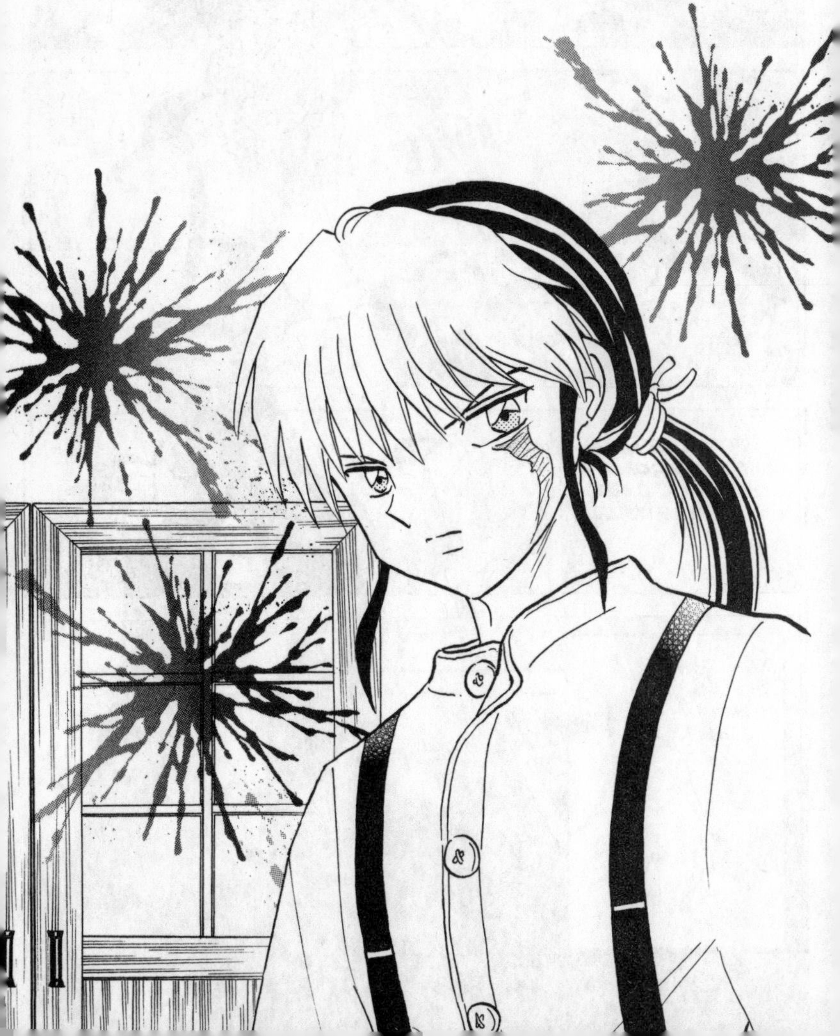

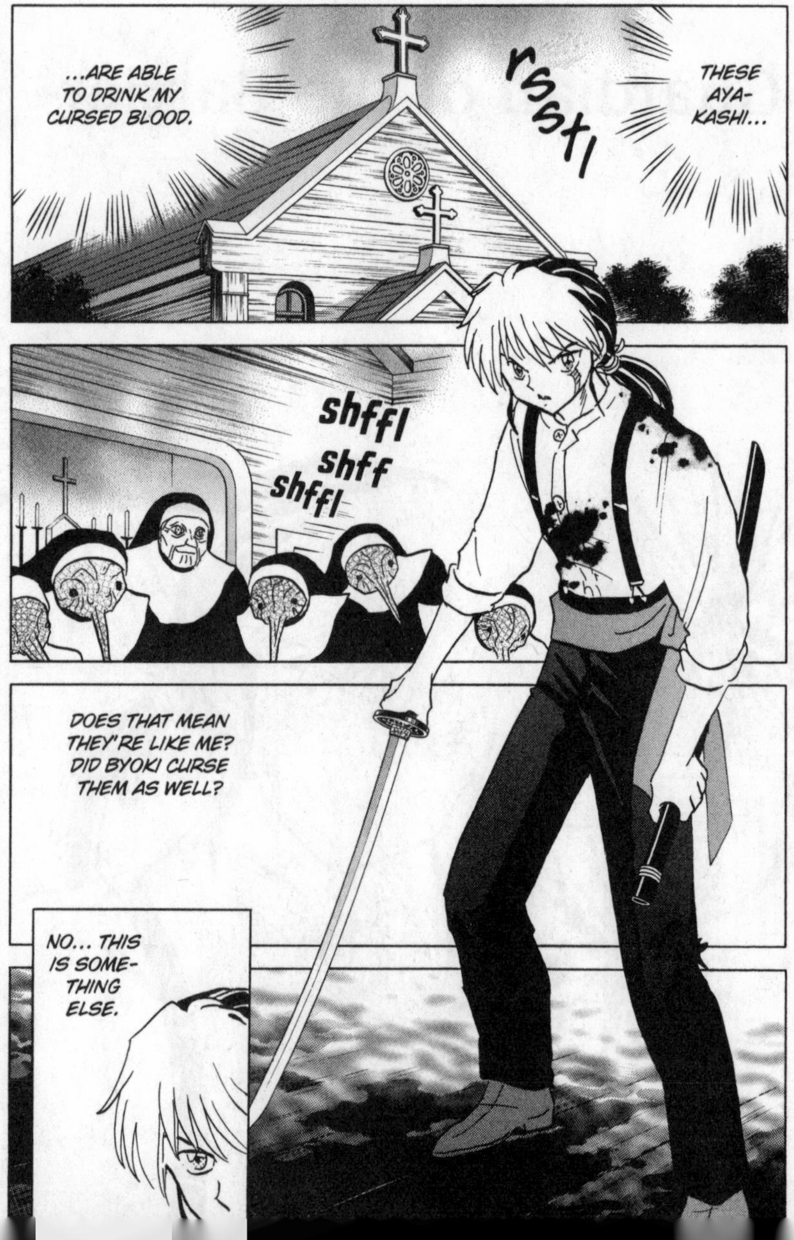
THESE AYA-KASHI...
rsstl
...ARE ABLE TO DRINK MY CURSED BLOOD.
shffl shff shffl
DOES THAT MEAN THEY'RE LIKE ME? DID BYOKI CURSE THEM AS WELL?
NO... THIS IS SOME-THING ELSE.

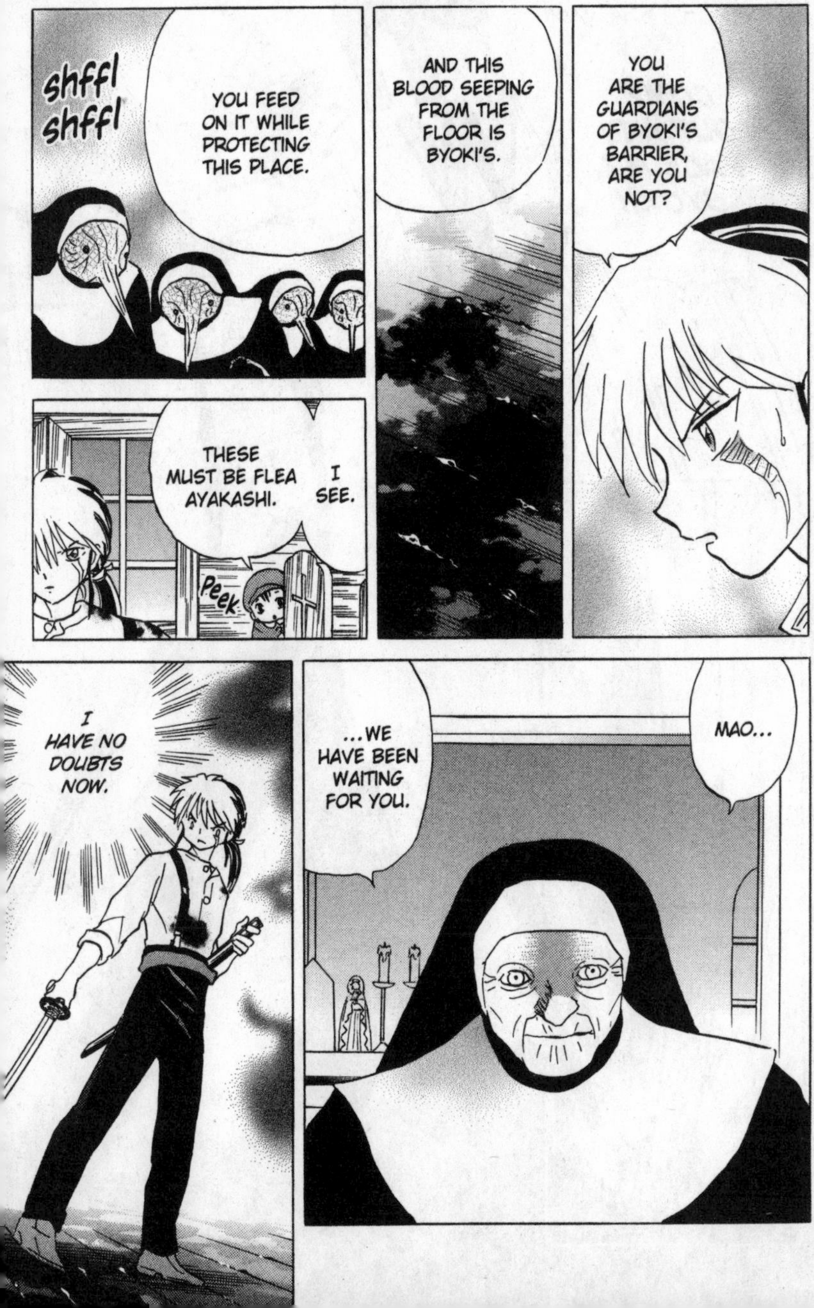
YOU ARE THE GUARDIANS OF BYOKI'S BARRIER, ARE YOU NOT?
AND THIS BLOOD SEEPING FROM THE FLOOR IS BYOKI'S.
YOU FEED ON IT WHILE PROTECTING THIS PLACE.
shffl shffl
I SEE.
THESE MUST BE FLEA AYAKASHI.
Peek
MAO...
...WE HAVE BEEN WAITING FOR YOU.
I HAVE NO DOUBTS NOW.

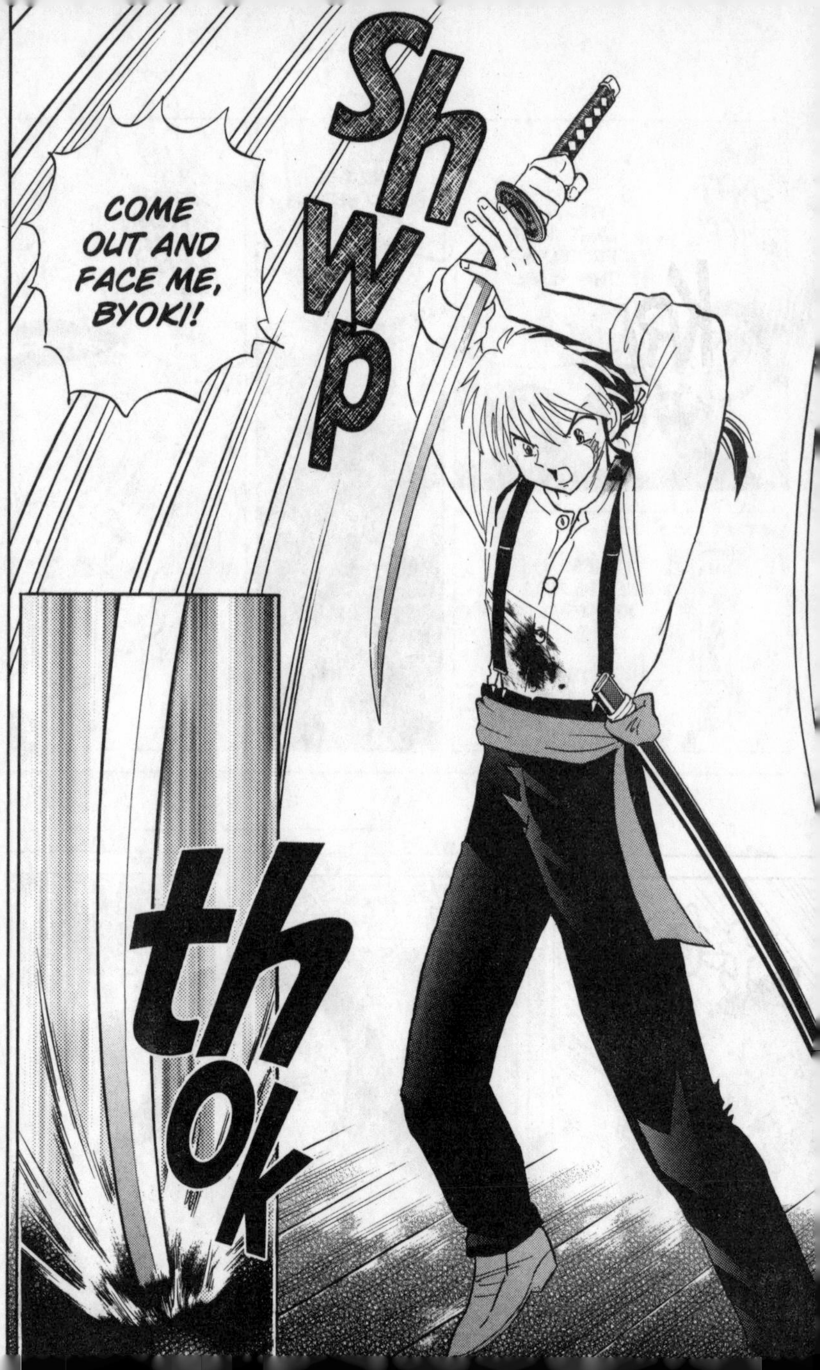
Shwp
COME OUT AND FACE ME, BYOKI!
thok

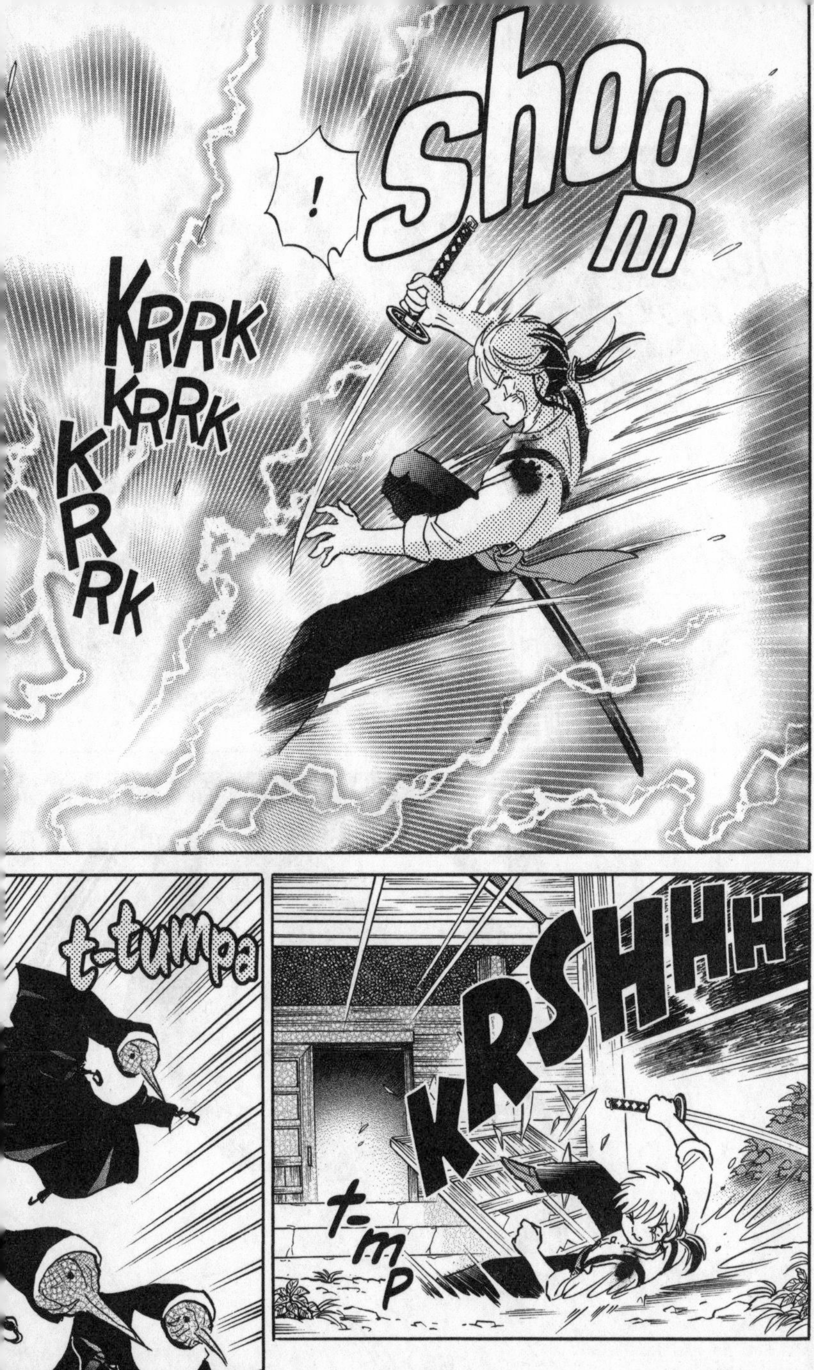

Shooom
!
KRRK KRRK KRRK
KRSHHH
t-mp
t-tumpa

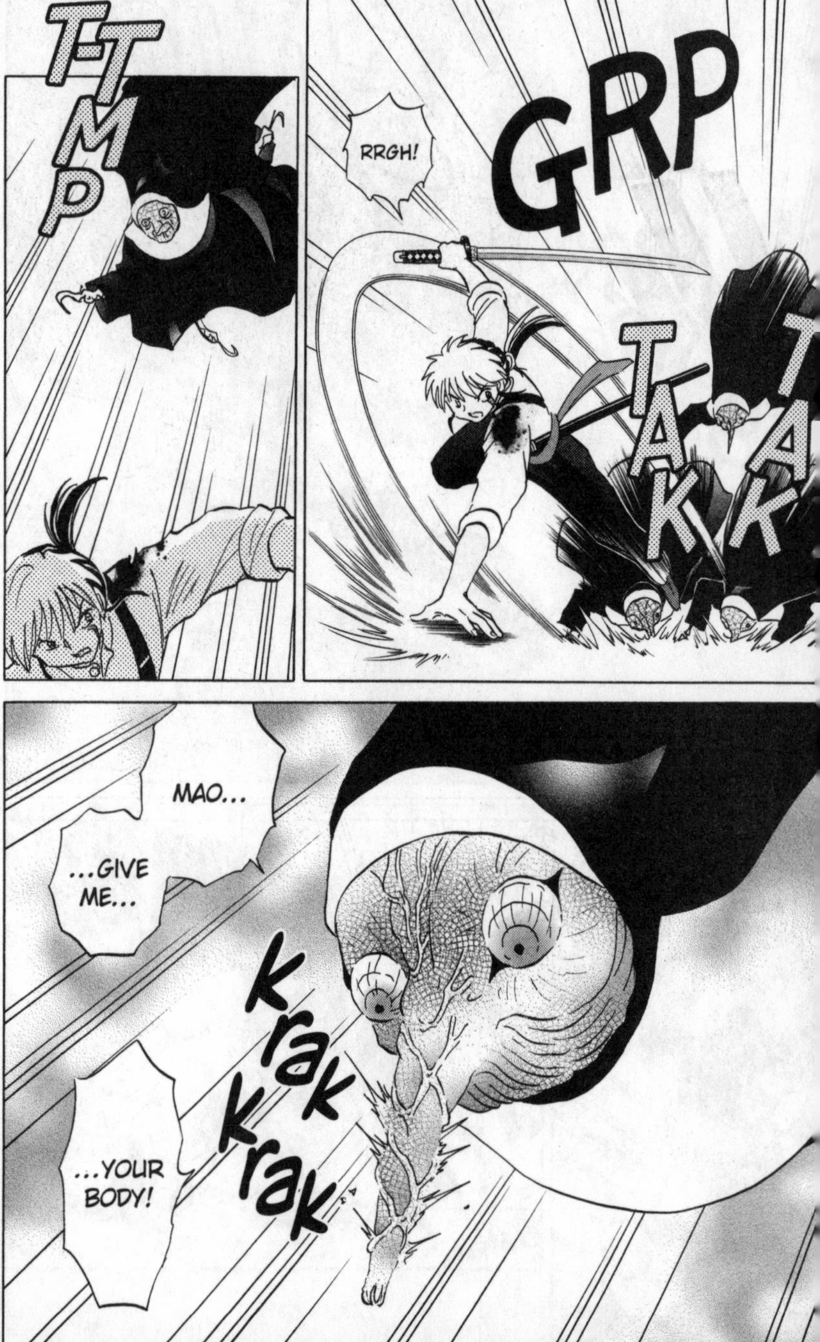
GRP
RRGH!
TAKK
TAKK
T-TMP
MAO...
...GIVE ME...
krak krak
...YOUR BODY!

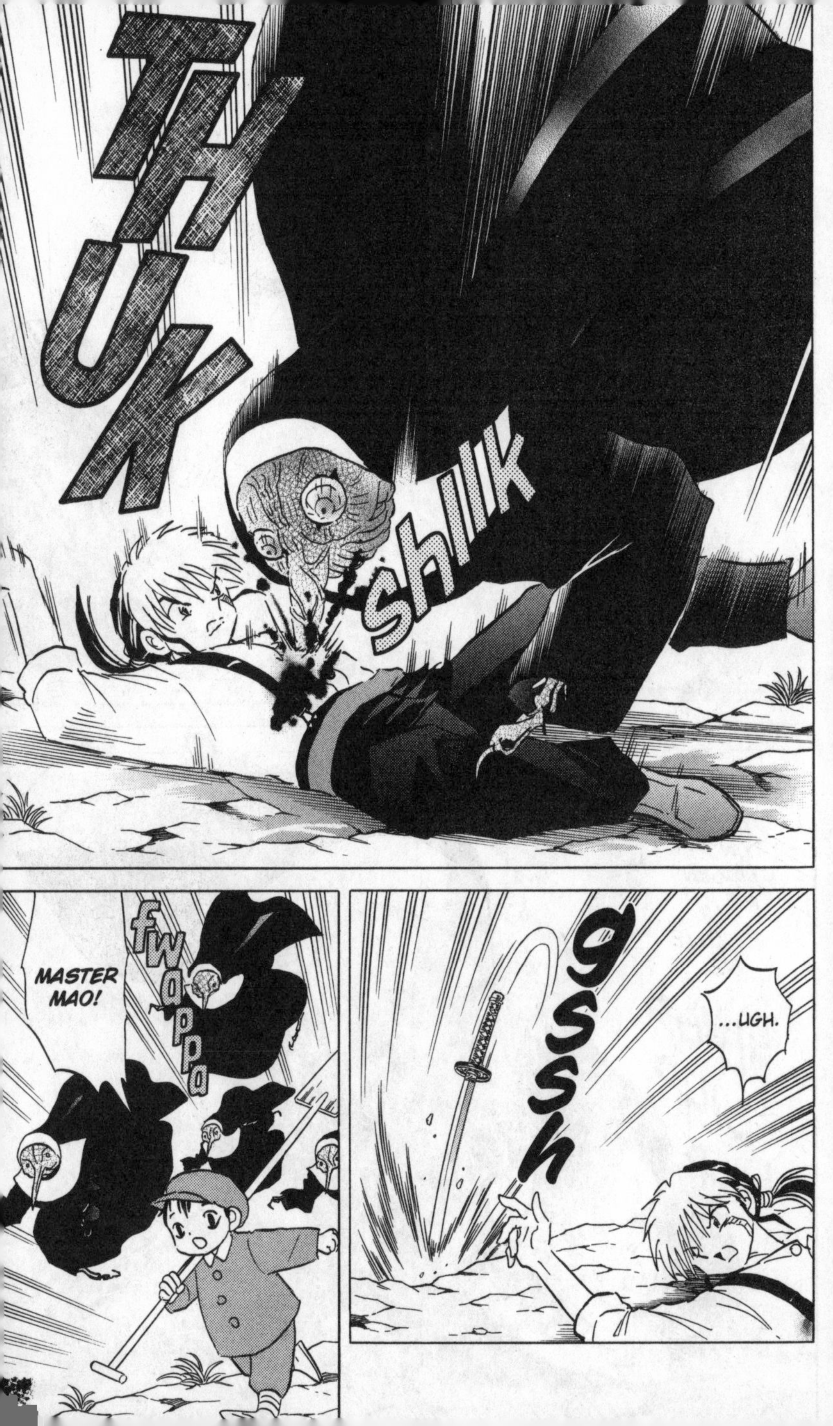
THUK
shllk
gssh
...UGH.
fwappa
MASTER MAO!

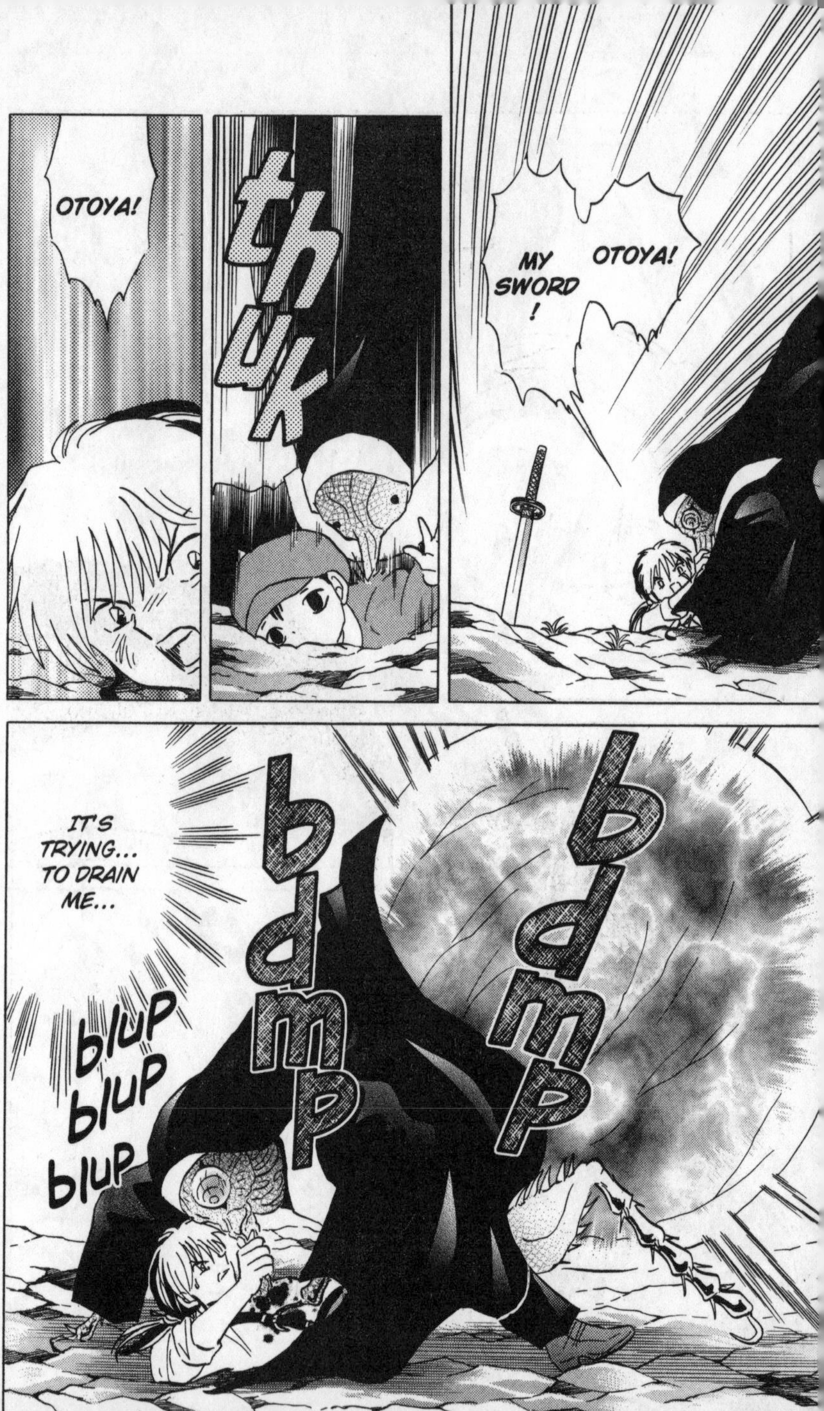
OTOYA!
MY SWORD!
thuk
OTOYA!
bdmp
bdmp
IT'S TRYING... TO DRAIN ME...
blup blup blup

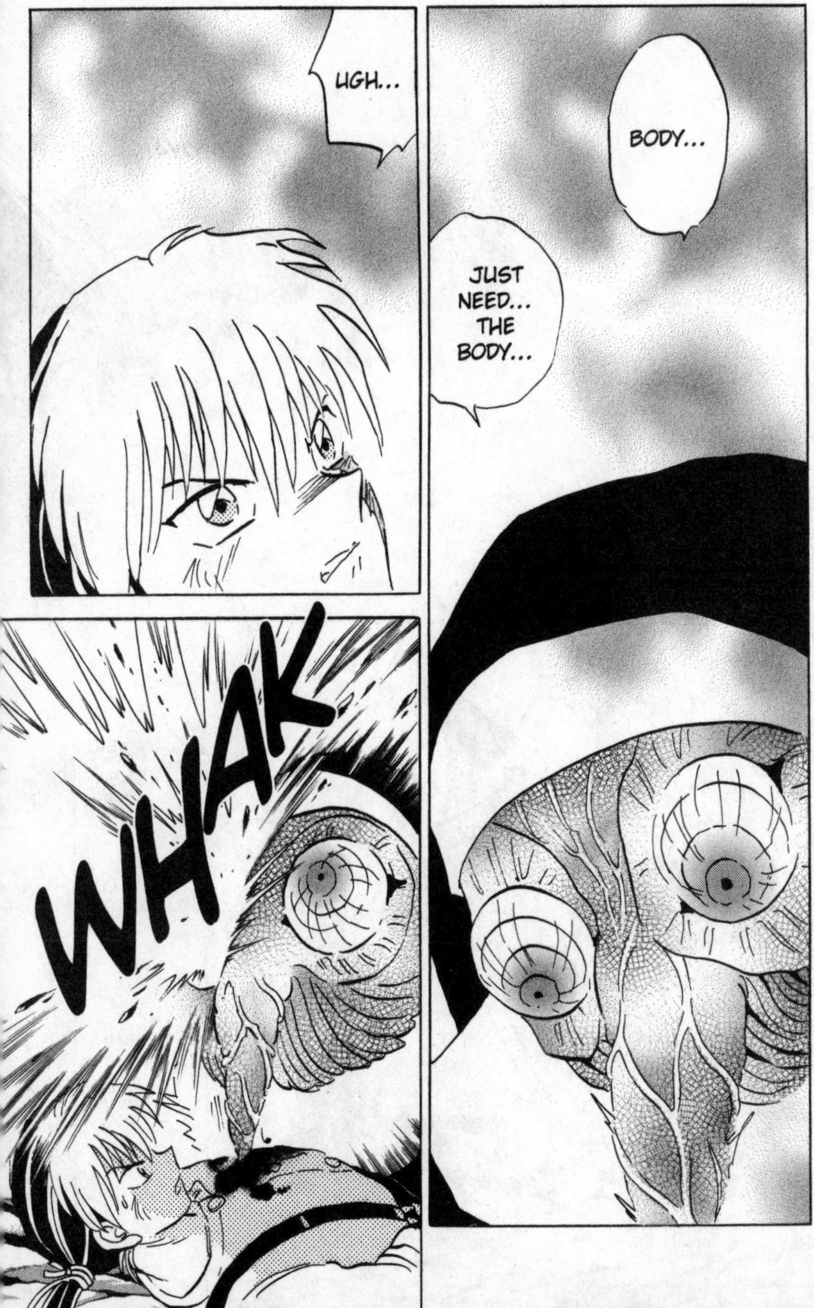
BODY...
JUST NEED... THE BODY...
UGH...
WHAK

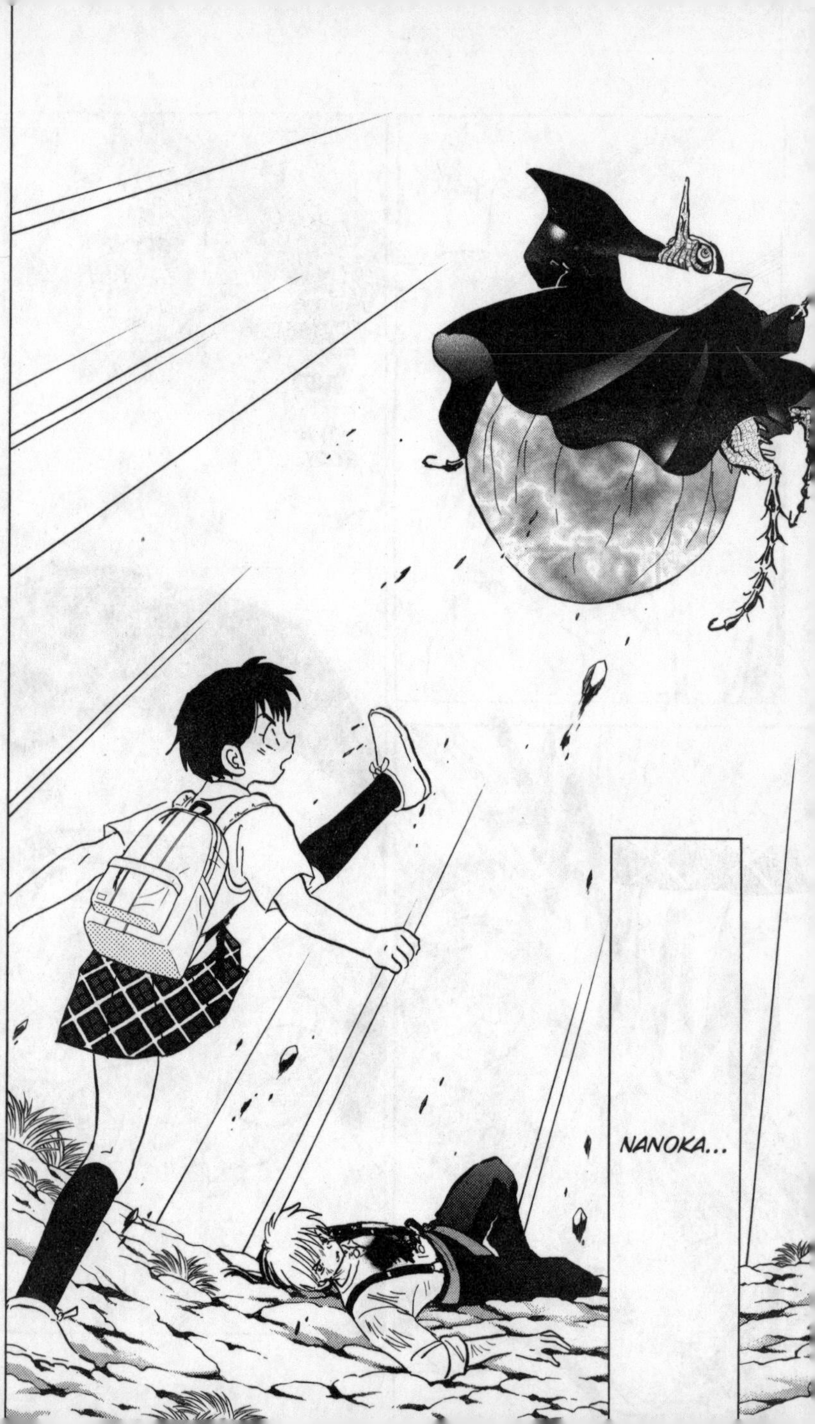
NANOKA...

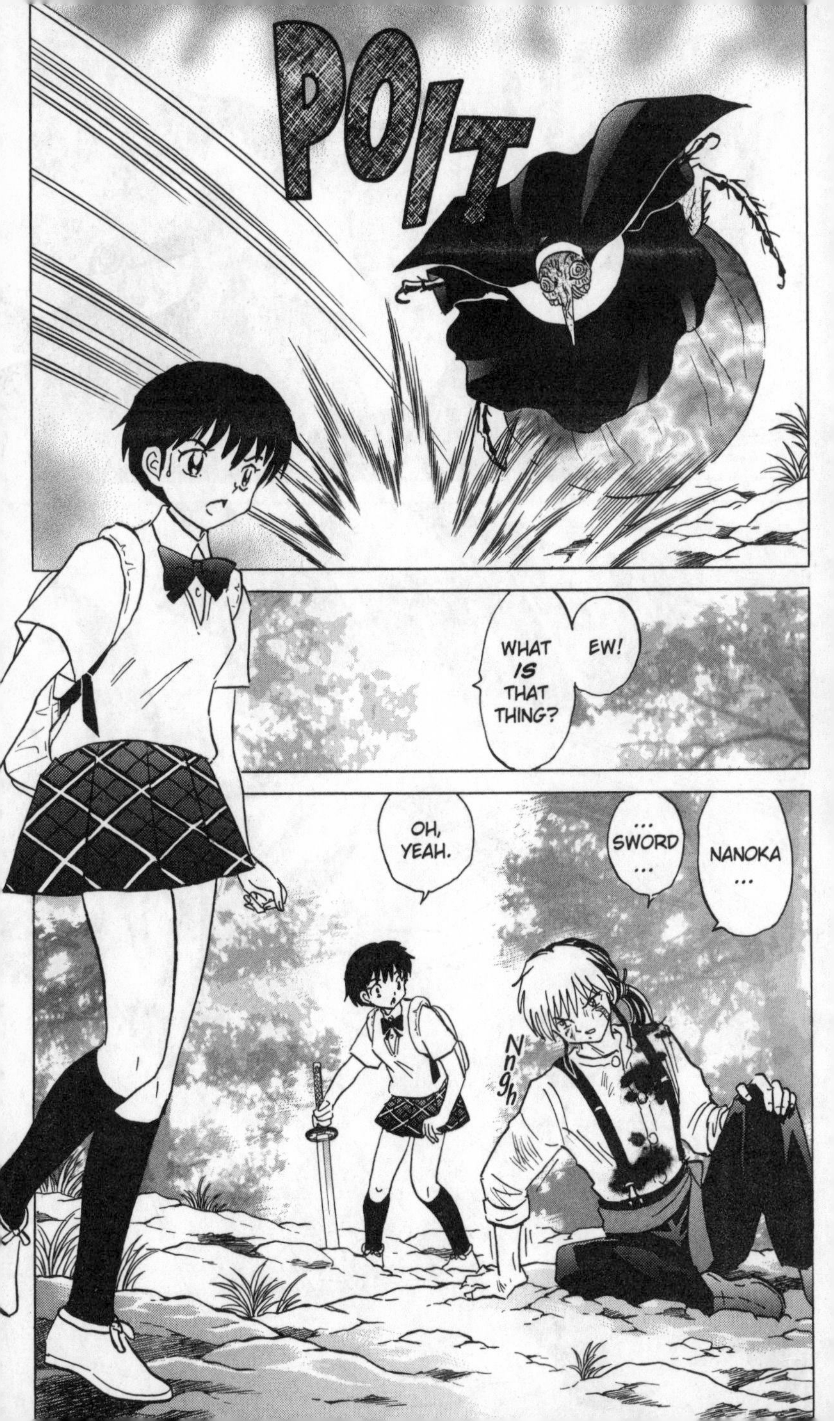
POIT
EW!
WHAT IS THAT THING?
NANOKA ...
... SWORD ...
OH, YEAH.
Nngh

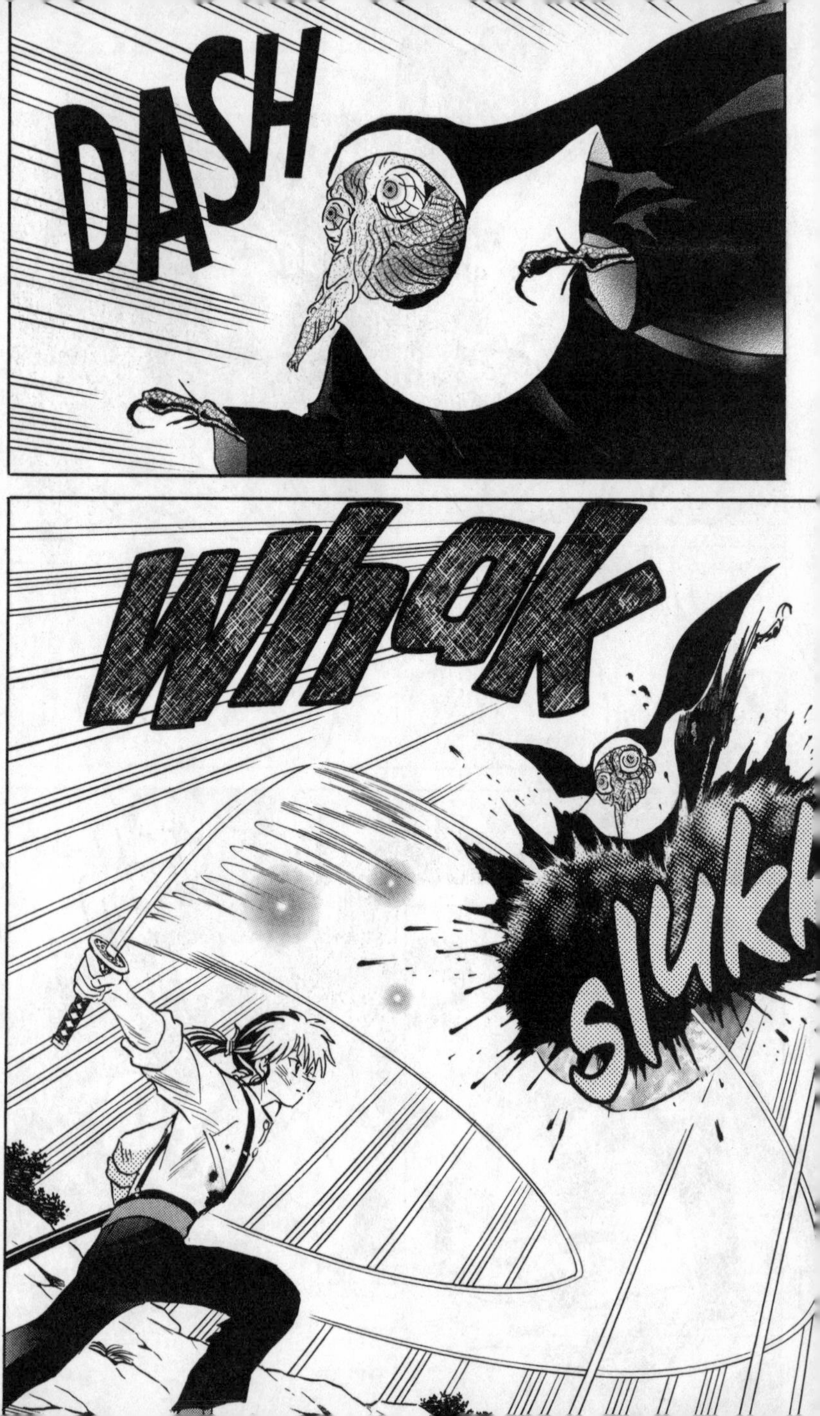
DASH
whak
sluk

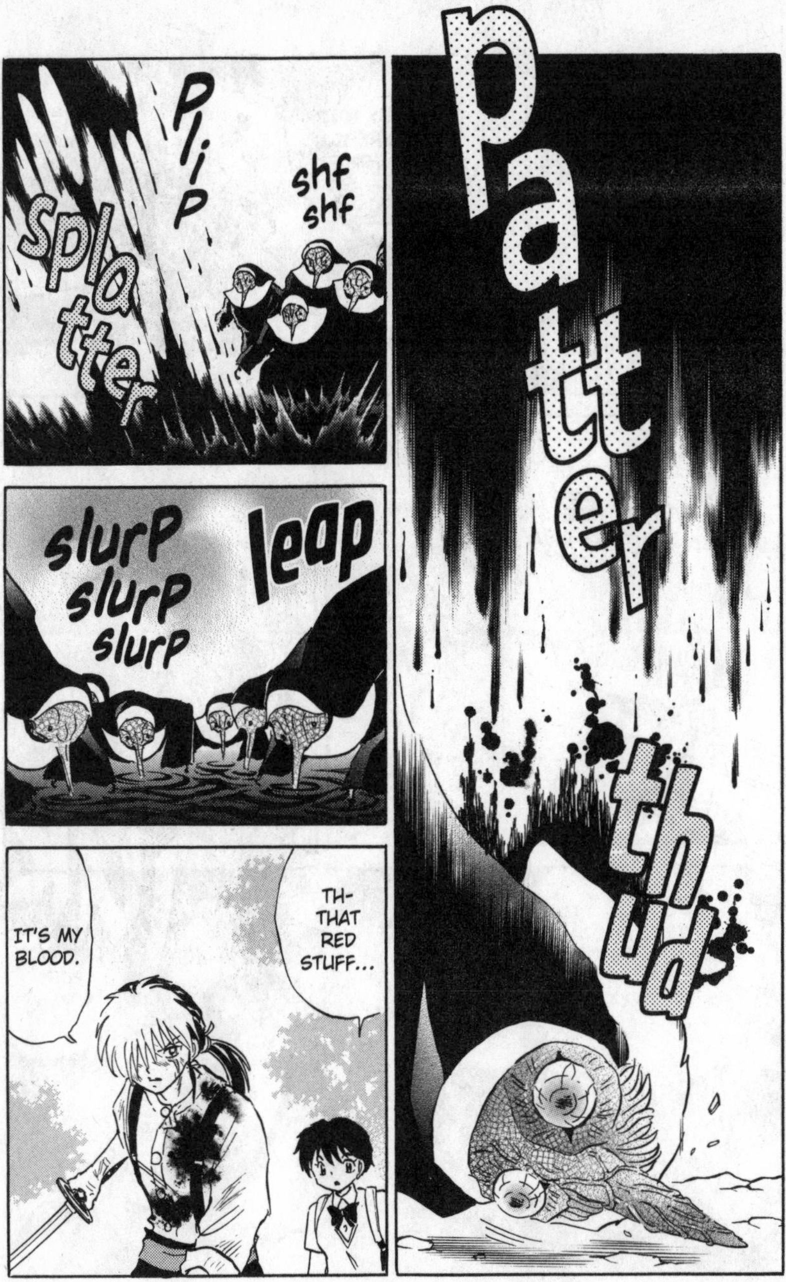
patter
thud
Plip
shf shf
splatter
leap
slurp slurp slurp
TH- THAT RED STUFF...
IT'S MY BLOOD.

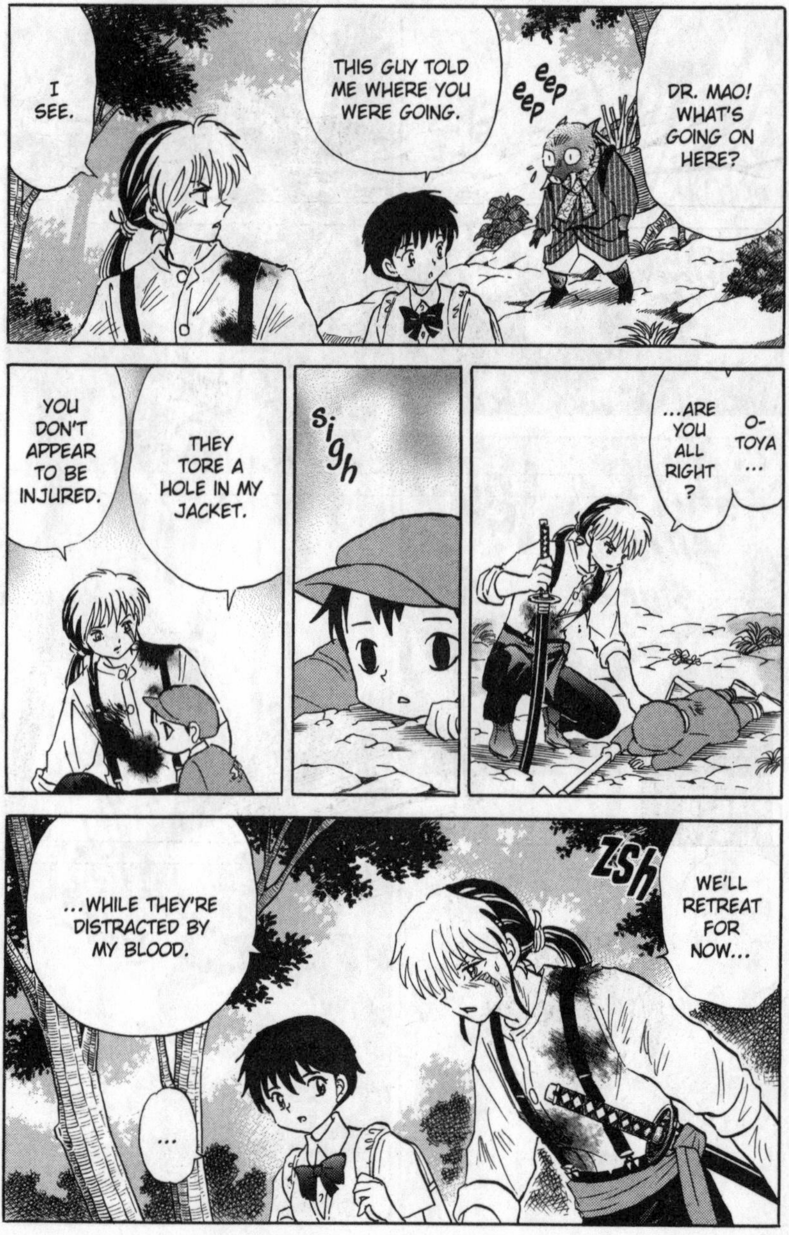
DR. MAO! WHAT'S GOING ON HERE?
eep eep
THIS GUY TOLD ME WHERE YOU WERE GOING.
I SEE.
O-TOYA...
...ARE YOU ALL RIGHT?
sigh
THEY TORE A HOLE IN MY JACKET.
YOU DON'T APPEAR TO BE INJURED.
WE'LL RETREAT FOR NOW...
zsh
...WHILE THEY'RE DISTRACTED BY MY BLOOD.
...

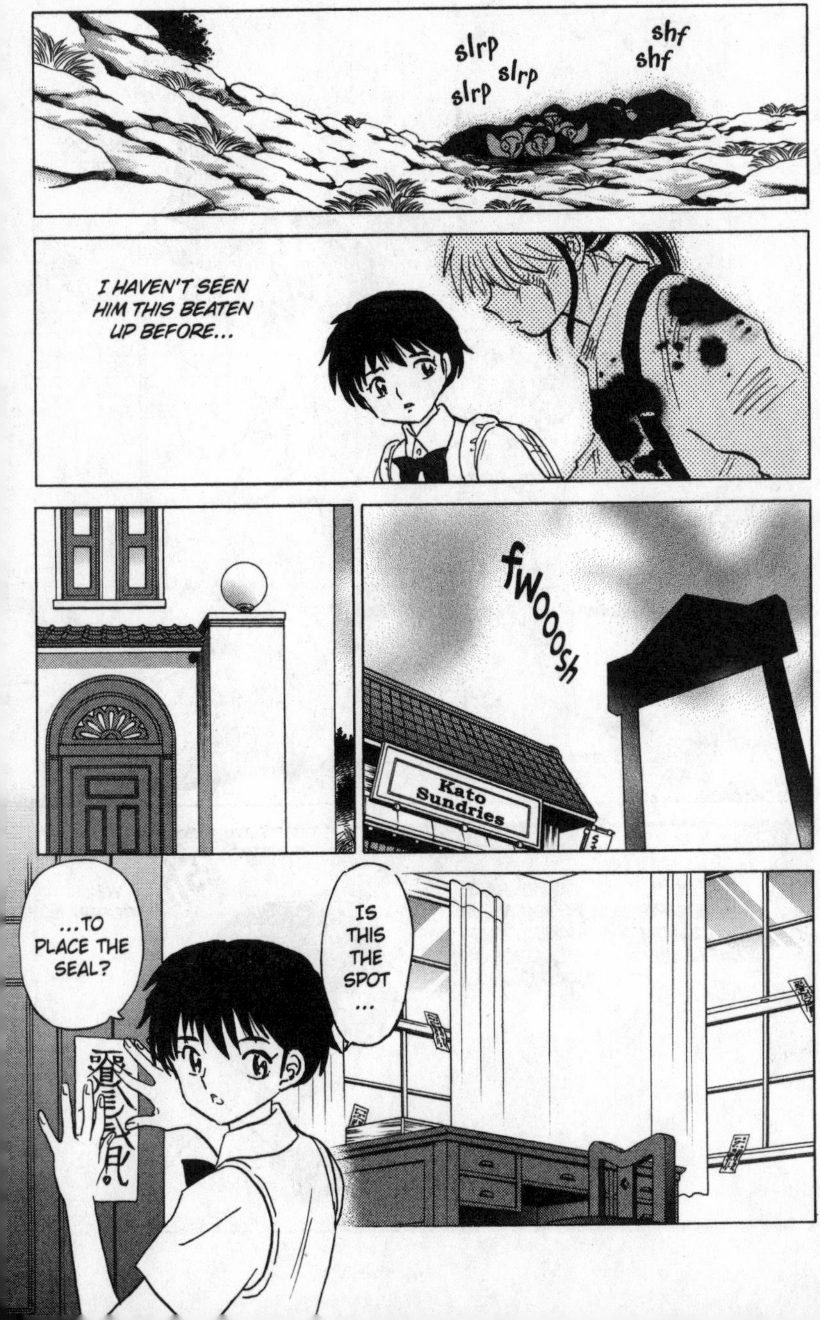
shf
shf
slrp
slrp
slrp
I HAVEN'T SEEN HIM THIS BEATEN UP BEFORE...
fwoooosh
Kato Sundries
IS THIS THE SPOT...
...TO PLACE THE SEAL?

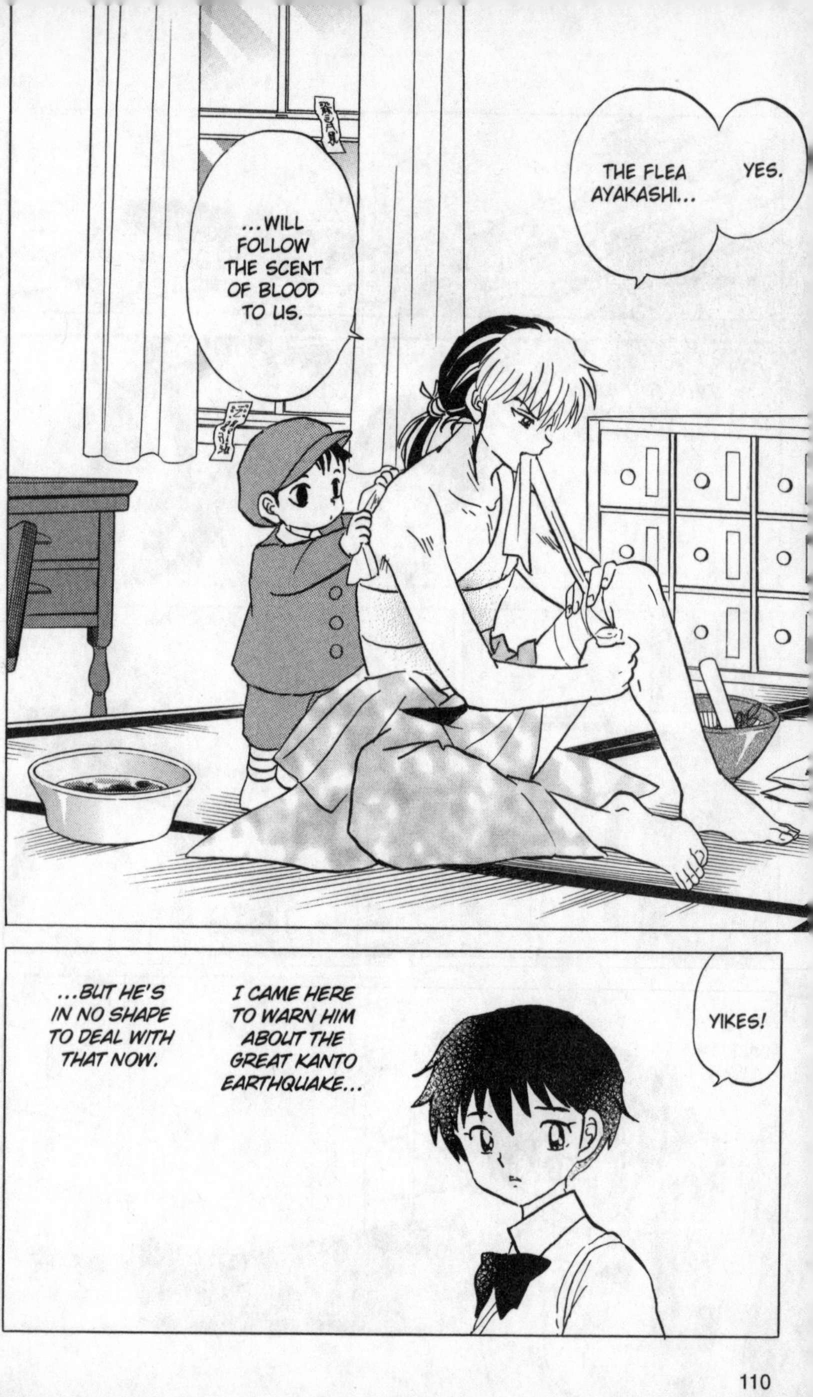
YES.
THE FLEA AYAKASHI...
...WILL FOLLOW THE SCENT OF BLOOD TO US.
YIKES!
I CAME HERE TO WARN HIM ABOUT THE GREAT KANTO EARTHQUAKE...
...BUT HE'S IN NO SHAPE TO DEAL WITH THAT NOW.

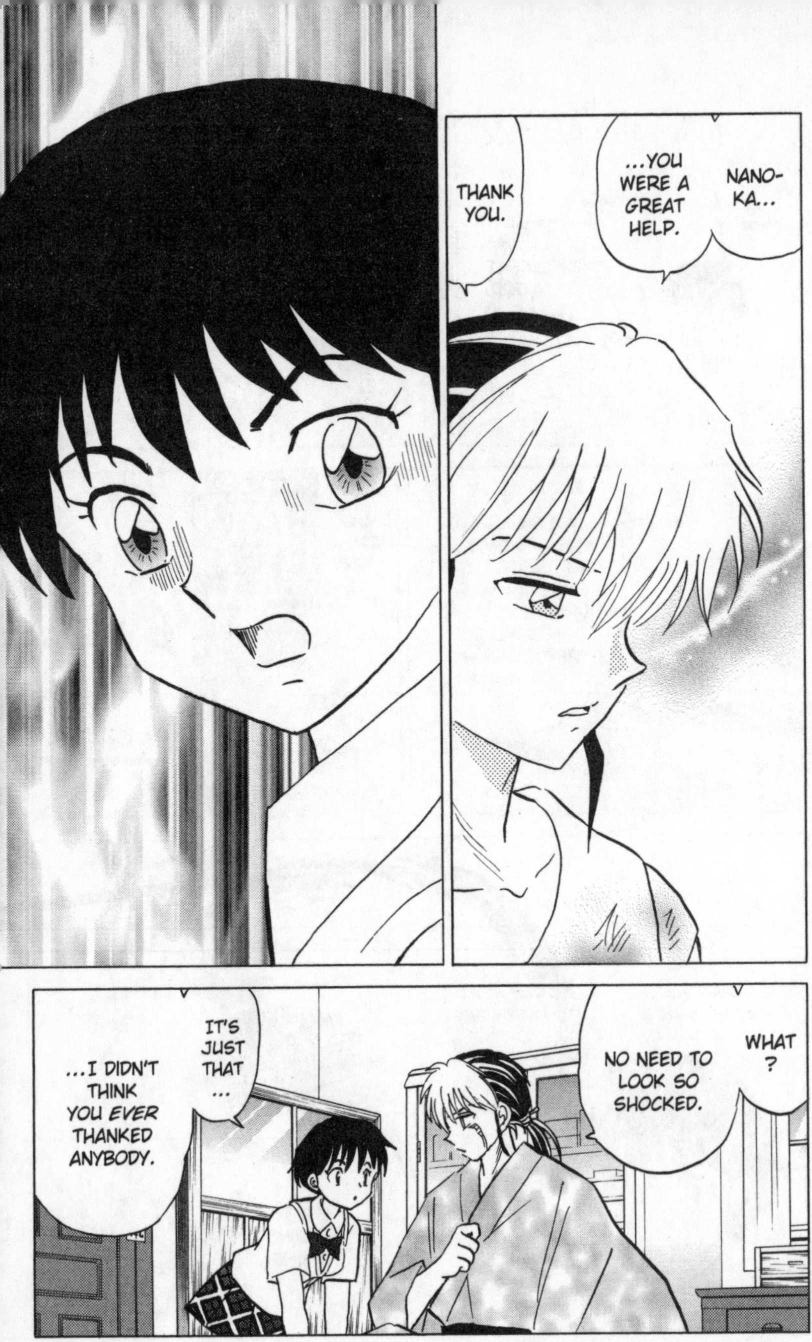
NANO-KA...
...YOU WERE A GREAT HELP.
THANK YOU.
WHAT ?
NO NEED TO LOOK SO SHOCKED.
IT'S JUST THAT ...
...I DIDN'T THINK YOU *EVER* THANKED ANYBODY.

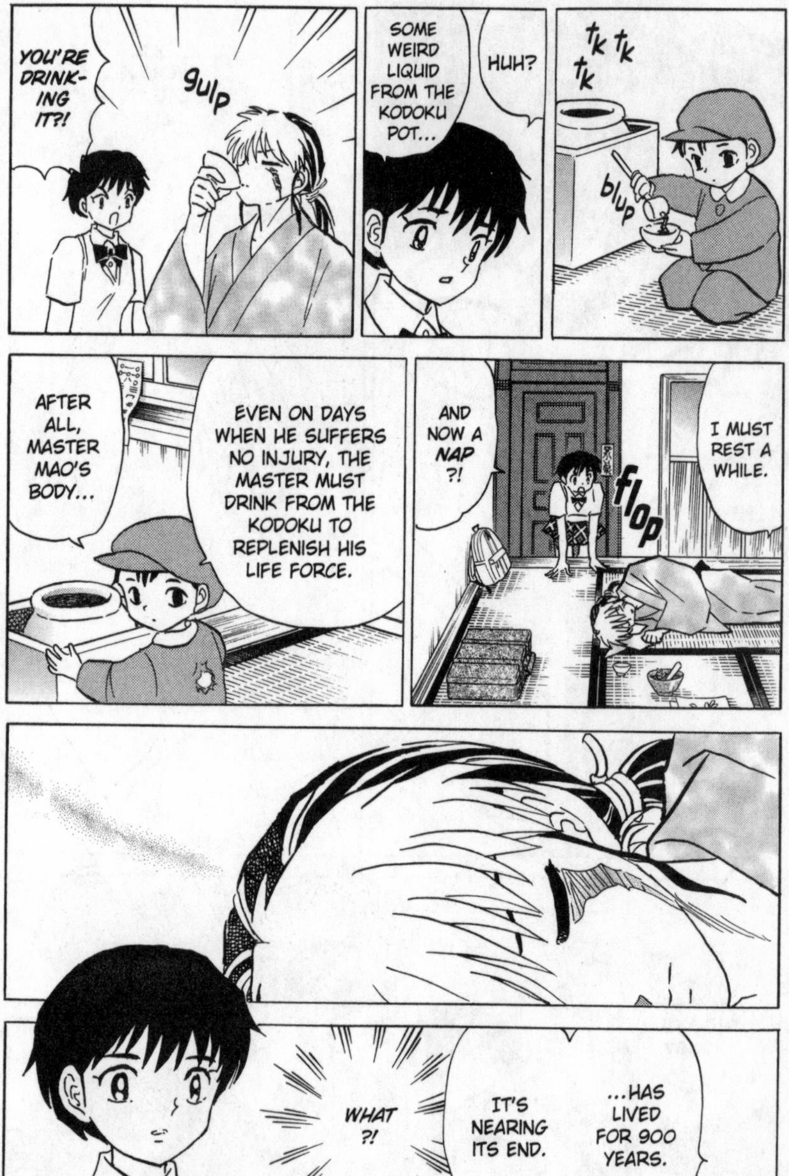
tk tk tk
blup
HUH?
SOME WEIRD LIQUID FROM THE KODOKU POT...
gulp
YOU'RE DRINKING IT?!
I MUST REST A WHILE.
flop
AND NOW A NAP ?!
EVEN ON DAYS WHEN HE SUFFERS NO INJURY, THE MASTER MUST DRINK FROM THE KODOKU TO REPLENISH HIS LIFE FORCE.
AFTER ALL, MASTER MAO'S BODY...
...HAS LIVED FOR 900 YEARS.
IT'S NEARING ITS END.
WHAT ?!

Chapter 7:
Bait

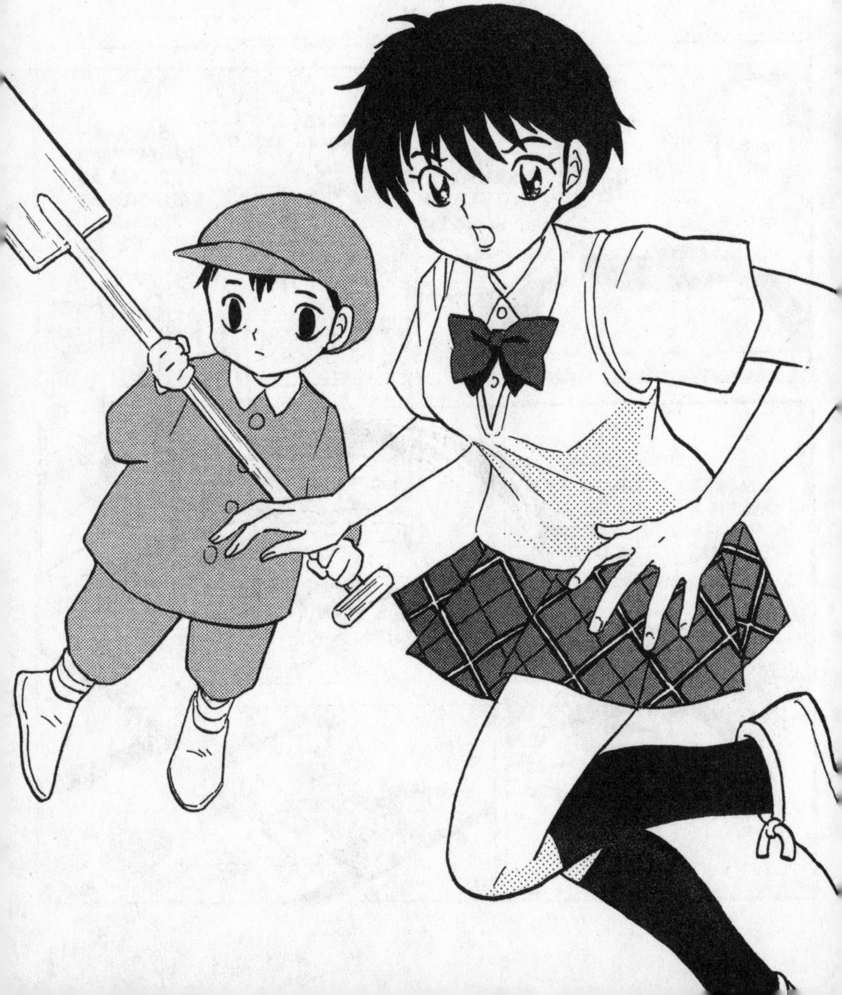

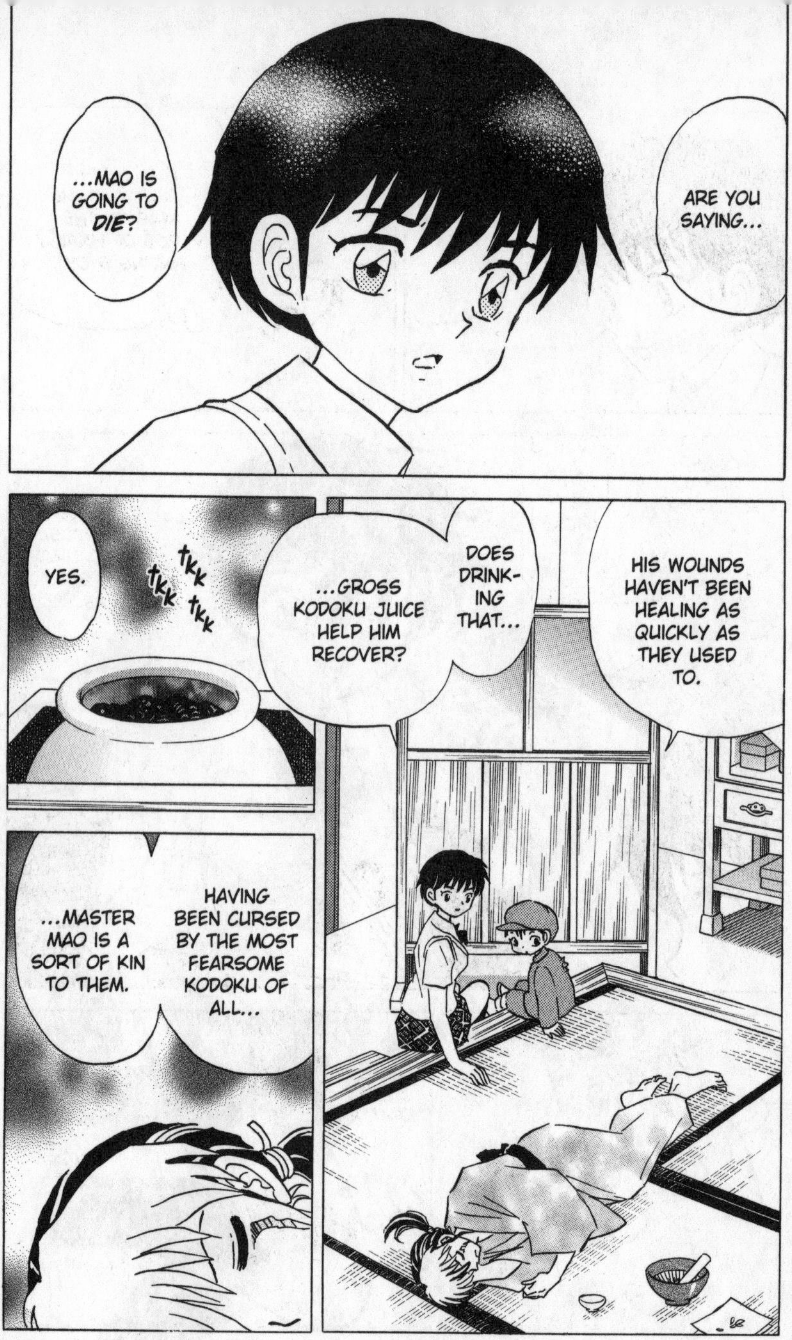
ARE YOU SAYING...
...MAO IS GOING TO DIE?
HIS WOUNDS HAVEN'T BEEN HEALING AS QUICKLY AS THEY USED TO.
DOES DRINKING THAT...
...GROSS KODOKU JUICE HELP HIM RECOVER?
YES.
tkk tkk tkk
HAVING BEEN CURSED BY THE MOST FEARSOME KODOKU OF ALL...
...MASTER MAO IS A SORT OF KIN TO THEM.

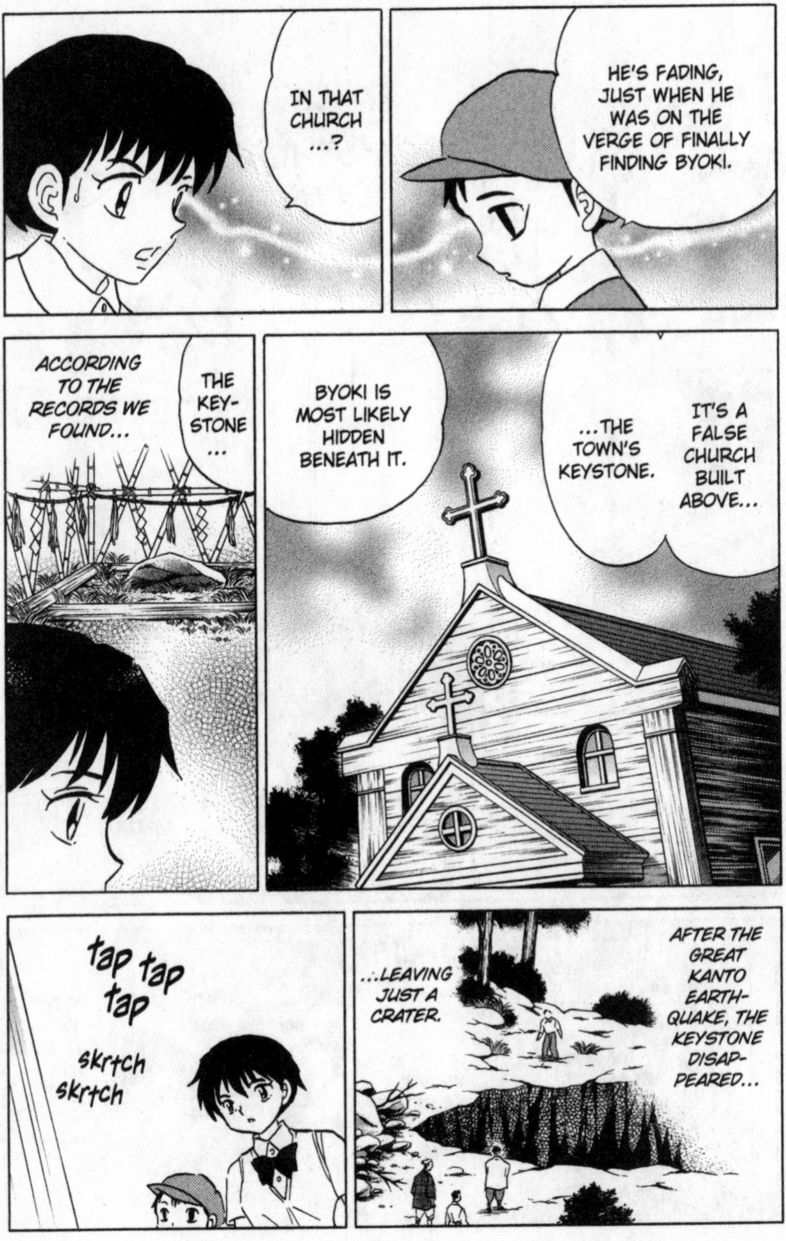
HE'S FADING, JUST WHEN HE WAS ON THE VERGE OF FINALLY FINDING BYOKI.
IN THAT CHURCH ...?
IT'S A FALSE CHURCH BUILT ABOVE...
...THE TOWN'S KEYSTONE.
BYOKI IS MOST LIKELY HIDDEN BENEATH IT.
THE KEY-STONE ...
ACCORDING TO THE RECORDS WE FOUND...
AFTER THE GREAT KANTO EARTH-QUAKE, THE KEYSTONE DISAP-PEARED...
...LEAVING JUST A CRATER.
tap tap tap
skrtch skrtch

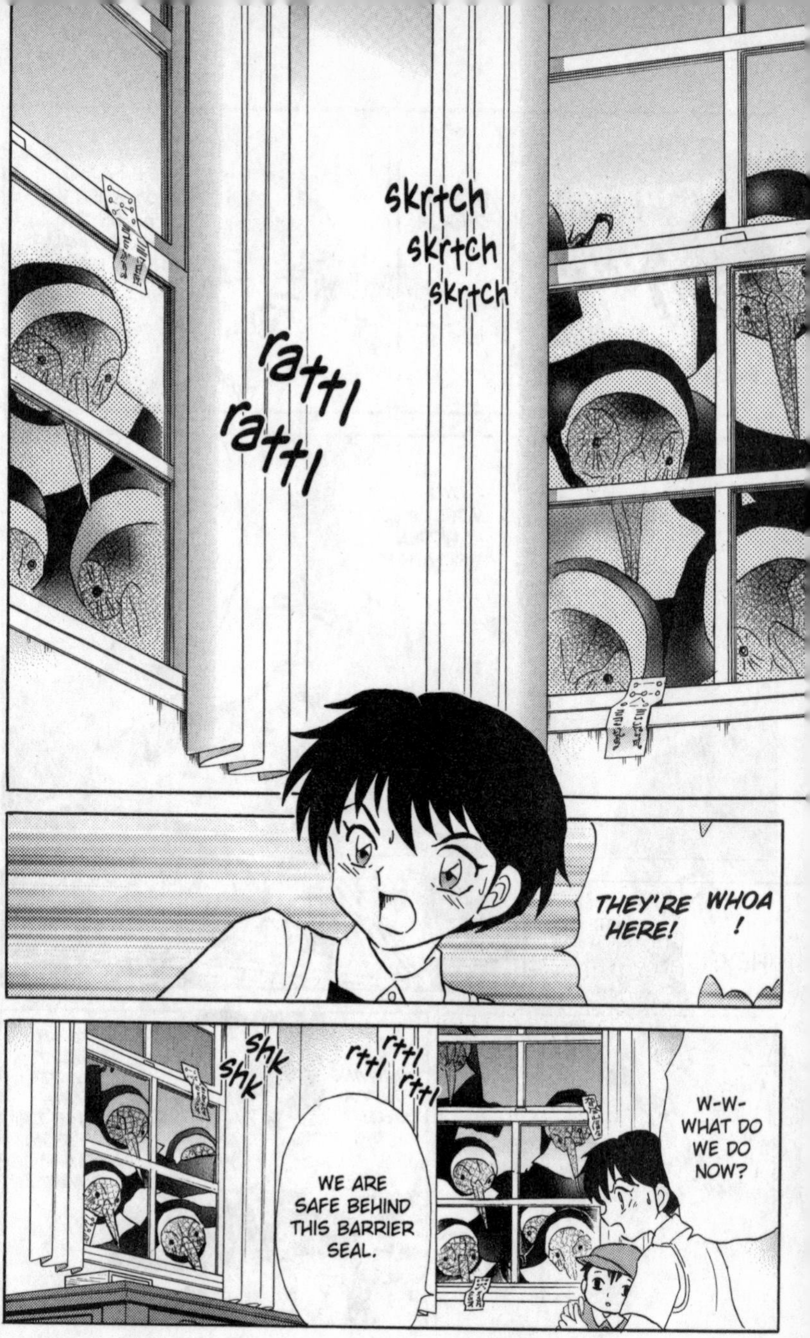
skrtch
skrtch
skrtch
rattl
rattl
WHOA!
THEY'RE HERE!
W-W-WHAT DO WE DO NOW?
rttl
rttl
rttl
shk
shk
WE ARE SAFE BEHIND THIS BARRIER SEAL.

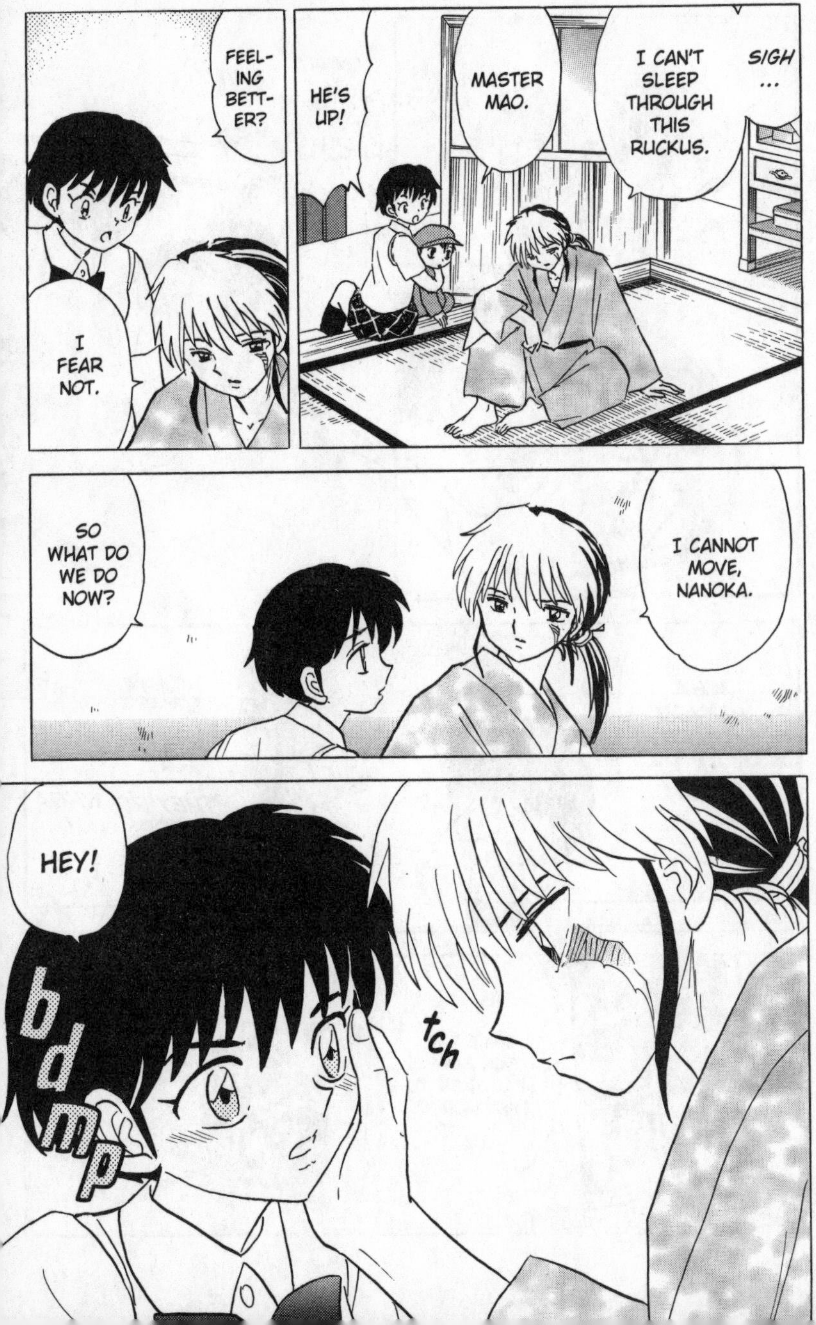
SIGH ...
I CAN'T SLEEP THROUGH THIS RUCKUS.
MASTER MAO.
HE'S UP!
FEEL-ING BETT-ER?
I FEAR NOT.
I CANNOT MOVE, NANOKA.
SO WHAT DO WE DO NOW?
HEY!
tch
bdmp

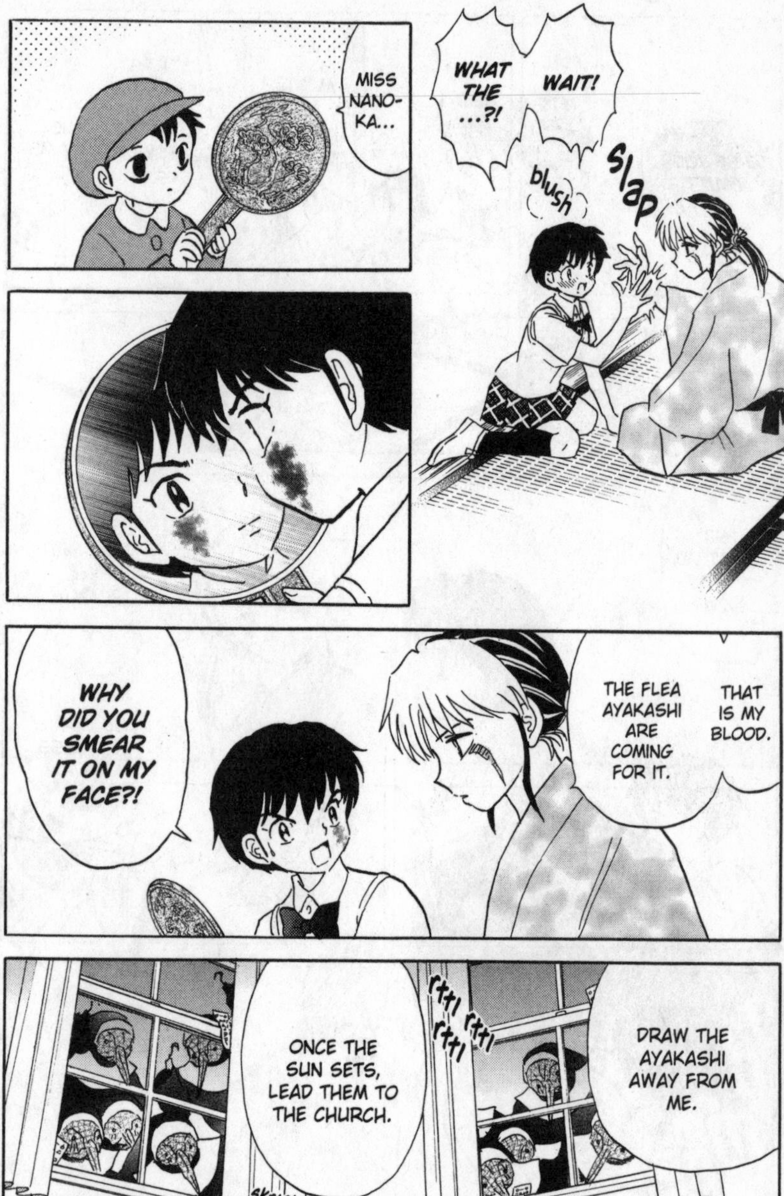
WAIT!
WHAT THE ...?!
slap
blush
MISS NANO-KA...
THAT IS MY BLOOD.
THE FLEA AYAKASHI ARE COMING FOR IT.
WHY DID YOU SMEAR IT ON MY FACE?!
DRAW THE AYAKASHI AWAY FROM ME.
rttl rttl rttl
ONCE THE SUN SETS, LEAD THEM TO THE CHURCH.
skrtch skrtch

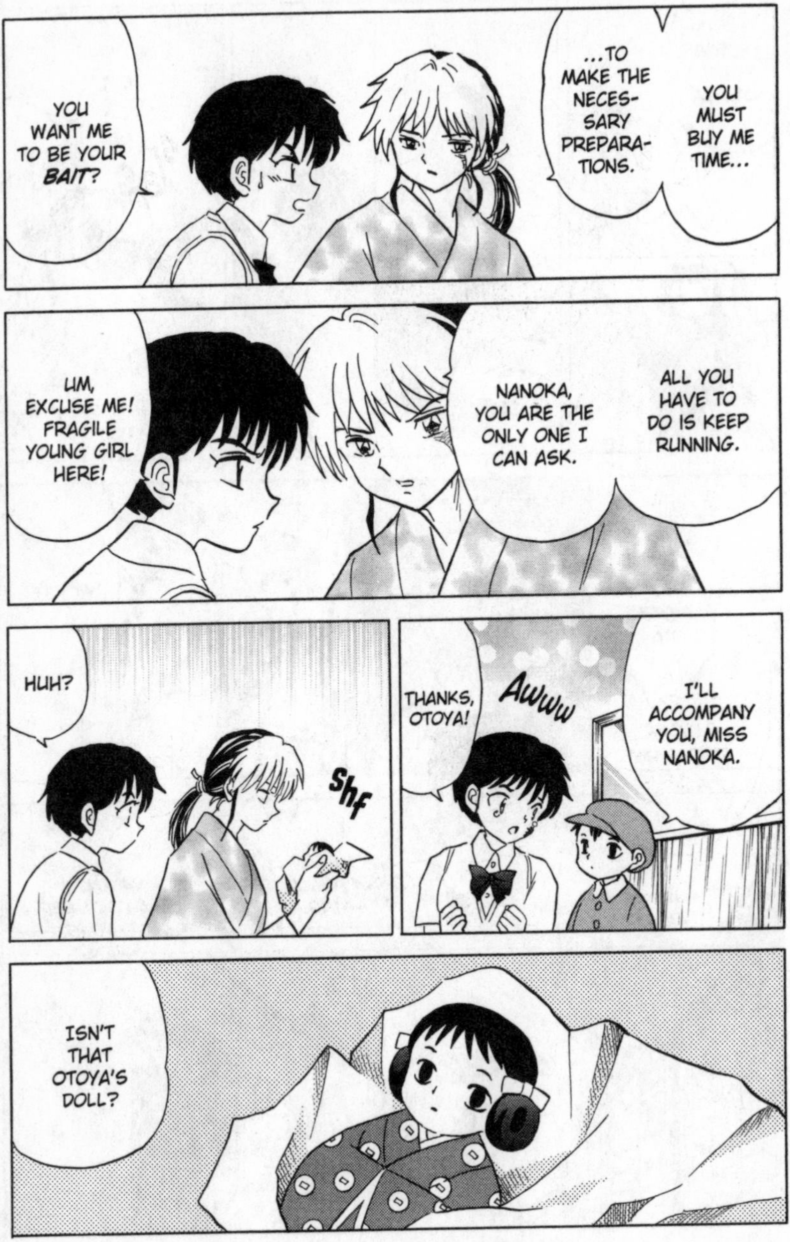
YOU MUST BUY ME TIME...
...TO MAKE THE NECES-SARY PREPARA-TIONS.
YOU WANT ME TO BE YOUR *BAIT*?
ALL YOU HAVE TO DO IS KEEP RUNNING.
NANOKA, YOU ARE THE ONLY ONE I CAN ASK.
UM, EXCUSE ME! FRAGILE YOUNG GIRL HERE!
I'LL ACCOMPANY YOU, MISS NANOKA.
Awww
THANKS, OTOYA!
Shf
HUH?
ISN'T THAT OTOYA'S DOLL?

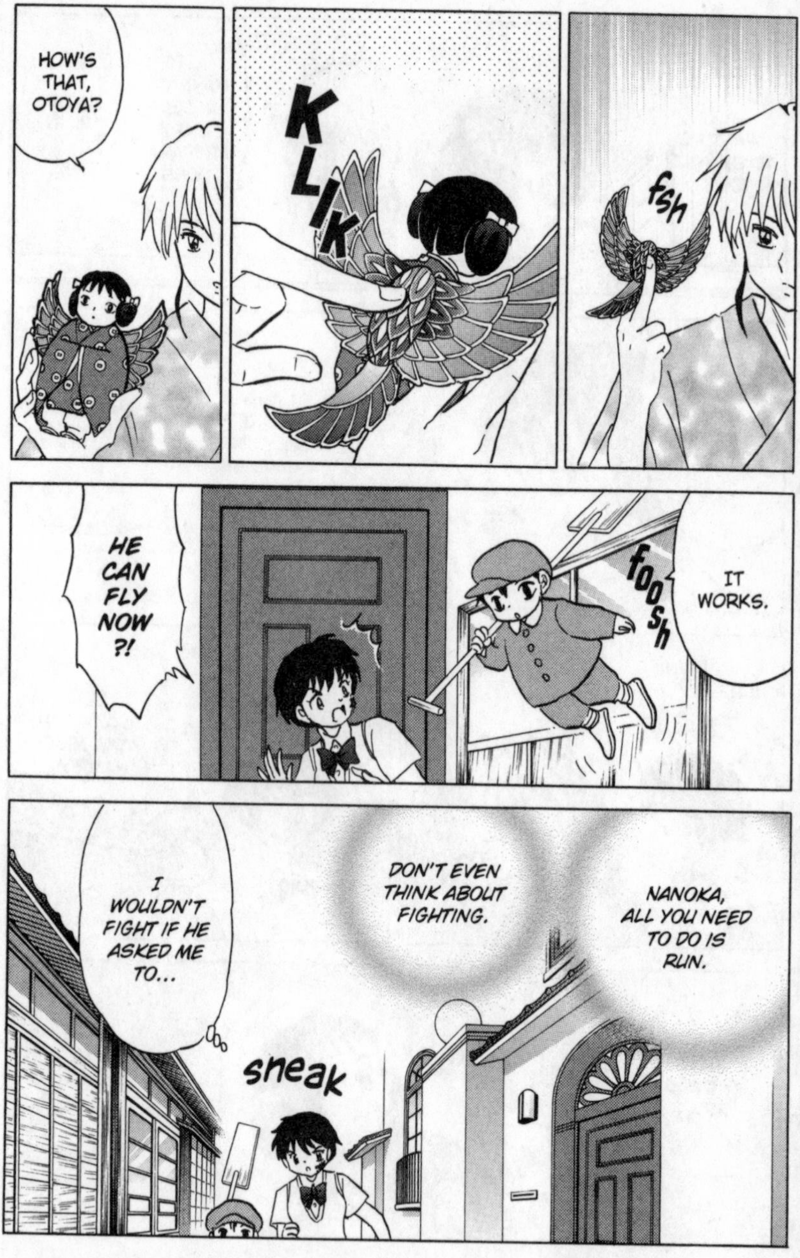
fsh
KLIK
HOW'S THAT, OTOYA?
IT WORKS.
foosh
HE CAN FLY NOW?!
NANOKA, ALL YOU NEED TO DO IS RUN.
DON'T EVEN THINK ABOUT FIGHTING.
I WOULDN'T FIGHT IF HE ASKED ME TO...
sneak

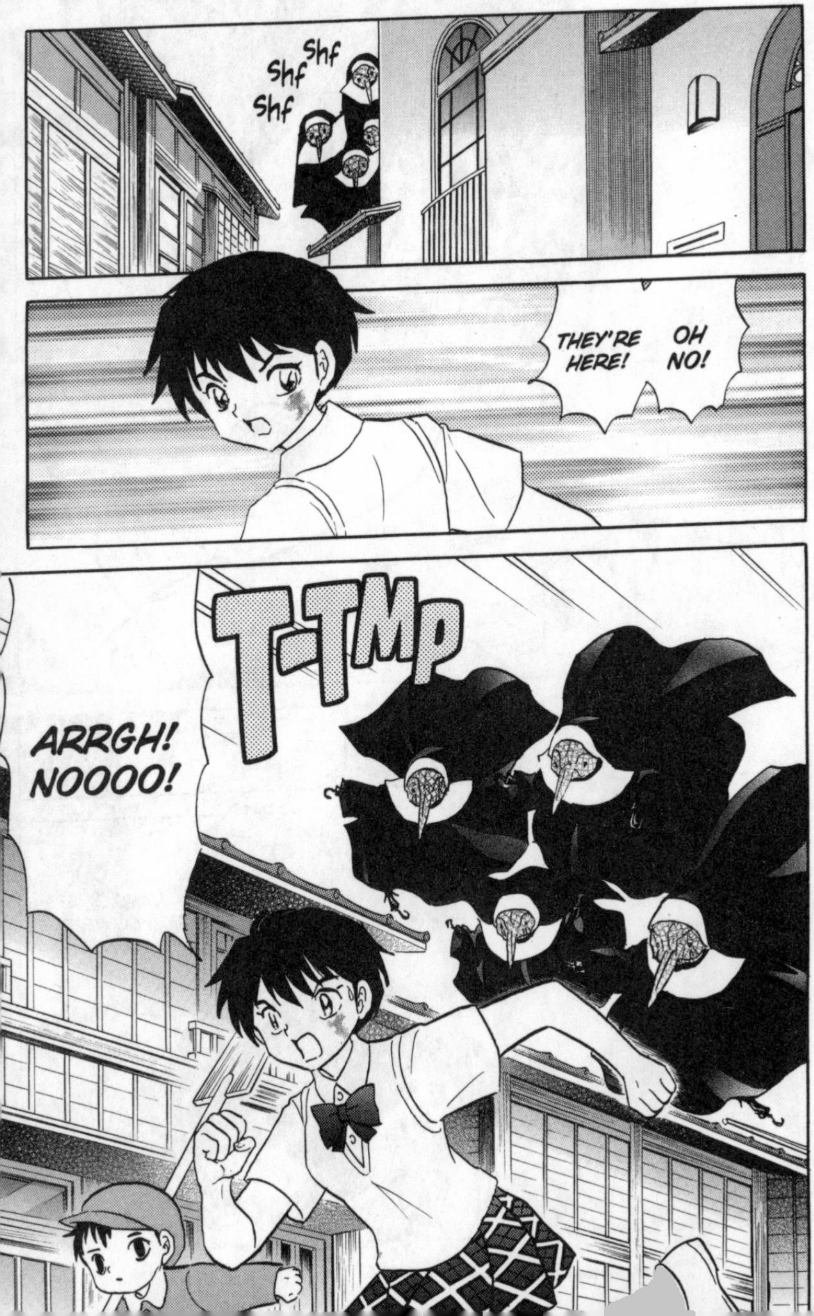
Shf Shf Shf
OH NO!
THEY'RE HERE!
T-TMP
ARRGH! NOOOO!

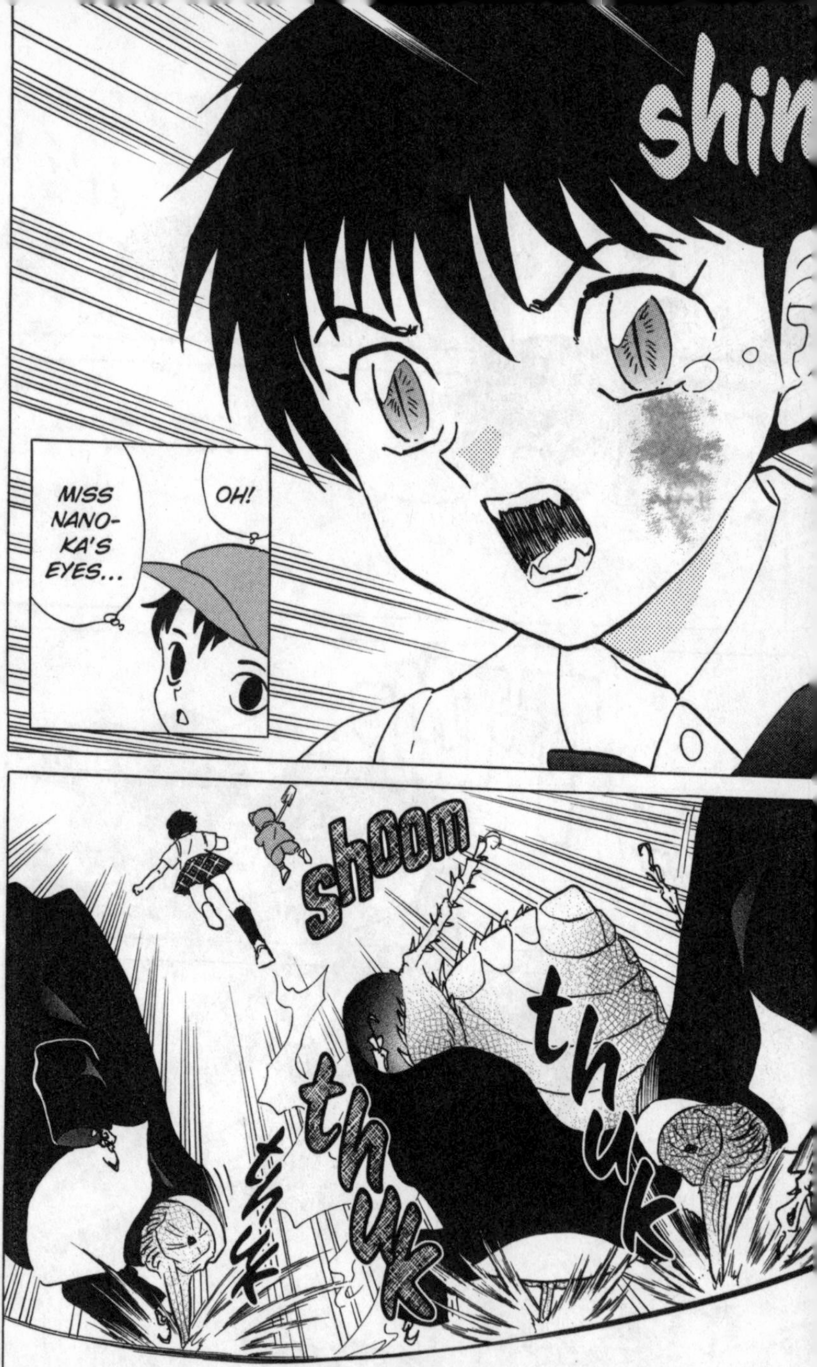
shin
OH!
MISS NANO-KA'S EYES...
shoom
thuk
thuk
thuk

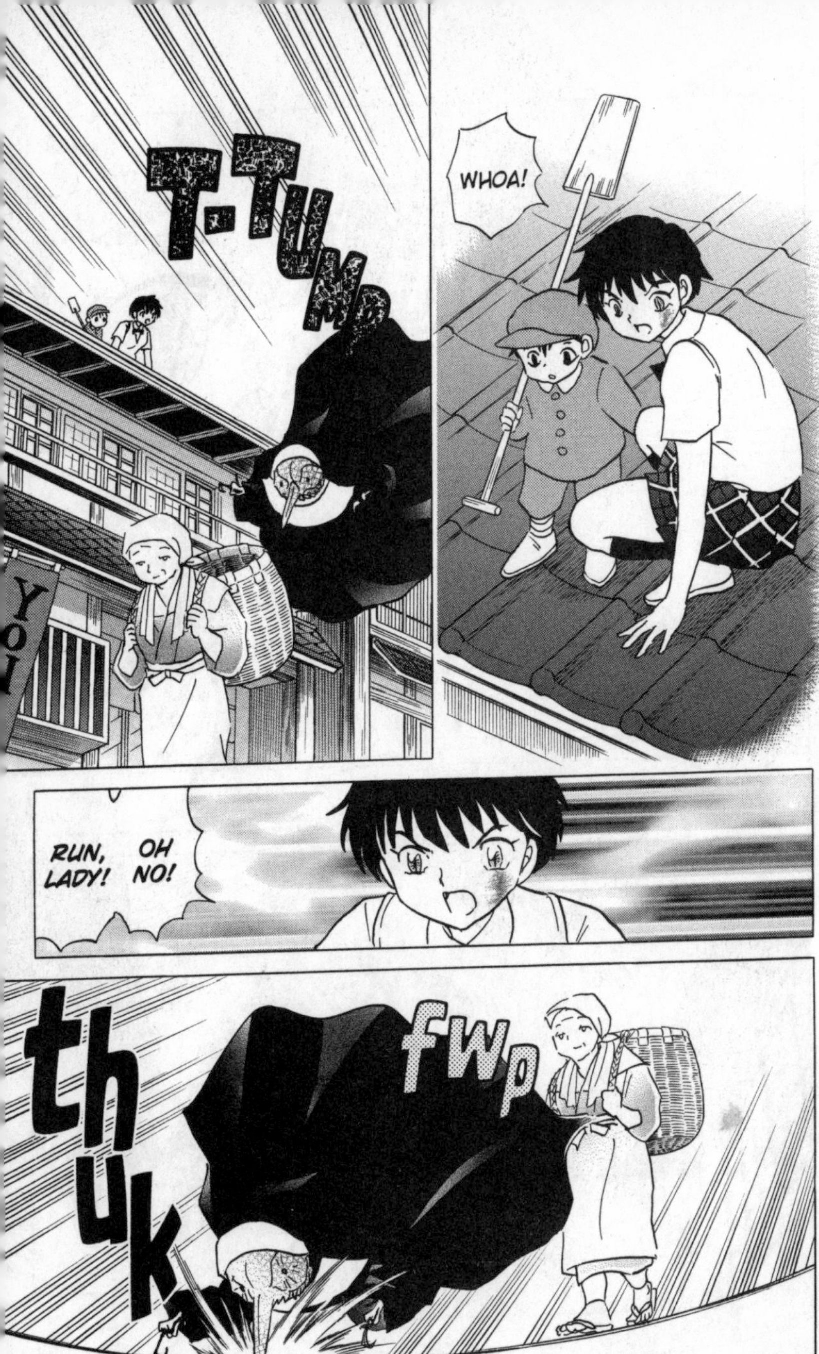
WHOA!
T-TUMP
OH NO!
RUN, LADY!
fwp
thuk

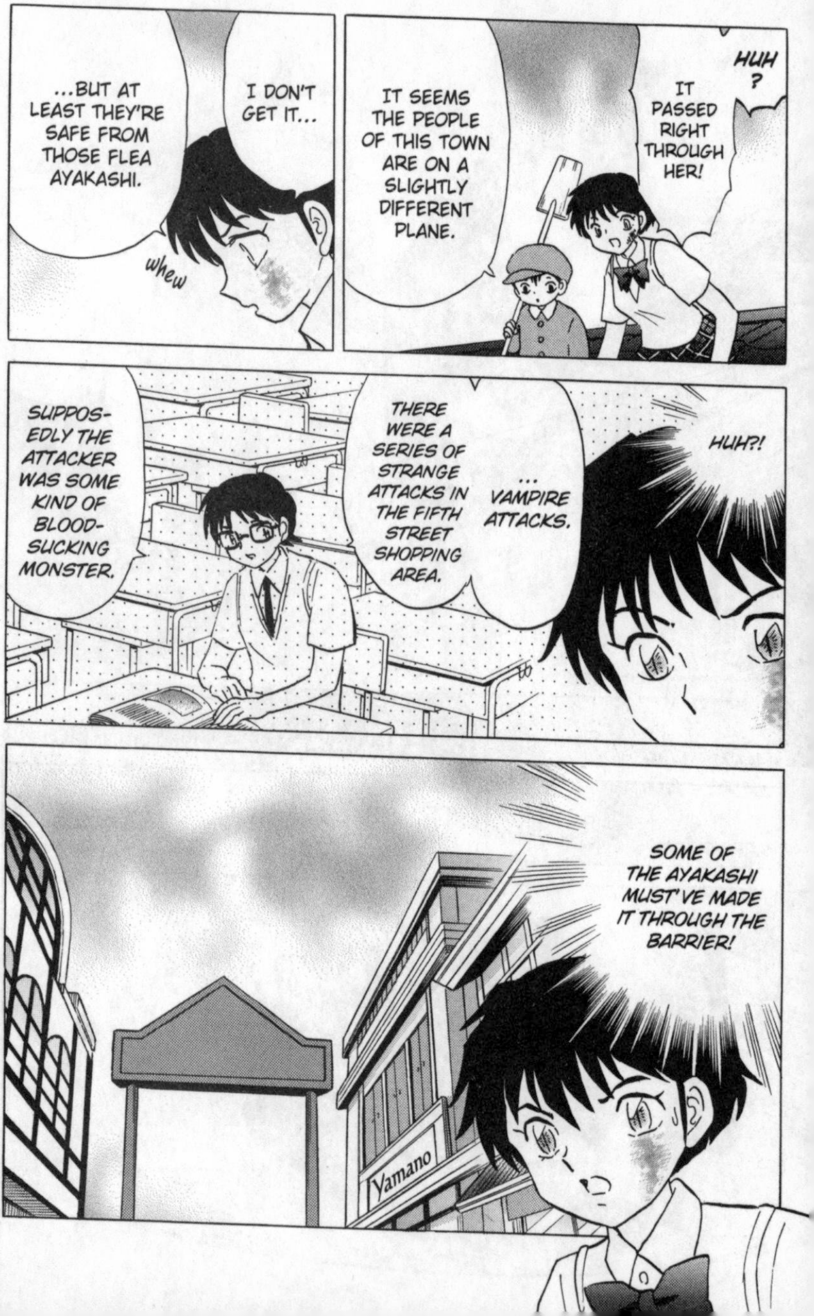
HUH ?
IT PASSED RIGHT THROUGH HER!
IT SEEMS THE PEOPLE OF THIS TOWN ARE ON A SLIGHTLY DIFFERENT PLANE.
I DON'T GET IT...
...BUT AT LEAST THEY'RE SAFE FROM THOSE FLEA AYAKASHI.
whew
HUH?!
... VAMPIRE ATTACKS.
THERE WERE A SERIES OF STRANGE ATTACKS IN THE FIFTH STREET SHOPPING AREA.
SUPPOS-EDLY THE ATTACKER WAS SOME KIND OF BLOOD-SUCKING MONSTER.
SOME OF THE AYAKASHI MUST'VE MADE IT THROUGH THE BARRIER!
Yamano

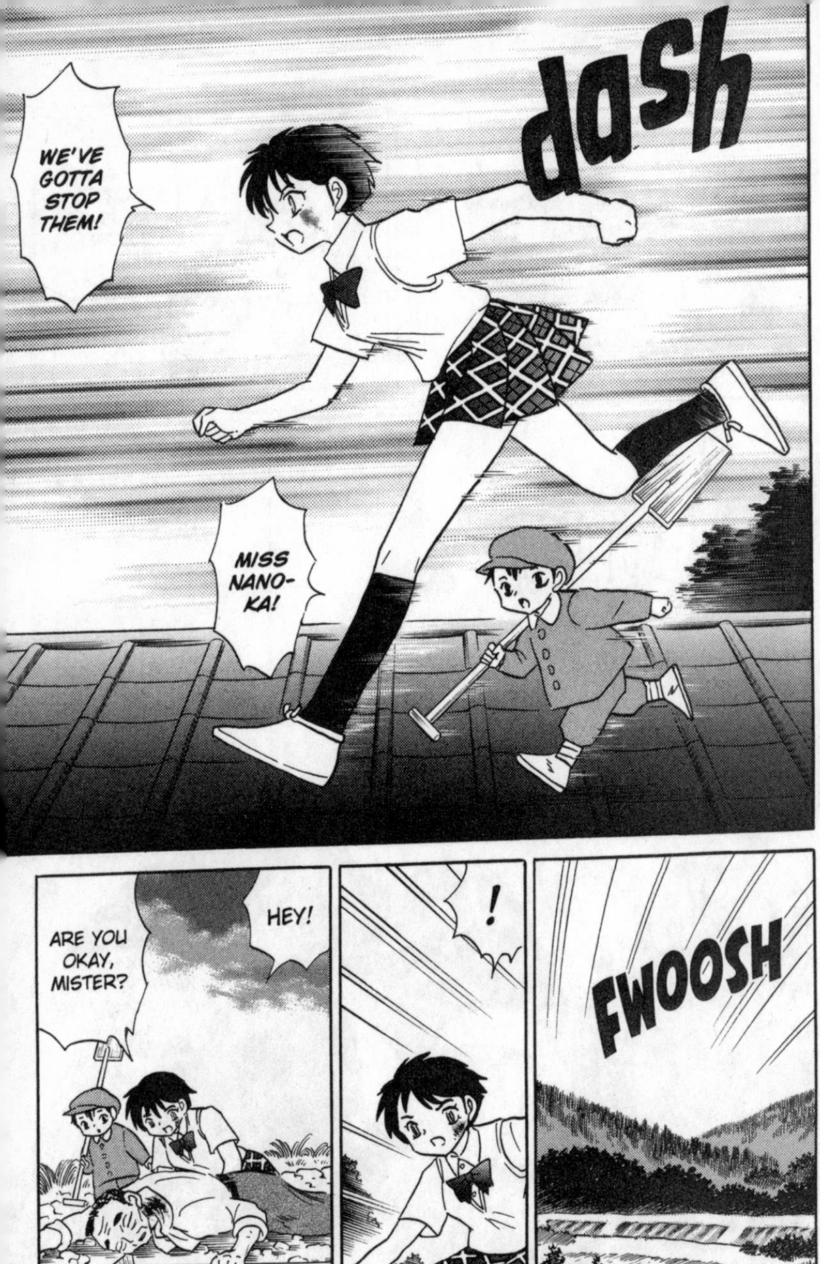
dash
WE'VE GOTTA STOP THEM!
MISS NANOKA!
FWOOSH
!
HEY!
ARE YOU OKAY, MISTER?

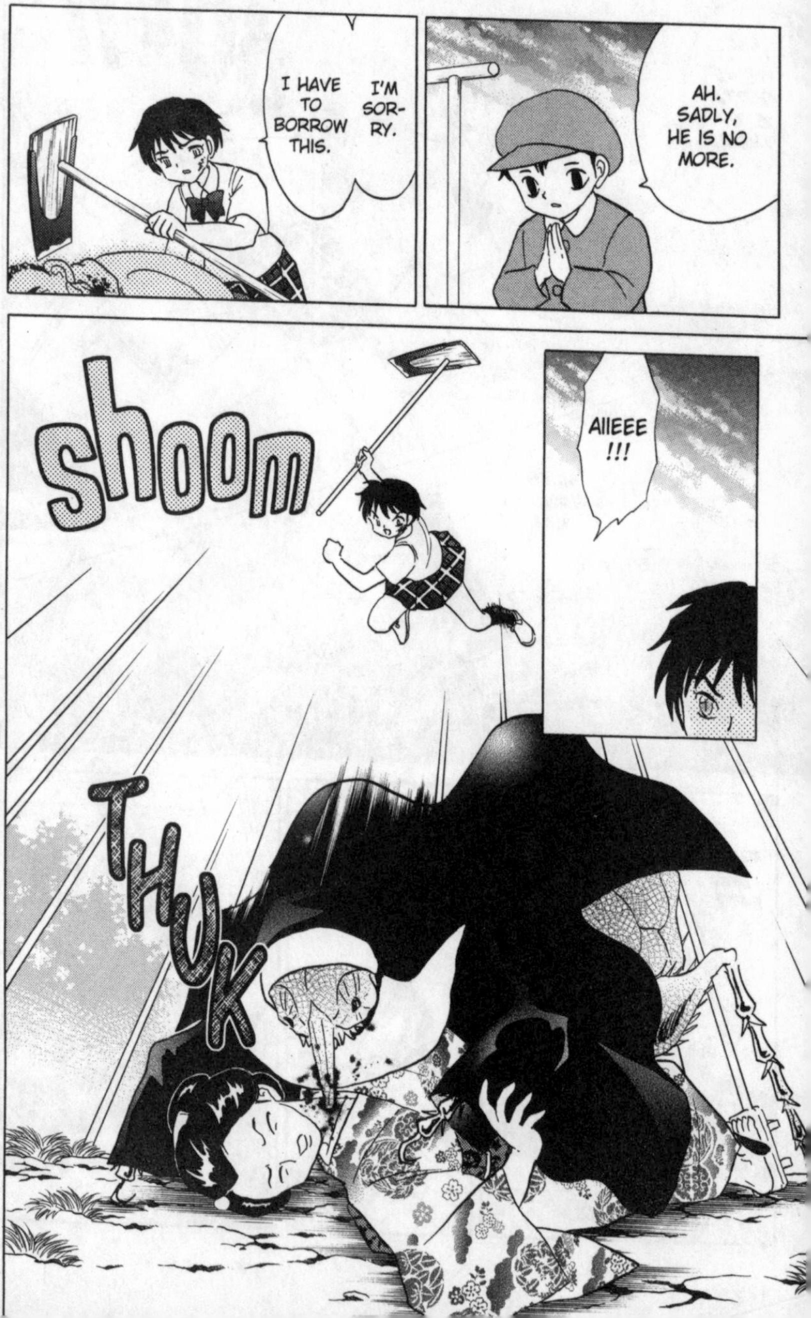
AH. SADLY, HE IS NO MORE.
I'M SORRY.
I HAVE TO BORROW THIS.
AIIEEE!!!
shoom
THUK

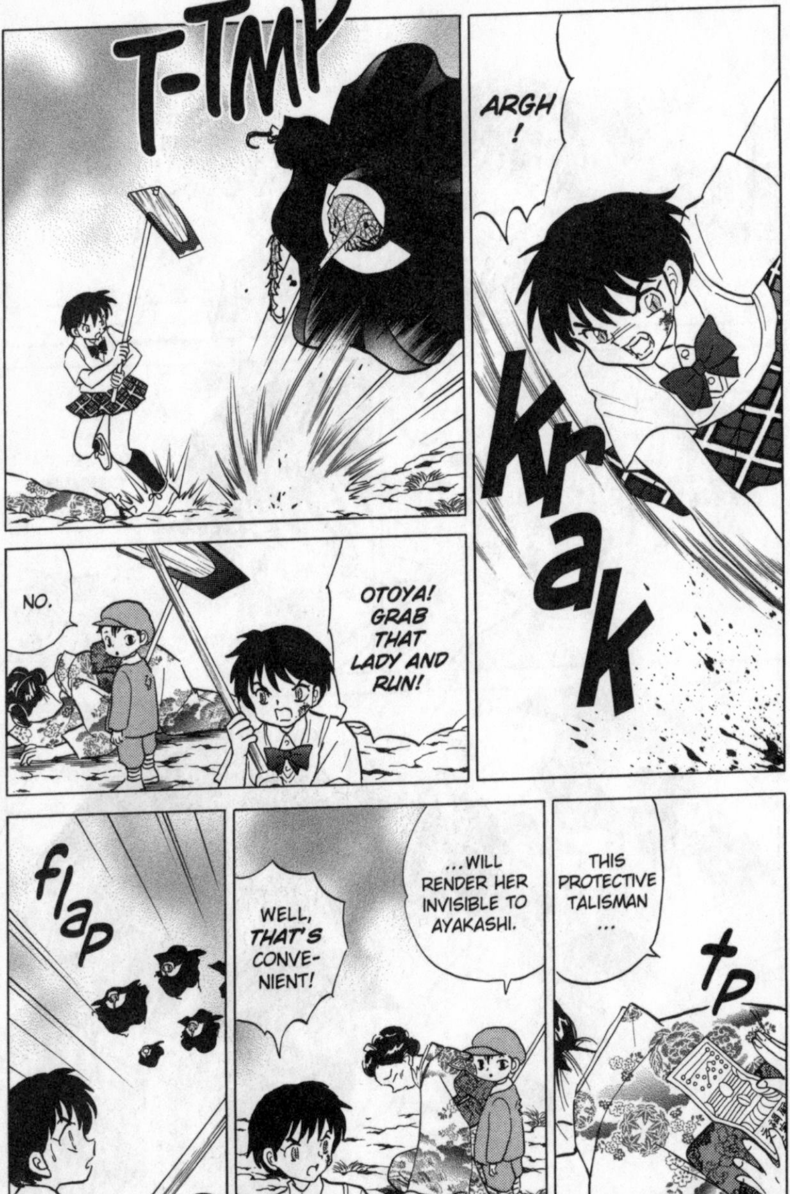
ARGH!
KRAK
T-TMP
OTOYA! GRAB THAT LADY AND RUN!
NO.
THIS PROTECTIVE TALISMAN ...
TP
...WILL RENDER HER INVISIBLE TO AYAKASHI.
WELL, THAT'S CONVE-NIENT!
FLAP

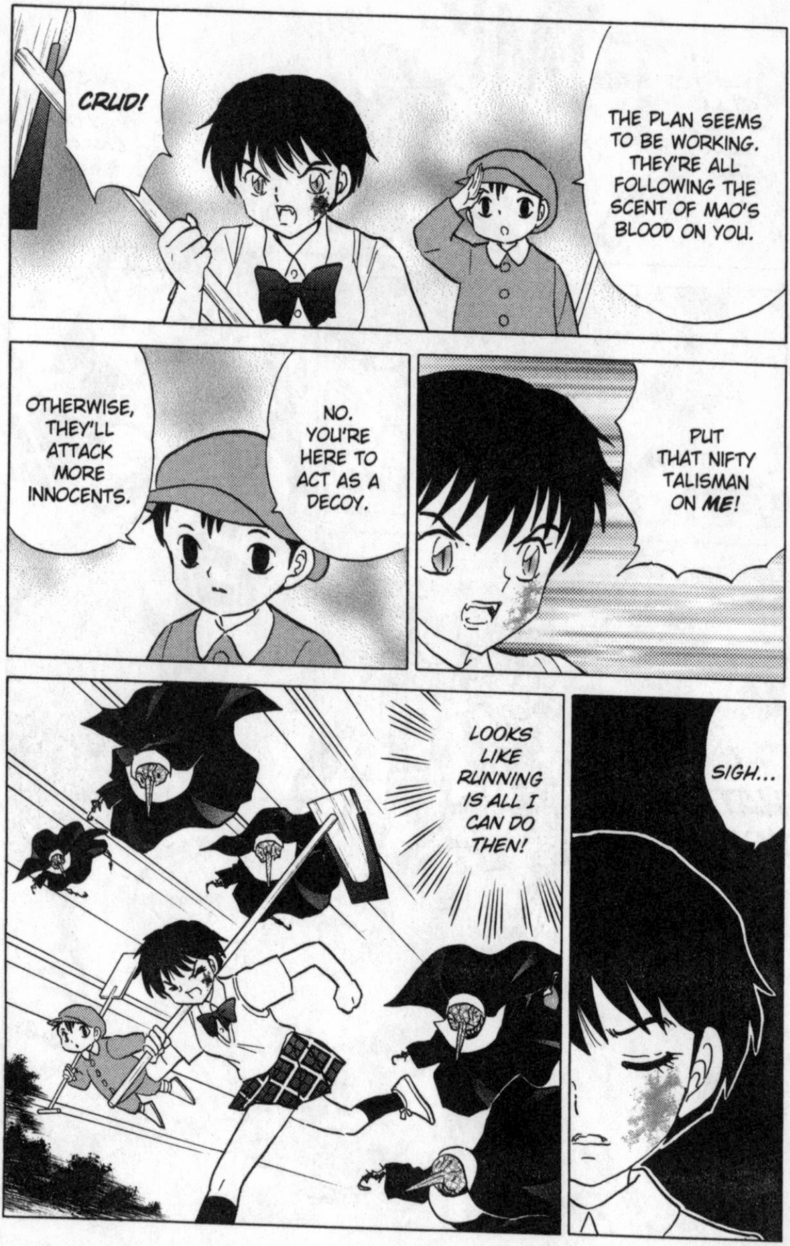
THE PLAN SEEMS TO BE WORKING. THEY'RE ALL FOLLOWING THE SCENT OF MAO'S BLOOD ON YOU.
CRUD!
PUT THAT NIFTY TALISMAN ON *ME*!
NO. YOU'RE HERE TO ACT AS A DECOY.
OTHERWISE, THEY'LL ATTACK MORE INNOCENTS.
SIGH...
LOOKS LIKE RUNNING IS ALL I CAN DO THEN!

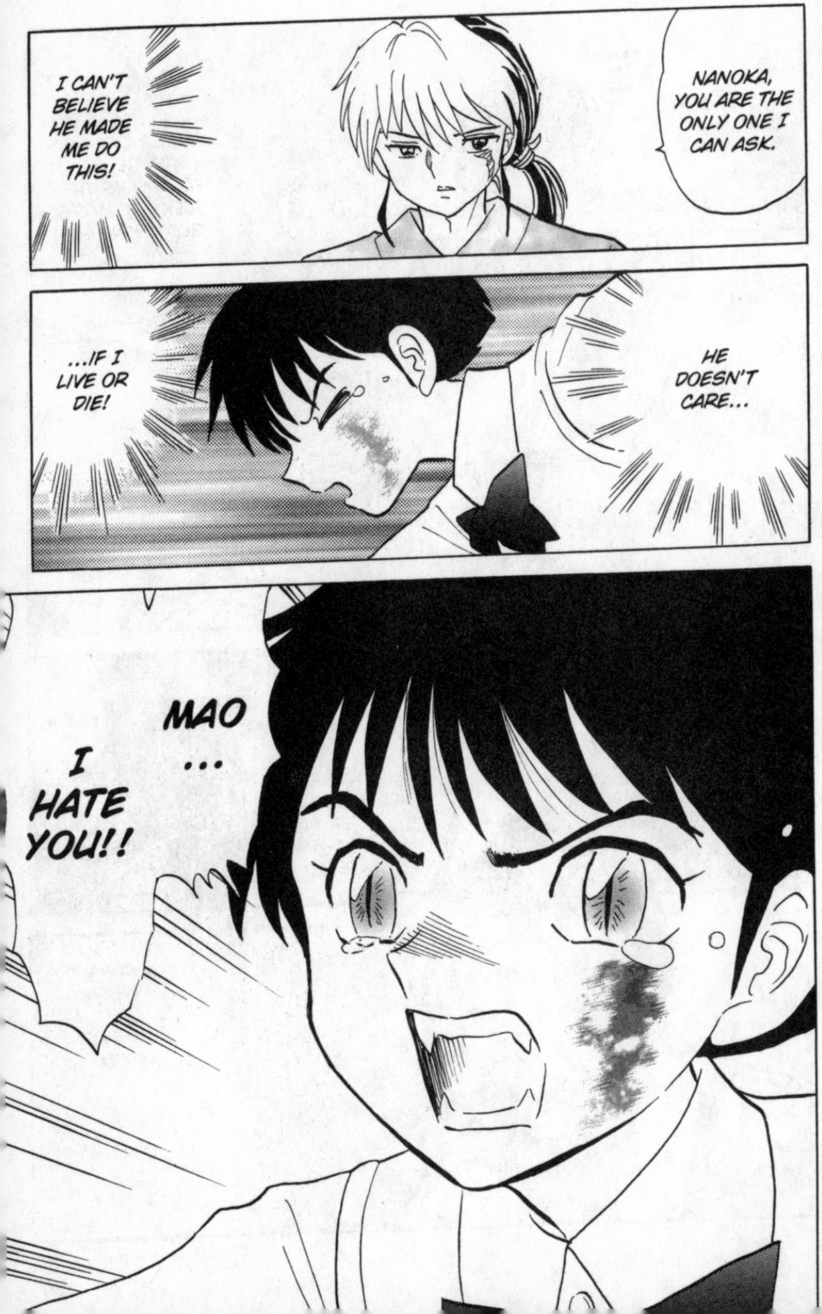
NANOKA, YOU ARE THE ONLY ONE I CAN ASK.
I CAN'T BELIEVE HE MADE ME DO THIS!
HE DOESN'T CARE...
...IF I LIVE OR DIE!
MAO...
I HATE YOU!!

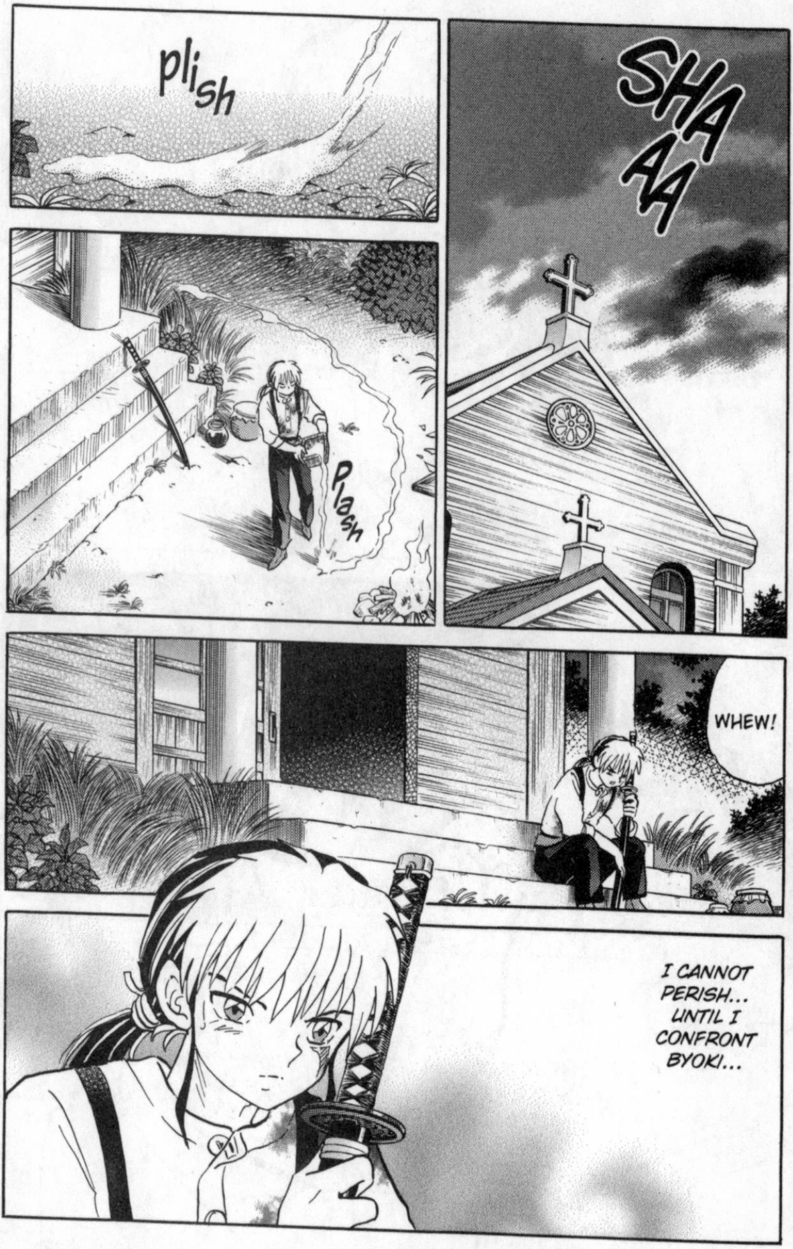
SHAAAA
plish
plash
WHEW!
I CANNOT PERISH... UNTIL I CONFRONT BYOKI...

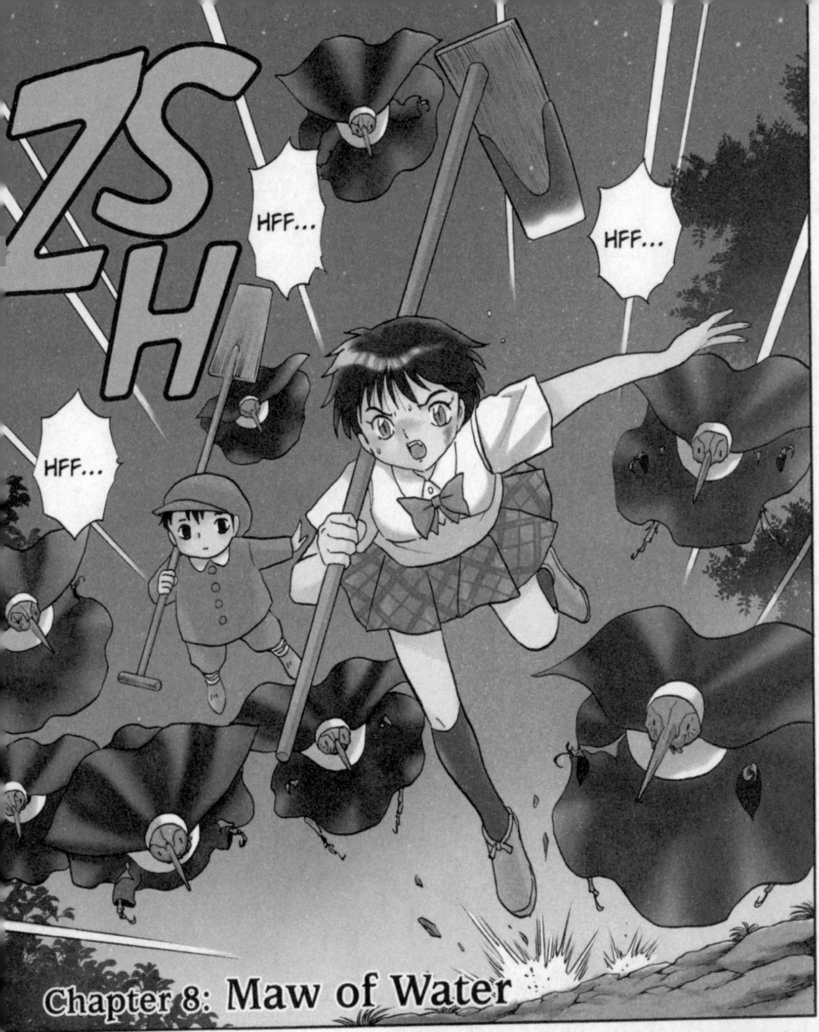
ZSH
HFF...
HFF...
HFF...

Chapter 8: Maw of Water

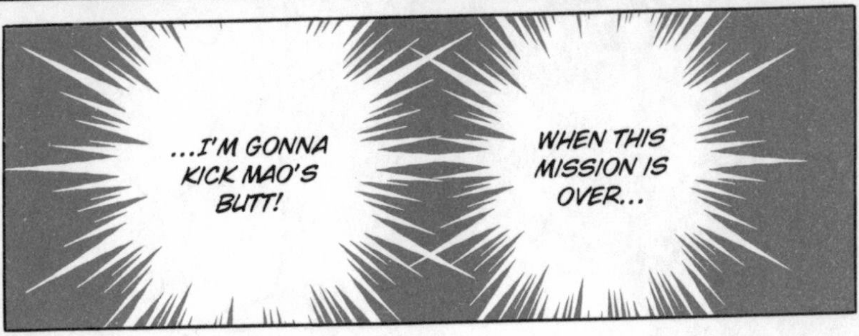
WHEN THIS MISSION IS OVER...
...I'M GONNA KICK MAO'S BUTT!

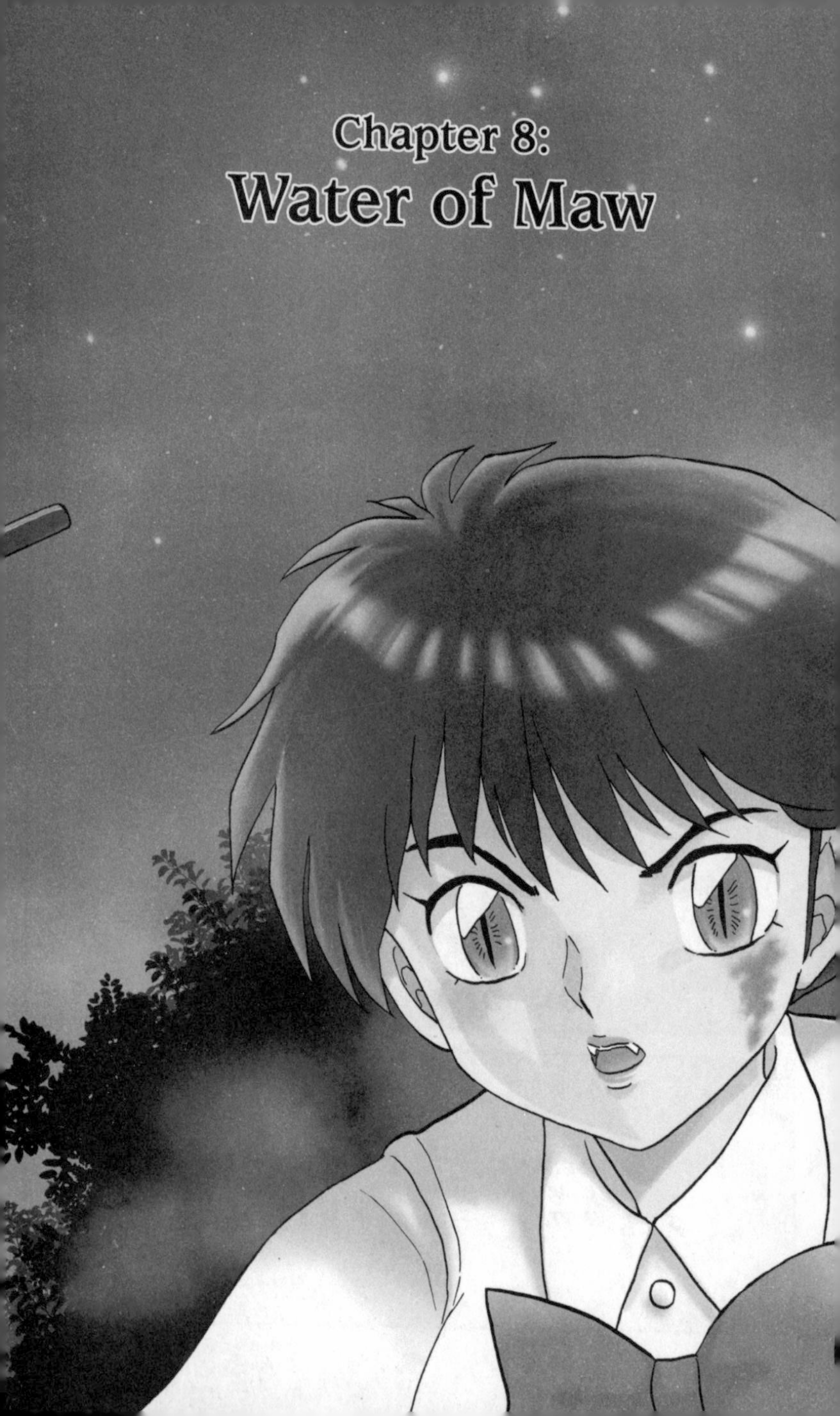
Chapter 8:
Water of Maw

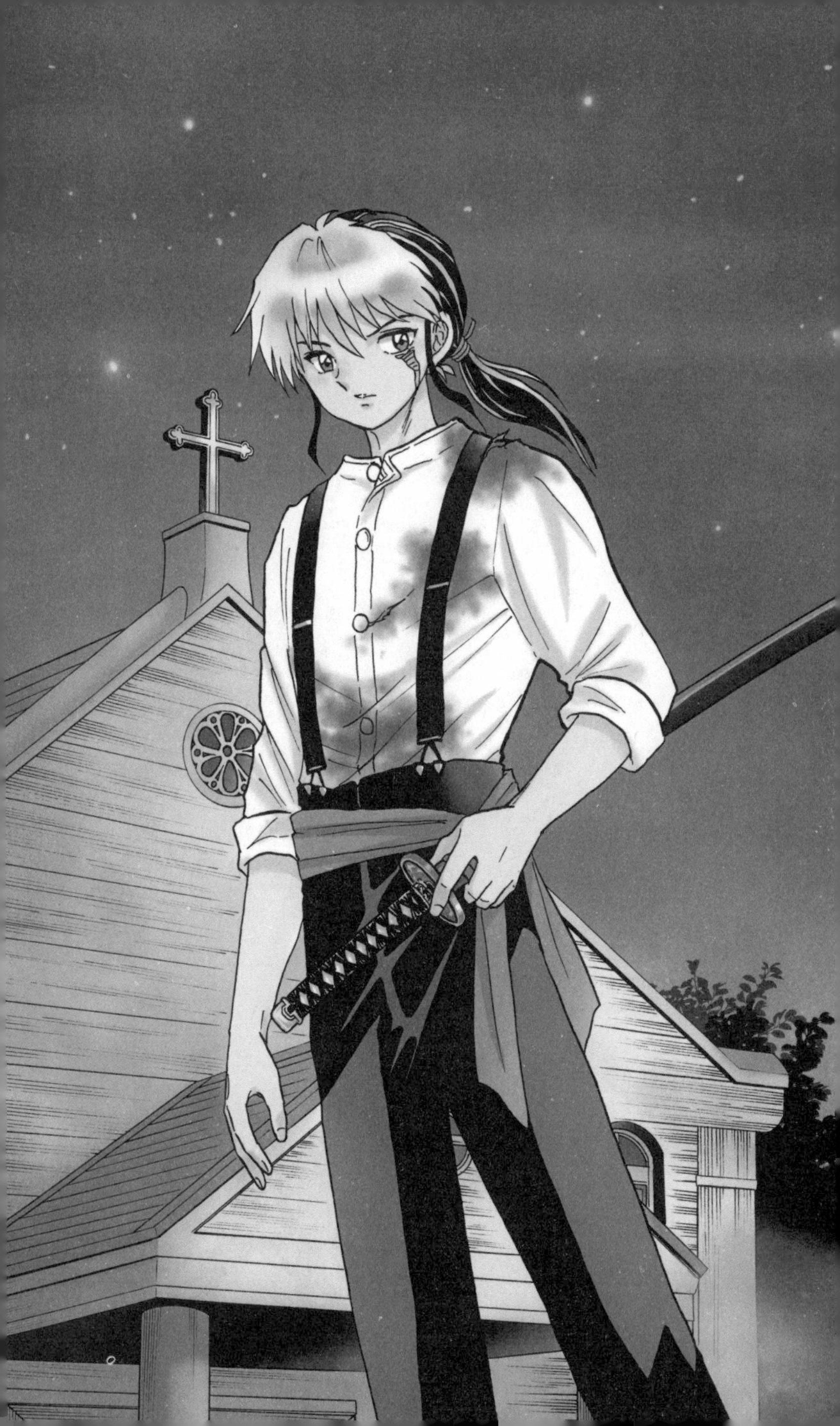

MAO

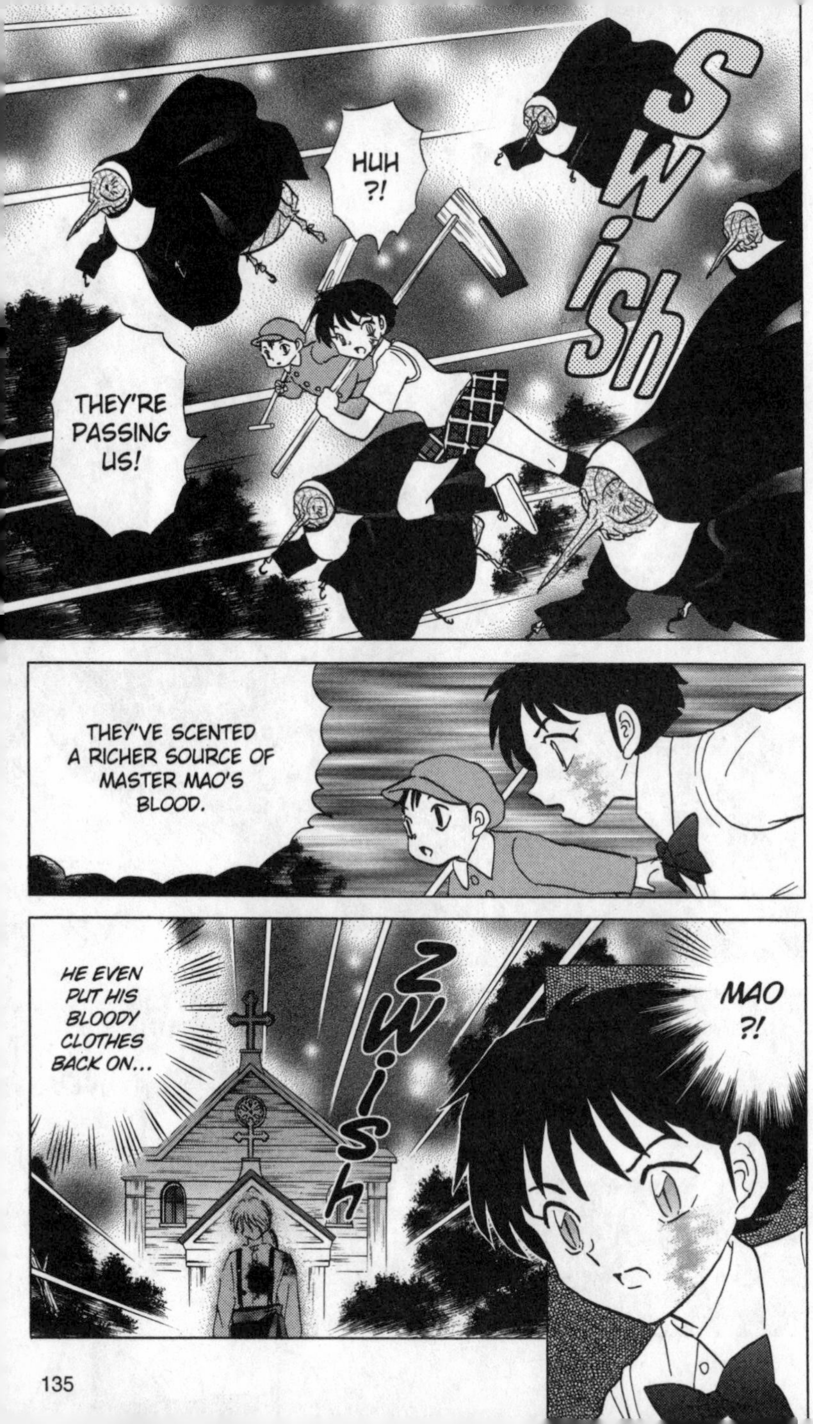
SWiSh
HUH ?!
THEY'RE PASSING US!
THEY'VE SCENTED A RICHER SOURCE OF MASTER MAO'S BLOOD.
MAO ?!
ZWiSh
HE EVEN PUT HIS BLOODY CLOTHES BACK ON...

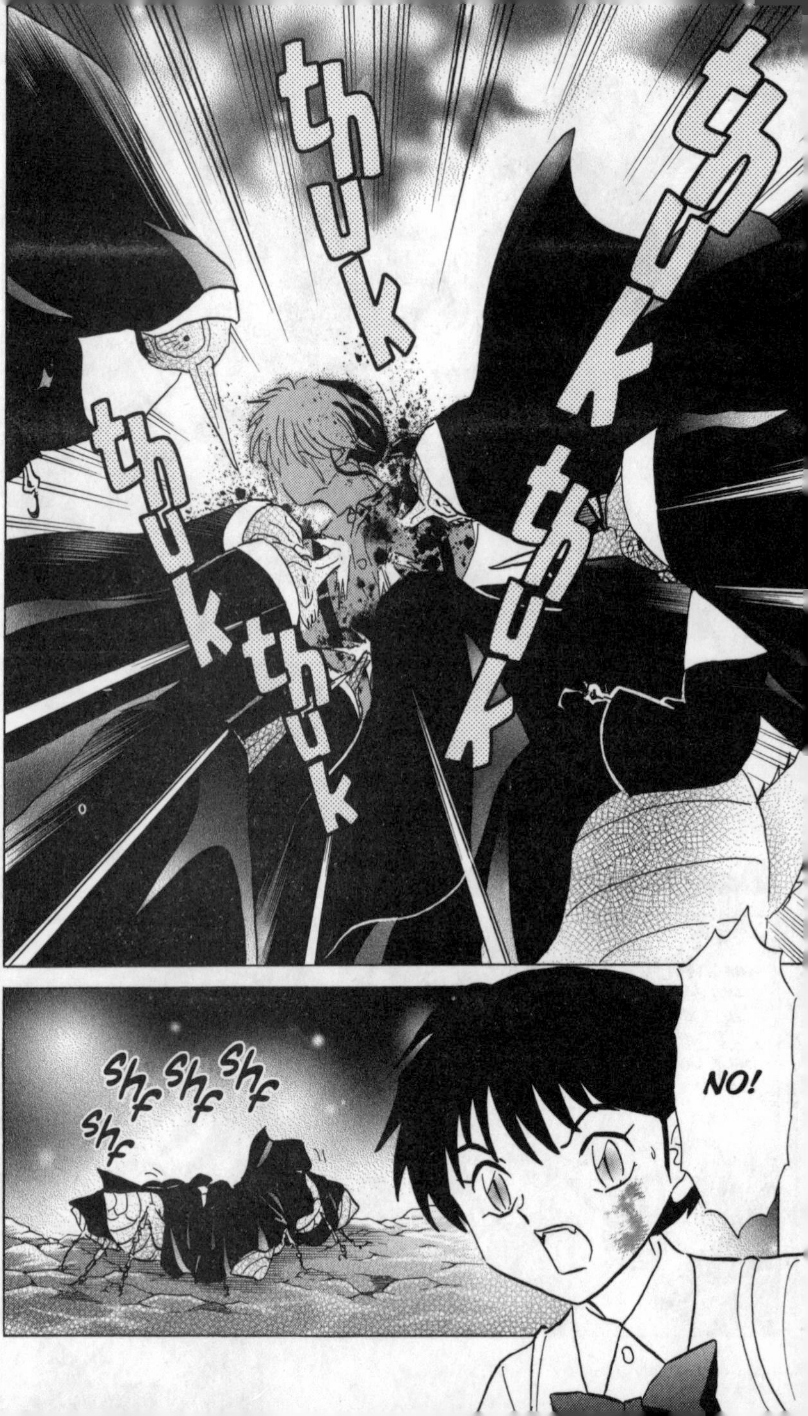
thuk thuk thuk
thuk
thuk thuk
NO!
shf shf shf shf

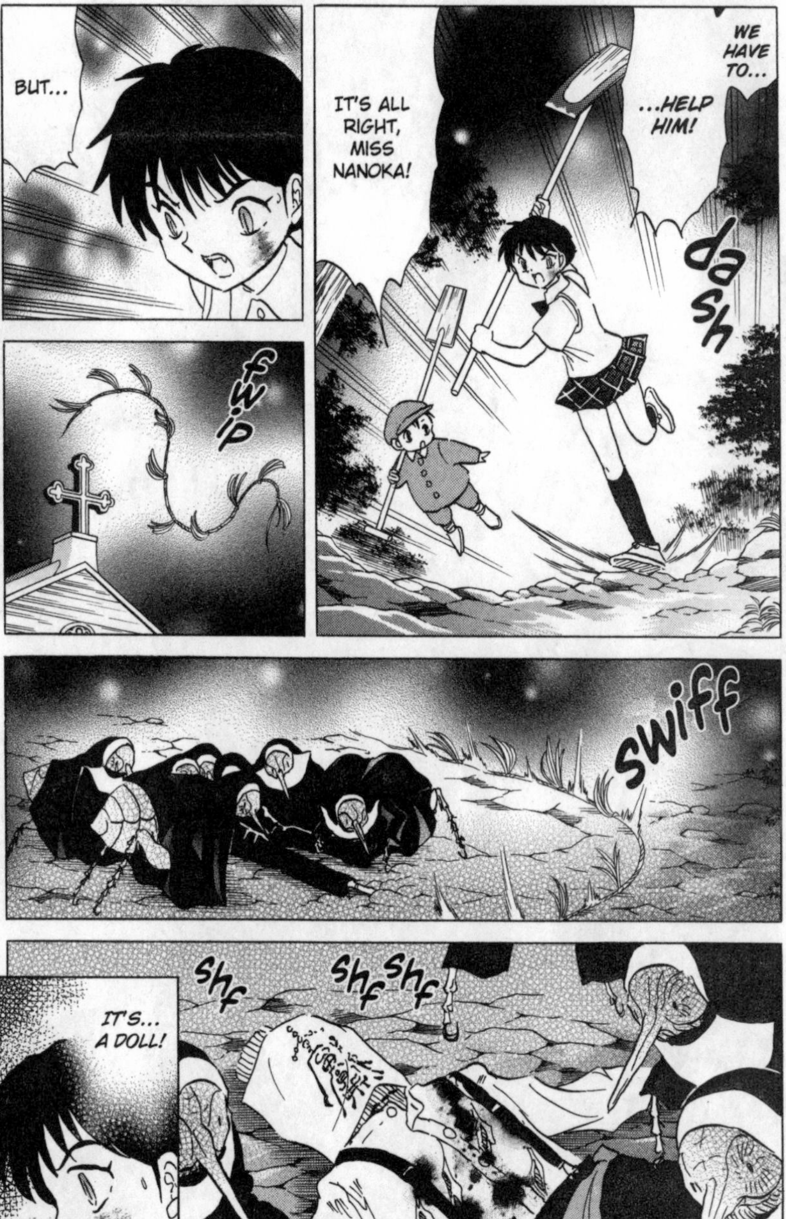
WE HAVE TO...
...HELP HIM!
IT'S ALL RIGHT, MISS NANOKA!
dash
BUT...
fwip
swiff
shf
shf shf
IT'S... A DOLL!

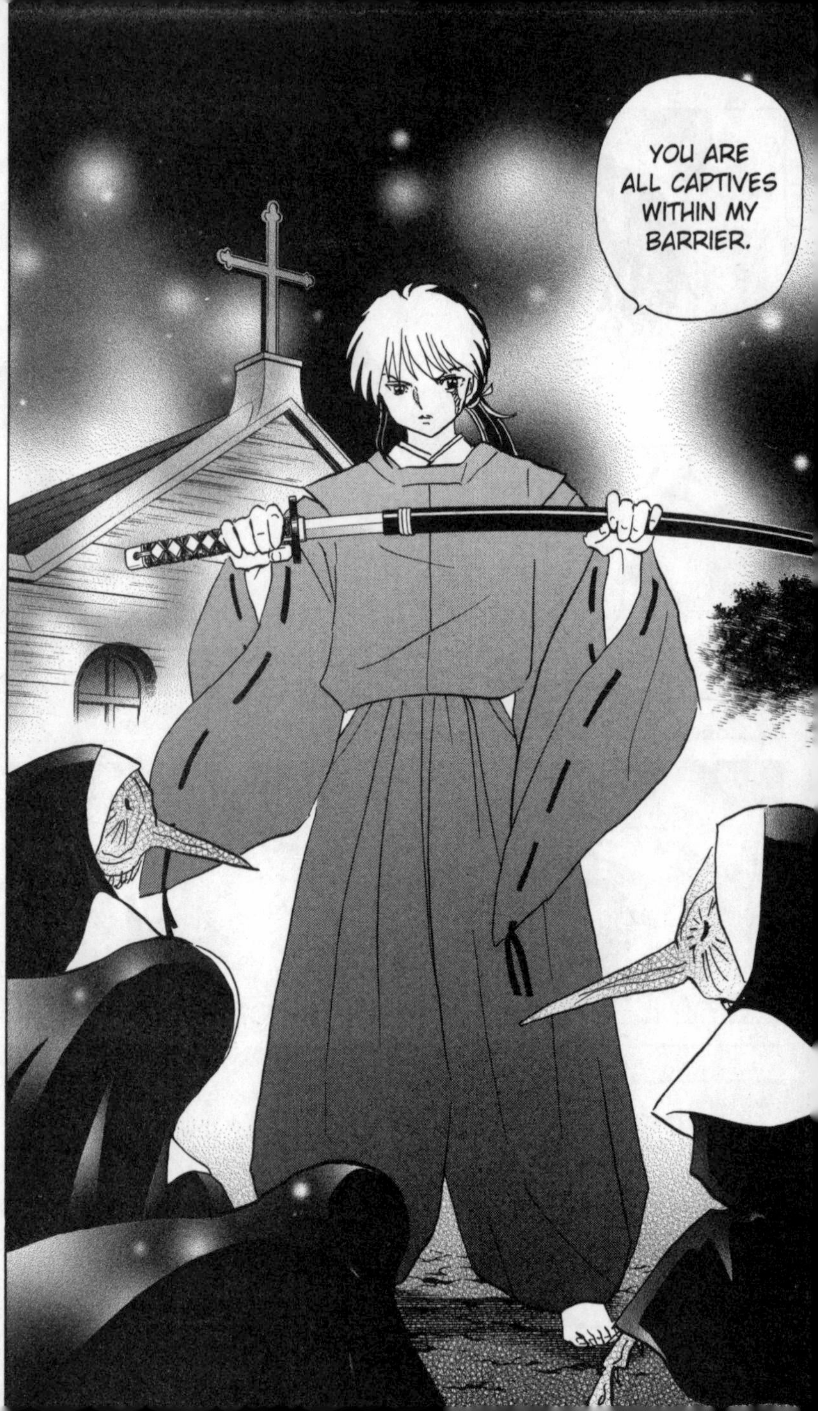
YOU ARE ALL CAPTIVES WITHIN MY BARRIER.

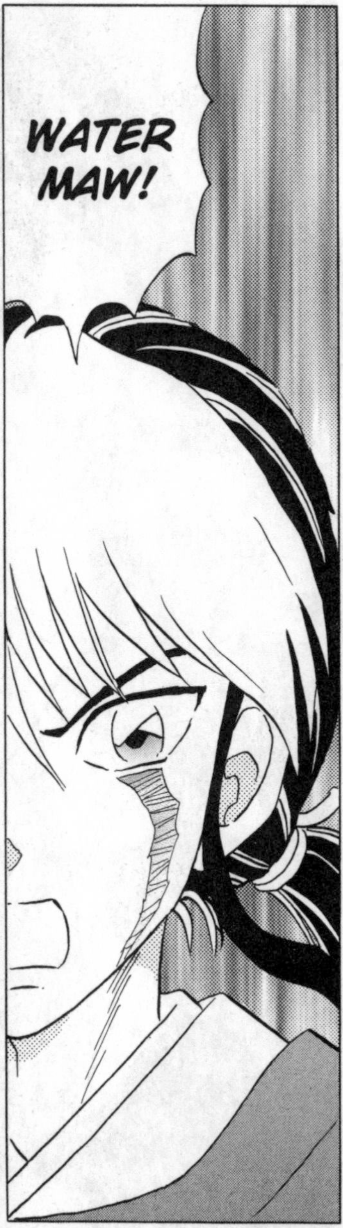
WATER MAW!
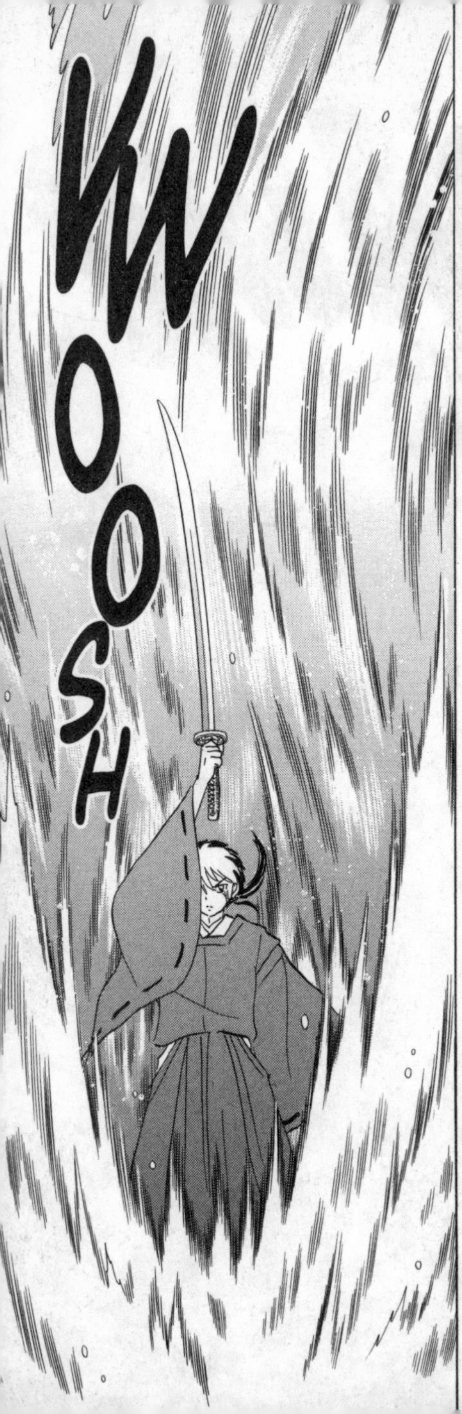
WOOOSH

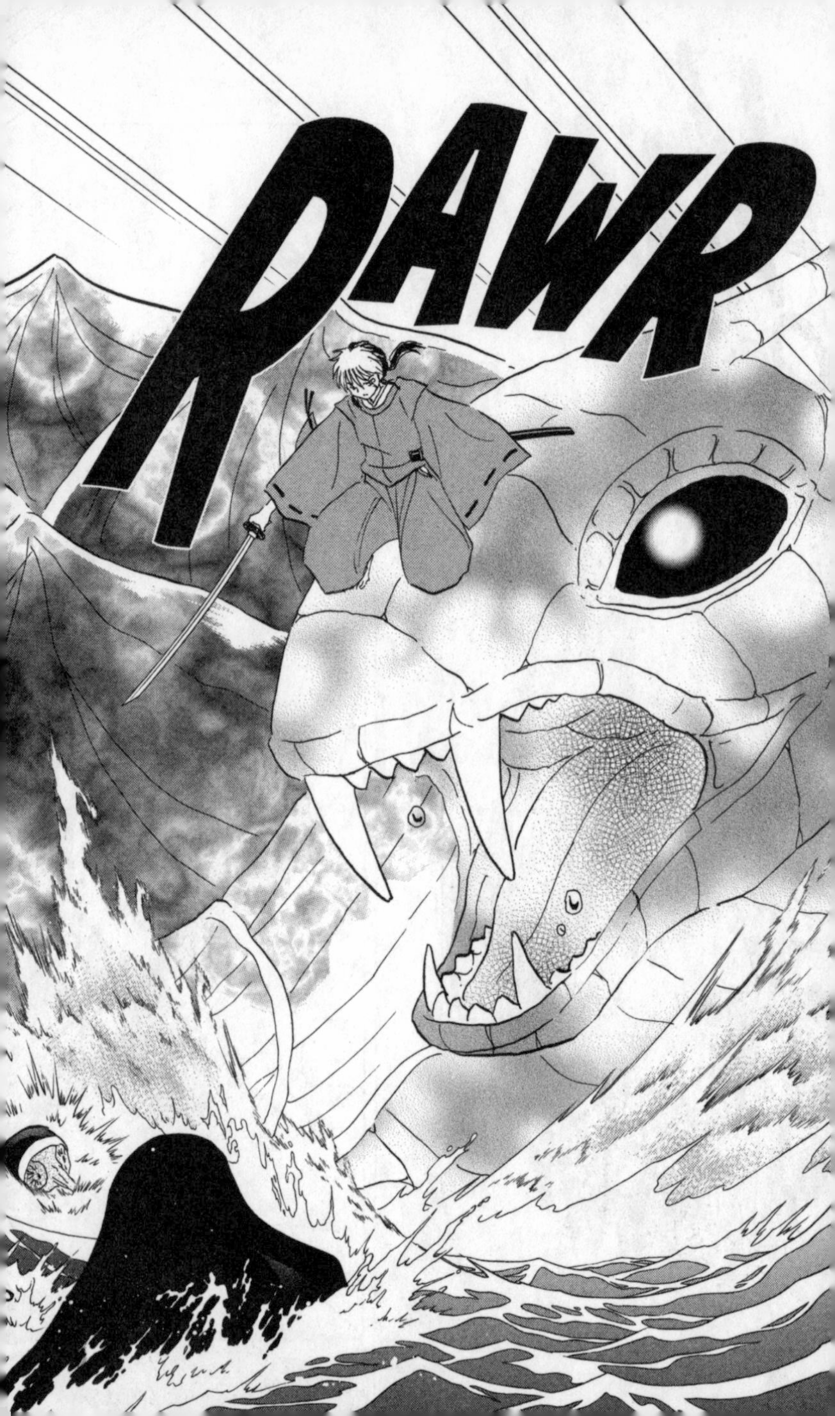
RAWR

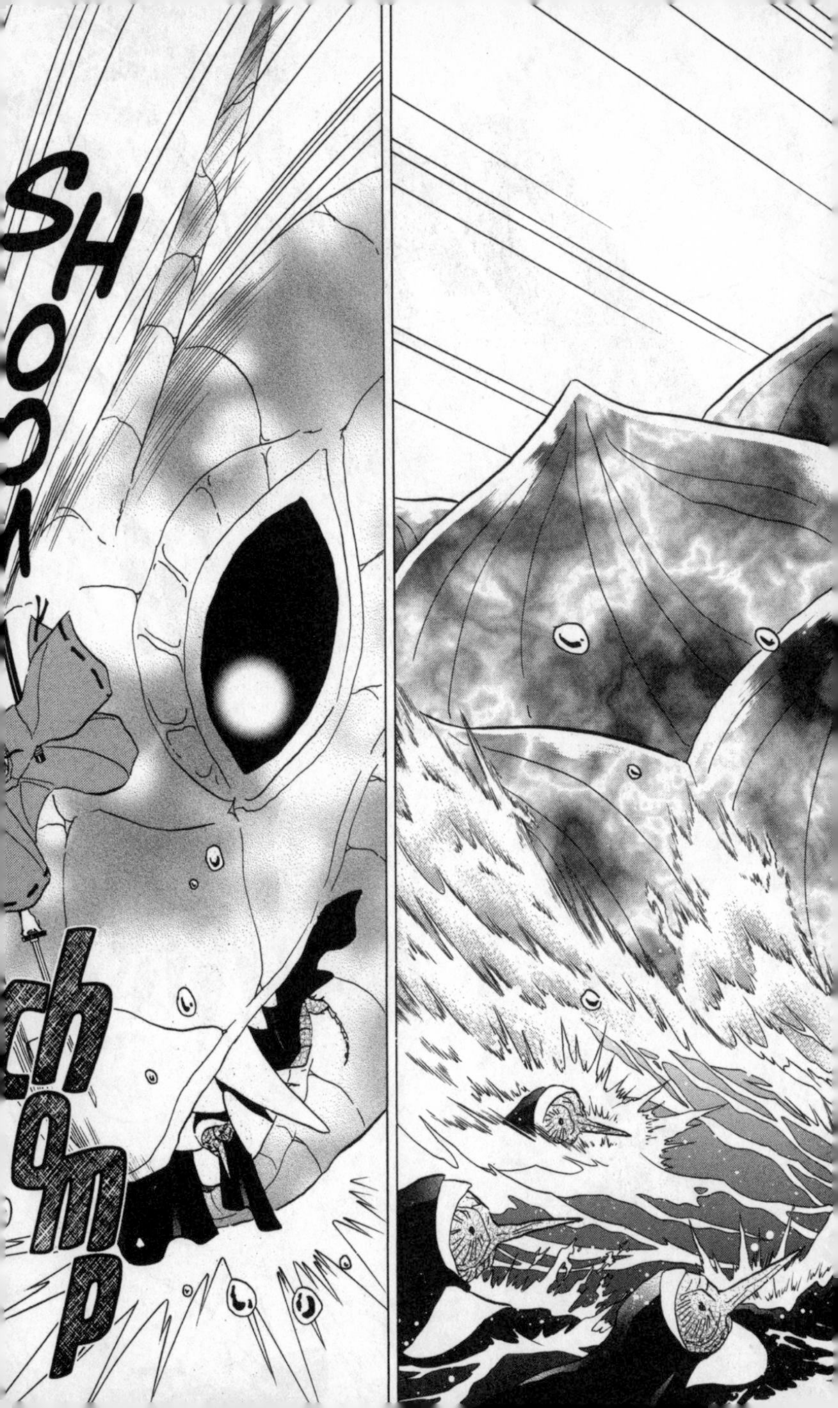
SHOOM
chomp

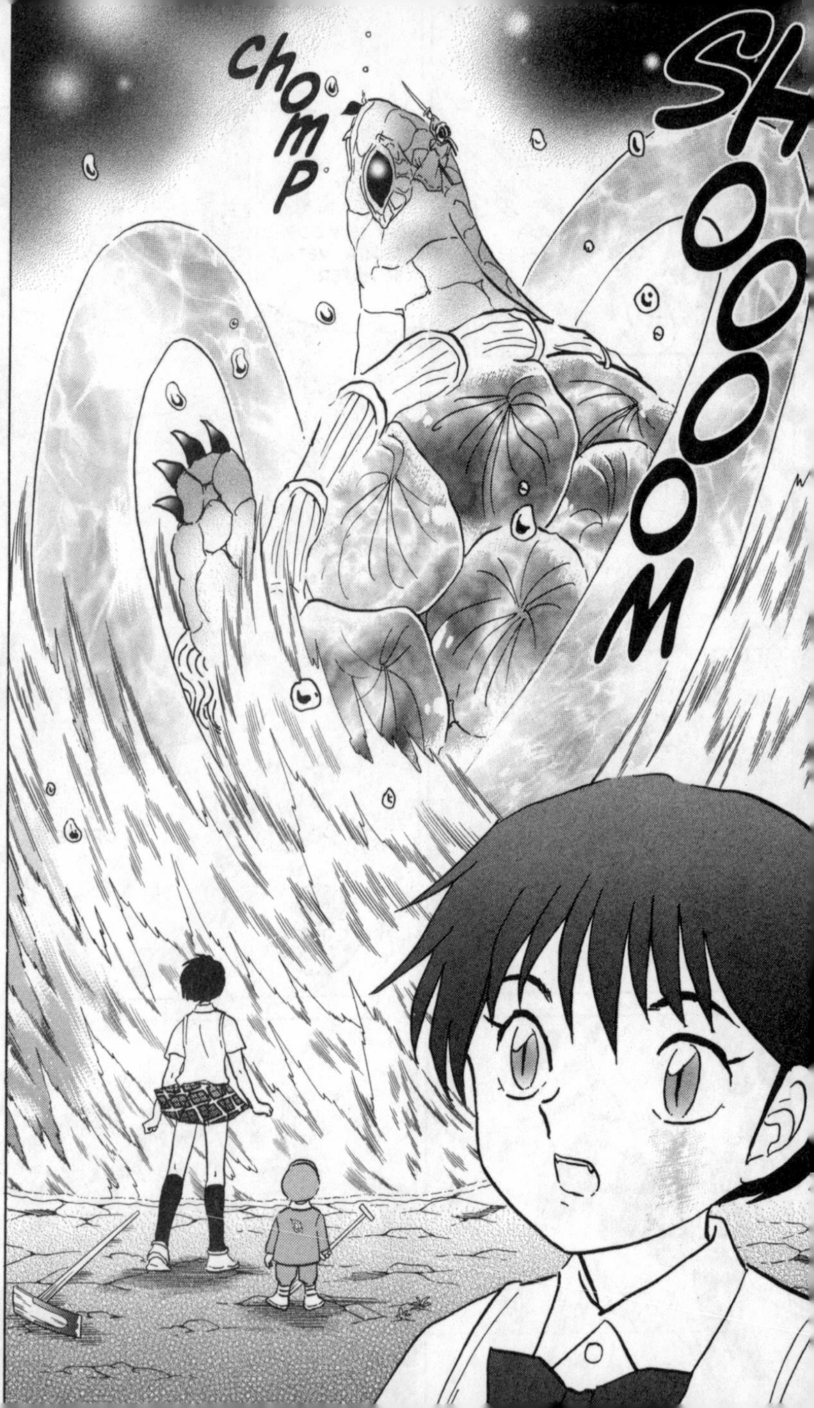
SHOOOOOM
CHOMP

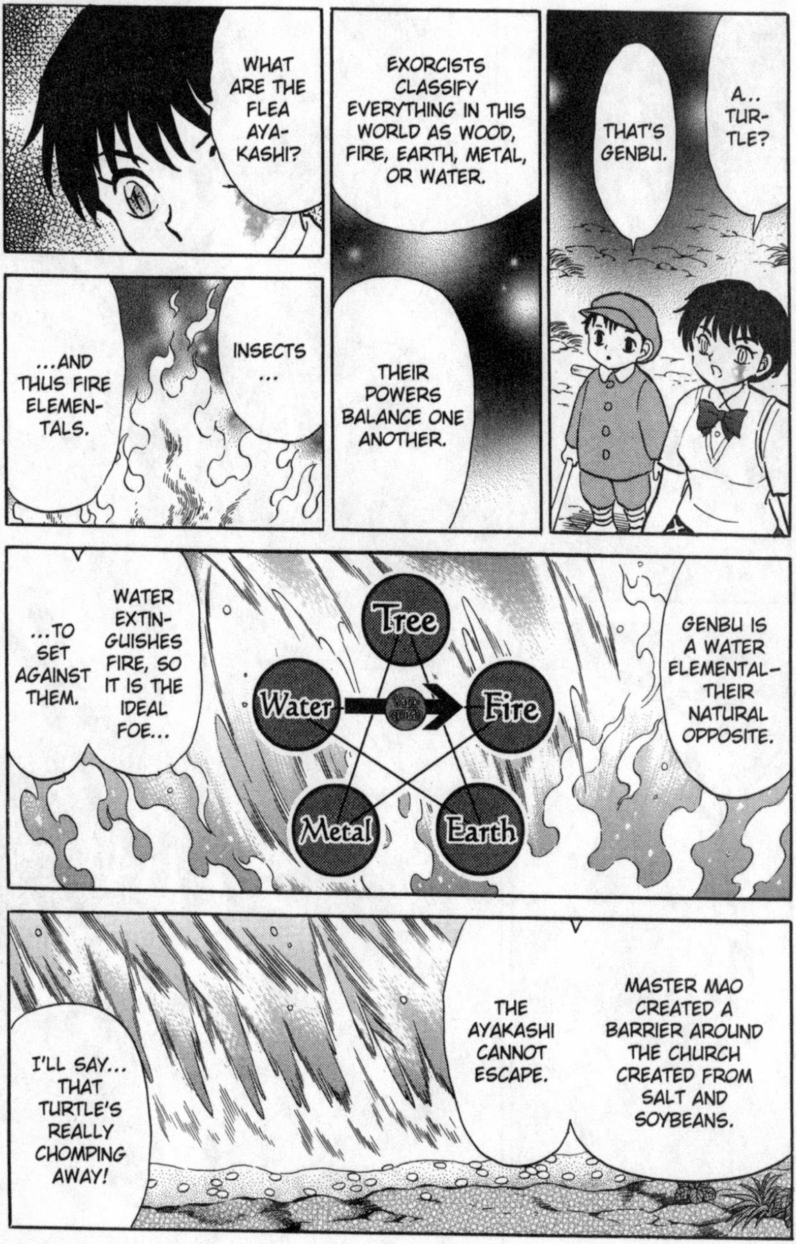
A... TURTLE?
THAT'S GENBU.
EXORCISTS CLASSIFY EVERYTHING IN THIS WORLD AS WOOD, FIRE, EARTH, METAL, OR WATER.
THEIR POWERS BALANCE ONE ANOTHER.
WHAT ARE THE FLEA AYAKASHI?
INSECTS...
...AND THUS FIRE ELEMENTALS.
GENBU IS A WATER ELEMENTAL-THEIR NATURAL OPPOSITE.
Tree
Water
Fire
Metal
Earth
WATER EXTINGUISHES FIRE, SO IT IS THE IDEAL FOE...
...TO SET AGAINST THEM.
MASTER MAO CREATED A BARRIER AROUND THE CHURCH CREATED FROM SALT AND SOYBEANS.
THE AYAKASHI CANNOT ESCAPE.
I'LL SAY... THAT TURTLE'S REALLY CHOMPING AWAY!

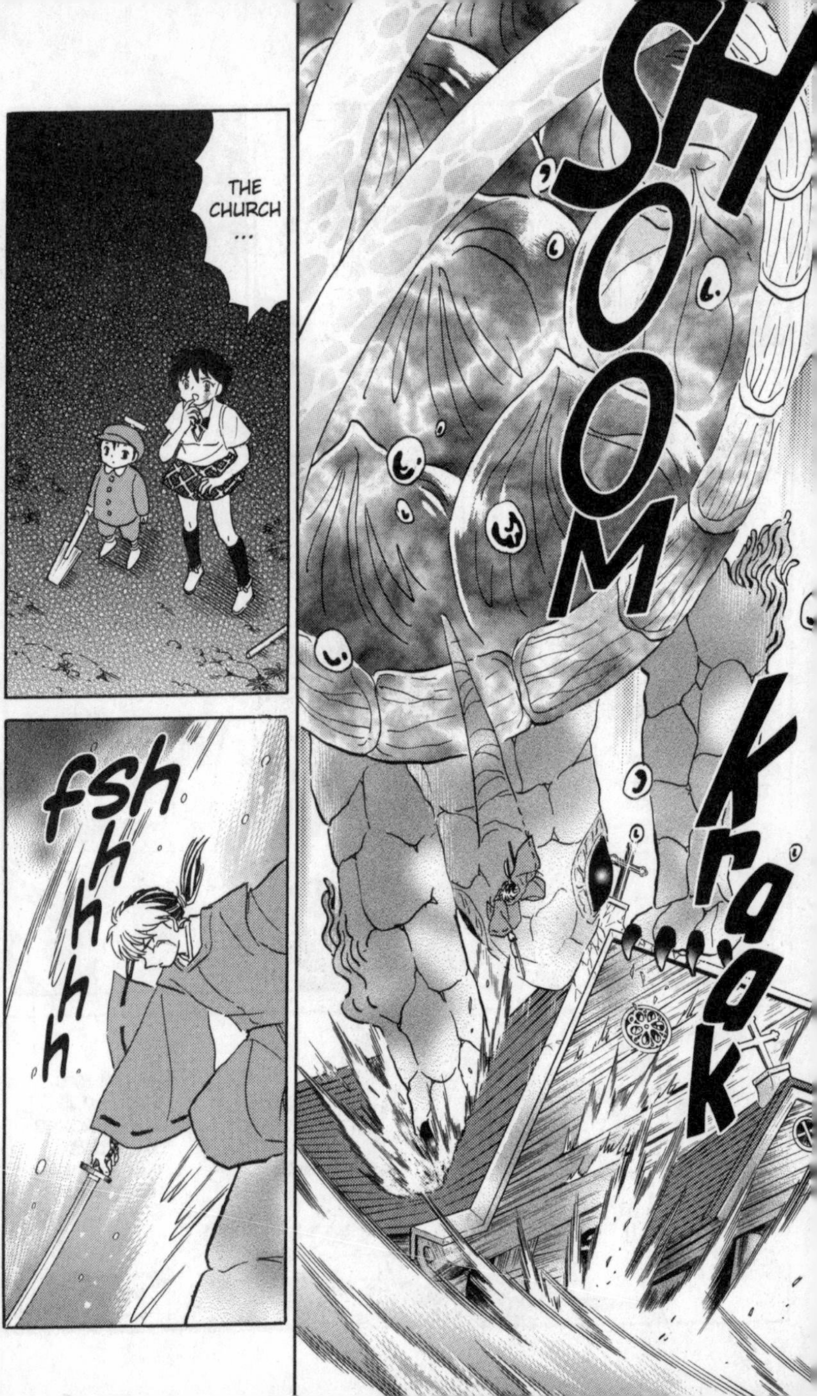
SHOOM
kraaak
THE CHURCH ...
fshhhhhh

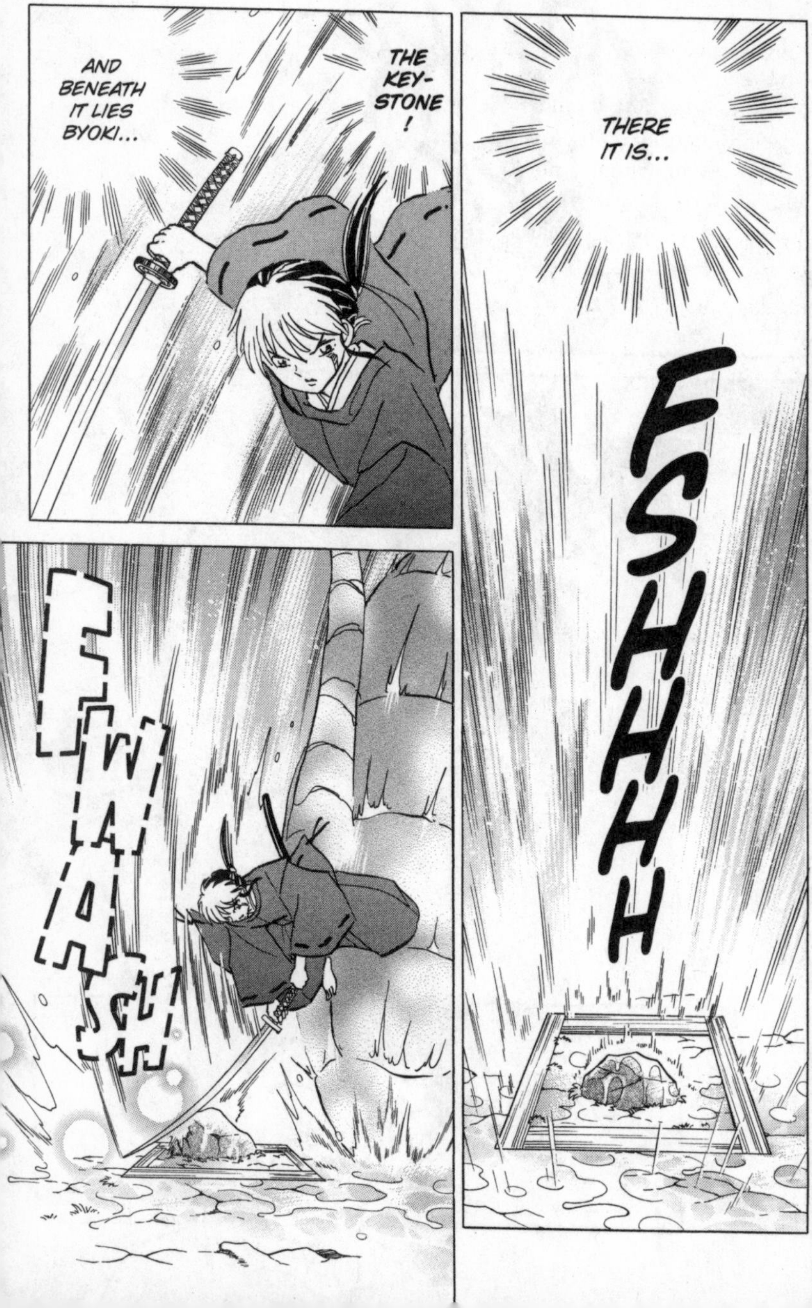
THERE IT IS...
FSHHHH
THE KEY-STONE!
AND BENEATH IT LIES BYOKI...
FWAASH

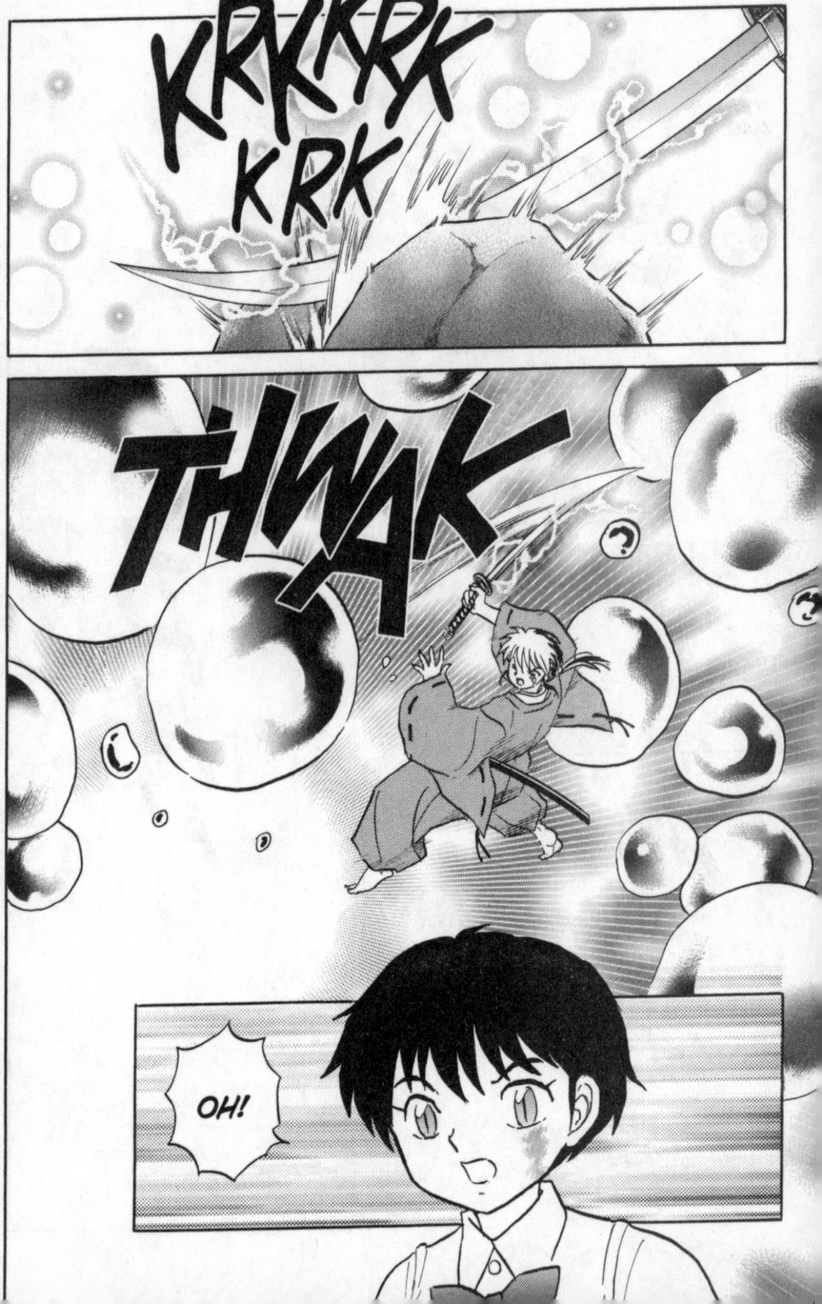
KRKKRK
KRK
THWAK
OH!

MAS-TER MAO!

YOU OKAY ?!

Splash

FSHHH

Splash

grp UGH...

THE CHURCH IS GONE.

shooo

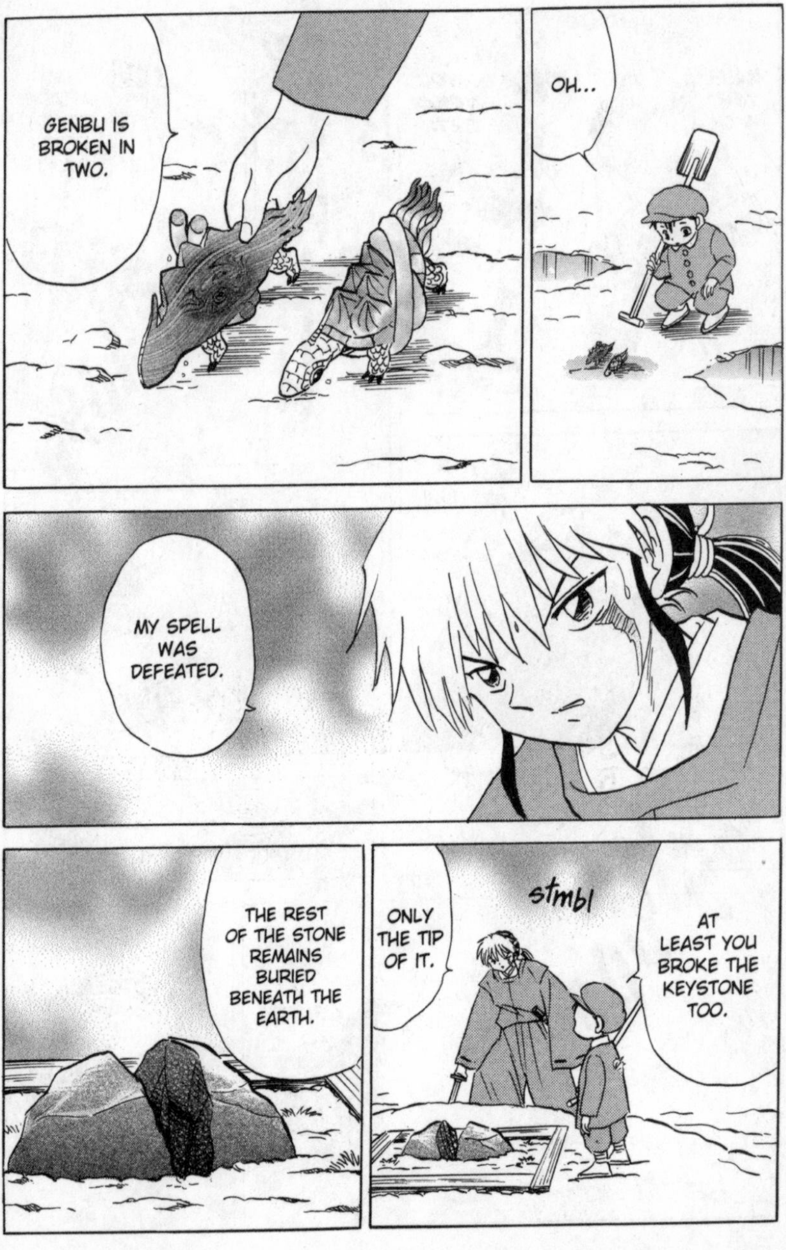
OH...
GENBU IS BROKEN IN TWO.
MY SPELL WAS DEFEATED.
AT LEAST YOU BROKE THE KEYSTONE TOO.
stmbl
ONLY THE TIP OF IT.
THE REST OF THE STONE REMAINS BURIED BENEATH THE EARTH.

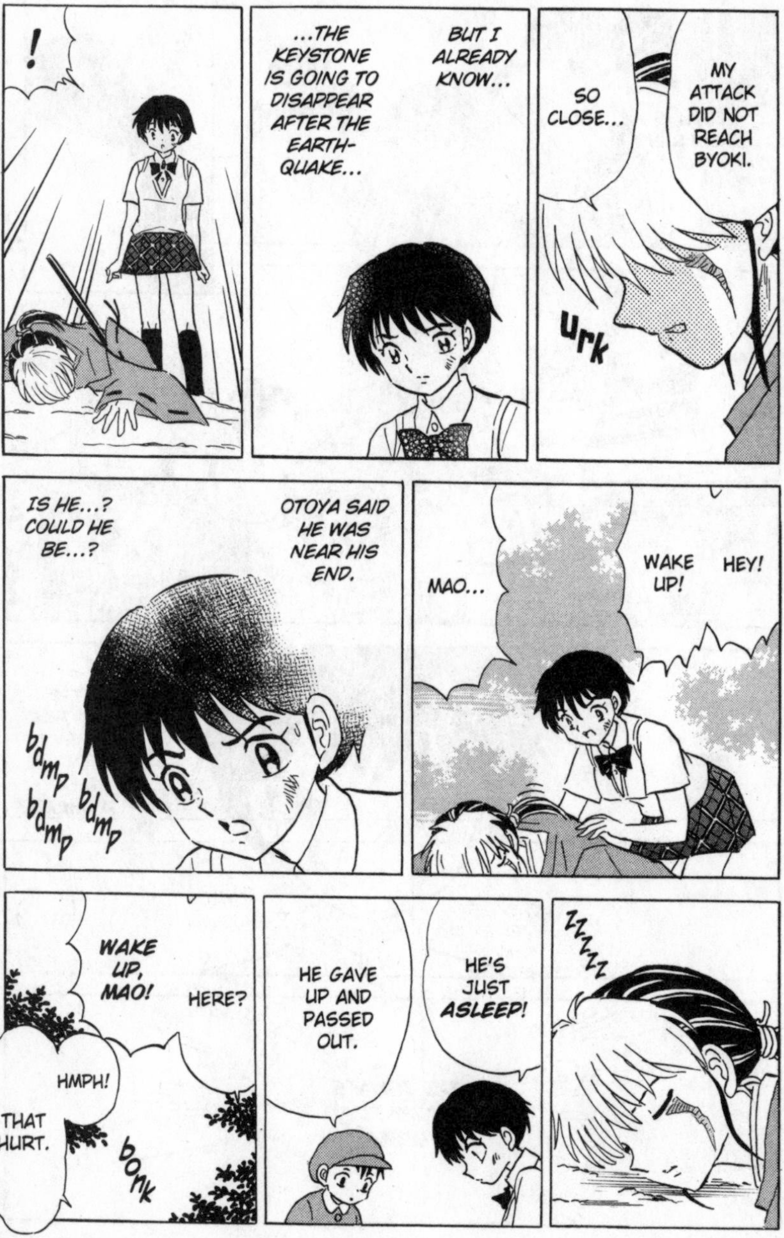
MY ATTACK DID NOT REACH BYOKI.
SO CLOSE...
urk
BUT I ALREADY KNOW...
...THE KEYSTONE IS GOING TO DISAPPEAR AFTER THE EARTH-QUAKE...
!
HEY!
WAKE UP!
MAO...
OTOYA SAID HE WAS NEAR HIS END.
IS HE...? COULD HE BE...?
bdmp bdmp bdmp
zzzzz
HE'S JUST ASLEEP!
HE GAVE UP AND PASSED OUT.
HERE?
WAKE UP, MAO!
HMPH!
THAT HURT.
bonk

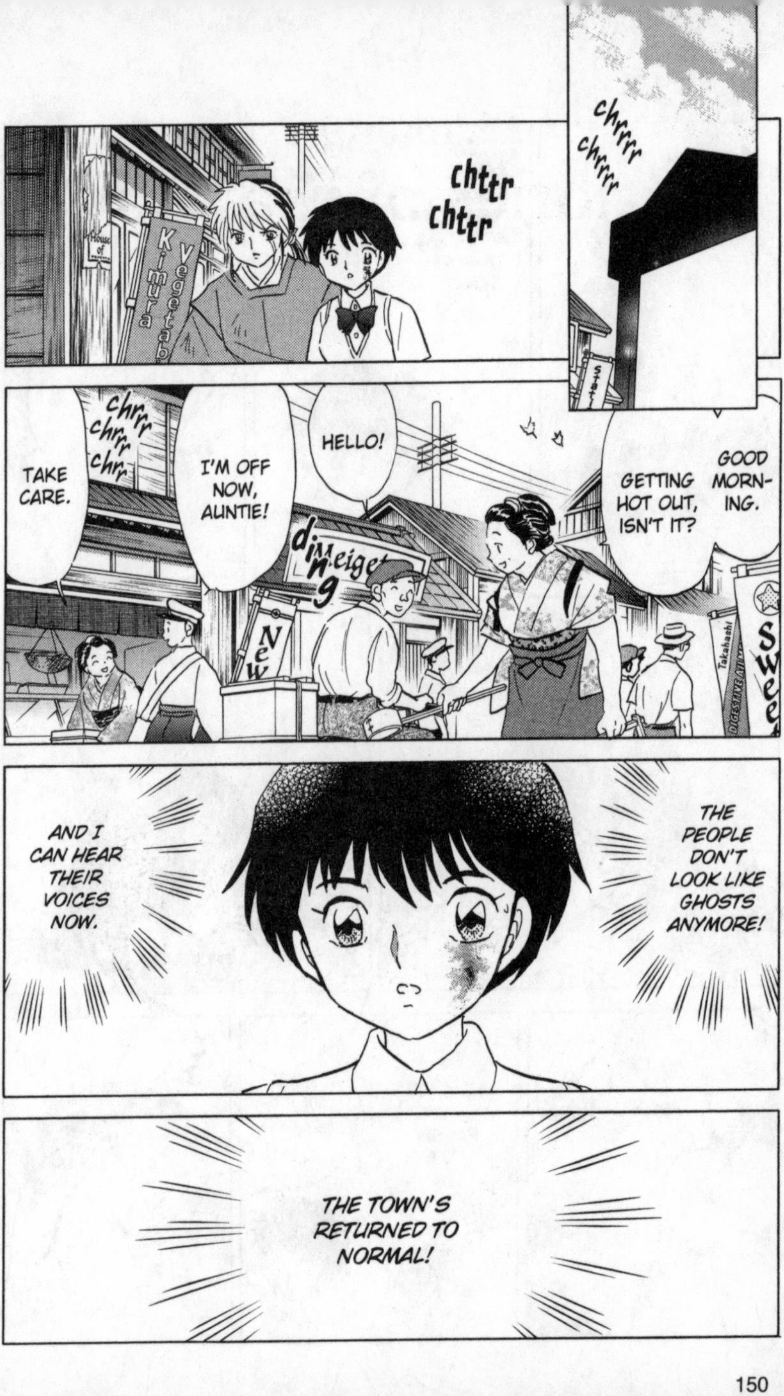
chrrrr chrrrr
chttr chttr
GOOD MORNING.
GETTING HOT OUT, ISN'T IT?
HELLO!
I'M OFF NOW, AUNTIE!
chrrr chrrr chrr
TAKE CARE.
THE PEOPLE DON'T LOOK LIKE GHOSTS ANYMORE!
AND I CAN HEAR THEIR VOICES NOW.
THE TOWN'S RETURNED TO NORMAL!

Chapter 9:
Memories of that Day

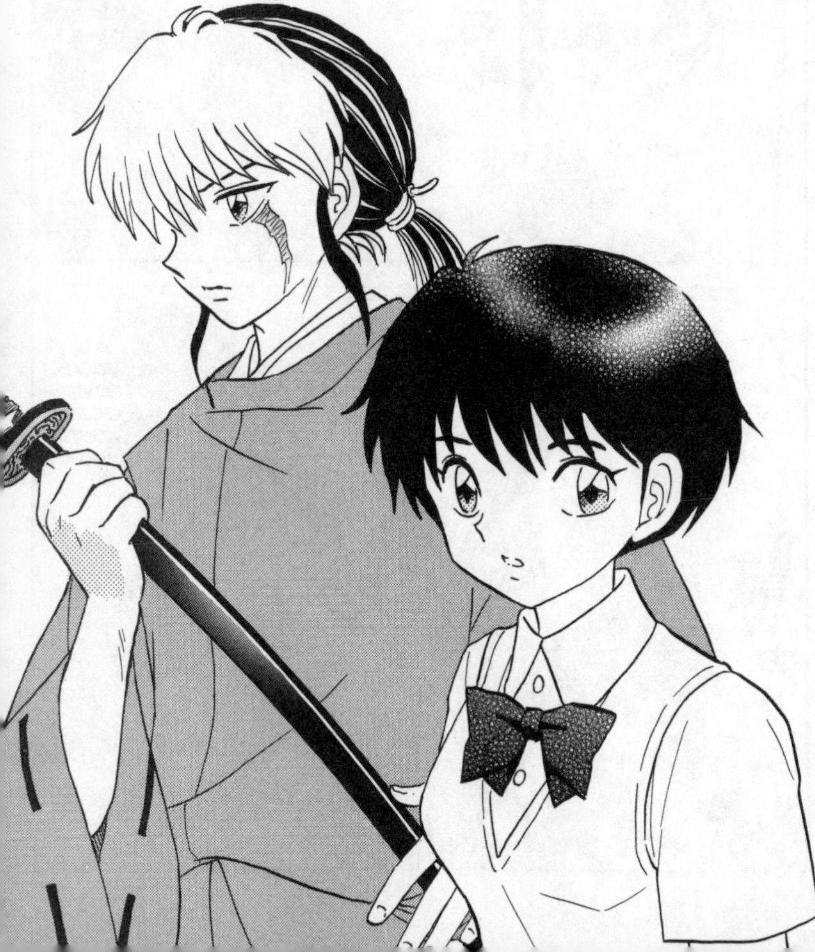

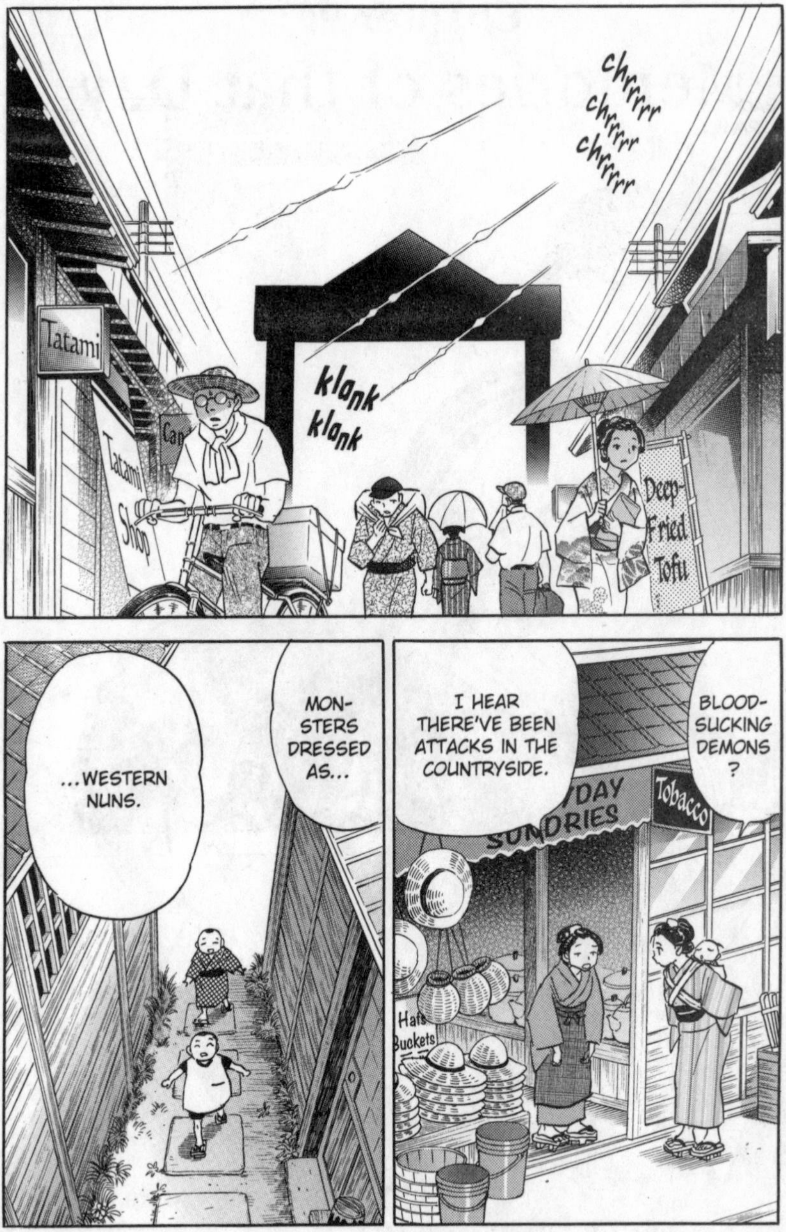
chrrrrr
chrrrrr
chrrrrr
klank
klank
Tatami
Tatami Shop
Deep-Fried Tofu
BLOOD-SUCKING DEMONS?
I HEAR THERE'VE BEEN ATTACKS IN THE COUNTRYSIDE.
Tobacco
SUNDRIES
Hats
Buckets
MON-STERS DRESSED AS...
...WESTERN NUNS.

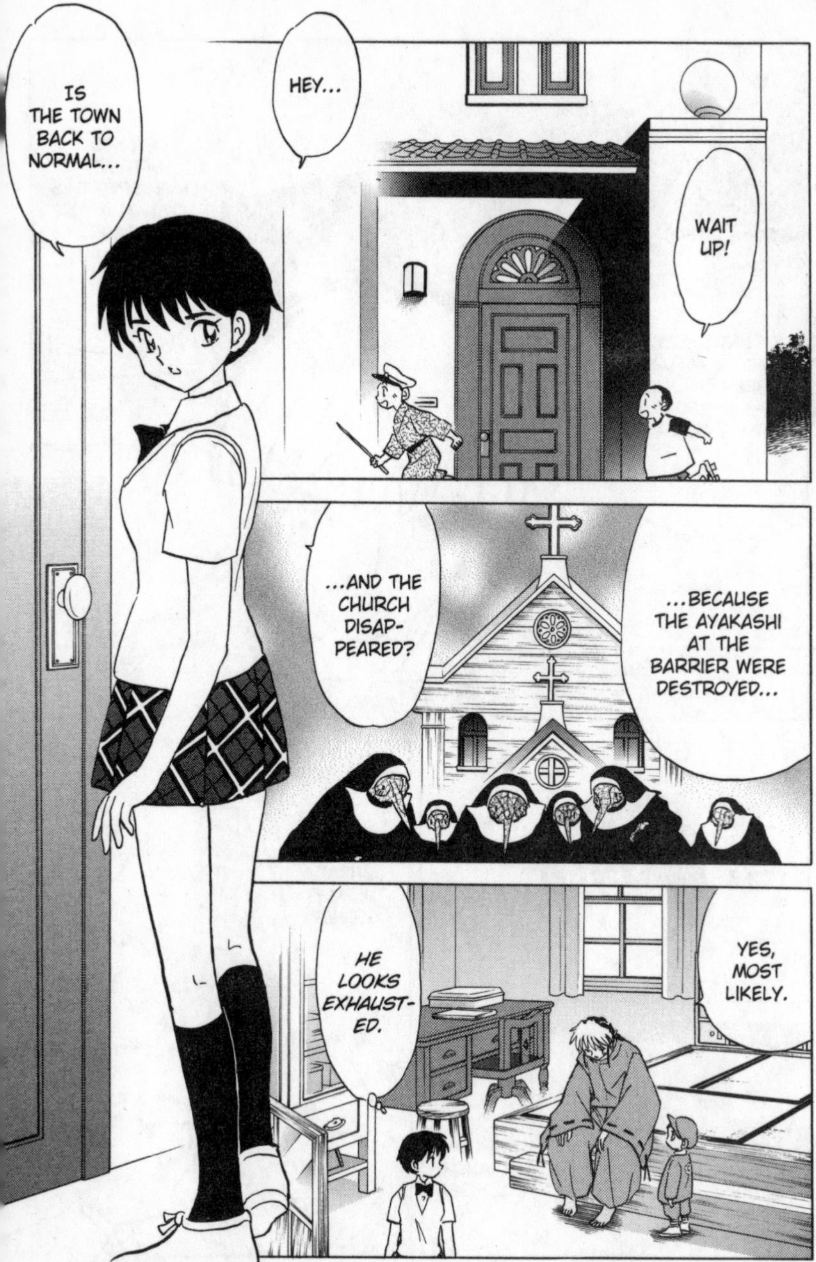
HEY...
IS THE TOWN BACK TO NORMAL...
WAIT UP!
...AND THE CHURCH DISAPPEARED?
...BECAUSE THE AYAKASHI AT THE BARRIER WERE DESTROYED...
YES, MOST LIKELY.
HE LOOKS EXHAUSTED.

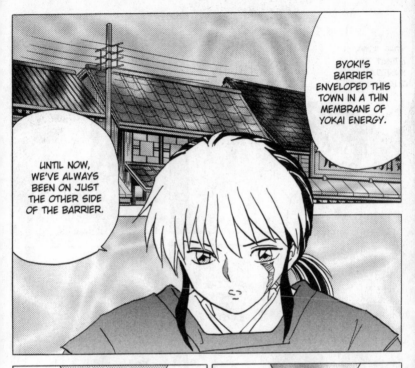

BYOKI'S BARRIER ENVELOPED THIS TOWN IN A THIN MEMBRANE OF YOKAI ENERGY.
UNTIL NOW, WE'VE ALWAYS BEEN ON JUST THE OTHER SIDE OF THE BARRIER.
IS BYOKI...
...STILL LURKING BENEATH THE KEY-STONE?
UM...
...ABOUT THAT KEY-STONE.
IT WON'T BE AROUND MUCH LONGER.
...?

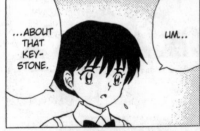

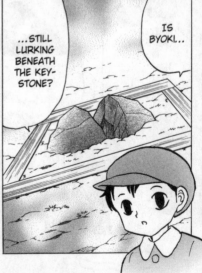

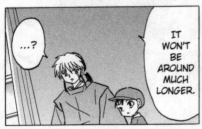

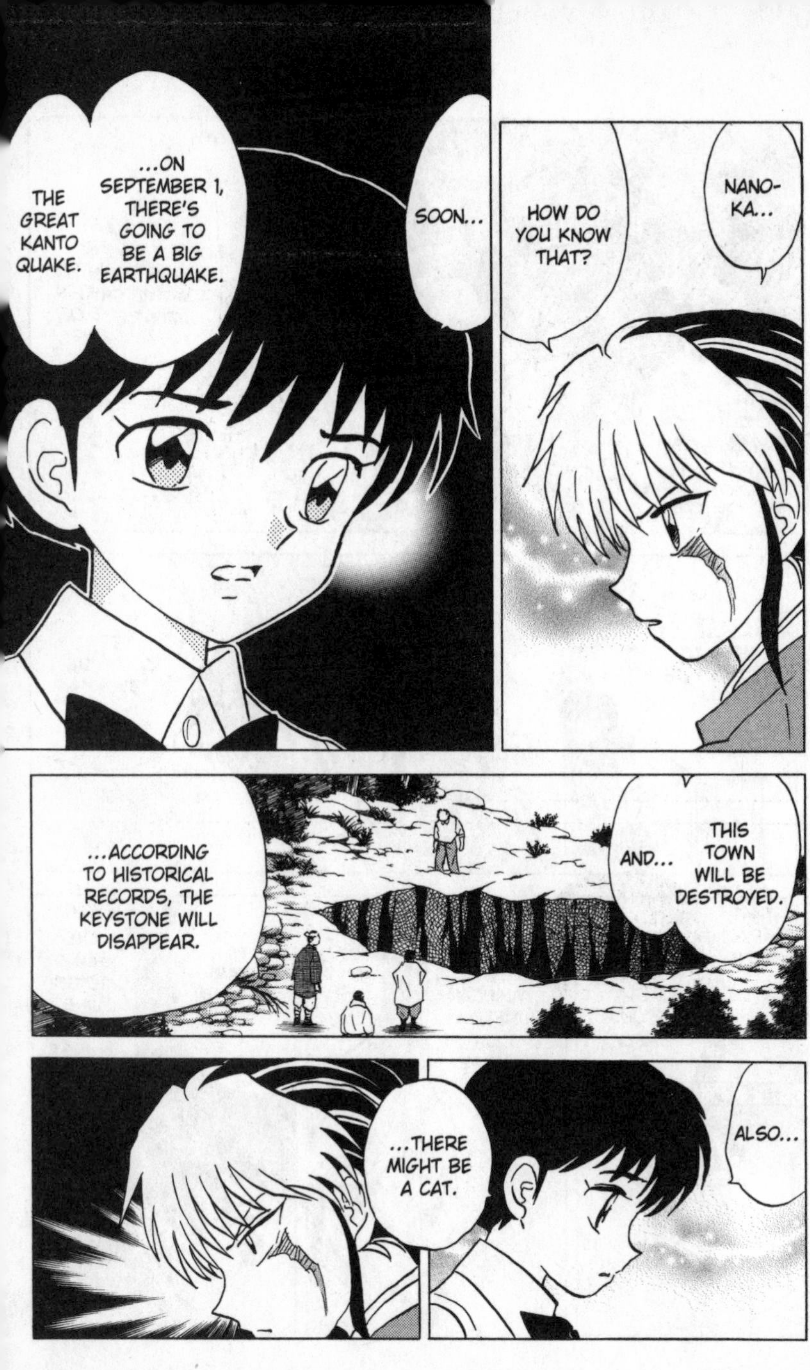
NANO-KA...
HOW DO YOU KNOW THAT?
SOON...
...ON SEPTEMBER 1, THERE'S GOING TO BE A BIG EARTHQUAKE.
THE GREAT KANTO QUAKE.
THIS TOWN WILL BE DESTROYED.
AND...
...ACCORDING TO HISTORICAL RECORDS, THE KEYSTONE WILL DISAPPEAR.
ALSO...
...THERE MIGHT BE A CAT.

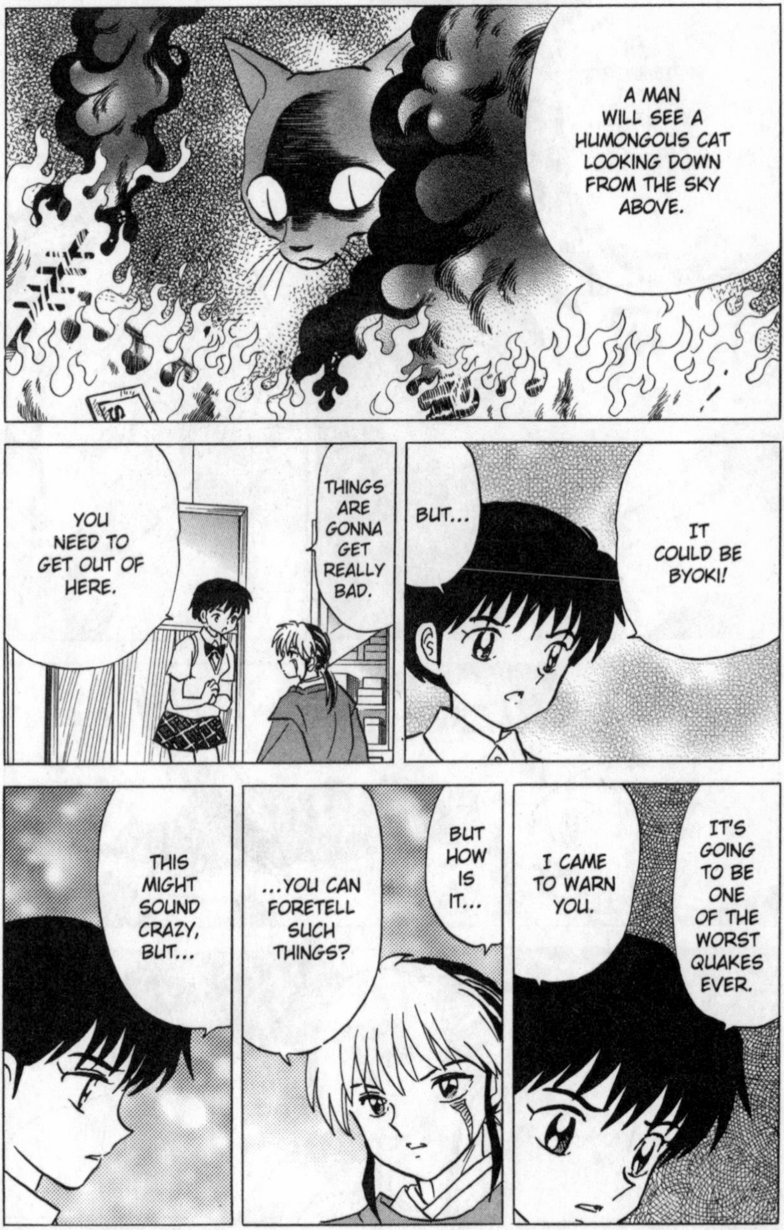
A MAN WILL SEE A HUMONGOUS CAT LOOKING DOWN FROM THE SKY ABOVE.
IT COULD BE BYOKI!
BUT...
THINGS ARE GONNA GET REALLY BAD.
YOU NEED TO GET OUT OF HERE.
IT'S GOING TO BE ONE OF THE WORST QUAKES EVER.
I CAME TO WARN YOU.
BUT HOW IS IT...
...YOU CAN FORETELL SUCH THINGS?
THIS MIGHT SOUND CRAZY, BUT...

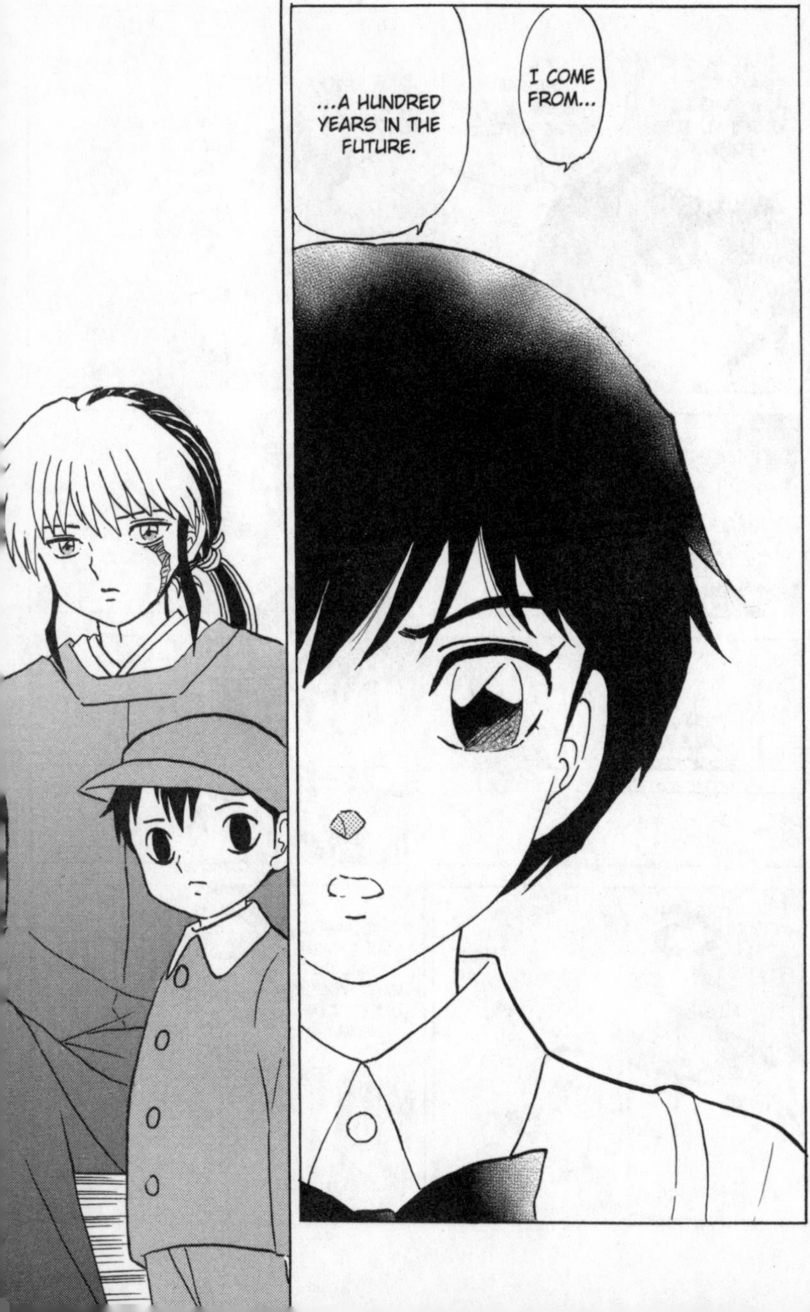
I COME FROM...
...A HUNDRED YEARS IN THE FUTURE.

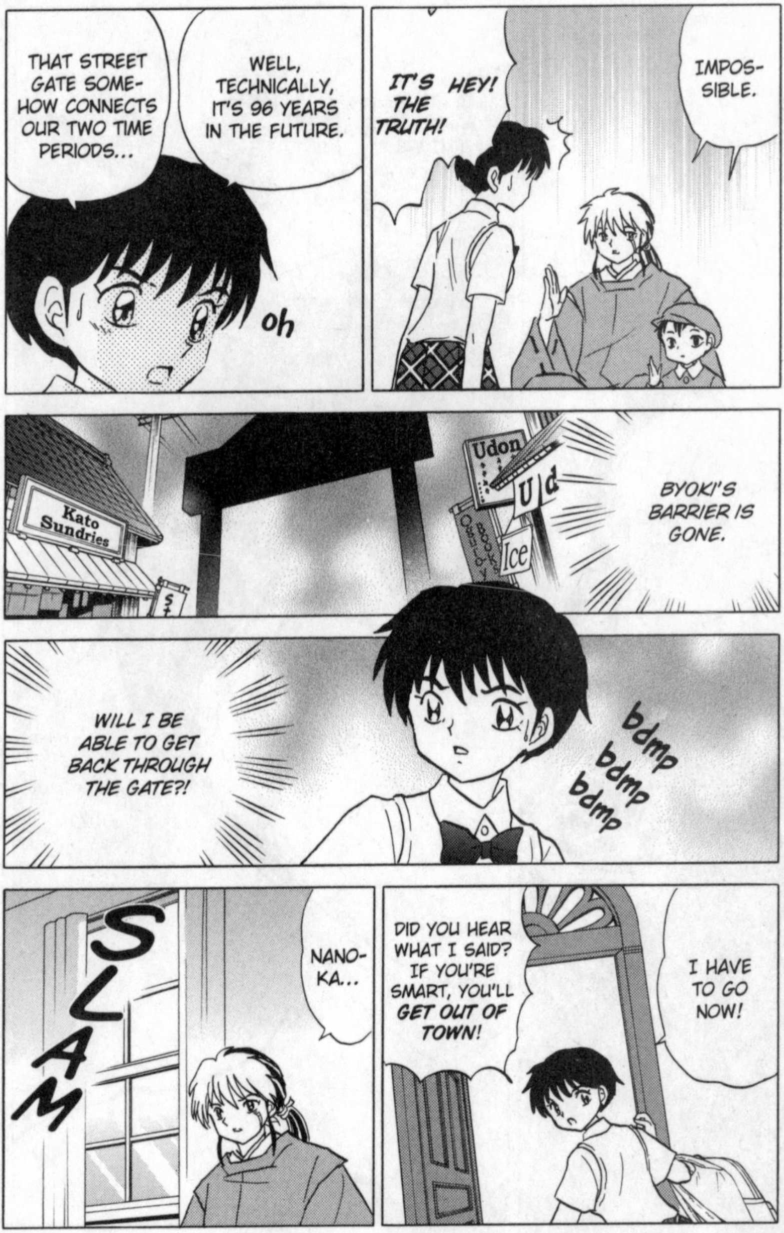
IMPOS-SIBLE.
HEY!
IT'S THE TRUTH!
WELL, TECHNICALLY, IT'S 96 YEARS IN THE FUTURE.
THAT STREET GATE SOME-HOW CONNECTS OUR TWO TIME PERIODS...
oh
BYOKI'S BARRIER IS GONE.
Udon
Ud
Ice
Kato Sundries
bdmp bdmp bdmp
WILL I BE ABLE TO GET BACK THROUGH THE GATE?!
I HAVE TO GO NOW!
DID YOU HEAR WHAT I SAID? IF YOU'RE SMART, YOU'LL GET OUT OF TOWN!
NANO-KA...
SLAM

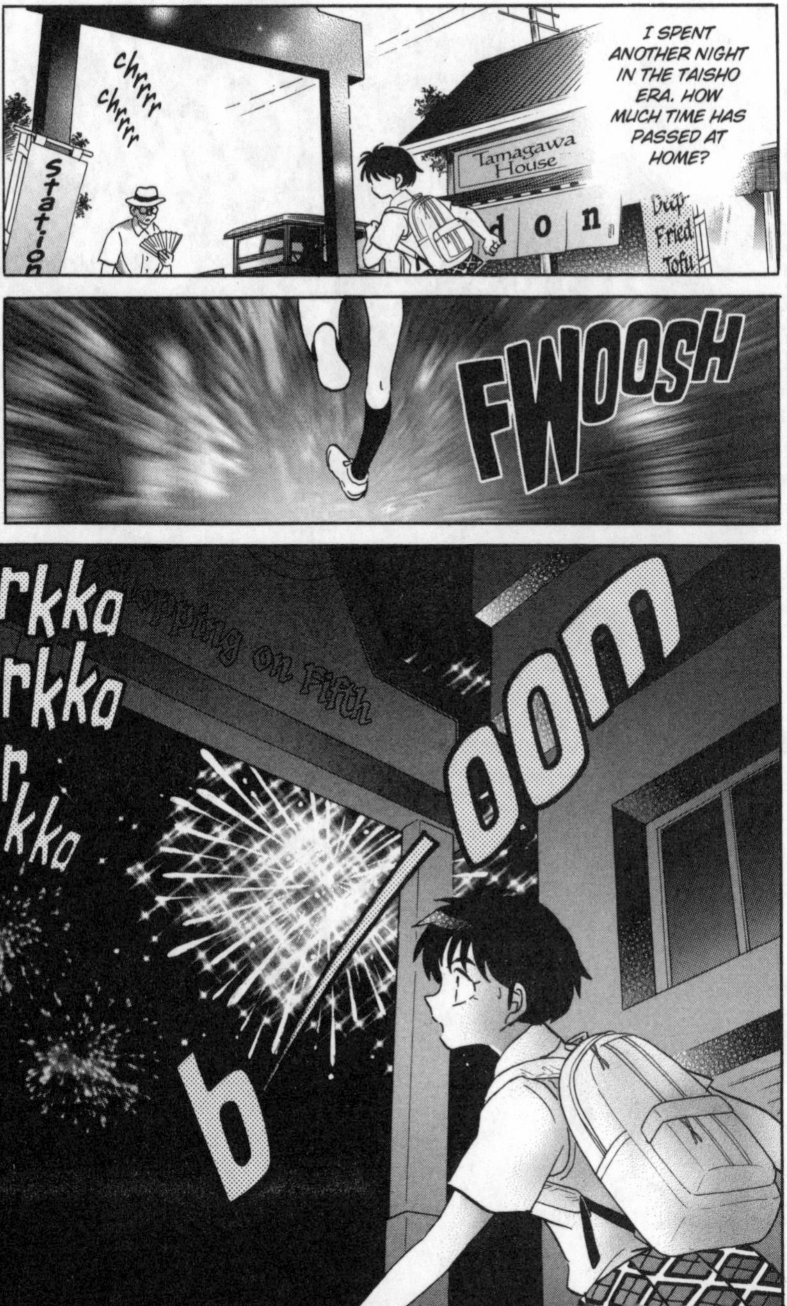
I SPENT ANOTHER NIGHT IN THE TAISHO ERA. HOW MUCH TIME HAS PASSED AT HOME?
Tamagawa House
Deep Fried Tofu
don
chrrrr chrrrr
Station
FWOOSH
oom
b
pping on Fifth
rkka
rkka
rkka

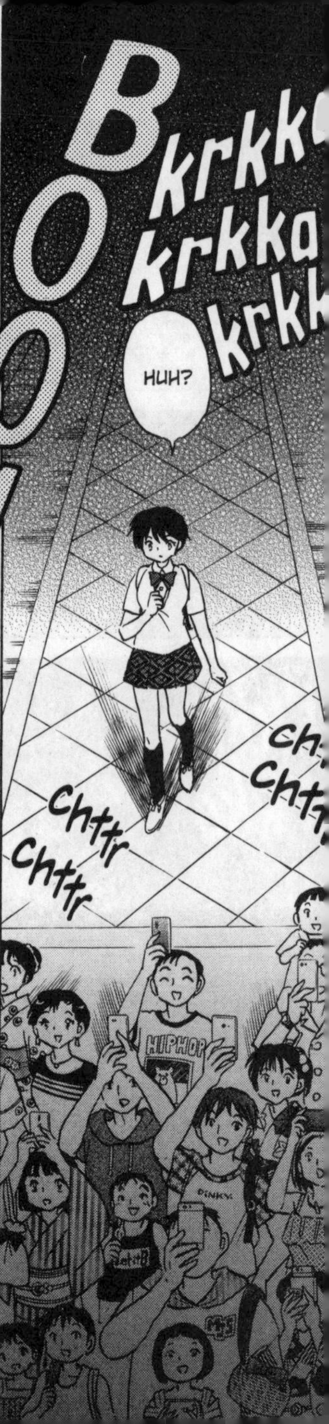
BOOM
krkka
krkka
krkk
HUH?
Chttr
Chttr

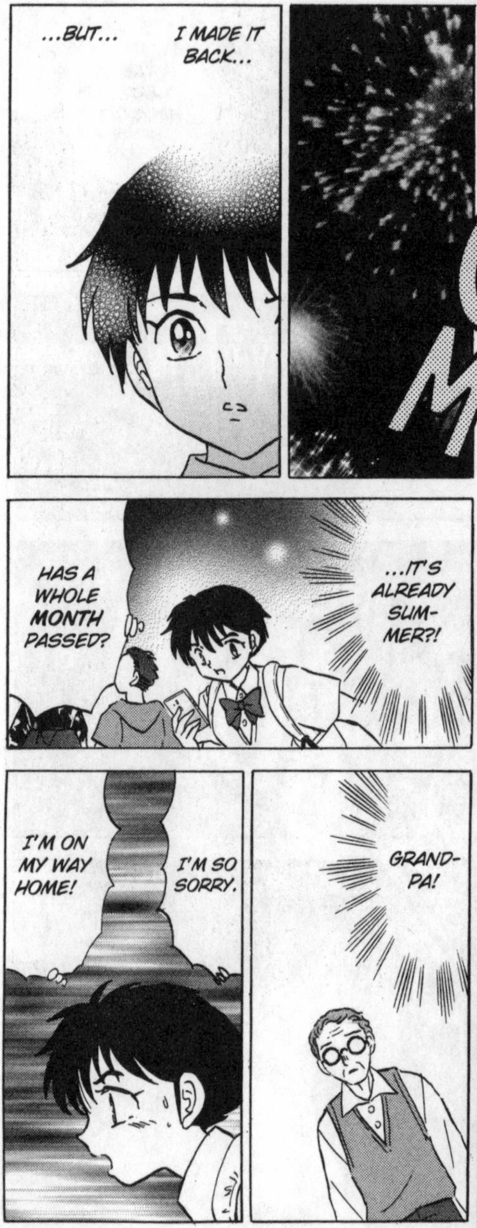
I MADE IT BACK...
...BUT...
...IT'S ALREADY SUM-MER?!
HAS A WHOLE MONTH PASSED?
GRAND-PA!
I'M SO SORRY.
I'M ON MY WAY HOME!

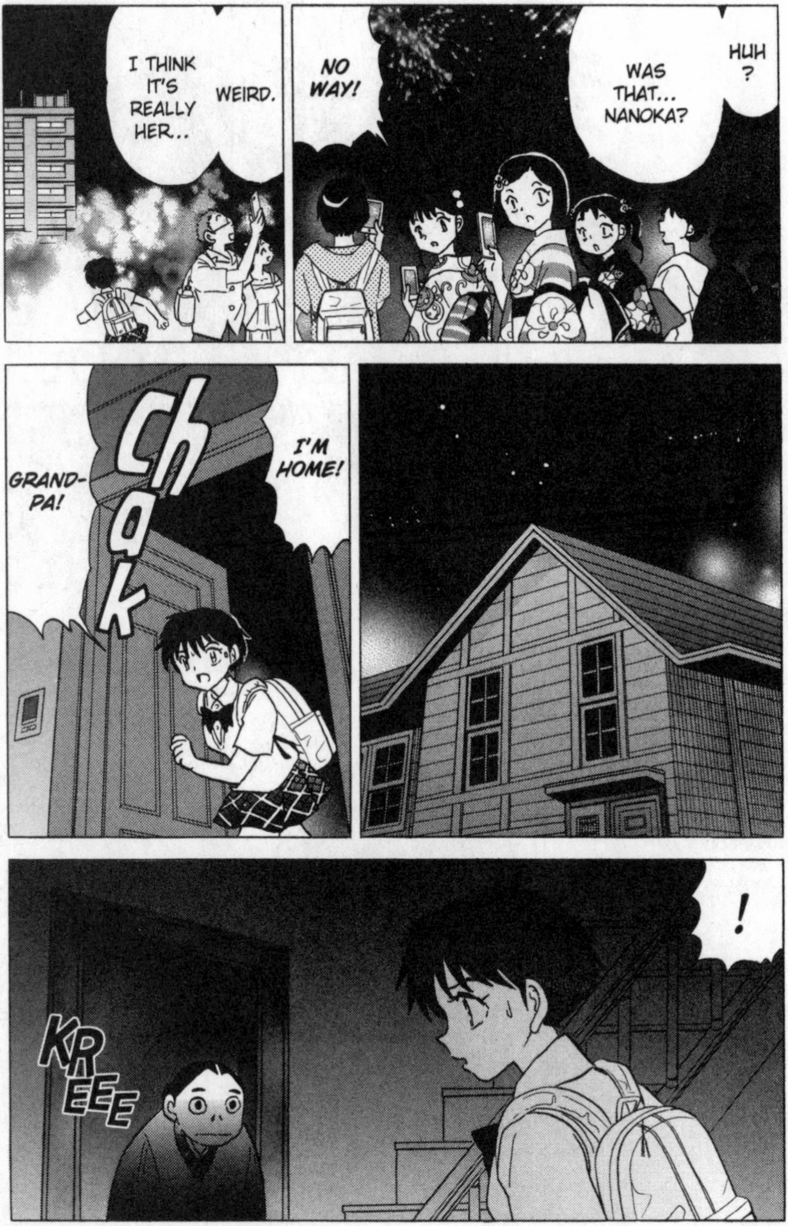
HUH ?
WAS THAT... NANOKA?
NO WAY!
WEIRD.
I THINK IT'S REALLY HER...
I'M HOME!
Chak
GRAND-PA!
!
KREEEE

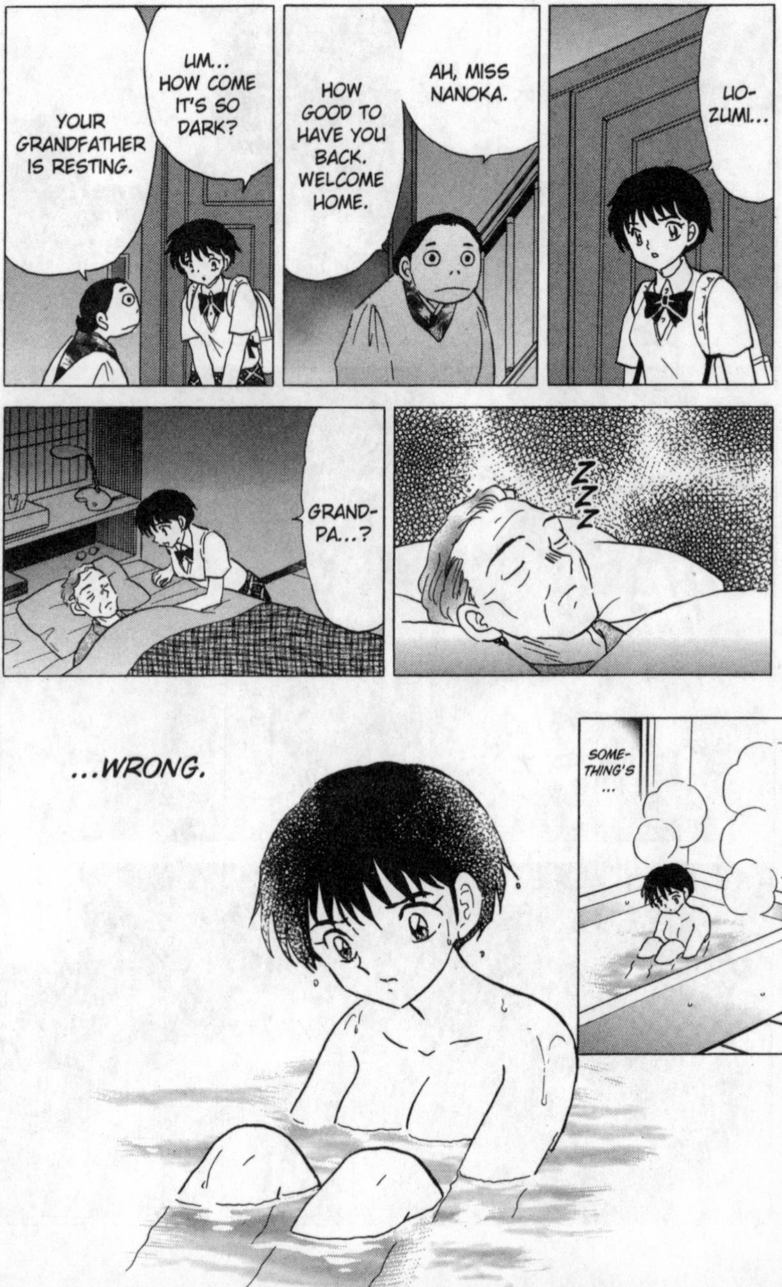
UO-ZUMI...
AH, MISS NANOKA.
HOW GOOD TO HAVE YOU BACK. WELCOME HOME.
UM... HOW COME IT'S SO DARK?
YOUR GRANDFATHER IS RESTING.
ZZZ
GRAND-PA...?
SOME-THING'S ...
...WRONG.

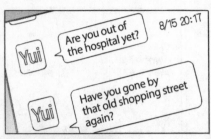

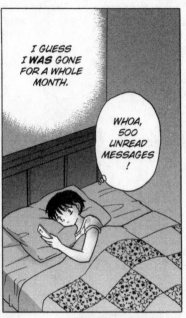

I GUESS I **WAS** GONE FOR A WHOLE MONTH.
WHOA, 500 UNREAD MESSAGES!
8/15 20:17
Yui
Are you out of the hospital yet?
Yui
Have you gone by that old shopping street again?
GRANDPA TOLD EVERYONE I'VE BEEN IN THE HOSPITAL.
chrrr chrrr
NANOKA! WHAT A RELIEF.
WHERE **WERE** YOU?

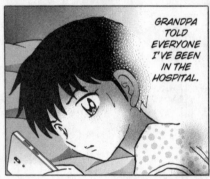

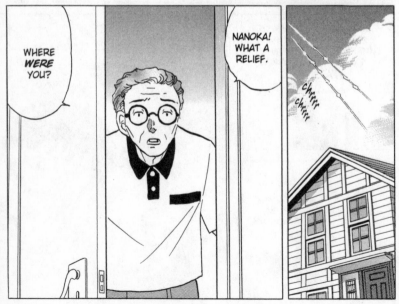

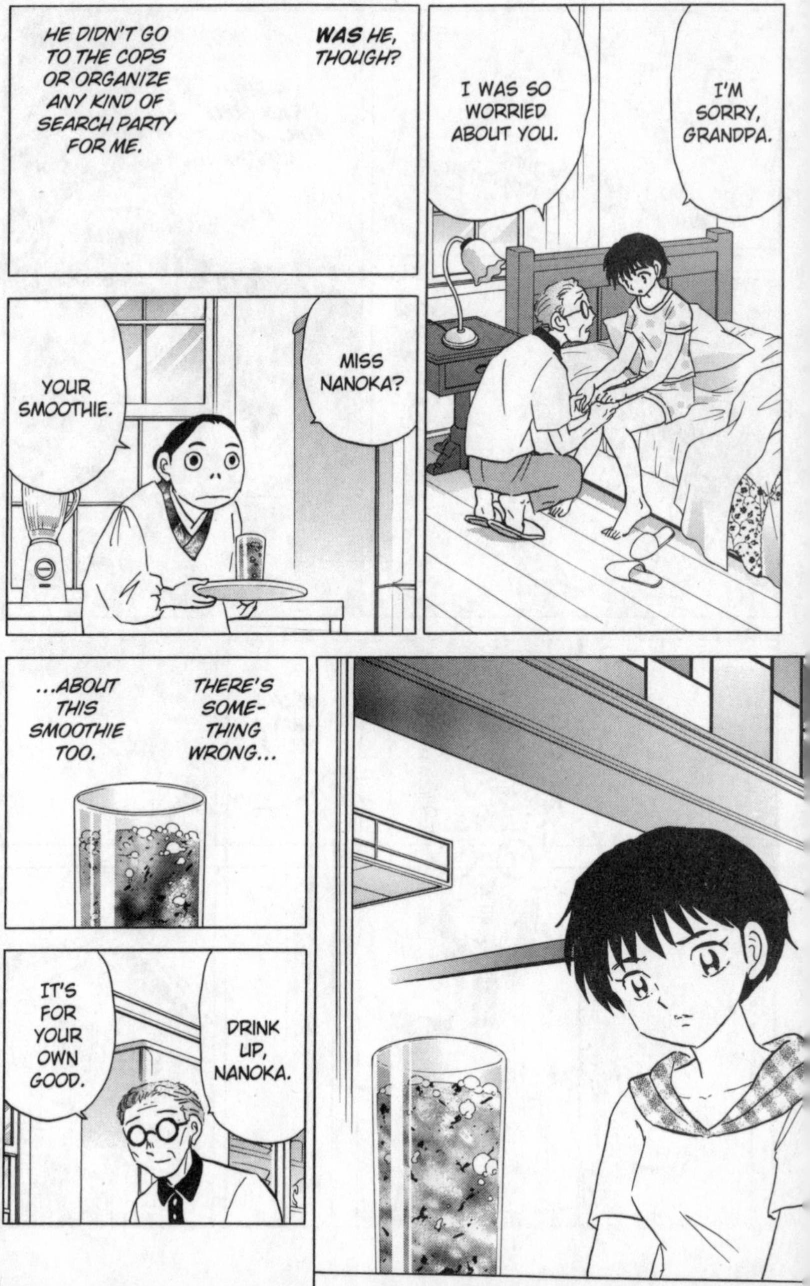
I'M SORRY, GRANDPA.
I WAS SO WORRIED ABOUT YOU.
WAS HE, THOUGH?
HE DIDN'T GO TO THE COPS OR ORGANIZE ANY KIND OF SEARCH PARTY FOR ME.
MISS NANOKA?
YOUR SMOOTHIE.
THERE'S SOME-THING WRONG...
...ABOUT THIS SMOOTHIE TOO.
DRINK UP, NANOKA.
IT'S FOR YOUR OWN GOOD.

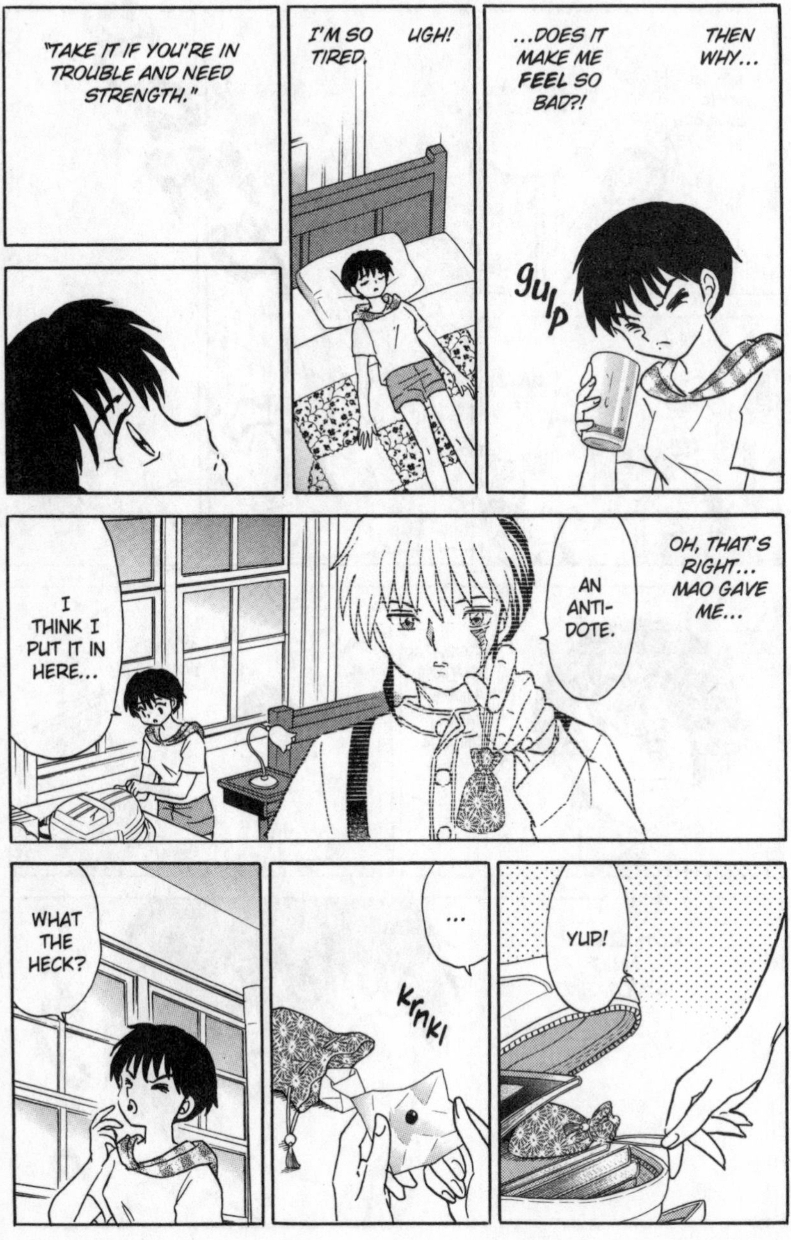
THEN WHY...
...DOES IT MAKE ME FEEL SO BAD?!
gulp
UGH!
I'M SO TIRED.
"TAKE IT IF YOU'RE IN TROUBLE AND NEED STRENGTH."
OH, THAT'S RIGHT... MAO GAVE ME...
AN ANTI-DOTE.
I THINK I PUT IT IN HERE...
YUP!
...
krnkl
WHAT THE HECK?

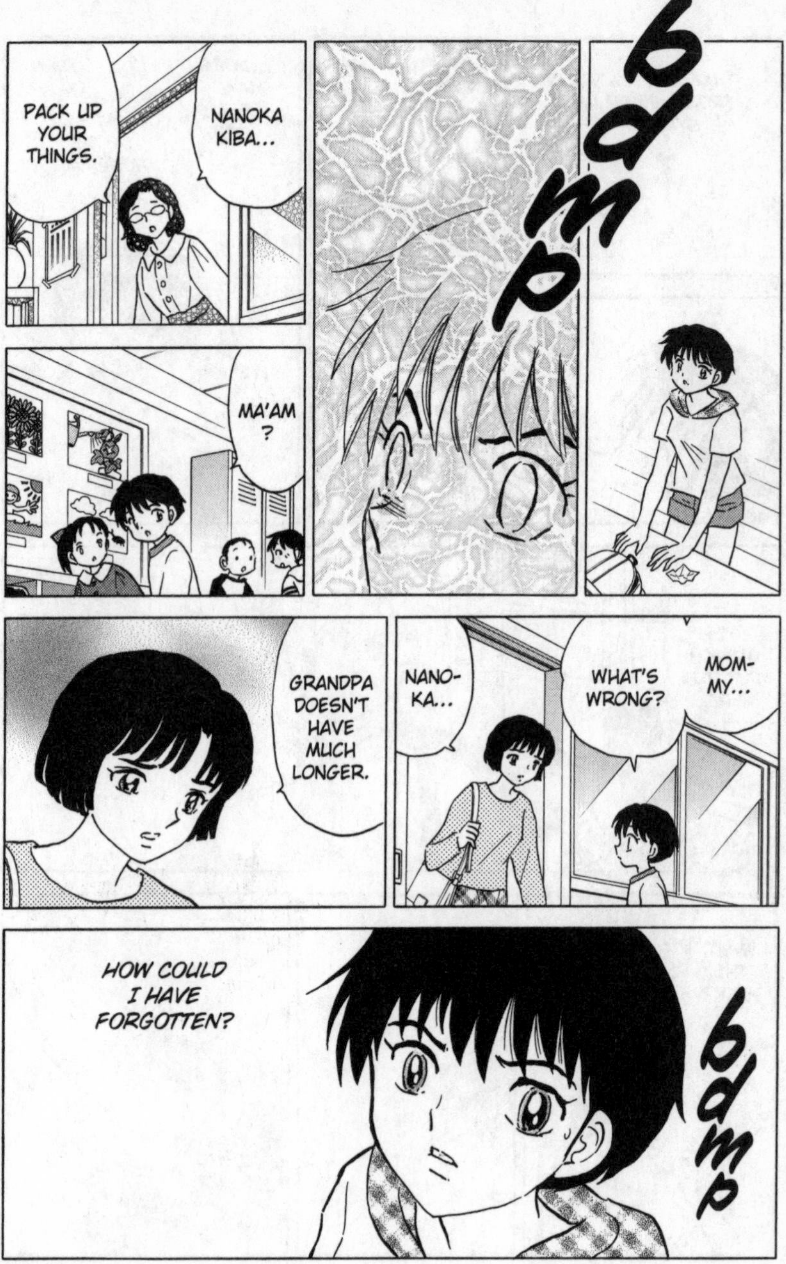
bdmp
NANOKA KIBA...
PACK UP YOUR THINGS.
MA'AM?
MOMMY...
WHAT'S WRONG?
NANOKA...
GRANDPA DOESN'T HAVE MUCH LONGER.
bdmp
HOW COULD I HAVE FORGOTTEN?

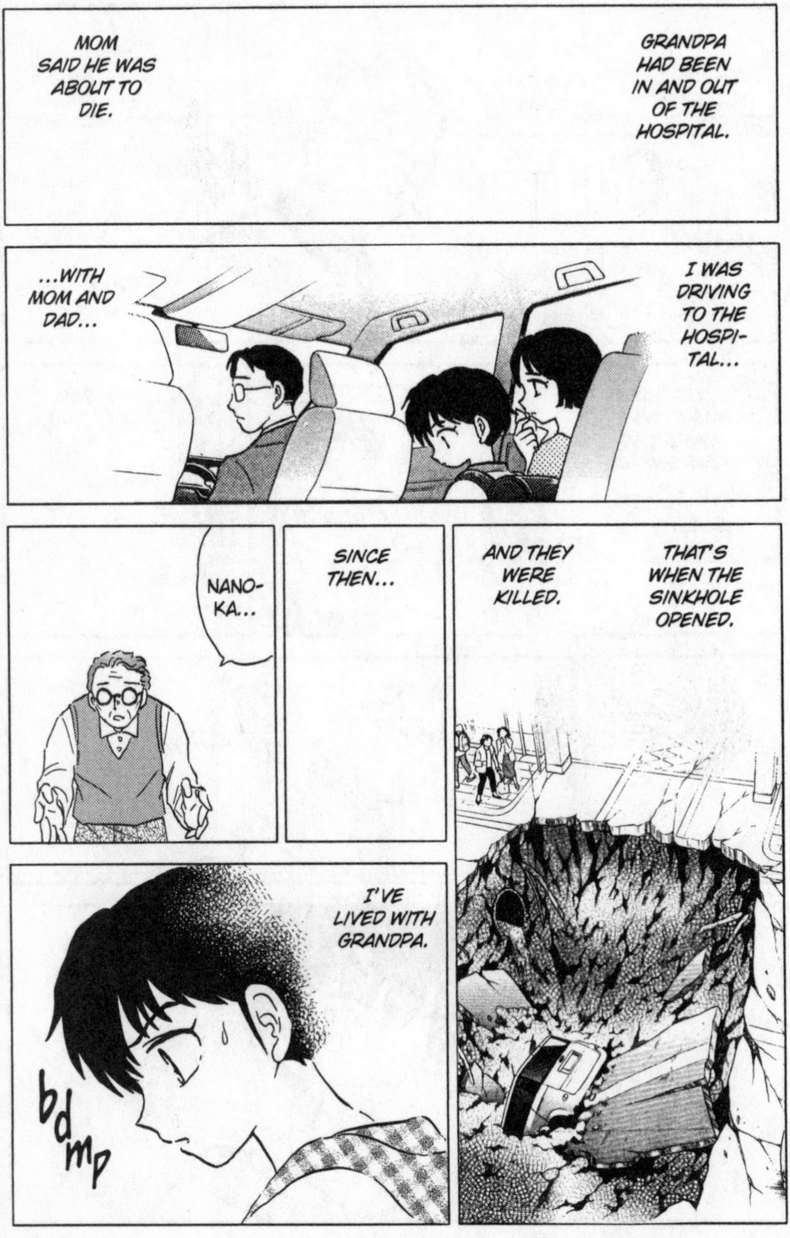
GRANDPA HAD BEEN IN AND OUT OF THE HOSPITAL.
MOM SAID HE WAS ABOUT TO DIE.
I WAS DRIVING TO THE HOSPI-TAL...
...WITH MOM AND DAD...
THAT'S WHEN THE SINKHOLE OPENED.
AND THEY WERE KILLED.
SINCE THEN...
NANO-KA...
I'VE LIVED WITH GRANDPA.
bdmp

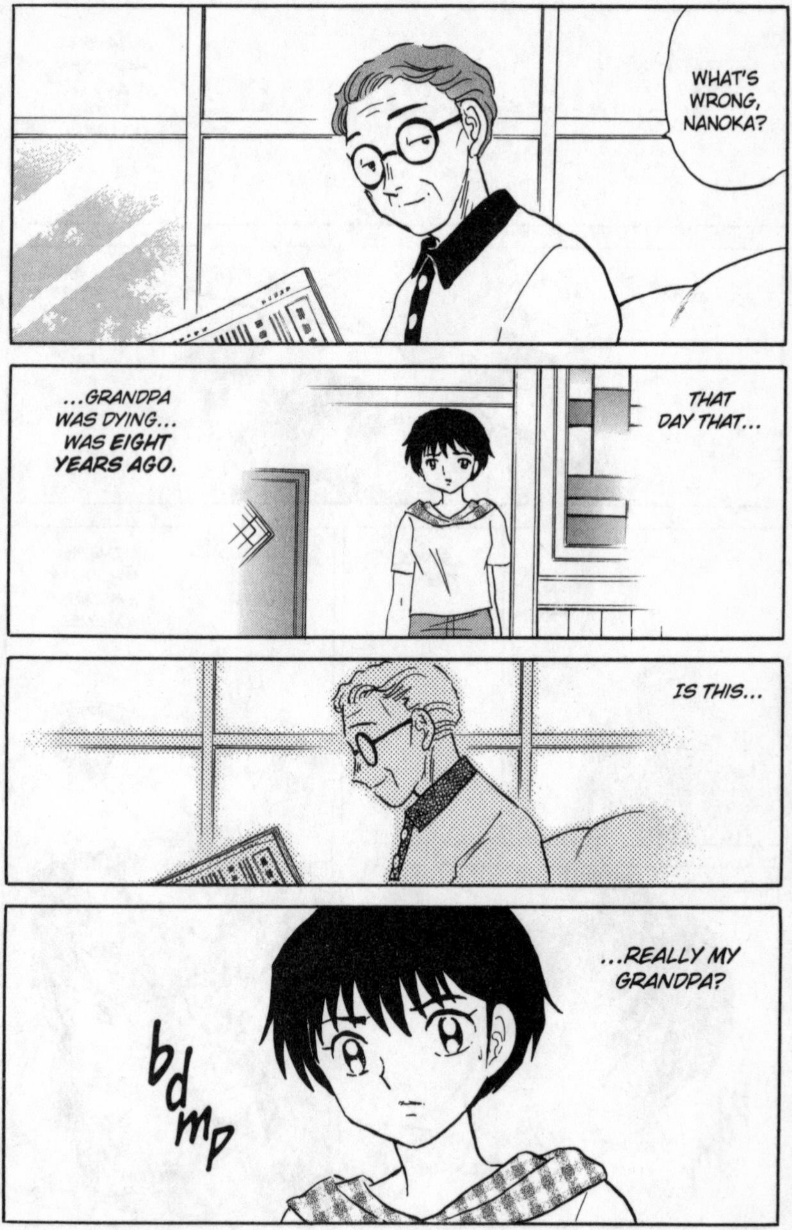
WHAT'S WRONG, NANOKA?
THAT DAY THAT...
...GRANDPA WAS DYING... WAS EIGHT YEARS AGO.
IS THIS...
...REALLY MY GRANDPA?
bdmp

Chapter 10:
The Beginning

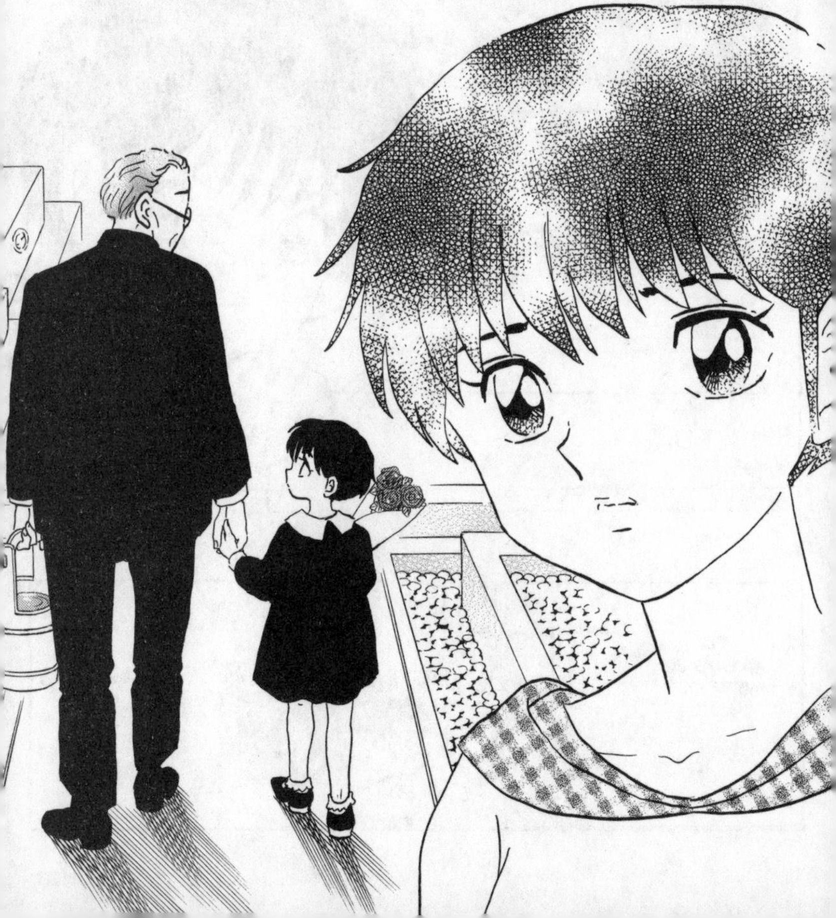

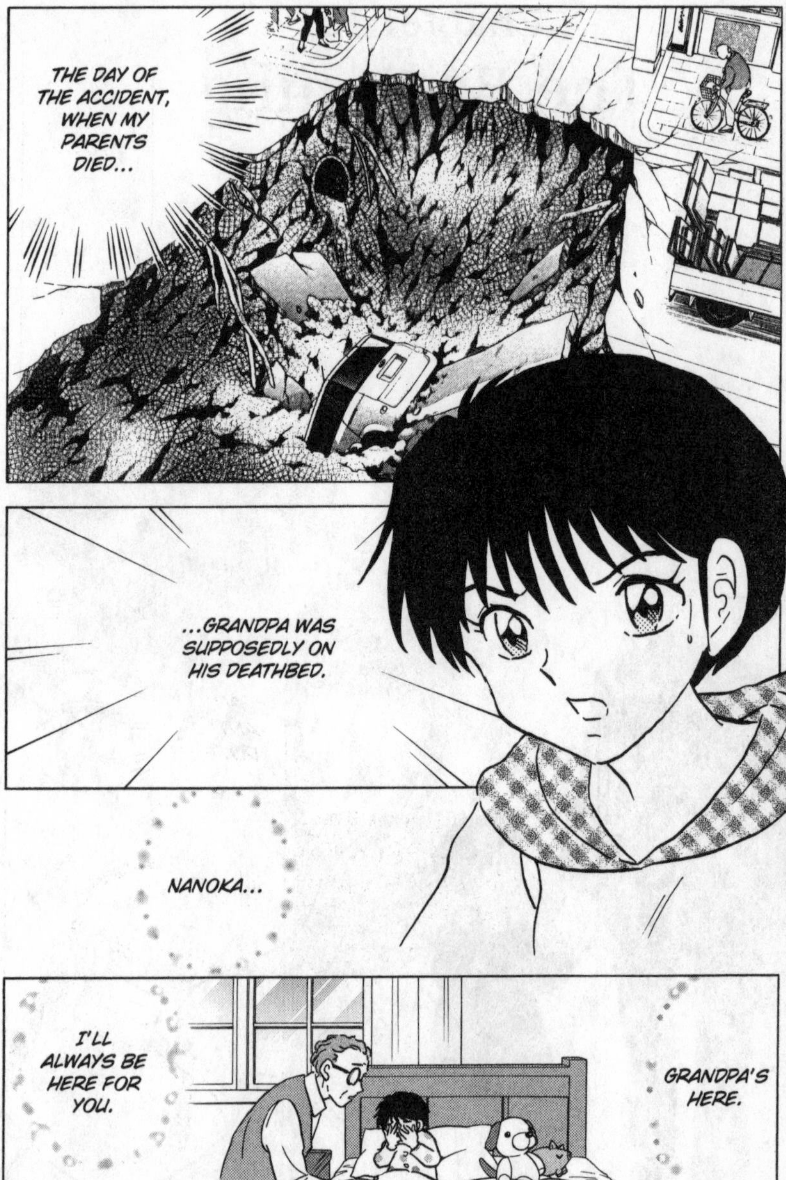
THE DAY OF THE ACCIDENT, WHEN MY PARENTS DIED...
...GRANDPA WAS SUPPOSEDLY ON HIS DEATHBED.
NANOKA...
GRANDPA'S HERE.
I'LL ALWAYS BE HERE FOR YOU.

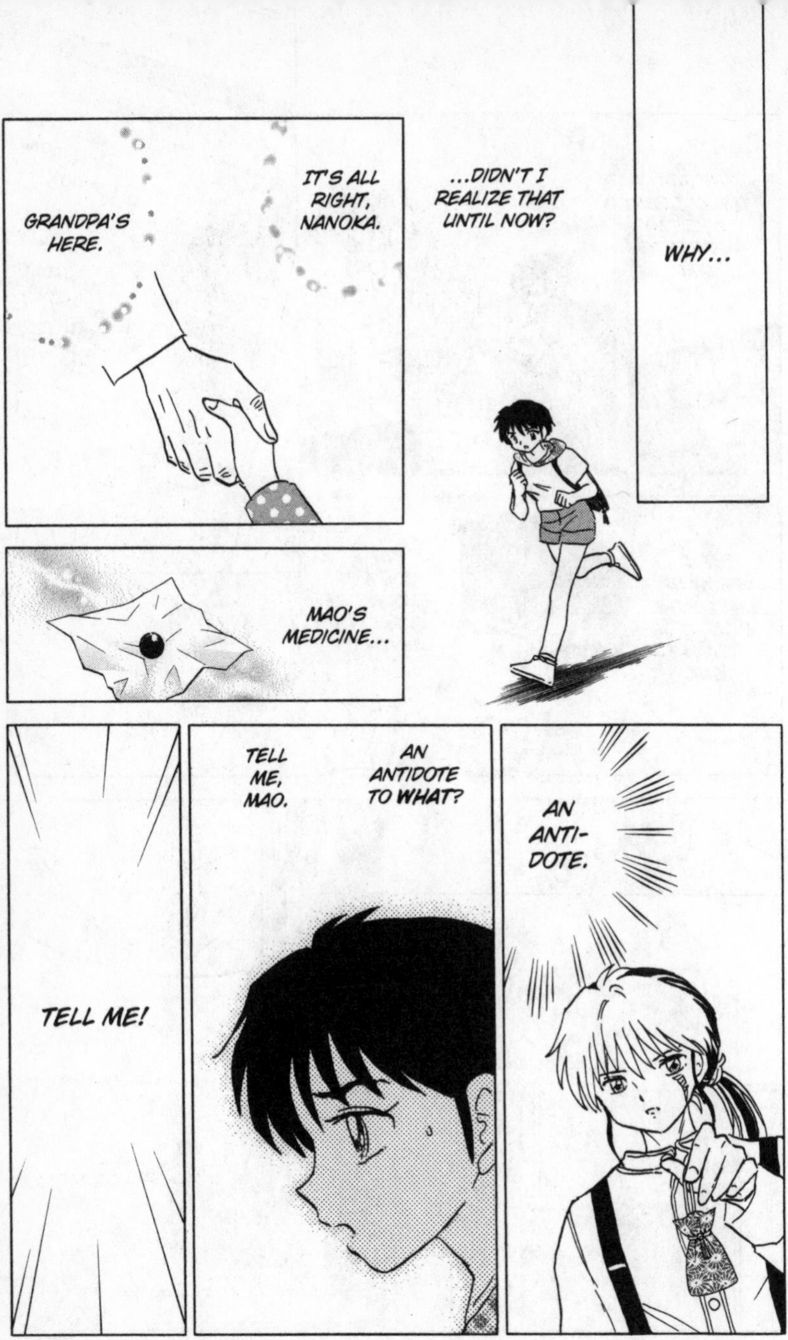
WHY...
...DIDN'T I REALIZE THAT UNTIL NOW?
IT'S ALL RIGHT, NANOKA.
GRANDPA'S HERE.
MAO'S MEDICINE...
AN ANTI-DOTE.
AN ANTIDOTE TO WHAT?
TELL ME, MAO.
TELL ME!

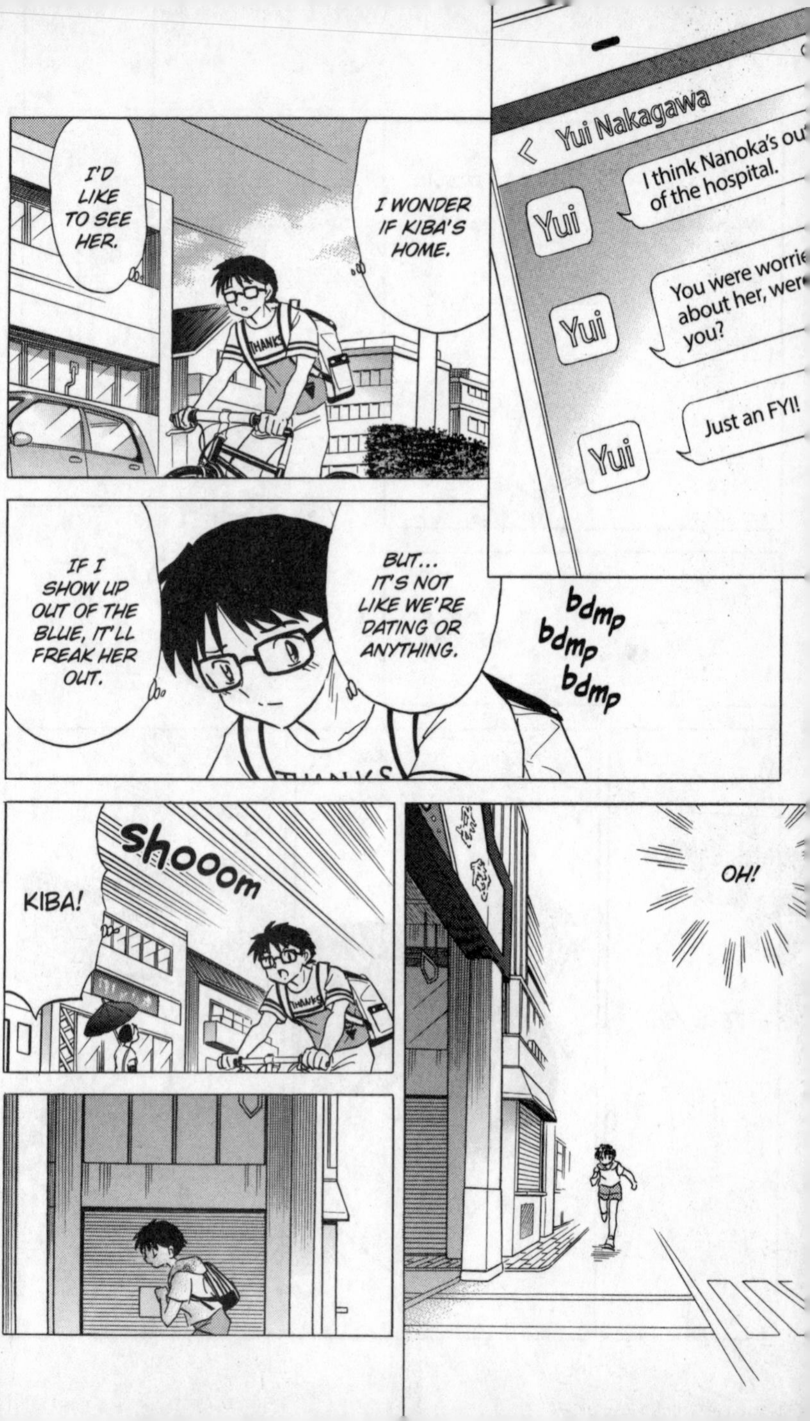
Yui Nakagawa
I think Nanoka's out of the hospital.
You were worried about her, weren't you?
Just an FYI!
I WONDER IF KIBA'S HOME.
I'D LIKE TO SEE HER.
bdmp bdmp bdmp
BUT... IT'S NOT LIKE WE'RE DATING OR ANYTHING.
IF I SHOW UP OUT OF THE BLUE, IT'LL FREAK HER OUT.
OH!
shooom
KIBA!

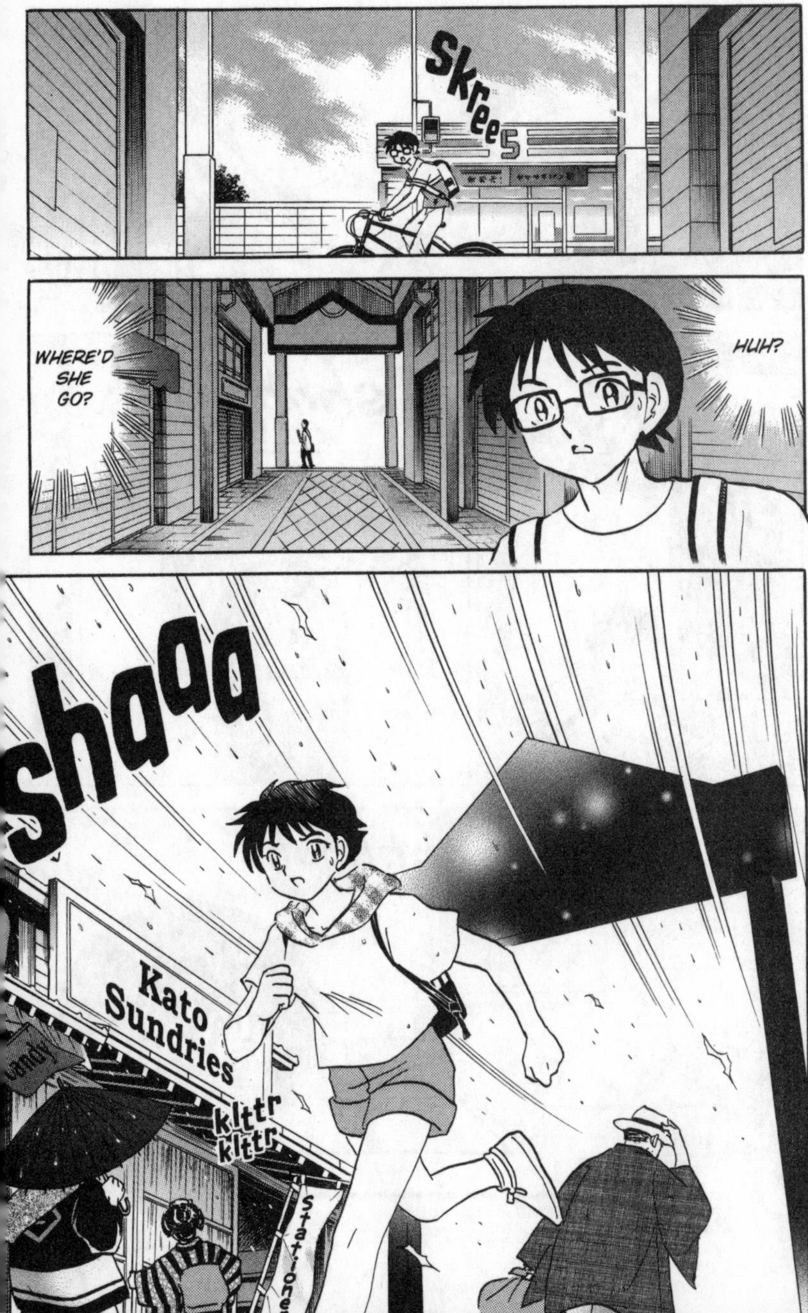
Skrees
HUH?
WHERE'D SHE GO?
shaaa
Kato Sundries
klttr klttr
Stationer

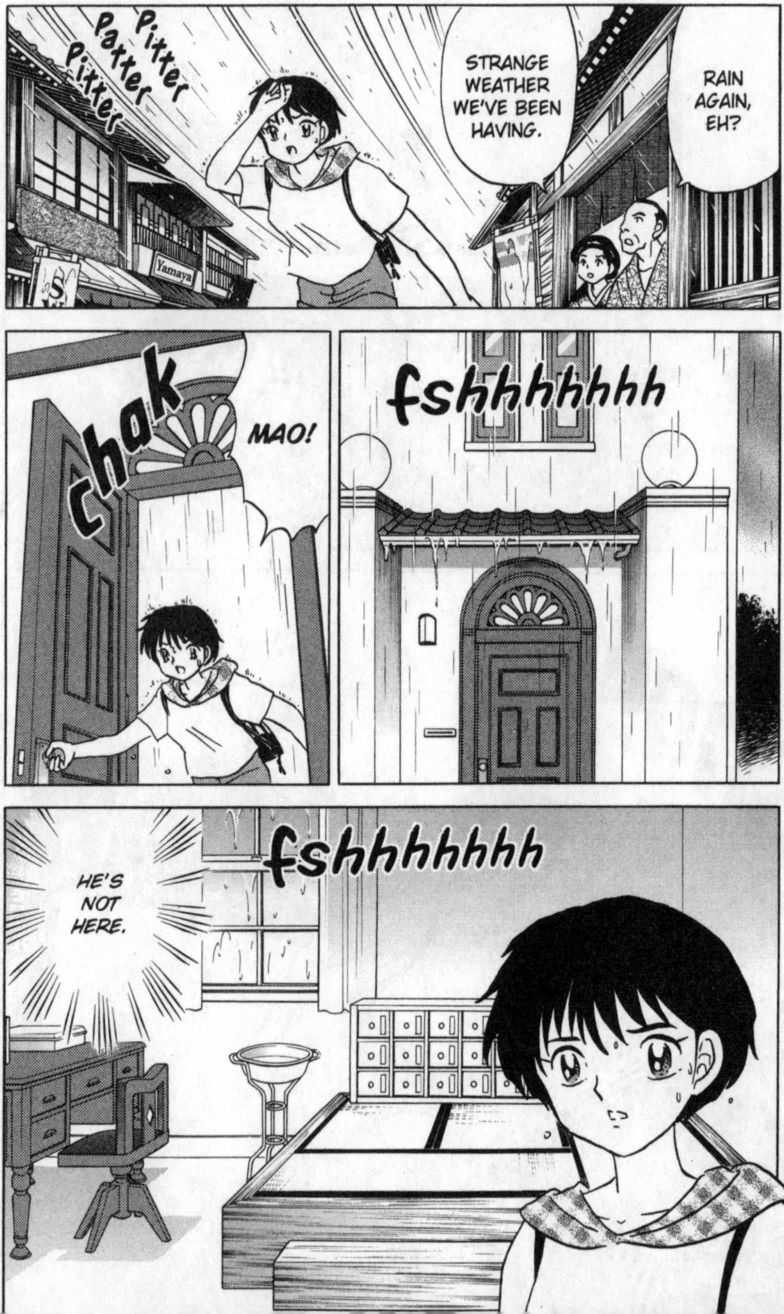
RAIN AGAIN, EH?
STRANGE WEATHER WE'VE BEEN HAVING.
Pitter Patter Pitter
Yamaya
fshhhhhhhh
MAO!
Chak
fshhhhhhh
HE'S NOT HERE.

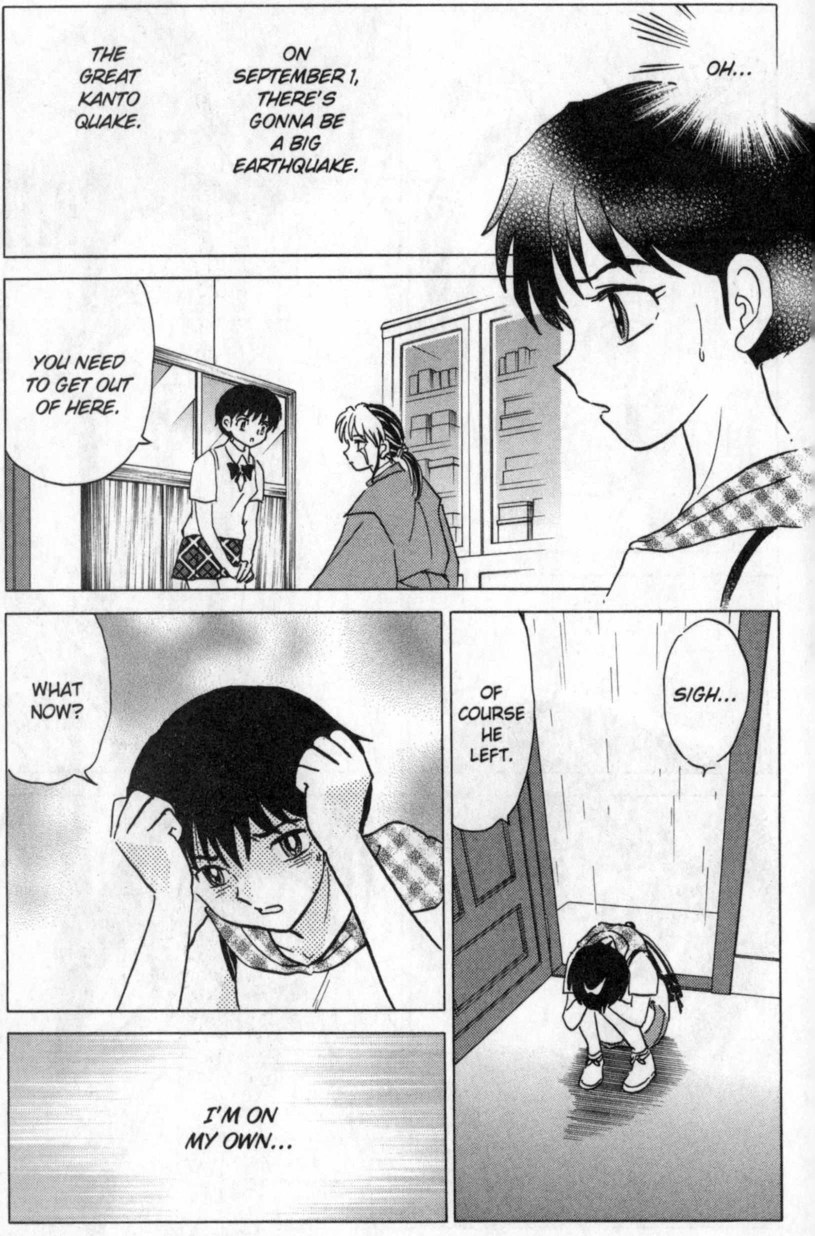
OH...
ON SEPTEMBER 1, THERE'S GONNA BE A BIG EARTHQUAKE.
THE GREAT KANTO QUAKE.
YOU NEED TO GET OUT OF HERE.
SIGH...
OF COURSE HE LEFT.
WHAT NOW?
I'M ON MY OWN...

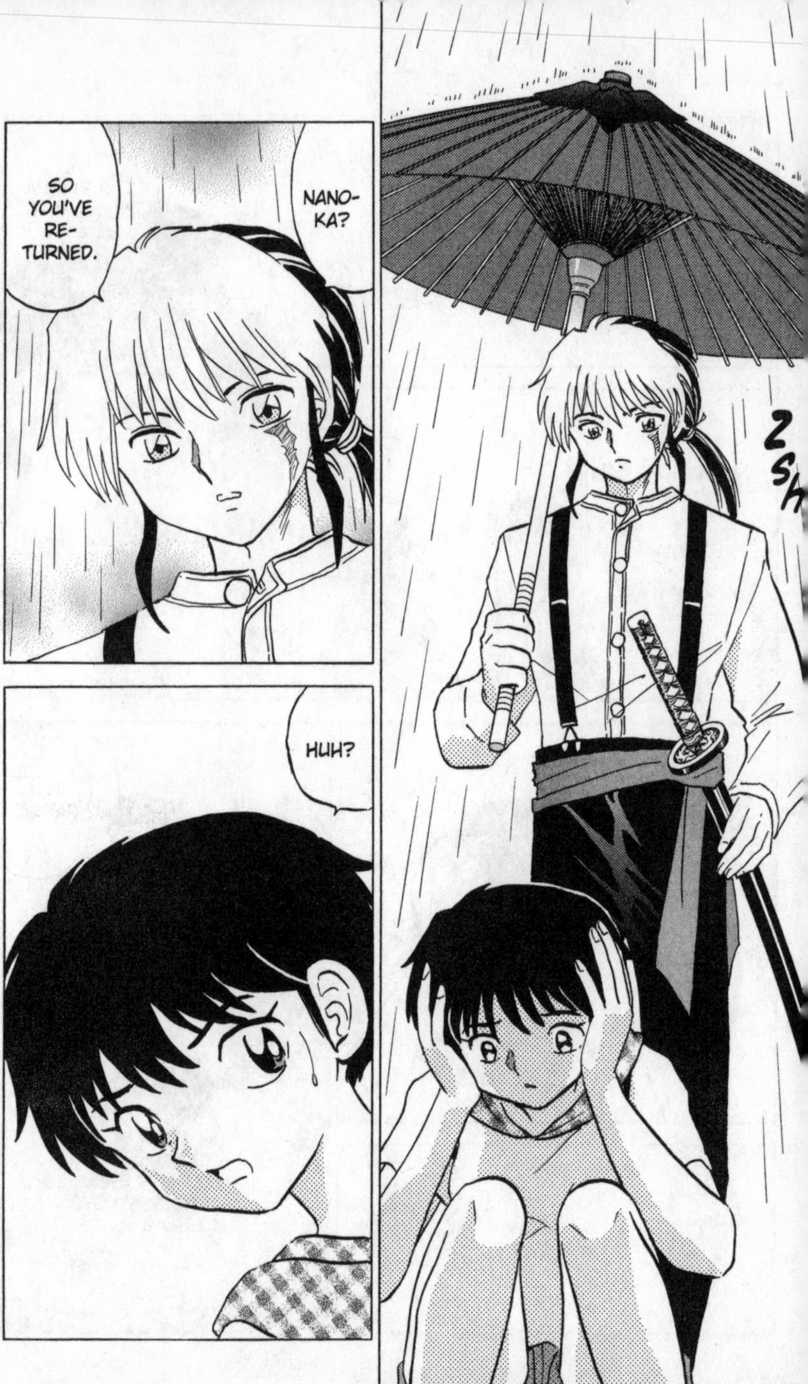
ZSH
NANO-KA?
SO YOU'VE RE-TURNED.
HUH?

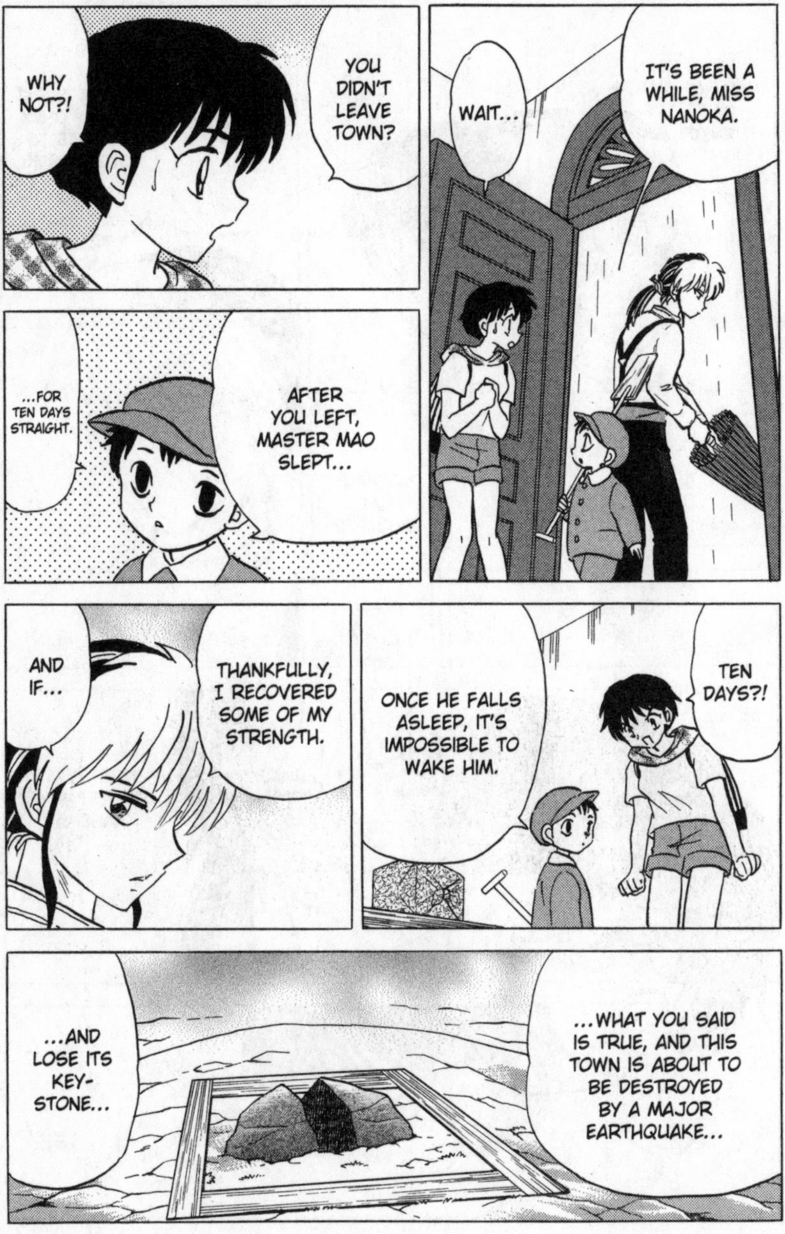
IT'S BEEN A WHILE, MISS NANOKA.
WAIT...
YOU DIDN'T LEAVE TOWN?
WHY NOT?!
AFTER YOU LEFT, MASTER MAO SLEPT...
...FOR TEN DAYS STRAIGHT.
TEN DAYS?!
ONCE HE FALLS ASLEEP, IT'S IMPOSSIBLE TO WAKE HIM.
THANKFULLY, I RECOVERED SOME OF MY STRENGTH.
AND IF...
...WHAT YOU SAID IS TRUE, AND THIS TOWN IS ABOUT TO BE DESTROYED BY A MAJOR EARTHQUAKE...
...AND LOSE ITS KEY-STONE...

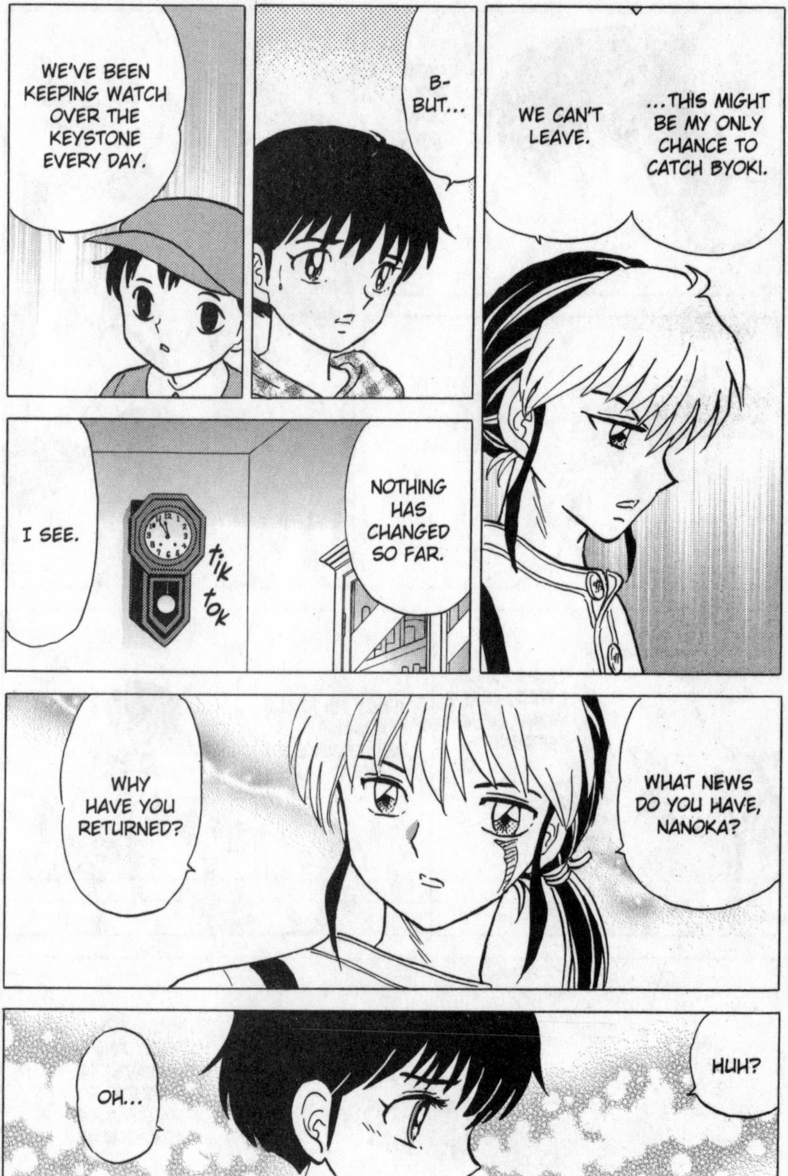
...THIS MIGHT BE MY ONLY CHANCE TO CATCH BYOKI.
WE CAN'T LEAVE.
B-BUT...
WE'VE BEEN KEEPING WATCH OVER THE KEYSTONE EVERY DAY.
NOTHING HAS CHANGED SO FAR.
tik tok
I SEE.
WHAT NEWS DO YOU HAVE, NANOKA?
WHY HAVE YOU RETURNED?
HUH?
OH...

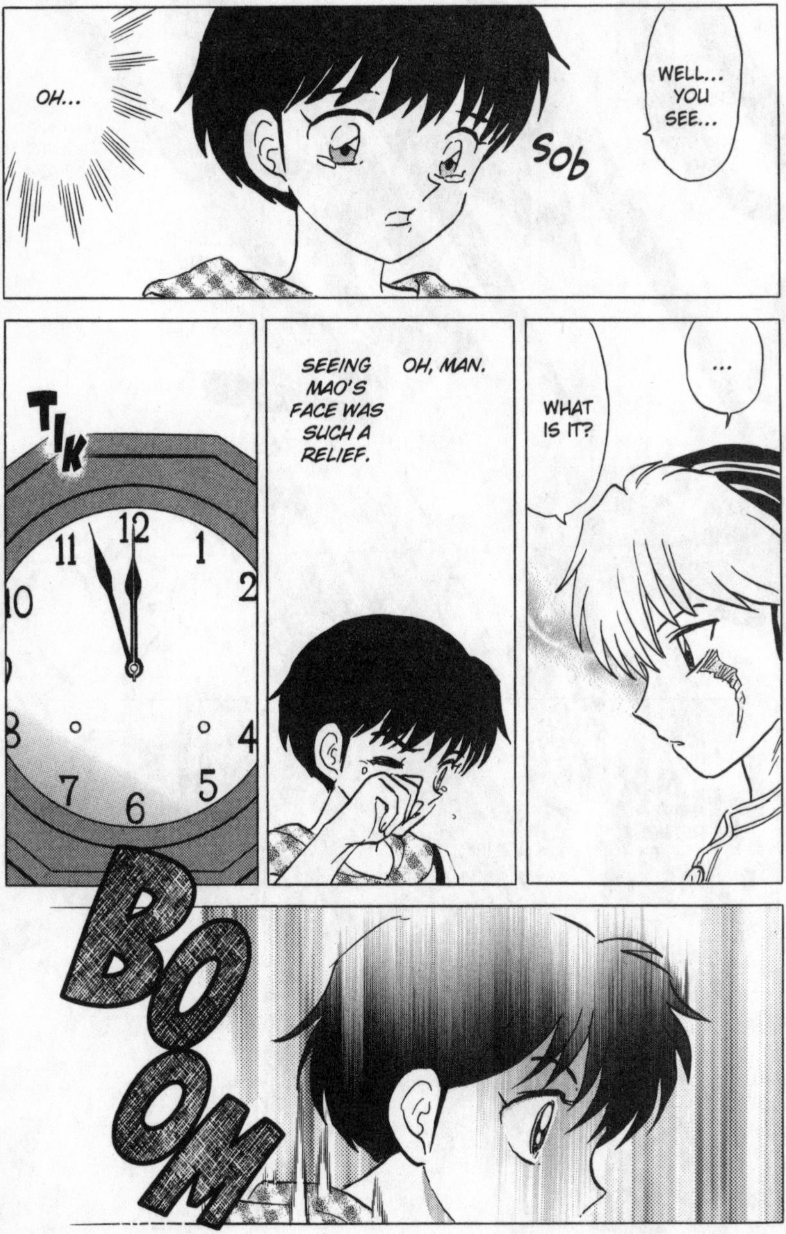
WELL... YOU SEE...
SOB
OH...
...
WHAT IS IT?
OH, MAN.
SEEING MAO'S FACE WAS SUCH A RELIEF.
TIK
BOOM

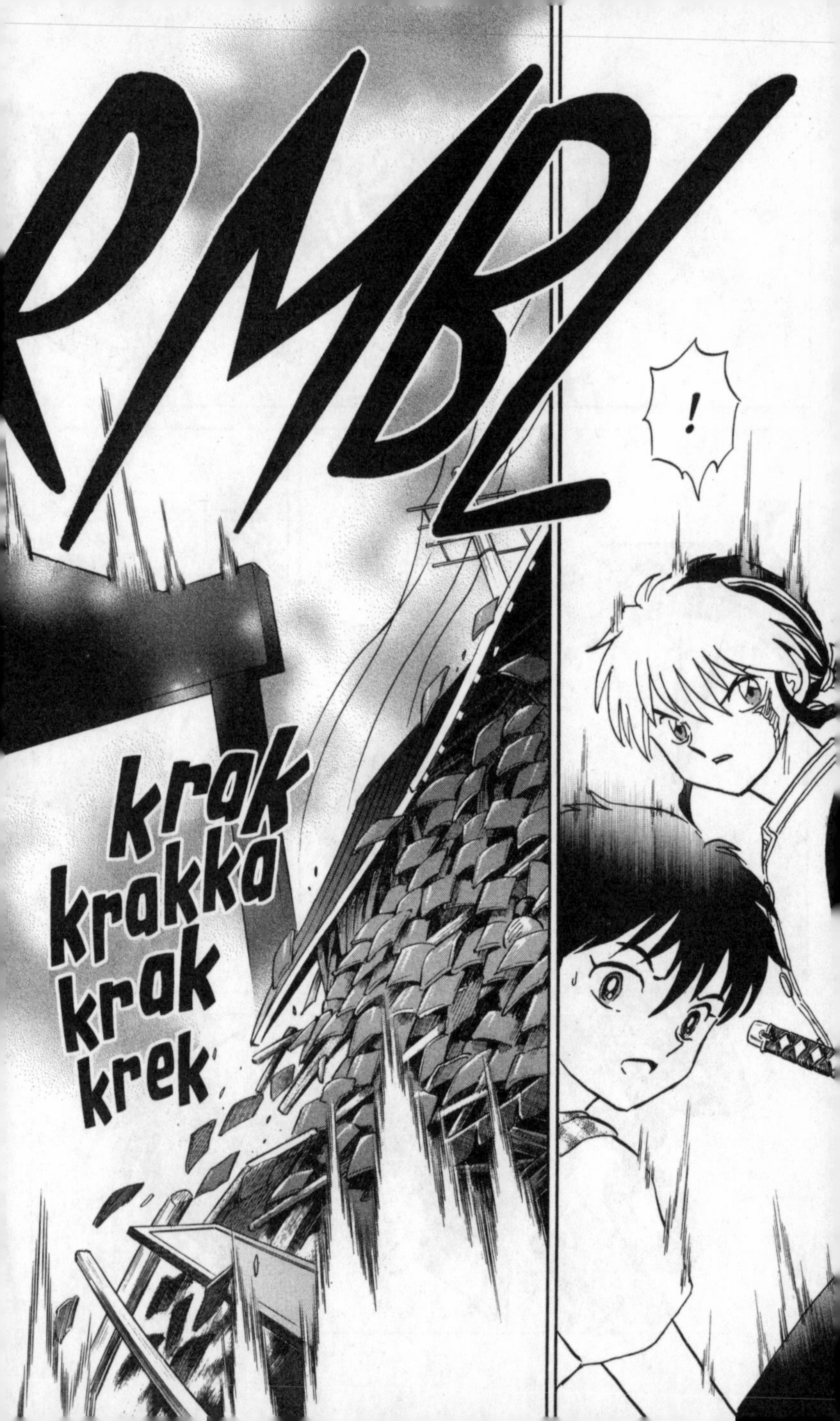
RMBL
!
krak krakka krak krek

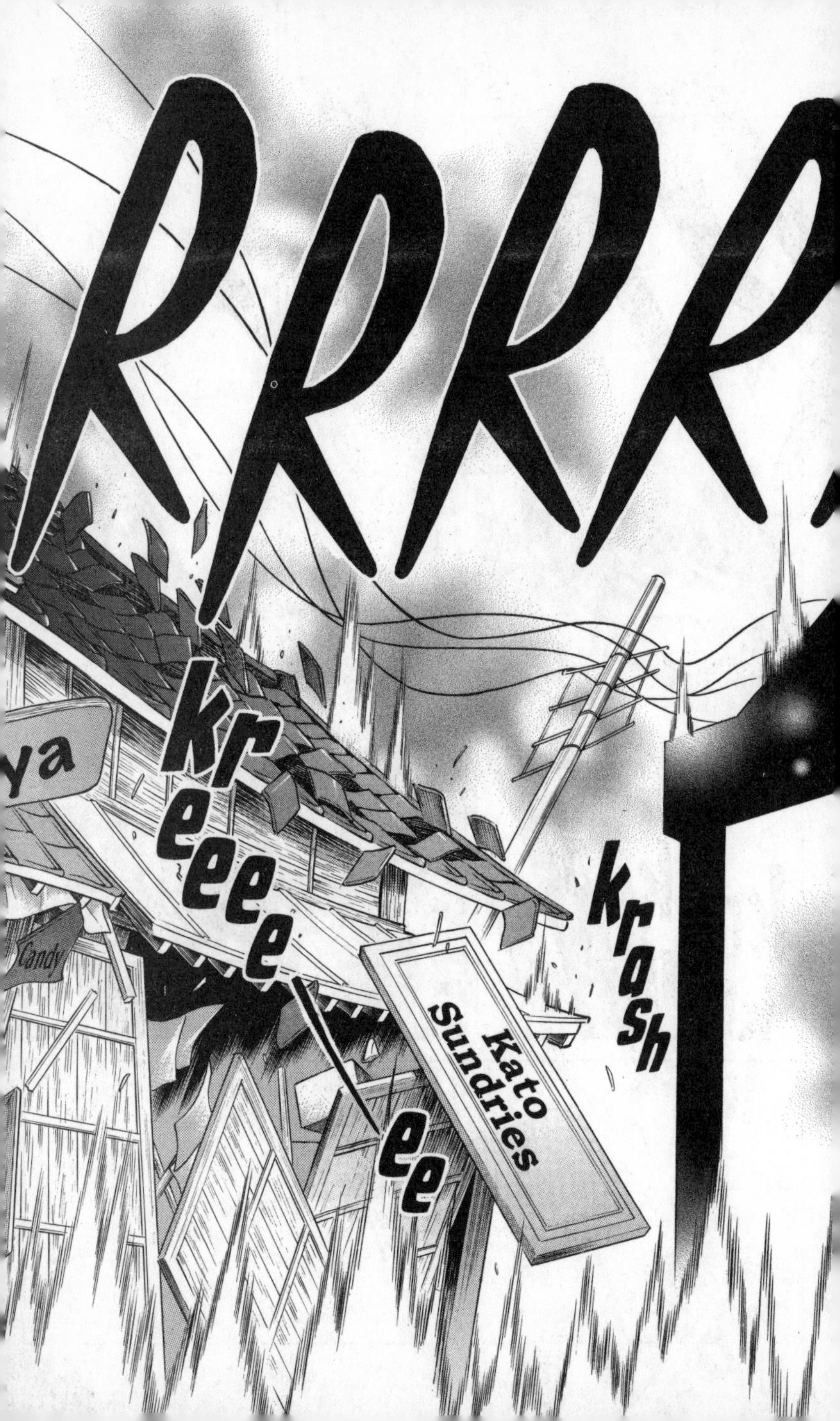
RRRR
krash
kreeeee
ee
Kato Sundries
ya
Candy

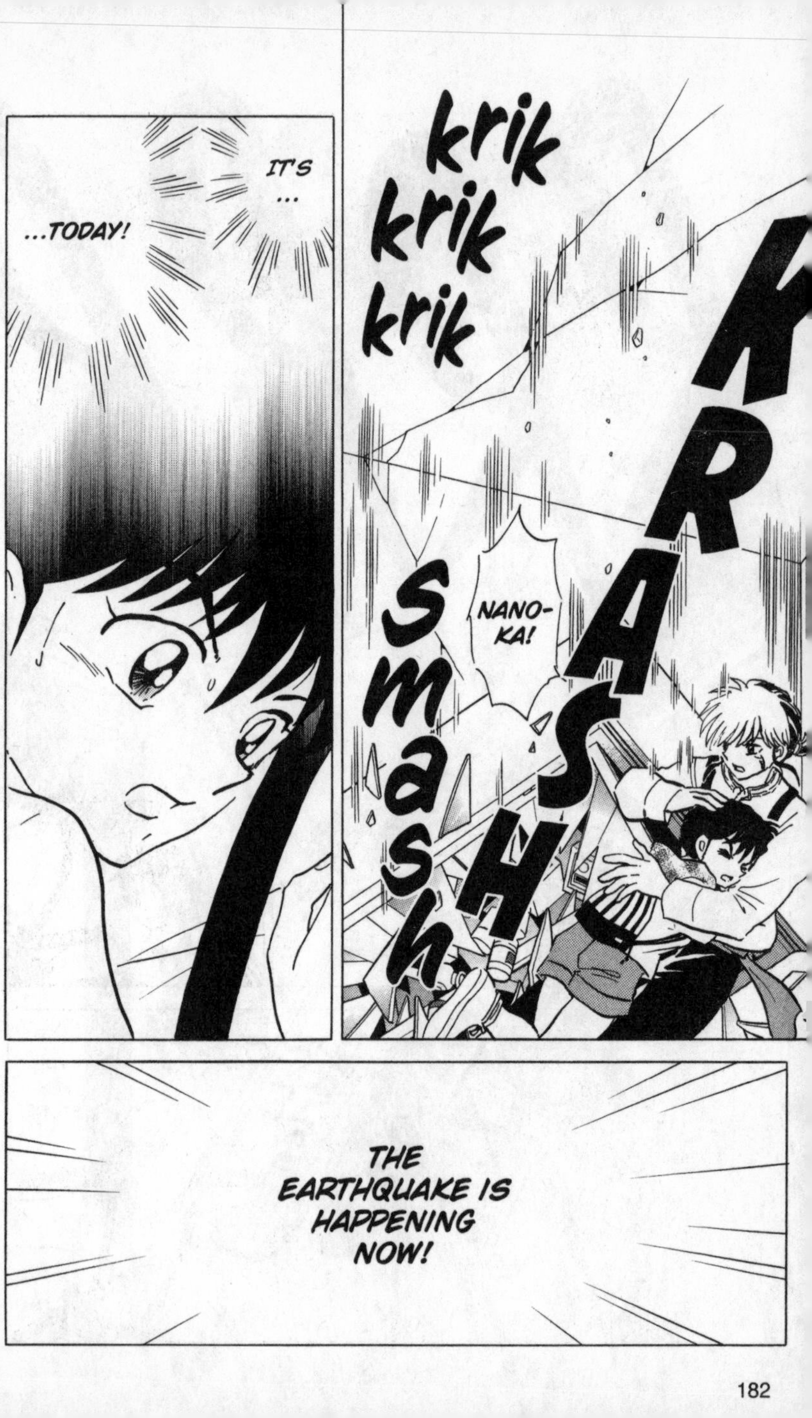
krik krik krik
KRASH
smash
NANO-KA!
IT'S ...
...TODAY!
THE EARTHQUAKE IS HAPPENING NOW!

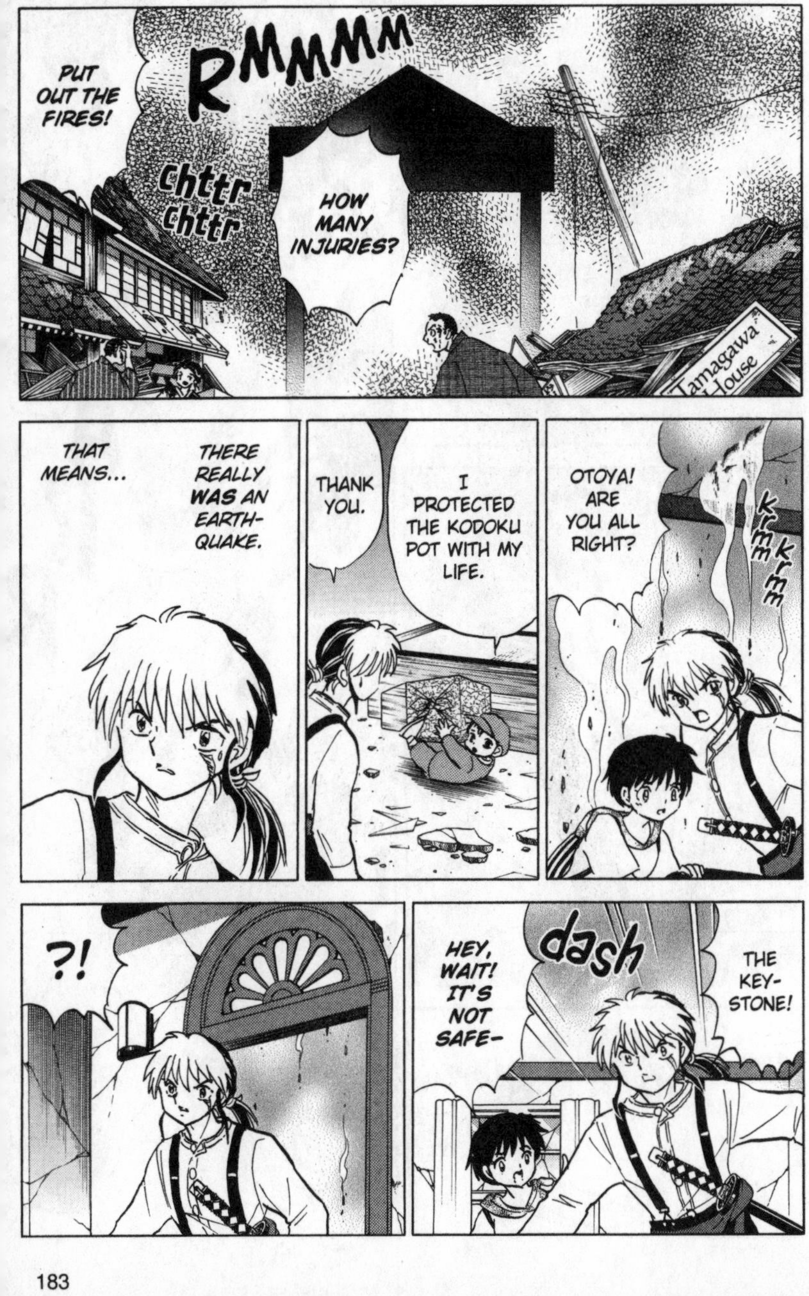
RMMMM
PUT OUT THE FIRES!
chttr chttr
HOW MANY INJURIES?
Tamagawa House
krmm krmm
OTOYA! ARE YOU ALL RIGHT?
I PROTECTED THE KODOKU POT WITH MY LIFE.
THANK YOU.
THAT MEANS...
THERE REALLY WAS AN EARTHQUAKE.
THE KEY-STONE!
dash
HEY, WAIT! IT'S NOT SAFE-
?!

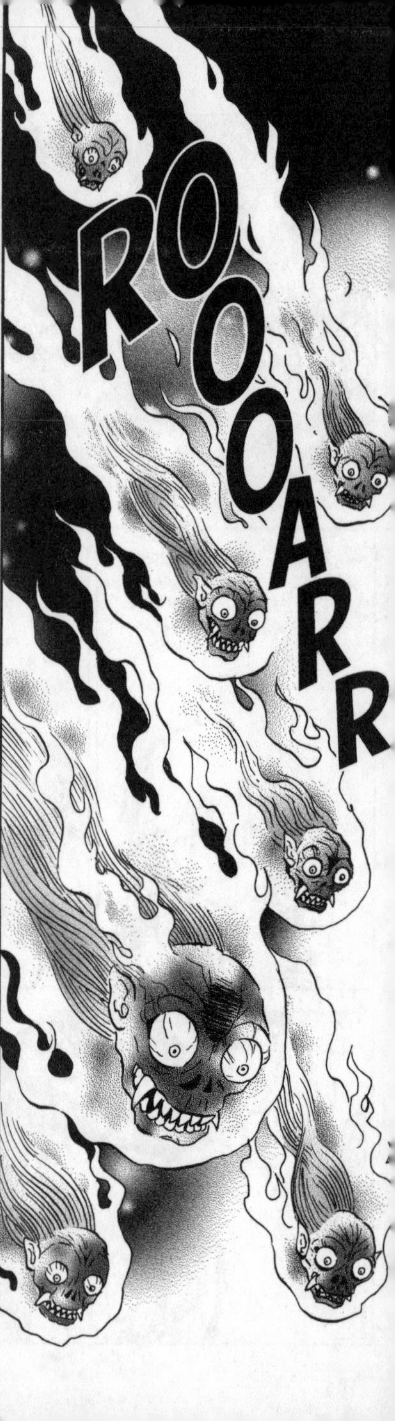
ROOOARR

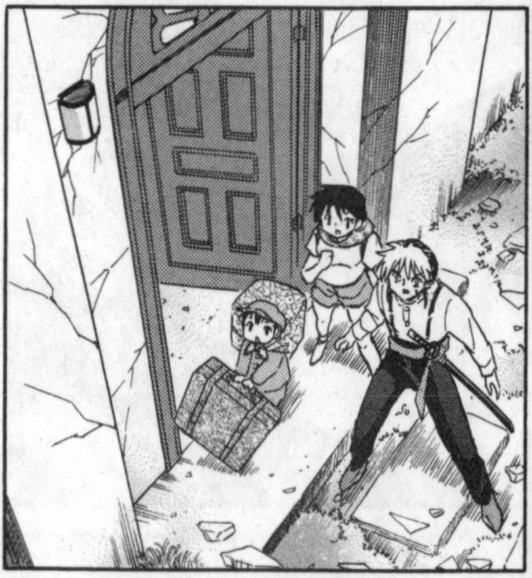

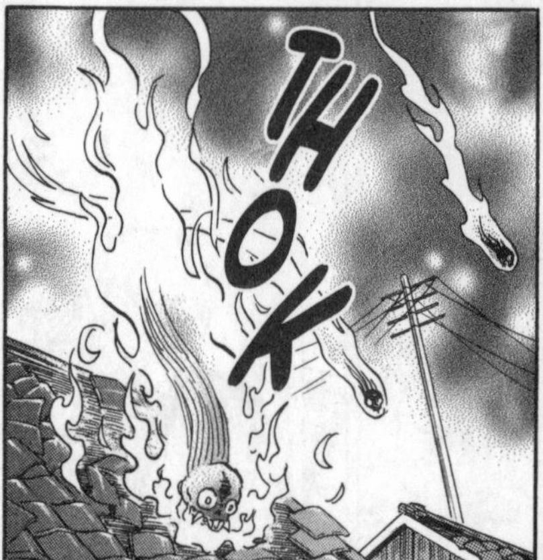
THOK

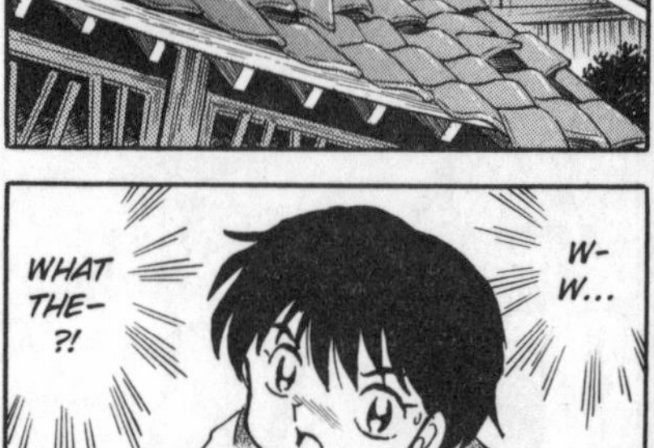
W-W...
WHAT THE—?!

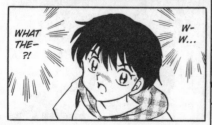

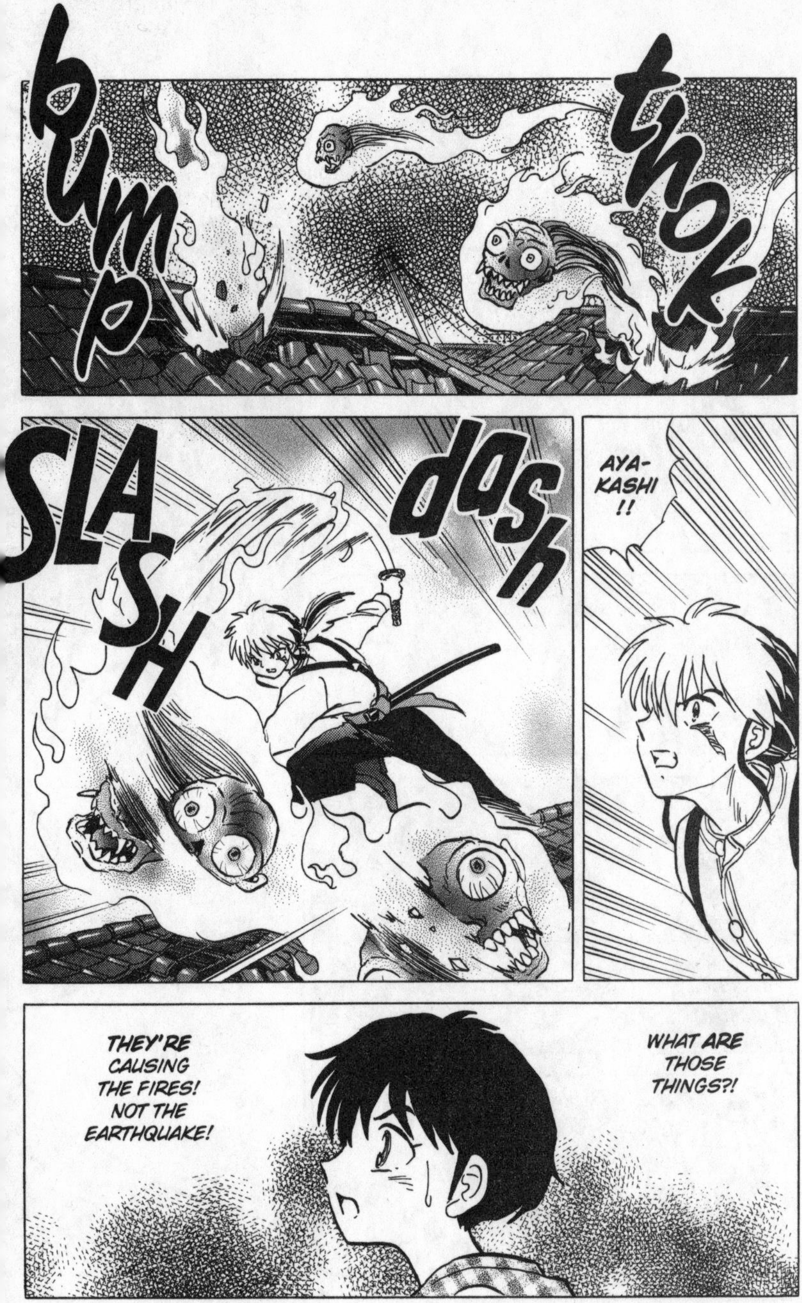
thok
bump
AYA-KASHI!!
dash
SLASH
WHAT ARE THOSE THINGS?!
THEY'RE CAUSING THE FIRES! NOT THE EARTHQUAKE!

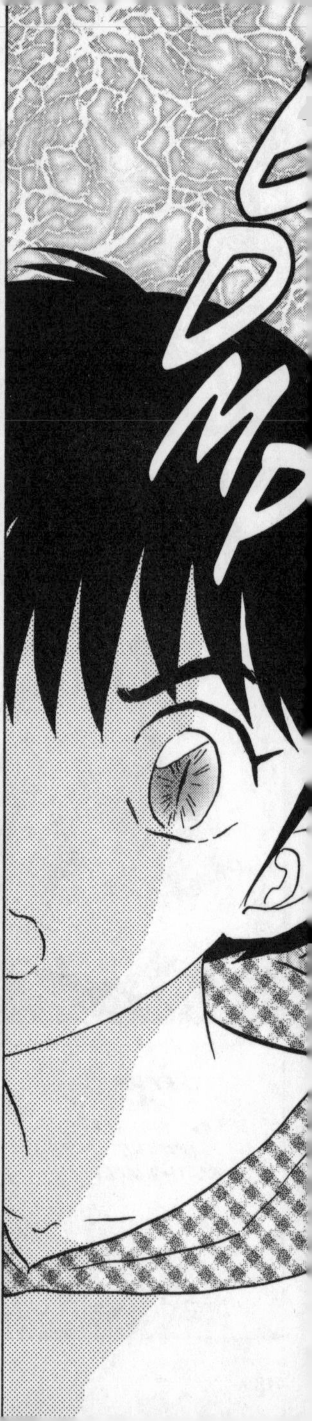
DMP

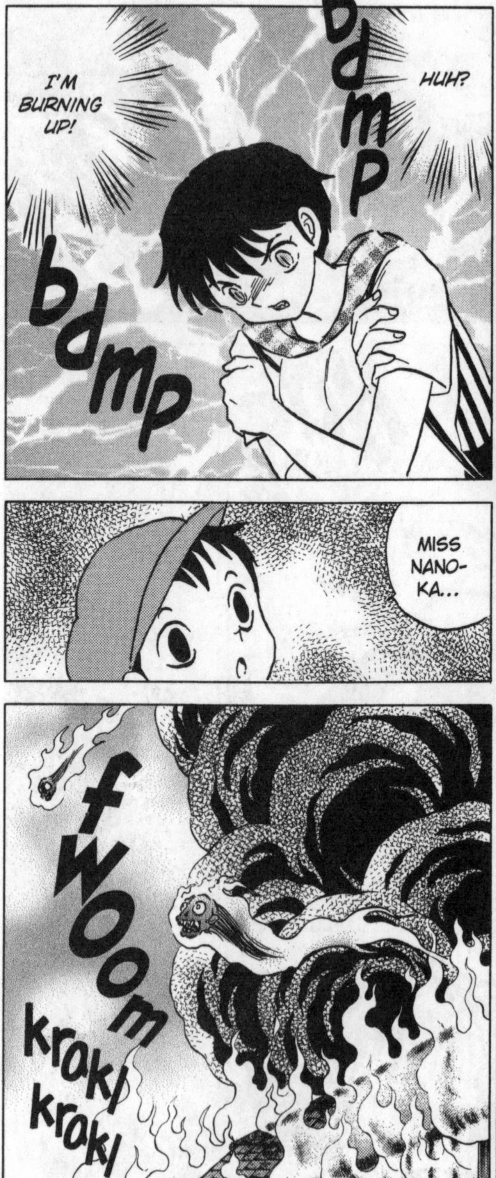
HUH?
bdmp
I'M BURNING UP!
bdmp
MISS NANO-KA...
fwoom
krakl krakl

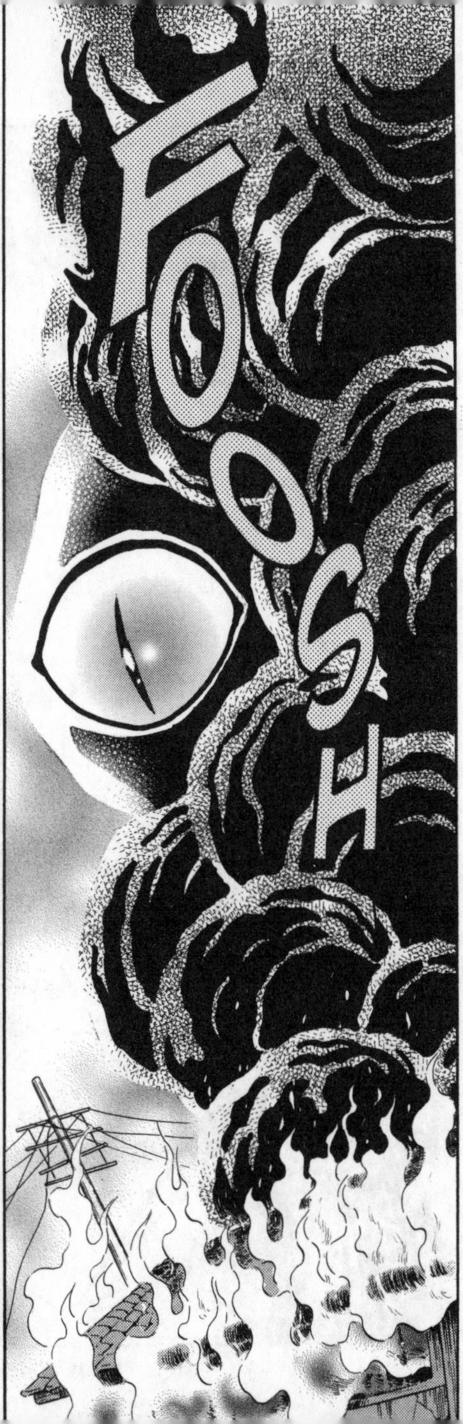
FOOOSH

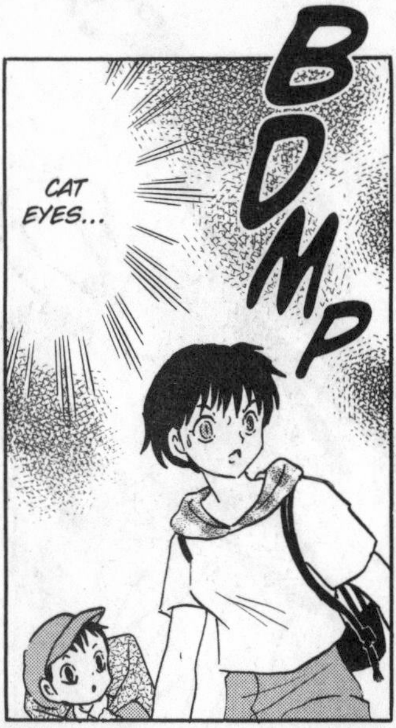
BDMP
CAT EYES...

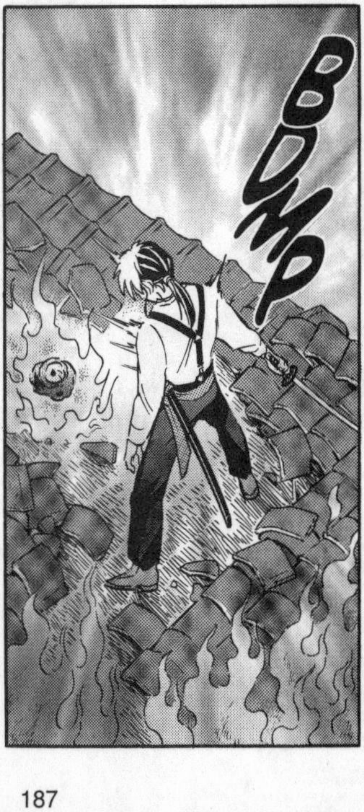
BDMP

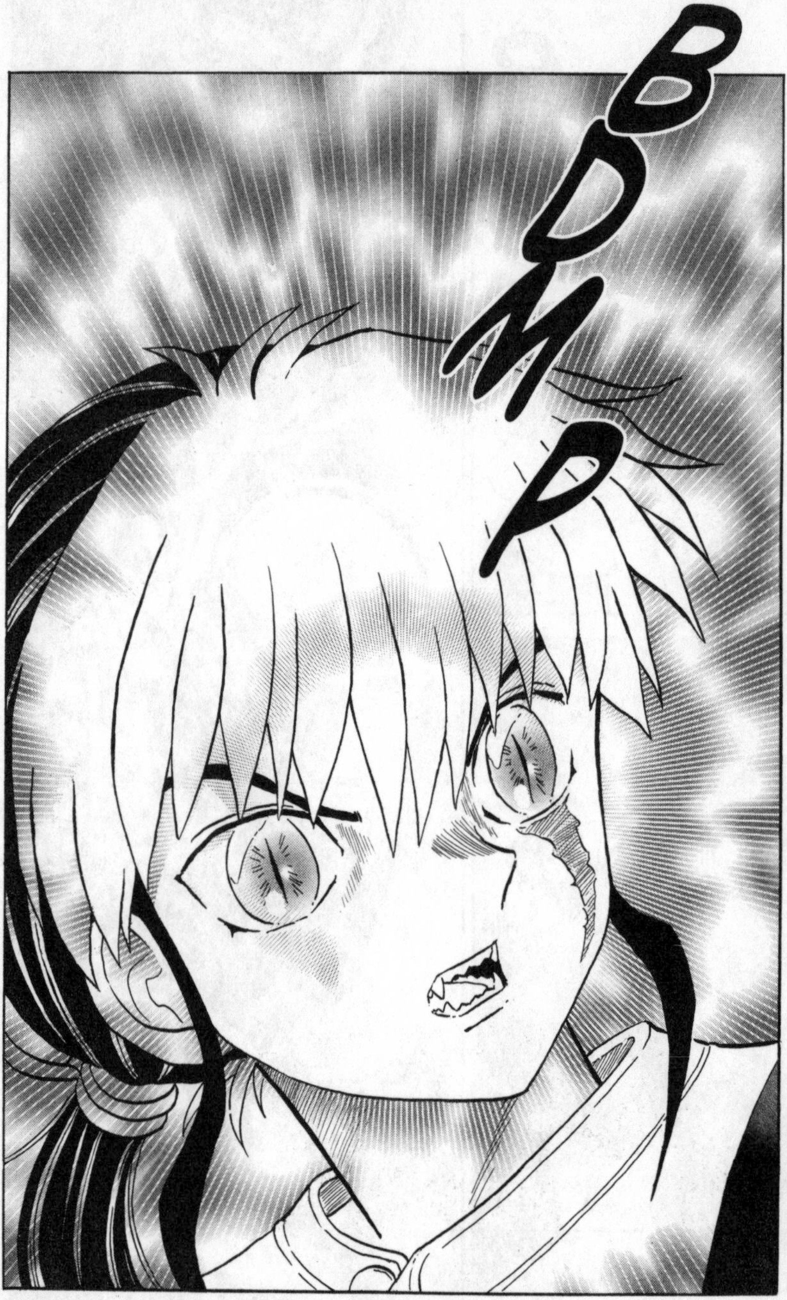
BDMP

TO BE CONTINUED...

MAO

Rumiko Takahashi

The spotlight on Rumiko Takahashi's career began in 1978 when she won an honorable mention in Shogakukan's prestigious New Comic Artist Contest for *Those Selfish Aliens*. Later that same year, her boy-meets-alien comedy series, *Urusei Yatsura*, was serialized in *Weekly Shonen Sunday*. This phenomenally successful manga series was adapted into anime format and spawned a TV series and half a dozen theatrical-release movies, all incredibly popular in their own right. Takahashi followed up the success of her debut series with one blockbuster hit after another—*Maison Ikkoku* ran from 1980 to 1987, *Ranma ½* from 1987 to 1996, and *Inuyasha* from 1996 to 2008. Other notable works include *Mermaid Saga*, *Rumic Theater*, and *One-Pound Gospel*.

Takahashi was inducted into the Will Eisner Comic Awards Hall of Fame in 2018. She won the prestigious Shogakukan Manga Award twice in her career, once for *Urusei Yatsura* in 1981 and the second time for *Inuyasha* in 2002. A majority of the Takahashi canon has been adapted into other media such as anime, live-action TV series, and film. Takahashi's manga, as well as the other formats her work has been adapted into, have continued to delight generations of fans around the world. Distinguished by her wonderfully endearing characters, Takahashi's work adeptly incorporates a wide variety of elements such as comedy, romance, fantasy, and martial arts. While her series are difficult to pin down into one simple genre, the signature style she has created has come to be known as the "Rumic World." Rumiko Takahashi is an artist who truly represents the very best from the world of manga.

MAO
VOLUME 2
Shonen Sunday Edition

STORY AND ART BY
RUMIKO TAKAHASHI

MAO Vol. 2
by Rumiko TAKAHASHI
© 2019 Rumiko TAKAHASHI
All rights reserved.
Original Japanese edition published by SHOGAKUKAN.
English translation rights in the United States of America,
Canada, the United Kingdom, Ireland, Australia and New
Zealand arranged with SHOGAKUKAN.

Original Cover Design: Chie SATO + Bay Bridge Studio

Translation/Junko Goda
English Adaptation/Shaenon Garrity
Touch-up Art & Lettering/Susan Daigle-Leach
Cover & Interior Design/Yukiko Whitley
Editor/Annette Roman

Printed in Canada

Published by VIZ Media, LLC
P.O. Box 77010
San Francisco, CA 94107

10 9 8 7 6 5 4 3 2 1
First printing, November 2021

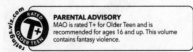

viz.com

shonensunday.com

Coming in Volume 3...

The battle rages on as Byoki tries to grasp the once-in-a-millennium opportunity to take over Mao's body. Nanoka witnesses the accident that orphaned her unfold and grows suspicious of her present day guardian. Can her beloved grandfather be trusted? What about Mao, who has no memory of his actions when in his hybrid form? Then, a former fellow apprentice to Mao's master attacks...with flaming heads! Was Mao really the golden child or... something else? Meanwhile, back in town, young women are disappearing. Who is the prime suspect?

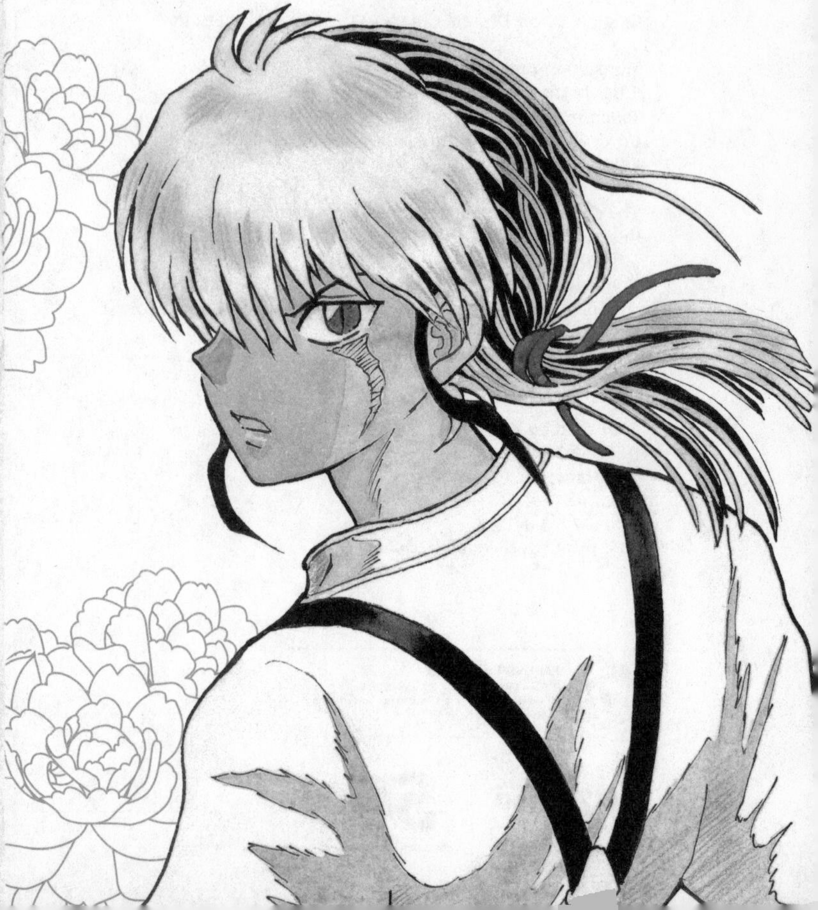